LOCOMOTIVE BUILDERS OF LEEDS

E.B. WILSON AND MANNING WARDLE

LOCOMOTIVE BUILDERS OF LEEDS

E.B. WILSON AND MANNING WARDLE

Mark Smithers

PEN & SWORD
TRANSPORT

First published in Great Britain in 2018 by
Pen & Sword Transport

An imprint of Pen & Sword Books Ltd
Pen & Sword Books Ltd Yorkshire - Philadelphia
47 Church Street
Barnsley
South Yorkshire
S70 2AS

ISBN 978 1 47382 563 5

A CIP catalogue record for this book is available from the British Library.

Typeset by Aura Technology and Software Services, India
Printed and bound by Replika Press Pvt. Ltd.

Pen & Sword Books Ltd incorporates the Imprints of Pen & Sword Archaeology, Atlas, Aviation, Battleground, Discovery, Family History, History, Maritime, Military, Naval, Politics, Railways, Select, Transport, True Crime, Fiction, Frontline Books, Leo Cooper, Praetorian Press, Seaforth Publishing, Wharncliffe and White Owl.

For a complete list of Pen & Sword titles please contact
PEN & SWORD BOOKS LIMITED
47 Church Street, Barnsley, South Yorkshire, S70 2AS, England
E-mail: enquiries@pen-and-sword.co.uk
Website: www.pen-and-sword.co.uk

CONTENTS

ACKNOWLEDGMENTS

The author acknowledges the assistance of several individuals and organisations during the compilation of this book. At an organizational level, these include in particular the National Railway Museum; the National Archive; West Yorkshire County Libraries; the Railway Correspondence and Travel Society; the Stephenson Locomotive Society; the Industrial Railway Society; the Industrial Locomotive Society Chasewater Railway Museum and the Hunslet Museum, Stafold Barn.

Individuals whose contributions deserve commendation include Dawn Whitehead and Anthony Coulls of the National Railway Museum; S.A. Leleux; Alan Baker; the late Ron Redman; Don Townsley; Russell Wear; Graham Lee, Henry Noon and Hazel Tomlinson of Statfold Barn Railway, and John Scott-Morgan.

INTRODUCTION

During a period spanning over 180 years following the appearance of the first steam locomotive on the Middleton Railway in Leeds in 1812, the locomotive building industry was to prove to be an important contributor to the city's prosperity through periods of peace and conflict. The Railway Foundry name had originated in the parish of Hunslet (Hunslet Lane) in 1837 with Todd, Kitson and Laird and it was retained, on a site adjacent to Pearson Street by Shepherd & Todd two years later. This enterprise, in its various forms, remained a significant player in the market throughout the 1840s and most of the 1850s and from the enlarged factory, in the guise of E.B. Wilson & Co. in 1846, emerged what was probably the best-known main-line locomotive design produced in the city, namely the *Jenny Lind* 2-2-2. The *Jenny Lind* was to have a major impact on domestic locomotive design during the succeeding years, mainly by reason of its use of a higher working boiler pressure than was hitherto customary, but also in its facilitation of the wider adoption of Stephenson link motion allied to an inside cylinder chassis layout.

On the back of this achievement, the second Railway Foundry (as distinct from the final Leeds-based concern to use the same name, namely Hudswell Clarke & Co. Ltd. which occupied part of the estate of the former Wilson site) became the birthplace of a small number of series-produced main-line locomotive specifications that went on to have a major impact on subsequent practice at home and overseas Unfortunately, technological success did not go hand-in-hand with financial solvency and, a dozen years later, the enterprise fell victim to economic difficulties going back to the financial crisis of 1847-8 that followed the first 'Railway Mania'. During the period of Trusteeship that followed, a small number of then seemingly insignificant locomotives produced during the 1850s sowed the seeds of a different direction for much of Leeds-based locomotive building following the eventual demise of the second Railway Foundry. These designs were developed by a new firm, Manning Wardle & Co., which was based on an adjacent site to the second Railway Foundry in the Boyne Engine Works. Manning Wardle & Co. (later Ltd.) went on to produce a range of related sturdy tank locomotive designs that found a ready market in the industrial sector, particularly with the contractors who built much of the domestic main-line network during the second 'Railway Mania' and beyond. Other representatives of these classes, some in modified form, also found markets abroad and notable examples within the scope of this volume survive in Norway and Uruguay.

The Manning Wardle standard classes were to become a major influence on the product policy of neighbouring manufacturers. Locomotives recognizably descended from the small but influential Railway Foundry designs of the 1850s continued to be built by other manufacturers following Manning Wardle's demise until after the end of the Second World War. Post-1926 representatives of the 'Manning Wardle standard' line of evolution continued to be constructed by the successors-in-title to the company's goodwill. Recognizably similar designs were also by produced by Hudswell Clarke & Co. Ltd., notably the inside-cylinder 'Countess of Warwick' class 0-6-0ST, the last examples of which were not completed until 1946. Following the demise of Manning Wardle as a physical entity in 1926 and a legal entity (as originally constituted) in 1931, the company's real estate was acquired by neighbouring concerns, including Hunslet Engine Co. Ltd. and part of the former Manning Wardle premises remained in use associated with railway equipment manufacture until the closure of Hunslet's Leeds base in 1995.

The purpose of this book is to give an enhanced overview of the known history and products of the second Railway Foundry, and of the standard inside cylinder 0-6-0ST and outside cylinder 0-4-0ST designs (and their close relatives) of British standard gauge and above produced at the Boyne Engine Works up to 1926, along with derivative locomotives produced by the two immediate successor companies in holding the Manning Wardle goodwill and drawings, Kitson & Co. Ltd. and Robert Stephenson & Hawthorns Ltd. Normally Manning Wardle locomotives covered by this volume were built with boilers not having domes on the barrel and exceptions to this rule will be confined to specimens built to variants of standard designs whose influence cannot be isolated from the wider flow of evolution of those classes.

CHAPTER 1

THE BEGINNINGS OF LOCOMOTIVE MANUFACTURE IN LEEDS

The most influential figure in the genesis of locomotive manufacture in the City of Leeds was Matthew Murray. Murray is believed to have been born in Newcastle-Upon-Tyne in 1765 and he spent more than two decades of his early life there, where he served his engineering apprenticeship in work associated with the textile industry. After moving to Leeds in 1788 he formed an initial partnership with David Wood in Holbeck in 1795 before moving to new premises at Water Lane in the same area at the turn of the eighteenth and nineteenth centuries. This move had largely been financed by colliery owner James Fenton Snr. and hence the manufacturing facility of Fenton, Murray and Wood was born. One of the buildings associated with this facility was built in the form of a rotunda and gave the factory its commonly used name of the 'Round Foundry'. Much of the firm's early work was, predictably, tied up with stationary engines and the textile industry and the early years of the nineteenth century were characterized *inter alia* by a fractious relationship with Messrs. Boulton & Watt of Birmingham over the originality of ideas and patents. In 1811, however, a new opportunity arose for the Holbeck manufacturer which was to have implications that were to extend far beyond the city's boundaries. In 1758, the owner of Middleton Colliery, Charles Brandling, obtained an Act of Parliament, the first of its kind, to construct a railway some 3½ miles in length, linking the colliery with a coal staithe situated close to the town centre, with the first horse-drawn traffic commencing on 20th September that year. By the first decade of the nineteenth century, draught horses of the type used on early railways, or 'waggonways' as they were known, were very much in demand for military purposes and thoughts were turning to their replacement by mechanized means of traction.

The earliest railway locomotives had been designed by Richard Trevithick using cast iron boilers, a 'single cylinder and flywheel' arrangement with the cylinder enclosed by the boiler and mounted either horizontally or vertically and smooth cast iron rails. Brandling's steward John Blenkinsop (1783-1831) had realised that the use of smooth brittle rails limited the feasible tractive effort/locomotive weight ratio of the period to uneconomic levels and his patent for a 'Tramway for Conveying Coals' (3431 of 1811) attempted to remedy the problem by using a driven toothed wheel to engage with a rack incorporated into the outer upright face of one of the running rails. Blenkinsop was not a steam technology engineer and for the design of his locomotives he turned to fellow 'Tyneside exile' Matthew Murray. The first of the new rack locomotives constructed at the Round Foundry was put into service in June 1812 and its operational debut was recorded by the *Leeds Mercury* for the 27th of that month:

> 'On Wednesday last a highly interesting experiment was made with a Machine constructed by Messrs. Fenton, Murray and Wood of this place under the direction of Mr. John Blenkinsop, the Patentee, for the purpose of substituting the agency of steam in the conveyance of coal on the Iron Railway from the mines of J.C. Brandling, Esq., at Middleton, to Leeds. This machine is in fact a steam engine of four horse power, which, with the assistance of cranks turning a cog-wheel and iron cogs placed at one side of the Railway, is capable of moving when lightly loaded, at the speed of ten miles an hour.
>
> 'At four o'clock in the afternoon, the Machine ran from the Coal Staith to the top of Hunslet Moor, where six, and afterwards eight waggons of coals, each weighing 3¼ tons, were hooked to the back part. With this immense weight, to which, as it approached the town, was superadded about fifty of the spectators mounted upon the waggons, it set off on its return to the Coal Staith, and performed the journey, a distance of about a mile and a half, principally on a dead level, in twenty-three minutes without the slightest accident.

'The experiment, which was witnessed by thousands of spectators, was crowned with complete success, and when it is considered that this invention is applicable to all Railroads, and that at the works of Mr. Brandling alone the use of fifty horses will be dispensed with, we cannot forbear to hail the invention as of vast public utility, and to rank the inventor amongst the benefactors of the country.'

The initial locomotive was originally unnamed but was eventually named *Salamanca* following the Duke of Wellington's forces' victory over the French during the Peninsular War battle there on 22 July 1812. *Salamanca* was soon followed another similar locomotive, *Prince Regent*, and it was claimed that one of these locomotives, which weighed approximately four tons each, was capable of hauling twenty loaded coal wagons, each of 3½ tons weight (giving a total train weight inclusive of engine of 74 tons) at 3½ miles per hour. Some ½ ton of coal was used during 12 hours of work whilst water consumption was 55 gallons per hour. The boiler required refilling every five miles (there apparently being no feed pumps) and the cost of each locomotive when new was £350. In common with Trevithick's designs, the first two locomotives as built possessed single flue cast iron boilers and cylinder steam/exhaust valves that were of the simple 'tap' variety, apparently worked by tappets from the piston rods. Unlike their Trevithick precursors, they

This drawing, originally published in Thomas Gray's *Observations on a General Iron Railway* in 1821 depicts one of the Middleton Railway rack locomotives and is considered to be an accurate representation of their early appearance. Another published drawing suggests that the earliest design of locomotives for the Middleton Railway possessed single-acting cylinders, but, given the lack of a flywheel, and the contemporary descriptions of the locomotives' early operational careers, it is extremely difficult to see how such an arrangement could have been employed in practice. (*Railway Magazine*)

possessed two cylinders set at 90 degrees to one another, hence they were self-starting and needed no flywheel – an early drawing purporting to show single-acting cylinders would appear to have been inaccurate, given the lack of a flywheel or any other assisted starting arrangements. They also possessed a distinct composite timber/iron underframe and only the pinion wheel was driven, the leading and trailing axles being for carrying purposes only. The gauge of the railway was 4ft 1in.

In late 1812, a further pair of locomotives was constructed at the Round Foundry on similar lines except that the oscillating plug valves were actuated by eccentrics mounted on each of the 'bellcrank' axles driving the pinion wheel. It is also thought that the silencer fitted to the exhaust steam pipe assembly, there being no connection to the main chimney and hence no blastpipe, made its first appearance at this stage. Although both of the locomotives were originally intended for the Middleton Railway, one was eventually diverted to John Watson for use at Willington Colliery near Newcastle-Upon-Tyne. This locomotive was named *Willington* whilst its twin sister was named, rather confusingly *Marquis Wellington*. The former locomotive was soon returned to the Middleton Railway to bring the Middleton's compliment of 'Round Foundry' locomotives to four, but two further similar locomotives were supplied to John Watson for use at Kenton and Coxlodge Collieries from Leeds shortly afterwards. These are recorded as being of 4ft 7½in gauge and having 8in diameter cylinders. The first of the two locomotives to enter service, presumably the Kenton specimen, did so on 2 September 1813, drawing 70 chaldron wagons containing an aggregate weight of 70 tons at an average speed of three miles an hour in the presence of a group of witnesses that included George Stephenson and several Killingworth Colliery employees. Despite the initial optimism associated with these locomotives, the Coxlodge engine was found to be unsteady in service and costly to use, eventually being taken out of use following a boiler explosion shortly after entry into service. Both locomotives had apparently fallen out of use by 1820.

This drawing of the 1812 Blenkinsop design for the Middleton Railway first appeared in *The Mechanic's Magazine* in 1829. Note that the drive to the valves from the 'coupling gear' axles is shown in some detail. (*The Mechanic's Magazine*)

There appears to be some doubt as to the true dimensions of the early Middleton Railway locomotives, E.R. Forward ARCSc in *Catalogue of Railways, Locomotives and Rolling Stock* states that the first pair had oval cross-section boilers (vertical axis 37in, horizontal 32in) with a length of 9ft 7in and a flue tube of 14in. diameter. The timber supporting frame was carried on four 'smooth' wheels of 3ft diameter (unflanged and running on cast iron edge rails) whilst the single rack pinion of 3ft 2in diameter was driven via gearing from the cylinders of 9in bore and 22in stroke. R. Young in *Timothy Hackworth and the Locomotive* (1923) suggested that all of the early Middleton locomotives were eventually rebuilt with larger boilers, 10ft 6in long and 4ft 2in diameter (presumably wrought iron and circular in section) and cylinders of 8in bore and 24in stroke. Whatever the truth of the matter, it was the Middleton Railway that was to give David Joy his first acquaintance with the steam railway locomotive. In 1832 he recorded:

> 'Living in Hunslet Lane on the London Road, the old coal railway from Middleton Pits into Leeds ran behind our house a few fields off, and we used to see the steam from the engines rise above the trees. Once, I remember, going with my nurse, who held my hand (I had to stretch up to hers, I was so little) while we stood to watch the engine with its train of coal wagons pass. We were told it would come up like a dash of lightening, but it only came lumbering on like a cart.'

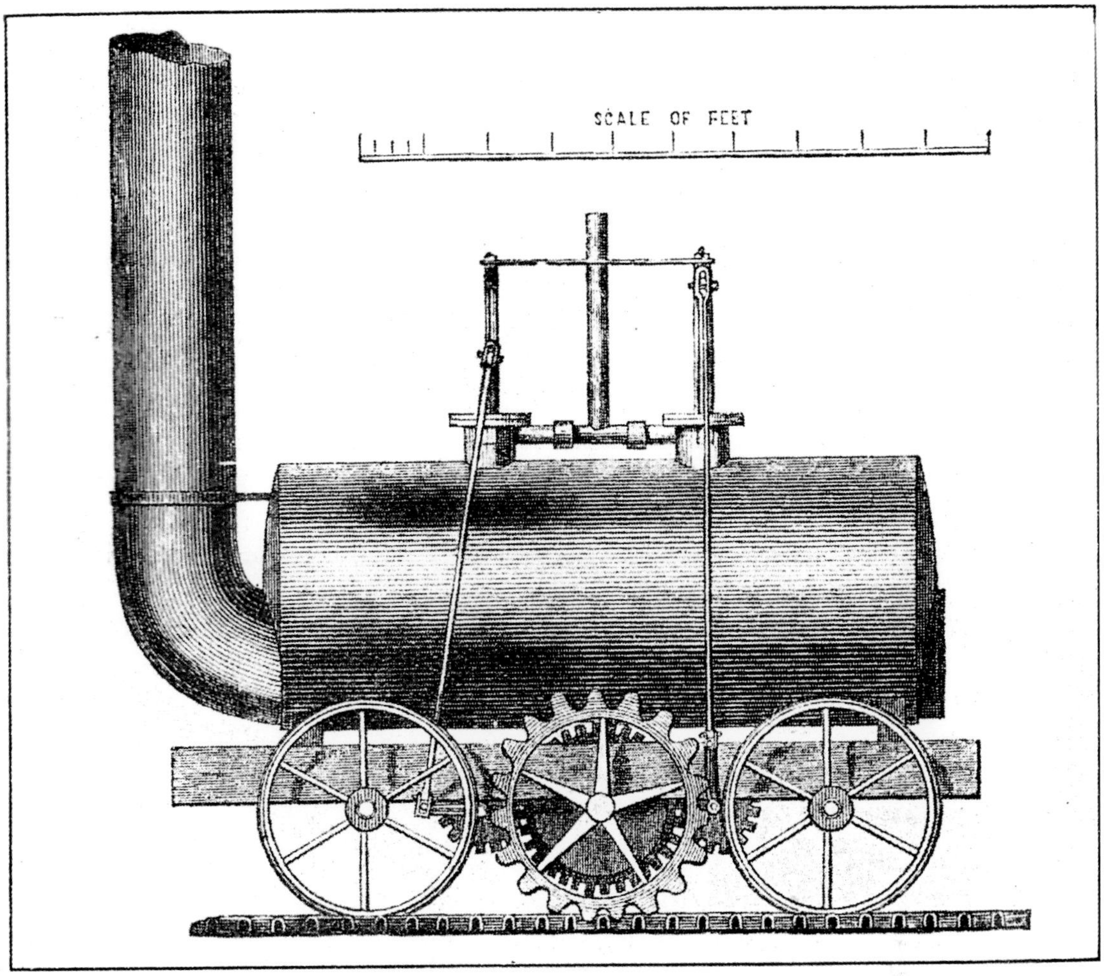

This later drawing appeared in Nicholas Wood's *A Treatise on Railroads* in 1831 and is believed to show the locomotives' design after boiler replacement and other alterations had taken place. The diameters of both the boiler barrel and internal flue (and associated chimney) have increased when compared to the previous drawing. The lower 'fish belly' portions of the cast iron rails have been omitted and certain locomotive details are missing. (*Railway Magazine*)

David Joy thus appeared less than impressed with his first experience of the steam locomotive's early fumblings and matters were not made any better by the fact that the careers of the 'Round Foundry' locomotives on the Middleton Railway were marred by two fatal boiler explosions. The first, on 28 February 1818 involved *Salamanca* and appears to have resulted from tampering with the safety valve. The second, in which the casualty was driver James Hewitt, was described in the *Leeds Mercury* for 15 February 1834:

> 'On Wednesday one of the locomotion engines of the Middleton Colliery, was burst by pressure of the steam. The shock produced by the explosion was so great that it was felt in almost every house in Hunslet and the unfortunate engine-driver was literally blown to atoms and his mutilated body scattered in all directions.'

All of the Middleton 'rack railway' locomotives fell out of use shortly afterwards, although the railway was destined to live on in more conventional form. A railway was built on Blenkinsop's principles to serve Orrell and Winstanley Colliery near Wigan using steam locomotives allegedly built by the Haigh Foundry and this is believed to have been in use for over thirty-five years, whilst other unsuccessful attempts were made at getting the system adopted in Germany and Russia. Although the Blenkinsop rack system was to be rendered obsolete by the development of steel rails and it was in any case open to the obvious objection that the tractive loads were 'lop sided', the 'Round Foundry' rack locomotives established steam rail locomotion as a commercial proposition. The 'rack railway' was also destined to make a reappearance later in the nineteenth century for specialist applications and several are still active today. As for Matthew Murray, he died on 26 February 1826 and is buried at St. Matthew's Church in Holbeck.

CHAPTER 2

EARLY SUCCESS AND FAILURE 1831-1843

Following the initial phase of 'rack railway' locomotive construction, no more locomotives were constructed at the Round Foundry for several years although other engineering work continued unabated. Following the death of David Wood in 1820, the name of the firm was changed to Fenton, Murray & Jackson, the new partner, Richard Jackson being Matthew Murray's son-in law. By the time of re-commencement of locomotive building, the steam locomotive had come of age and the early experiments of Trevithick, Murray, Hedley, the Stephensons and others had given way in the forefront of technology to the Planet class

2-2-0. This design featured many of the refinements that one would normally associate with more modern

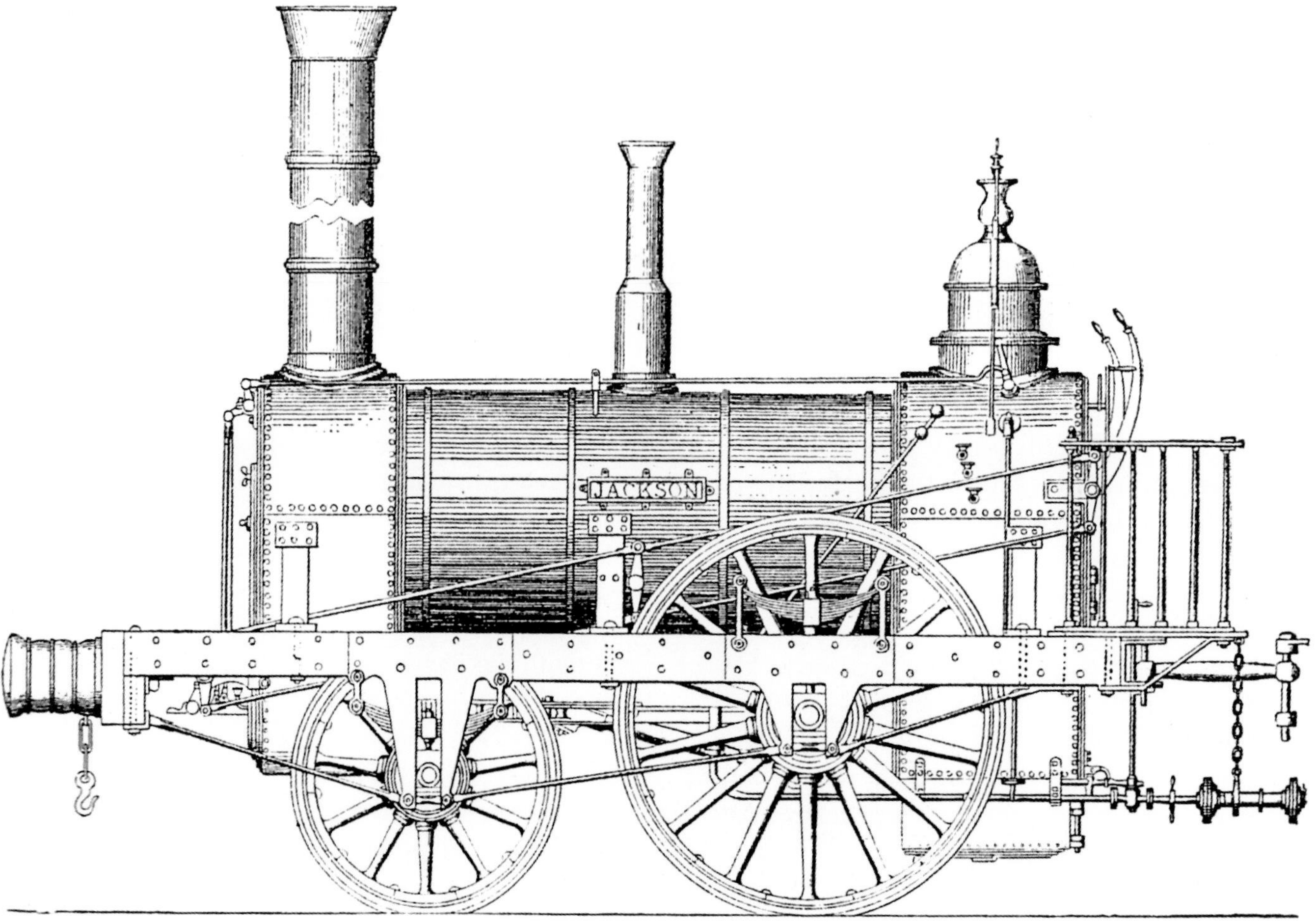

Fenton Murray and Jackson commenced locomotive building during the year following the introduction of the Planet class 2-2-0 on the Liverpool and Manchester Railway by Robert Stephenson & Co. This example was constructed at the Round Foundry in 1836 and although originally shown in *Railway Magazine* as being built for the Sheffield and Rotherham Railway (later part of the Midland Railway), it was in fact supplied to the Paris and Versailles Railway. (*Railway Magazine*)

steam locomotives such as a distinct full length 'chassis'; the cylinders at the leading end; a separate purpose-made smokebox, and a multitubular boiler with a suitably proportioned firebox wrapper. A major item still missing at this stage was the provision of valve gear equipped to make full use of the expansive nature of steam throughout the stroke of the cylinder. Be that as it may, the year 1831 saw two members of the Planet class completed at the Round Foundry for the Liverpool and Manchester Railway (L&MR) as No. 19 *Vulcan* and No. 21 *Fury* with a further example for the same customer following in 1833 as No. 33 *Leeds*. Although not long lived by modern standards, the trio had a respectable lifespan on the L&MR. by the standards of their contemporaries, being disposed of in 1840-1. Locomotives of the same basic type were also constructed for other customers in Britain and France during the ensuing years including the Leeds & Selby Railway, Paris & Versailles Railway and Montpellier & Cette Railway. Locomotives of this type continued to be supplied until 1839 with the early examples at least being sub-contracted from Robert Stephenson & Co. Typically, they had 3ft diameter leading wheels, 5ft diameter driving wheels and cylinders 11in bore by 18in stroke.

The Planet class was to have two important 'spin-off' designs, the 0-4-0 Samson and the 2-2-2 Patentee. Fenton, Murray and Jackson was to be involved in the production of both of these types. The Samson type was produced for the Roanne & Andrezieux system in 1832 and again for the Lyon & St. Etienne for export to the Lyon & St. Etienne Railway in in 1835 whilst at least two other examples are believed to have been constructed for the home market. The Patentee type of locomotive, which proliferated during the latter half of the 1830s proved in its various forms to be the most significant 'chunk' of the locomotive product output of the Round Foundry, from which its earliest examples appeared in 1836. The first domestic customer was the Leeds and Selby Railway, which took delivery of two specimens in 1836-7. The export market was not forgotten and at around the same time two

This drawing shows the other side of an 1834-vintage Planet class but otherwise differs little from the previous illustration save for the fact that the leading wheels have 12 rather than 11 spokes. (*Origine de la Locomotive: Broise and Coutier, Paris, 1886*)

The Stephenson 2-2-2 Patentee design is illustrated to advantage by this drawing which shows that it differed from the Planet class mainly by reason of its larger overall dimensions and the need for a trailing axle. The Planet's main features such as the basic boiler and smoke box design, inside cylinders, sandwich frames and 'gab' motion (albeit redesigned) were all still present, although the driving wheels in this instance were unflanged. This locomotive was a Robert Stephenson & Co. product, *Victory* for the Sheffield and Rotherham Railway in 1838. (*Stephenson Locomotive Society*)

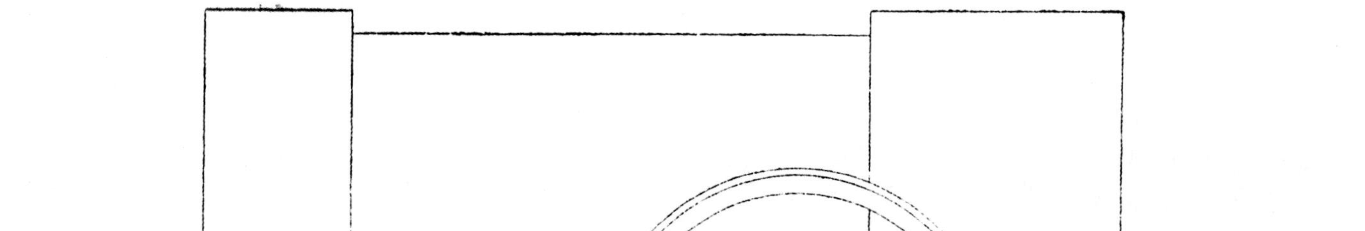

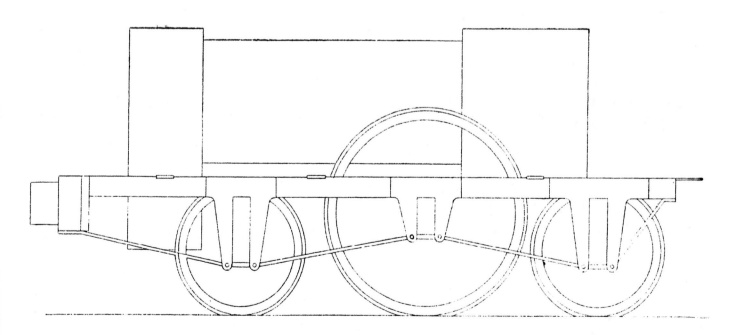

The Sheffield and Rotherham Railway ordered a similar locomotive early in 1839 from Fenton, Murray and Jackson and this was delivered on 23 April as *Agilis*. Unlike *Victory, Agilis* was fitted with flanged wheels throughout as shown in this rudimentary sketch. (*Stephenson Locomotive Society*)

further examples, *Vulkan* and *Mars* made their appearance on the Munich & Augsberg Railway. The early examples of the type had 13in by 18in cylinders and 5ft 6in driving wheels but later specimens were suitably enlarged to cope with increasing traffic demands. In all, two more variants of the basic type were to be produced for the Leeds & Selby Railway; one for the Sheffield & Rotherham Railway (with a similar engine sub-contracted to another manufacturer); four for the London & Southampton Railway; nine for the North Midland Railway; two for the Paris & Orleans Railway and one each for the Paris & Versailles Railway and Belgian State Railways. The six Hull & Selby specimens were built with 12in by 18in cylinders and 5ft 6in driving wheels. These six locomotives bore the names *Kingston, Exeley, Selby, Collingwood, Andrew Marvel* and *Wellington* with all but the last being taken over by the York & North Midland Railway (Y&NMR) in 1846 and the last survivor, *Andrew Marvel*, being numbered successively 59 and 44 by that railway before becoming N.E.R 279 in 1853 prior to replacement in 1868.

One particular variation on the basic theme was destined to constitute the best known and most successful class of locomotive to emerge from the Round Foundry. Following the successful use of a large Patentee, *North Star* originally constructed by Robert Stephenson & Co. for the 5ft 6in gauge New Orleans Railway in the U.S.A. but converted to 7ft 0¼ in gauge for the Great Western Railway, and the construction of eleven similar locomotives for the 'broad gauge' concern, Daniel Gooch

The strong reliance by Fenton, Murray and Jackson on Robert Stephenson designs continued right up to the construction of the Great Western Fire Fly class and this class of 2-2-2 for the North Midland Railway was no exception. Recorded in David Joy's Diaries in 1844 in sketch form, the design is shown in more detail in this side view drawing. In all essentials, the design is a Patentee with a 'Gothic firebox' boiler. Dimensions quoted by David Joy were: cylinders 14 in. by 18 in.; driving wheels 6 ft. diameter; heating surface: tubes (121 2 in. diameter) 532 sq. ft. and firebox 52 sq. ft. The working pressure was 60psi and the weight in working order was about 12 tons. These dimensions correspond to North Midland Railway Nos. 15-17 but three further locomotives with 13in by 16in cylinders and 5ft 6in driving wheels were also built at the Round Foundry as NMR Nos. 21-23. (*Railway Magazine*)

designed the 62-strong Fire Fly class of locomotives constructed on similar principles but with a 'Gothic' (vaulted arch) raised firebox wrapper and twenty of these were built by Fenton, Murray and Jackson and delivered between May 1840 and August 1842. This class of locomotive certainly made its impact upon David Joy, who in 1842 was employed in his father's oil-crushing works in Leeds and recorded in his Diaries around May that year:

> 'It soon became evident that oil-crushing was not my vocation and I was asked if I would like to be an engineer. And the authority set my chief friend, the millwright John Kirk, to sound me, and to take me to see the engine works of Messrs. Fenton, Murray and Jackson, of Leeds. This happened one fine sunny afternoon – and all looked couleur de rose. There were several big locomotives building for the Great Western Railway, of the "Argus" type – in all stages of completion. Of course I was caught and on my return frankly admitted how much I had been delighted and how I would like to be an engineer. As my next brother was just coming from school at the June holiday, it was soon arranged that he should take my place at the Oil Mills and that I should go to "the foundry". Meanwhile, a gentleman's son, who was an apprentice at the same works was asked by the governor to supper to initiate me.'

After giving an account of his early hard experiences as a shop apprentice, Joy went on:

'However, I got accustomed to the "skinning" and then got at the interest in the engines. These were the Great Western Railway passenger engines, 16in by 20in cylinder; 7ft wheel. They were a very handsome engine with bright brass dome [in fact the casing for the raised 'vaulted arch' firebox wrapper] and wheel splashers – old fork and gab motion – and I fitted one of these forks, having learnt to file and chip [he adds] to mash my knuckles with the hammer. At this time, all such work – fork ends of eccentrics, etc., was done by hand, the

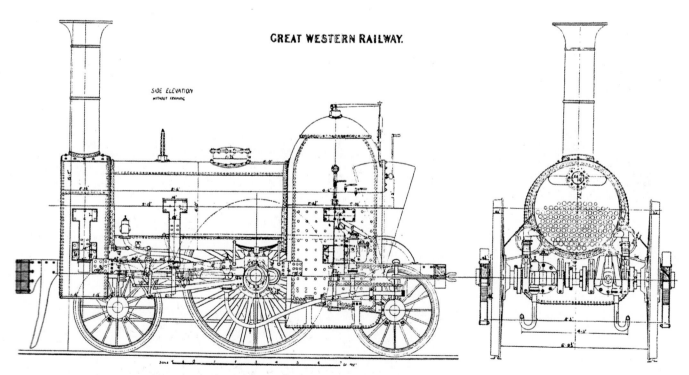

FIG. 6. GOOCH'S STANDARD LOCOMOTIVE.

The best-known products of Fenton, Murray & Jackson were the twenty Fire Fly class 2-2-2s completed between 1840 and 1842 at the Round Foundry. The Great Western Railway's first successful standard class of locomotive, their basic design is illustrated here by these sectional drawings. The Railway Foundry-built batch could be distinguished when new from the other members of the class by the provision of a manhole in the leading face of the 'Gothic' firebox wrapper. (*The Engineer*)

forging was chipped and filed and set to truth by a small set-square; and a pair of callipers for outside measures, and below for inside. Every fellow made his own in company's time and each fellow prided himself on the high finish of his pocket tools.'

In August 1842, Joy recorded:

'After all the work of a day, I well remember staying over hours to see one of these engines (at last) tried in steam. It was placed on special rails with struts in front and behind and the middle wheels resting on underground pillars [rollers] which they drive round, and to which was attached a counter to show the revolutions per minute, or miles per hour. After that test a dynamometer was yoked on at the trailing buffer and the hauling power noted. Any way now, I was in my element, and happy, and I forgot to be tired. The steam pressure was only 60 lbs. – and no lap on the valve.'

The Official Dimensions for the Fenton, Murray and Jackson Fire Fly locomotives showed some variance from Joy's figures and the cylinders were shown as being 15in bore by 18in stroke, although Joy had stated the driving wheel diameter correctly. The boiler barrel was 8ft 6in long and 4ft diameter whilst the firebox casing was 4ft 6in wide and 4ft 8in long with 131 tubes of 2in diameter. The working boiler pressure when new was quoted at lower than Joy's figure, namely 50psi, whilst the wheelbase was 13ft 4in equally divided. The weight of the locomotives in working order was approximately 24 tons of which 11¼ rested on the driving axle. The Fire Fly class proved an instant success and the Fenton, Murray and Jackson

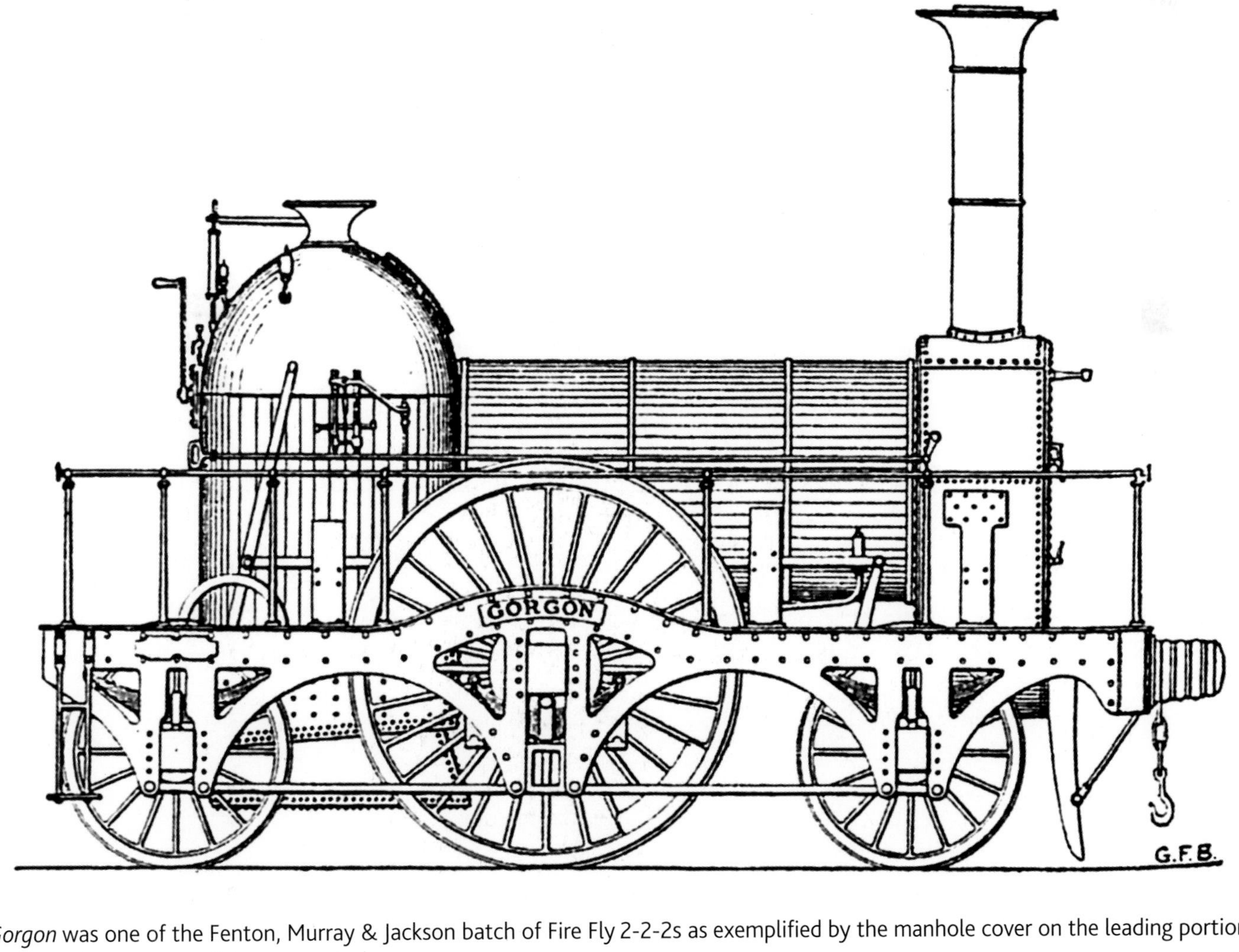

Gorgon was one of the Fenton, Murray & Jackson batch of Fire Fly 2-2-2s as exemplified by the manhole cover on the leading portion of the firebox wrapper. (*The Locomotive*)

locomotives were regarded as the best of the class. Two members of the batch achieved celebrity status: *Phlegethon* (maker's No. 46) which, with Daniel Gooch as driver accompanied by Brunel, took Queen Victoria's first railway journey from Slough to Paddington on 13 June 1842 in a time of 25 minutes for the 18¼ miles covered. *Ixion* (maker's No. 31) represented the broad gauge at the Gauge Commission Trials of December 1845 and undertook three return journeys between London Paddington and Didcot, achieving a maximum of 53 miles per hour with an 80 ton loading on the Didcot-bound journey and 60 miles per hour on the London-bound trip. With a 60 ton loading, the latter trip was undertaken in 63 minutes and 34 seconds at an average speed of 50 miles per hour with a maximum of 60, the latter figure increasing to 61 on the Didcot-bound run.

The standard gauge case was made by a series of tests between York and Darlington and although inferior results were achieved, the level of adoption of standard gauge at the time of the tests proved to be the deciding factor in ultimately sounding the death-knell for the Great Western's broad gauge. Nonetheless, during their period of operation, the Fire Fly class was to be seen all over the Great Western system including on the early Exeter expresses; all except three class members received 16in by 20in cylinders and seventeen, including ten of the Fenton, Murray and Jackson batch were rebuilt with lengthened mainframes and domeless boilers of more typical Great Western 'broad gauge' pattern. The final class member to be withdrawn from service was Fenton, Murray and Jackson-built *Ixion* in July 1879 whilst four of its Leeds-built sisters, *Charon*, *Gorgon*, *Lethe* and *Ganymede* were recorded as being surplus to the requirements of the Metropolitan Board of Works in the early years of the twentieth century, having found employment in London as stationary boilers following withdrawal from GWR service. All of these had, however, been extensively altered at Swindon during their operational careers.

Despite the success of the Round Foundry's products for the Great Western Railway, Fenton, Murray and Jackson was not destined to be a long-lived locomotive manufacturer. Shortly after the delivery of the last member of the batch Joy recorded:

> 'These engines finished slack times began and autumn and winter passed drearily. There were three of us apprentices in the works, and, being too far from home to return for meals, we fed in one of the workman's houses nearby. Breakfast 8 to 8.30; dinner 12 to 1; afternoon tea 4 to 4.30; works closing at 6 and opening at 6 a.m. Catering thus together we did it for about 6s. 6d. per week. Saturday closing time was 4 p.m.'

Joy paid a visit to the shops of the Manchester and Crewe Railway at Longsight, where John Ramsbottom was Superintendent, shortly after Christmas 1842, where he saw several products of Sharp, Roberts & Co., but his days at the Round Foundry were numbered. He further recorded early in 1843:

> 'Spring came and times were slacker. Finally Mr. Jackson sent for me to tell me that they were going to close the works so I should not be wanted.'

Fenton, Murray and Jackson thus passed into history shortly afterwards, but not before ensuring that locomotive manufacture in Leeds had made the transition from the experimental to the era of mainstream development. The direction of that development during the ensuing few years is a matter for the next chapter. As for the immediate material legacy of Fenton, Murray and Jackson, although the Round Foundry itself is long gone, having been demolished in 1875, other buildings that formed part of the complex are still extant. Two of the locomotive designs that formed part of the firm's product range, the Planet and the Fire Fly, have also been recreated in full size replica form and can be found at the Manchester Museum of Science and Industry and Didcot Railway Centre respectively.

CHAPTER 3

THE ORIGINS OF E. B. WILSON & CO.

In order to understand the history of E.B. Wilson & Co. and its products in detail one has to go back nearly a decade from the appearance of its name on the commercial scene. In 1837, one of the former apprentices at Fenton, Murray and Jackson, Charles Todd, joined forces with fellow engineer, James Kitson, and financial backer, David Laird, to set up a new manufacturing enterprise in Leeds. The *Leeds Mercury* for 1 September that year recorded:

> 'TODD, KITSON, and LAIRD, Engineers, BRASS & IRON FOUNDERS, RAILWAY FOUNDRY, HUNSLET LANE, LEEDS, Manufacturers of Locomotive Steam-Engines, Tenders, Carriage and Waggon Wheels, Axles, Springs, Stationary Steam Engines and Boilers, on the High and Low Pressure Principles, for Inclined Planes, Warehouses, Mills, &c. Also, Shafting and Gearing, Cranes, Turn-Tables, Pedestals or Chairs for Rails, Force and Lift Pumps, Cocks, Valves, Brass, Copper, and Iron Pipes, and Brass and Iron Castings of every Description.
>
> 'TODD, KITSON and LAIRD beg leave to announce that they are now commencing the above Business in all its Branches, on the most improved Principles, and in entirely new Buildings erected for the Purpose; and trust that their Capabilities and assiduous Attention will enable them with regard to Facility, Punctuality and superior Workmanship, to give Satisfaction to all who may favour them with their Orders. Railway Foundry, Hunslet Lane, Leeds, Sept. 1st 1837.'

The first locomotives completed at the new works were six specimens for the Liverpool and Manchester Railway. They were built in pairs to three different designs: 0-4-2 'Luggage Engines' *Lion* and *Tiger* (L&MR Nos. 57-8 respectively); 2-2-2 'Passenger Engines' *Leopard* and *Panther* (L&MR Nos. 62 and 64) 0-4-2 'Banking Engines' *Elephant* and *Buffalo* (L&MR Nos. 65 and 67). The first two pairs were delivered in 1838 with *Leopard* and *Panther* being delivered during the following year. These locomotives were all constructed on the principles pioneered with the Planet class, the last pair basically being Patentees whilst the other four essentially followed the pattern set by Stephenson's 0-4-2s for the Leicester & Swannington and Stanhope & Tyne Railways in 1832. Following a rebuild in 1841 and withdrawal from service in 1857, *Lion* was sold by the L&MR two years later for £400 to the Mersey Docks and Harbour Board and after over six decades of operation as a stationary engine was restored under London, Midland & Scottish Railway (LM&SR) auspices in time for the L&MR Centenary in 1930. Now no longer in working order, the engine is currently on display in Liverpool Museum.

The Todd, Kitson & Laird partnership was short-lived and as a consequence of the break-up late in 1839 and the appearance of a new protagonist, John Shepherd (born on 26 May 1811 and, according to his marriage certificate of 11 July 1839, a solicitor by profession), two new enterprises came into existence. Kitson & Laird set up on the north side of Pearson Street in what became the Airedale Foundry, whilst Shepherd & Todd was located on the south side of Pearson Street with its works inheriting the Railway Foundry name from the original manufacturer. The site for the new concern was purchased partly by means of a mortgage of £10,000 advanced to John Shepherd by his namesake father. The earliest locomotives constructed by Shepherd & Todd appear to have been three 0-4-2 tender locomotives for the Manchester & Leeds Railway. A sketch in David Joy's Diaries apparently illustrating these locomotives shows that they had chassis arrangements at least that were similar to *Lion* and *Tiger* of the Liverpool & Manchester Railway, although the boiler was of the front dome variety with only a modestly raised firebox wrapper. The cylinders were inside and, as with their Stephenson-designed precursors, arranged to drive upwards towards the rear coupled axle, and once again 'gab' motion was used. The cylinders were 14in bore by 20in stroke, coupled wheels 5ft diameter with 3ft 6in trailing wheels and the general appearance of the class was very similar to the still-extant *Ajax* built in 1841 by Jones, Turner & Evans in the Vienna Technical Museum as built.

The early arrangement of slide valves, with no lap, and valve gear with no provision for variable expansive

The Jenny Lind design was largely derived from this 2-2-2 design credited to John Gray with the first examples being supplied by Shepherd & Todd to the Hull & Selby Railway in 1840. The design featured framing similar in structure to the Stephenson Patentee class but the boiler was equipped with two domes and Gray's expansive motion was employed. Other locomotives of this type were also supplied to the York & North Midland Railway in the same year but in August 1845 when John Gray (then Locomotive Superintendent of the LB&SCR) was called upon to obtain similar locomotives for that railway, he had to turn to Timothy Hackworth of Shildon. Fourteen such locomotives were eventually supplied between September 1846 and November 1848, but the two earliest members of the class required completion work at Brighton Works. Dogged by poor workmanship and the fact that the design was already outdated by the time most of the class entered service, all had been radically rebuilt by January 1855. This drawing shows York & North Midland Railway No.9 *Antelope* in original condition. The use of Gray's valve gear necessitated a relatively high boiler pitch, a measure that was out of line with mainstream thinking on locomotive design in the United Kingdom at the time, a fact noted by David Joy (*The Late J.M. Fleming*).

working may have served the steam locomotive adequately during the 1830s but by the end of the decade attention was already turning to the economic advantages associated with variable expansion (facilitated by valves incorporating lap) and the use of lead (i.e. admission of live steam to the cylinder in advance of 'dead centre'), in the latter case particularly where locomotive speeds were increasing. John Gray, a former Liverpool & Manchester employee who had become Locomotive Superintendent of the Hull & Selby Railway patented his expansive motion at this time, which was the first viable attempt to address these problems. This motion comprised an expansion link pivoted at its lower end with a groove on each side. By means of a cam and roller mechanism, the forward and reverse eccentric rods could be alternatively engaged in their appropriate grooves. Although it was theoretically possible to obtain variable expansion in either direction of motion by using the expansion link, in practice the reversing mechanism was arranged to give variable expansion in forward gear only, owing to the fact that the normal pattern of smooth 'fore-and-aft' reversing lever movement associated with

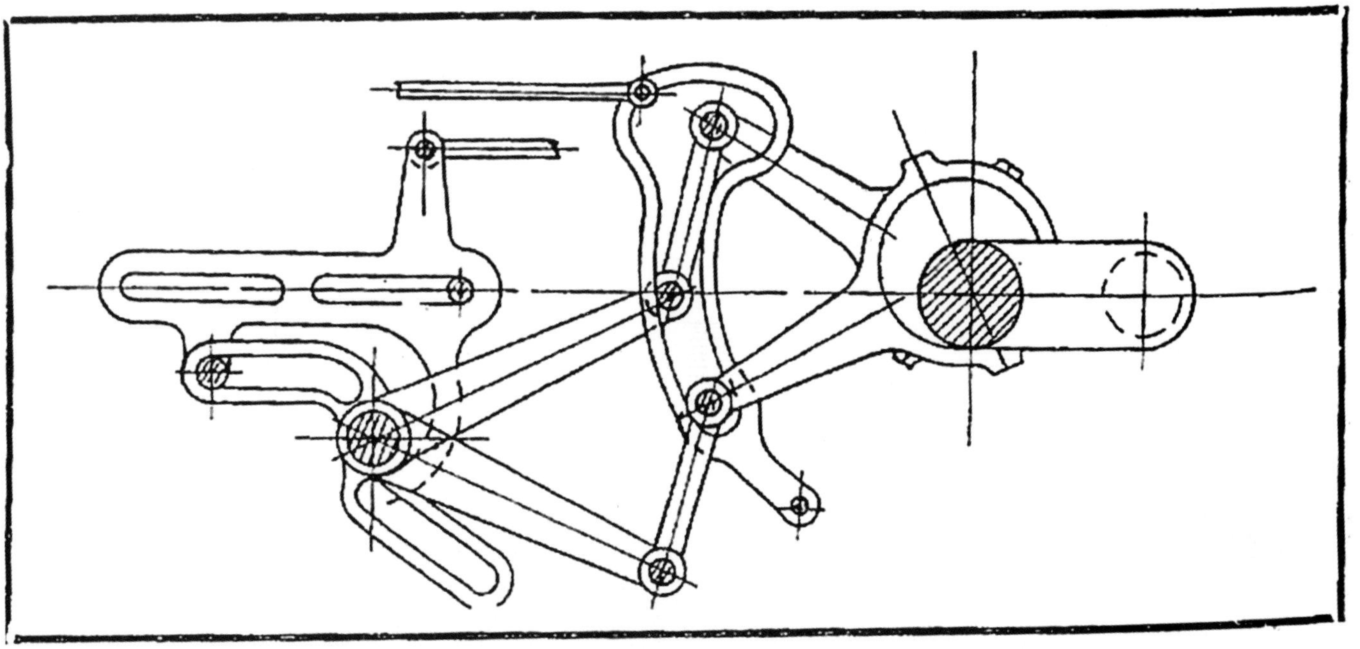

This sketch shows Gray's expansive motion (sometimes termed 'Horse Leg Motion') in detail, along with its cam-and-roller reversing mechanism. Sadly, in this view, the guide pin for the leading slot in the roller cradle has been omitted, but it can be seen that pulling the cradle backwards will pull the lower eccentric rod (which engages with the 'visible' slot on the expansion link) out of mesh with the expansion link, hence disengaging reverse gear. At the same time, the upper eccentric rod, whose slot is obscured from the reader, is brought into mesh and can progressively be brought closer to the expansion link fulcrum, thereby obtaining the variable 'cut-off' function. It will be noted that in reverse, only full gear was obtainable, not variable expansive working. (*Railway Magazine*)

later expansive valve gears was not possible with Gray's system. In 1840, six 2-2-2 locomotives were constructed for the Hull & Selby Railway with 12in or 13in by 24in cylinders, and at least two of these are believed to have possessed Gray's Motion. Five survived to be taken over by the Y&NMR in 1846 as Nos. 53-7 (later 38-42) with all being scrapped by 1854.Two further examples so fitted (with a cylinder bore or 13in) were completed for the Y&NMR in September of the same year as No. 9 *Antelope* and 10 *Ariel*. These locomotives all had 6ft diameter driving wheels, 'mixed' framing (i.e. outside bearings for the carrying wheels and inside for the driving wheels) and 'double dome' boilers. The same pattern of valve gear and basic boiler arrangements were used for four 0-6-0 goods locomotives completed for the Hull & Selby Railway with inside cylinders of 16inby 24in and 5ft 6in coupled wheels around 1842. These had the peculiarity of inside bearings for the intermediate and trailing wheelsets and outside bearings for the leading one. In consequence, the coupling rods transmitted their drive to the leading wheelset by means of return cranks. The reason for incorporating this measure was to allow for a wide spacing of the leading springs in order to reduce the tendency of the locomotive to 'roll' at the leading end whilst in motion. One of these locomotives bore the name *Hercules* whilst two others came into North Eastern Railway (NER) ownership in 1853, the longest-lived (on paper at least) being rebuilt in 1861 and replaced in 1882.

The coming of the North Midland Railway main line between Derby and its original terminus, Hunslet Lane in July 1840 facilitated the linking of both the Railway Foundry and the Airedale Foundry to the main railway network and this was accomplished by means of a connection, employing a rather unwieldy track layout, taken from a siding close to Hunslet Lane. The latter terminus was closed to passengers in 1846 following the opening of Leeds Wellington Station, but remained in use for the handling of goods until 1976, causing retention of the connection at Hunslet Junction that was latterly known as 'Hunslet Goods'. This, as will be seen, was to prove an important asset not only to the Railway Foundry of the 1840's and 1850's but also its successors during the ensuing years.

Eastern Counties Railway 'Long Boiler' 2-4-0s Nos. 37-41 were supplied by the Railway Foundry between December 1846 and March 1847. These locomotives possessed the following dimensions: coupled wheels 6ft.; leading wheels 3ft 8in.; cylinders 15in bore and 22 in stroke (laterally spaced at 6ft 2in between centres); engine wheelbase 11ft 8in (5ft 6in+6f. 2in); boiler barrel 13ft 7in long with an external diameter of 3ft 4in containing 107 non-ferrous tubes 1⅞in diameter. The firebox wrapper was 4ft long and 3ft 8½ in wide. The inside firebox was 3ft 2½in long and 3ft 0½in wide, whilst the total engine weight was 23.7 tons (6.925+7.1125+9.6625) and the maker's standard tender of the period was fitted. Despite Joy's poor view of the 'Long Boiler' type gained from operational experience, the five locomotives all survived to be rebuilt at Stratford between November 1863 and January 1868 and whilst many components, including the wheels and boiler, were renewed, the 'Long Boiler' configuration endured to the end, with the last survivor, No. 41, being scrapped in January 1882. (*The Locomotive*)

Following the collapse of Fenton, Murray and Jackson and a short period in the late spring of 1843 apparently without useful employment David Joy continued in his diaries:

'By the summer it was arranged that I should go to Shepherd and Todd, locomotive builders, Railway Foundry, as an office apprentice paying £200 premium, and to work for nothing 'till I was 21 – so I had not quite three years of it to look to. Here, with vastly increased advantages, I just worked the harder. Hours 9 to 5.30 and half an hour's walk home to dinner. The work in the shop was only two of Gray's six-coupled engines for the Hull and Selby Railway fitted with "Gray's Patent Expansion Valve Gear". Here was my fate again – "valve gears".'

Joy's fascination with expansive valve gears was to continue, for during the autumn of the same year he worked out a scheme for an expansive gear of his own design. According to Joy, this gear was later re-invented by Thomas Russell Crampton but it never saw the light of day in practical form under either name. Joy gave credit to Charles Todd for teaching him everything he needed to know during the slack period of late 1843 and early 1844, but in June 1844 the partnership of Shepherd and Todd ended when Charles Todd walked out leaving the former as sole proprietor. A new manager was brought in, a Mr. Buckle, who was not a locomotive engineer by trade but, in the words of Joy, 'gave us a temporary taste for marine engines.' Later entries in Joy's diaries suggest that in his case, the taste was to turn out not to be so temporary. In August 1844, whilst returning from a holiday in Wales, Joy took the opportunity to visit the Crewe Works of the Grand Junction Railway where he was able to meet Locomotive Superintendent Francis Trevithick and become familiar with the 'Crewe Type' locomotives then under construction which were, as we shall see, later to be manufactured for export at the Railway Foundry. By this stage, the Stephenson link valve motion had been invented, the first locomotive so fitted being Midland Railway No. 359 delivered by Robert Stephenson & Co. to the Midland Railway (MR) on 15 October 1842. A locomotive employing Dodd's Wedge motion had been delivered by the same maker in the preceding month which became MR No. 358. At this general stage in locomotive evolution, Joy noted, the age of the 'Stephenson Long Boiler' locomotive had been reached, locomotives characterized by three axles, outside cylinders, inside mainframes and a firebox, usually of the 'Gothic' (vaulted arch) pattern, located behind all of the axles. Joy drew particular attention to two examples, the notorious South Eastern Railway 2-2-2 *White Horse of Kent* which disgraced itself by frequent derailments owing to poor riding characteristics, on occasions with fatal results. The second was the 4-2-0 locomotive *Great A* which represented the standard gauge in the 'Battle of the Gauges' trials referred to in Chapter Two. These trials gave Joy his first opportunity to undertake a footplate ride on a steam locomotive. He recorded in the spring of 1845:

> 'We pupils used to frequent the railway station [Leeds] very much and one afternoon, watching the 4 p.m.

This drawing shows one of the Hurst/Hawkshaw 2-2-2 locomotives originally designed for the Manchester & Leeds Railway just prior to its 1847 absorption into the Lancashire & Yorkshire Railway, which continued building and ordering locomotives of the same design. In all, 81 of these locomotives were built between 1846 and 1849, some thirty-one at Miles Platting Works,twenty-one by Fairbairn and twenty-nine by Bury, Curtis and Kennedy of Liverpool. The coupled wheels were 5ft 9in diameter with a total wheelbase of 13ft 2in with cylinders 15in bore by 20 in stroke. David Joy, by the date of the reference in his Diaries must have been referring to the class prototype, No.37 when mentioning his acquaintance with the class, but despite its teething problems, the design was to influence Joy in two ways: in his redesigning of the erstwhile 'Stephenson Long Boiler' 2-2-2s to create the Jenny Red Legs; and in his adoption of the raised wrapper/back dome boiler in the initial design work on the 'Cambrian' system locomotive *Albion*. (*The Engineer*)

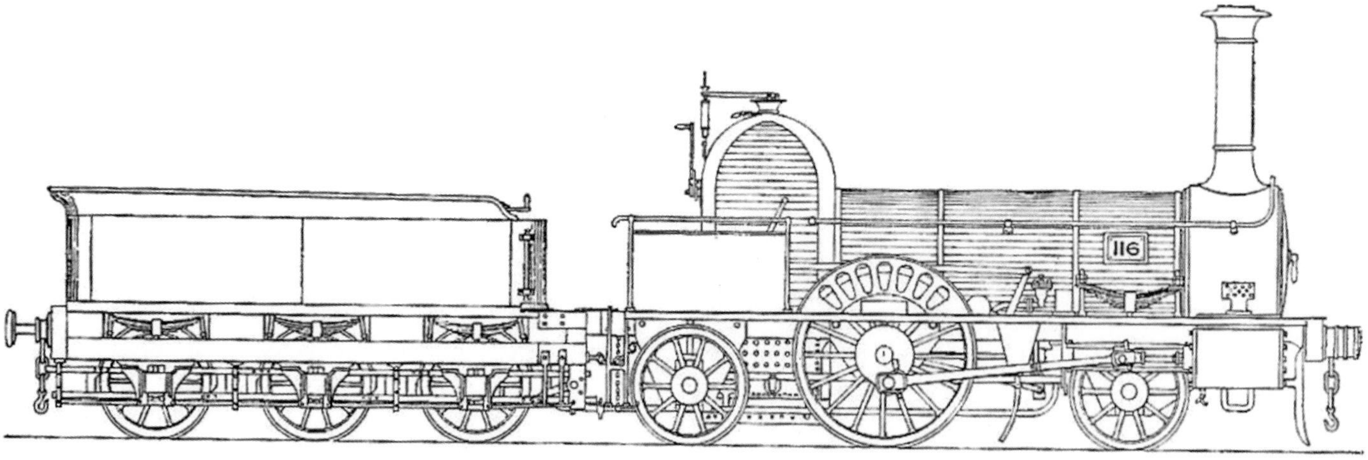

Eastern Counties Railway Jenny Red Legs 2-2-2 No.116 is seen in this drawing in company with an E.B. Wilson standard six-wheel tender of the mid-1840s period. The influence of the Manchester & Leeds design shown in the previous illustration on the chassis proportions of this locomotive is immediately apparent. This locomotive and its sister, No.117 were built in 1847, renumbered respectively 215-6 in 1854 and converted to 2-4-0STs (as Nos. 18-19) during the following year. (*The Locomotive*)

York express start, the driver Sid Watkins asked me if I would like a ride. (Will a duck swim, Rather). No coat, nothing on, I popped on to the engine and away we went, so jolly. This was my first fair run on an engine with a train; only to Castleford, still it was fine. I had many another like it. And this was "Great A".'

Back in November, the turbulent history of personnel in charge of the Railway Foundry had taken another twist and Shepherd sold out his interest in the business, being succeeded by Edward Brown Wilson (1818-1874), a member of the Hull-based Wilson shipping line family. At this stage, Wilson was sole proprietor of the business, but not of the premises whose legal status remained a complex affair. In January 1845, an order was received for ten locomotives for the Manchester, Bury and Rossendale Railway (later absorbed into the Lancashire and Yorkshire Railway). Joy recorded:

'Dutton, our manager, knew nothing about locomotives so I had to take all particulars from the railway's engineer, Mr. Cawbey, and I made all the drawings of the engine, going to the station to copy details from Stephenson's engines chiefly.'

In the event, it appears that only four of these outside cylinder 'long boiler' locomotives were ever built in the form intended. Eight further 2-4-0 'long boiler' specimens were built for the Y&NMR (together with a sister engine 'diverted' to the Midland Railway), with four further examples for the Eastern Counties and three more for the Sheffield, Ashton-under-Lyme and Manchester Railways (see next chapter), all completed by June 1848. Joy's apprenticeship ended in January 1846 and at the same time he referred to a new type of locomotive brought out by the Manchester and Leeds Railway that was in his words 'a beast' as it started out three times from Manchester before reaching Leeds but nonetheless became the standard type for the railway at that time. The class of locomotive to which Joy was referring was the Hirst/Hawkshaw outside cylinder 2-2-2 and it was destined to have a significant influence on subsequent events at the Railway Foundry, initially by reason of its general layout and later as a consequence of its boiler design as we shall see. Two Stephenson 'long boiler' inside cylinder 0-6-0 specimens with 15in by 24in cylinders and 4ft 9in coupled wheels were completed at this stage, one for the Sheffield, Ashton-under-Lyme and Manchester Railway (No. 13) and the other for the York & North Midland Railway (No. 39). As with the other contemporaneous Shepherd & Todd products, it would appear that 'Gothic' pattern fireboxes were utilized.

In order to satisfy Wilson's ambitions at this time, consolidation and expansion of the Railway Foundry was necessary. Prior to obtaining additional freehold land, on 25 September 1845 Wilson took out a lease of

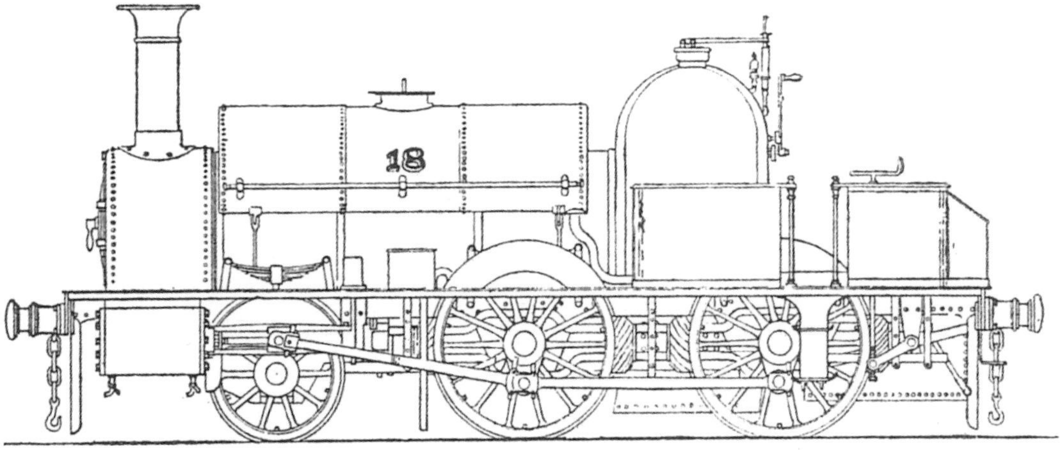

This drawing shows the erstwhile No. 116 in rebuilt form as 2-4-0ST No. 18. (*The Locomotive*)

fourteen years on the original 'Quadrangle' portion of the property hitherto used by Shepherd & Todd (bounded by Pearson St, Russell St, Yarmouth St and Jane St) from John Fretwell, from whom the neighbouring Kitson & Co. also leased land. Although the terms of this lease were honoured, it is clear from the events of the following fourteen months as recorded by Joy that all was not well and that relations between Wilson and certain other parties at the Railway Foundry at this stage were far from cordial.

On 4 March 1846, free of his apprenticeship and with his twenty-first birthday a day behind him, Joy sought permanent employment at the Railway Foundry but there were no paid posts on offer at the time. During the next five weeks or so, he also sought employment in Manchester at the Manchester & Leeds Railway and at Sharp, Roberts & Co. also without success, but whilst these efforts were in progress, E.B. Wilson had distanced himself from the Railway Foundry and the day to day running of affairs was in the hands of a new partnership. One of the new leading lights was James Fenton (1815-1863), the son of one of the partners in the Round Foundry and a former Locomotive Superintendent of the Manchester and Leeds Railway and Acting Engineer of the Leeds and Thirsk Railway. The other prominent figure was John Chester Craven (1813-1887). Craven was a native of Leeds, having been born in Hunslet and he had served his apprenticeship at the Round Foundry, where he remained gainfully employed until 1837. During this time, he had supervised the 'second wave' of locomotive construction from the age of 19. After nearly a year working in London for Messrs. Maudslay, Craven returned to Leeds, firstly joining Todd, Kitson & Laird and then spending a three-year term as Works Manager for Shepherd & Todd before serving under James Fenton (Jnr.) as Locomotive Foreman on the Manchester and Leeds Railway. In consequence of this 'break-up' as Joy termed it, and change of leading personnel, Joy was offered a draughstman's position and immediately took up employment, despite being somewhat disappointed with the remuneration. At this stage, the Railway Foundry was trading as Fenton & Craven, a title that was to persist throughout most of the remainder of 1846.

By May 1846, it was clear that the shortcomings of the Stephenson 'long boiler' type were becoming apparent, especially in relation to passenger locomotives. In relation to alterations ordered for the Y&NMR (the 'long boiler 2-4-0 locomotive previously referred to as diverted to the M.R. was in reality taken into that company's stock on 9 September 1846 and converted to a double framed inside cylinder locomotive approximately two years later), Joy recalled:

> 'Long boiler engines were going out; the engines did well but they were bad rollers. One dreary afternoon the driver came and said Mr. Carby wanted to see them. Willis and I went and left with the 4 p.m. express to York, a wet afternoon with driving rain... And did not that engine tumble about. She rolled like a ship in a gale. But we put balance weights on the wheels and she went all right then and so did all the others when balanced. We were now busy scheming engines for the Leeds and Dewsbury Railway of which Jimmy Fenton was boss. The only idea in favour was the Manchester, Bury and Rossendale Railway engine, or some sort of long boiler-but we ended by putting the cylinders outside and the trailing wheels behind the firebox.'

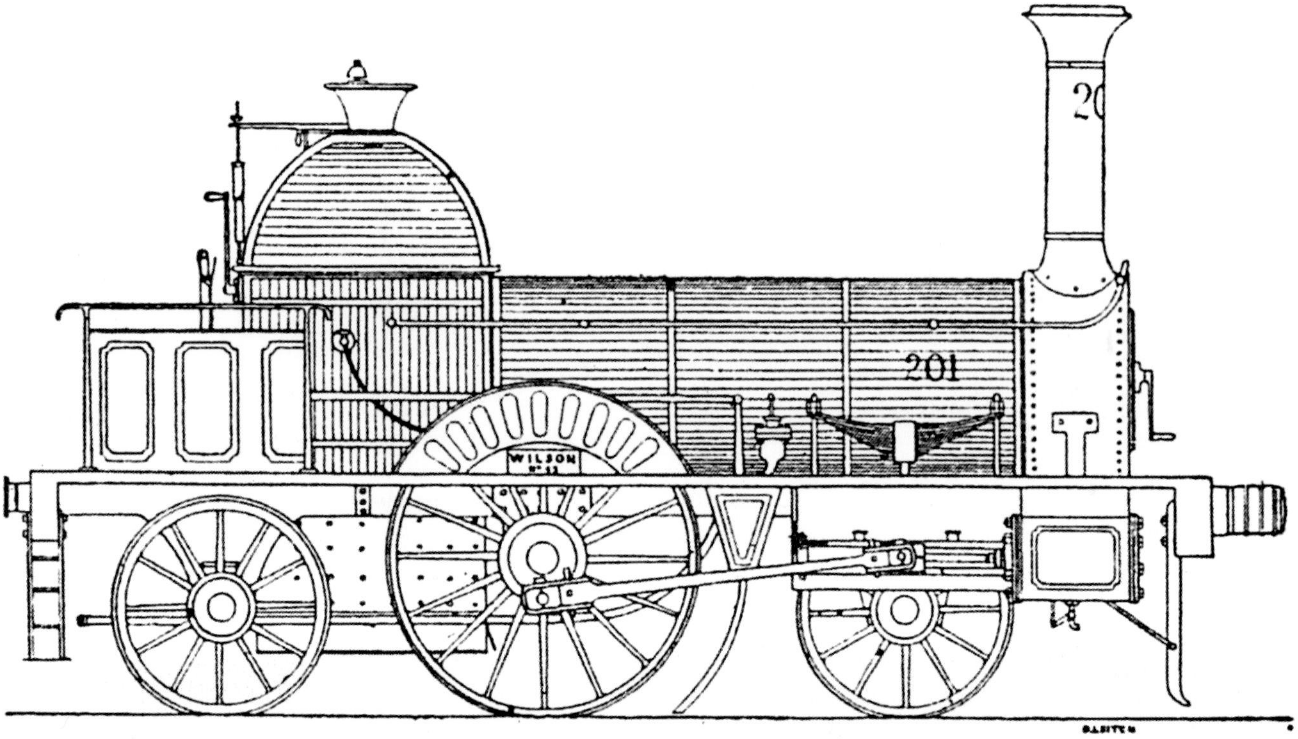

The Jenny Red Legs class also found its way to the Southern Division of the L&NWR where the livery, with its red wheel spokes, gave rise to the nickname. The quoted dimensions were: driving wheels 6ft diameter and carrying wheels 4ft 6in; cylinders 15in bore and 20in stroke; wheelbase 15ft (8+7) boiler heating surface 562sqft. As with the ECR examples, the boiler lagging was painted mahogany and the locomotives, numbered 201-4 by their owners, were delivered in 1848. Shortly after delivery, Nos.202-4 were sold to the Leeds & Thirsk Railway leaving only No.201 to spend much of its revenue-earning career on banking duties between Euston and Camden. Successively renumbered 801 and 1192 in 1861 and 1863 respectively, it was scrapped in 1867. (*The Locomotive*)

It would appear that the four 2-2-2s ordered by the Leeds, Dewsbury & Manchester Railway (LD&MR), along with two others, which were purchased by the Eastern Counties Railway (with which Craven has some form of association at this time) were constructed using the cylinders, wheels and other material intended for the previously mentioned curtailed order for 'long boiler' locomotives for the Manchester, Bury and Rossendale Railway. The LD&MR. was absorbed prior to opening by the London & North Western Railway (L&NWR) (Northern Division) to whom its four specimens were delivered where they were numbered 201-4. In relation to six goods engines supplied at the same time, Joy goes on record that:

> 'The goods [locomotives] were inside cylinders, six coupled inside frames, cylinders below leading axle; a bad engine, like Railway Foundry's first lot of six coupled for [the] Great Northern Railway. There should have been plenty of room for bearings but there was not. And the cry now was for low engines.'

These locomotives were given the numbers 35-39 & 43 by the L&NWR (Northern Division). They were equipped with 16in by 24in cylinders and 5ft wheels and all had disappeared from L&NWR service by the early part of 1865.

On Saturday 30 November 1846, David Joy returned to work at the Railway Foundry following a two week holiday in the Isle of Wight. He found E.B. Wilson back in power. A new, and vitally important chapter in the history of locomotive building in Leeds was about to begin.

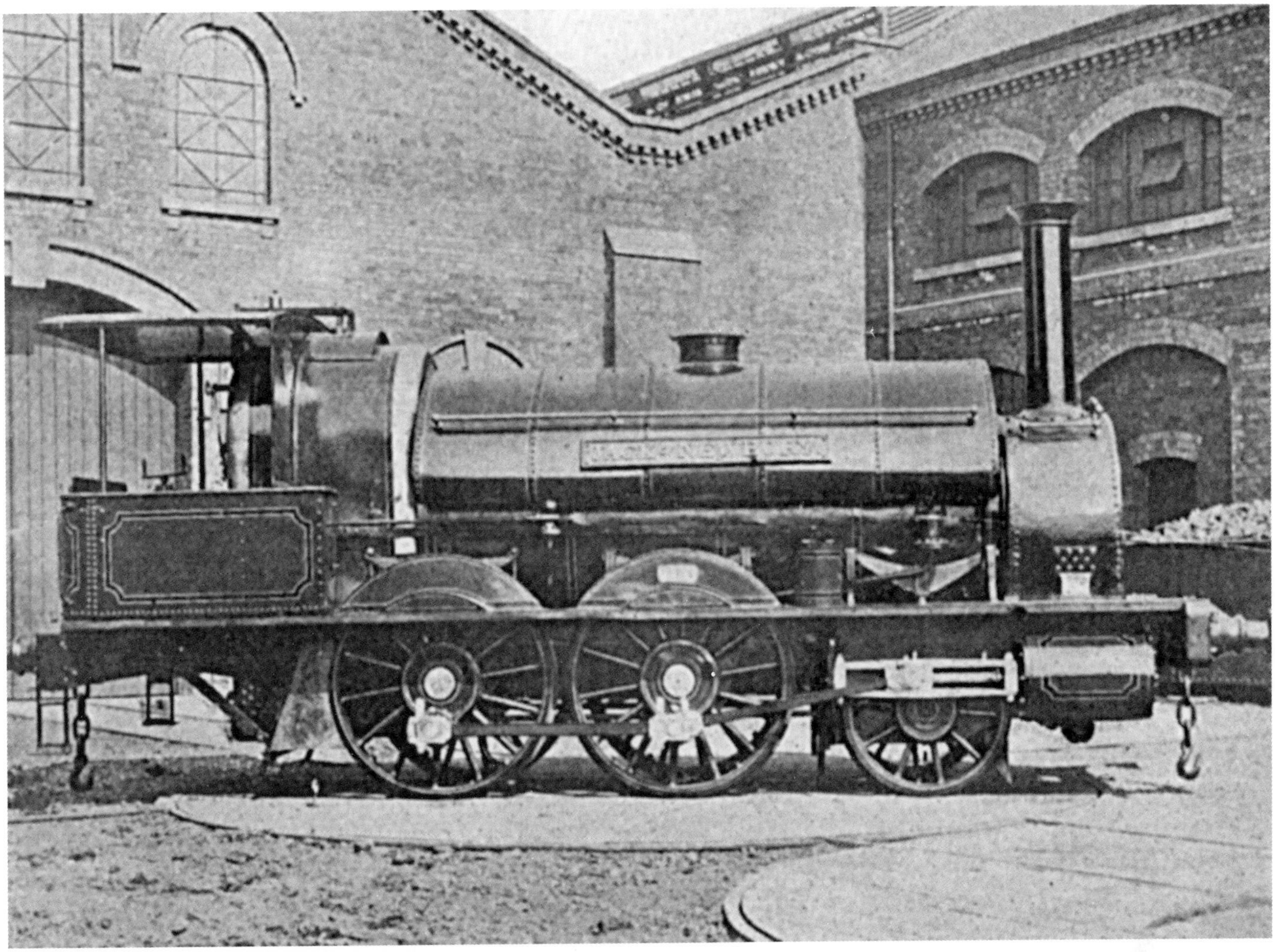

The locomotive *Jack of Newbury* (used by the Tredwells, the contractors who built the Worcester-Stourbridge; Stourbridge-Dudley, and Dudley-Tipton sections of the OW&WR) was described by David Joy as a White Horse of Kent (long-boiler outside cylinder 2-2-2 type), but appears always to have been a 2-4-0. The engine was delivered to the contractors John and Thomas Tredwell at Newbury on 26 May 1846, having been constructed at a cost of £2,000 by Fenton & Craven at the Railway Foundry. When new, the locomotive was equipped with a tender and would effectively have been a smaller version of Eastern Counties Railway Nos. 37-41. It appears to have been used on the building of the Reading-Hungerford and Reading-Basingstoke lines in 1847-8. It remained in Tredwell family ownership until 1874, having been used on a variety of contracts, including the L&NWR's Eccles-Tyldsley-Wigan line in 1861-4 before undergoing a rebuild at Vulcan Foundry's workshops. Following sale to Messrs Llewellins & James in 1874, another rebuild followed and it appears that the accompanying photograph was then taken at the Midland Railway's sheds at Bristol. This was the rebuild that resulted in the locomotive becoming a saddle tank, but the firebox wrapper design at this stage is also of interest, given the fact that the original would have been of the 'vaulted arch' White Horse of Kent pattern. The revised design suggests that at some stage in its career the locomotive had made either a return visit to the Railway Foundry or a visit to Boyne Engine Works for a new boiler. Be that as it may, the last known existential reference to *Jack of Newbury* was in an advertisement placed by Llewellins & James in *The Engineer* in December 1881, although the locomotive was mentioned in *The Locomotive* for 15 November 1907 where it was described as having 14in by 20in cylinders, 3ft leading wheels and 4ft 9in coupled wheels. (*Via Russell Wear*)

CHAPTER 4

THE JENNY LINDS AND THEIR IMMEDIATE DERIVATIVES

On the evening of being informed of Edward Brown Wilson's return to the Railway Foundry, David Joy, by now Chief Draughstman, was detailed to travel to London and thence to Brighton to see John Gray, who was now Locomotive Superintendent of the London, Brighton & South Coast Railway (LB&SCR), about an order for ten new locomotives. He continued in his Diaries:

> 'Arrived at Brighton on Sunday Night [1 December]. Spent three weeks taking tracings all day, and receiving instructions from Gray after 7 p.m. at night. He gave me an engine pass, so I went all over the line on the various engines-to Chichester on "Satellite", a little engine by Rennies [George & John Rennie].'

Whilst on the LB&SCR, Joy took the opportunity to take a ride on Bodmer's four-piston 'balanced' engine from Brighton to Lewes via a descent at Falmer Bank, where he recorded how the same locomotive derailed on the same descent a few years later, killing both members of its crew. He further recorded:

> 'Had a spin to London on one of the Gray engines built by Hackworth to the same drawings that I was taking.'

At this stage, therefore, it was clear that what was envisaged for the LB&SCR order was a batch of ten 2-2-2s of similar pattern to the Shepherd & Todd products for the Y&NMR. and Hull & Selby Railway and fitted with Gray's valve motion. The late delivery of the Hackworth locomotives, in spite of attempts to remedy the situation, did not commend Gray to the Brighton system's Directors, however, and Gray was given three months' notice, departing at the end of January 1847 being succeeded immediately by Thomas Kirtley, formerly locomotive Superintendent of the North Midland Railway, and (following the latter's death) on the 15 November 1847 by none other than John Chester Craven. Joy continued in his account:

> 'I had hardly started on the Gray drawings when word came that Gray was "out" and we were to design a new engine. I as Chief Draughstman, had it to do so set off scheming by order of Fenton, of course, on the lines of the last engine we had, Leeds and Dewsbury, short boiler (11ft. 6in.), outside cylinders, drivers far back, trailing wheels behind the firebox, and as much heating surface as possible in tubes, and 60 sq.ft in firebox if possible. Got out 10 or 12 schemes in a week, and threw all aside-after dissension. Then-12 noon, Saturday-Fenton came in to me and said "Try another, and give inside cylinders, 15in by 20in, and 6ft wheels and again the biggest surface possible". I was sick of it and bolted for my Saturday afternoon.'

It is clear from this entry that, with Gray out of the picture, Joy's initial thoughts turned to building a batch of locomotives similar to the Jenny Red Legs design to satisfy the Brighton order. Fenton, however, whilst taking on board some of the criticisms of the Gray design still had some regard for its chassis design with its inside cylinders and combination of outside bearings for the carrying wheels and inside ones for the drivers. The stage was thus set for one of the most important episodes in nineteenth century steam locomotive evolution. Joy continued:

> 'Arrived at home. I thought over the engine to go for-and at once struck me what a pretty engine it would make. So abandoned the Leeds and Dewsbury type, and all the feeling in favour of the long boiler class. This was going back to the old engine, and my inoculation into Gray's ideas at once biased me in favour of that type. I had studied very well for three weeks

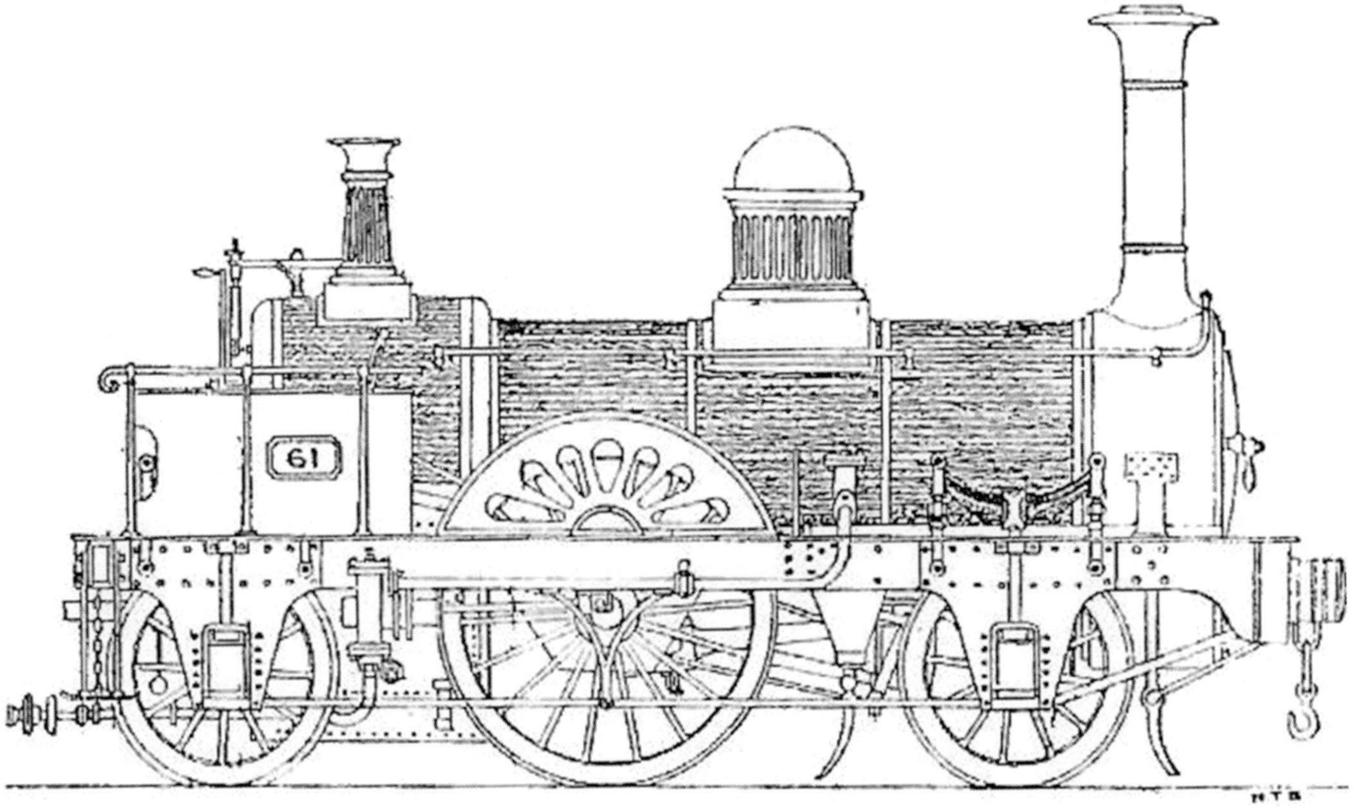

The first of David Joy's Jenny Linds was supplied by the Railway Foundry to the L.B. & S.C.R. as No. 60 in June 1847 and nine further locomotives of similar design followed during the ensuing 14 months, with the class taking the numbers 61-70 (the prototype being renumbered 70). The design proved a major advance upon their Gray-designed precursors and, apart from Nos. 62-3, which were effectively renewed by Craven in 1869 and 1865 respectively as 0-4-2Ts), they retained their 2-2-2 configuration throughout their operational careers, with No. 67 being the last withdrawal in this condition in April 1879. This drawing shows No. 61 as built and emphasizes the attractive lines of the design, with its combination of inside and outside frames, polished mahogany boiler lagging and fluted boiler mountings (a feature that found its way onto non-Wilson L.B. & S.C.R. types of the period). The boiler feed pumps on all but the last-built locomotive, No. 69, were driven from a crankpin mounted on the driving wheel boss (*The Locomotive*).

and had ferreted among all the types of engines on the Brighton Railway, and had ridden on most of them, with the idea to get a definite opinion of my own on what was best for the speeds. So, having a sheet of double elephant [drawing paper sheet size 26½in by 40in] mounted ready, as I mostly had now (as I spent all my evenings at drawing any engine I could get outside dimensions of) I set to work and drew out with Gray tendencies, a 10ft 6in boiler as big in diameter as I could get it, and as low down as I could possibly get it, for the cry was one for low centres of gravity to secure steadiness, though Gray did not seem to care for it [at this stage in the proceedings it should be noted that Gray was constrained from using a low boiler pitch for his locomotive designs as a consequence of incorporating his design of motion into them. Joy was not destined to adopt this measure]. Cylinders 15in by 20in; driving single, and as far back as possible, 6ft diameter. Inside frames which must be made to carry the cylinders, the [inside] frames stopped at the firebox, so that the firebox was got as wide as the wheels would allow it. This, of ordinary length, gave 80sqft of surface, and with 124 tubes 2in. diameter gave 730sqft of surface, or a total of over 800sqft. Then I put on Gray's outside bearings for the leading and trailing wheels, 4ft diameter, giving the bearings below, thus making a firm wheel base with no overhanging weight.

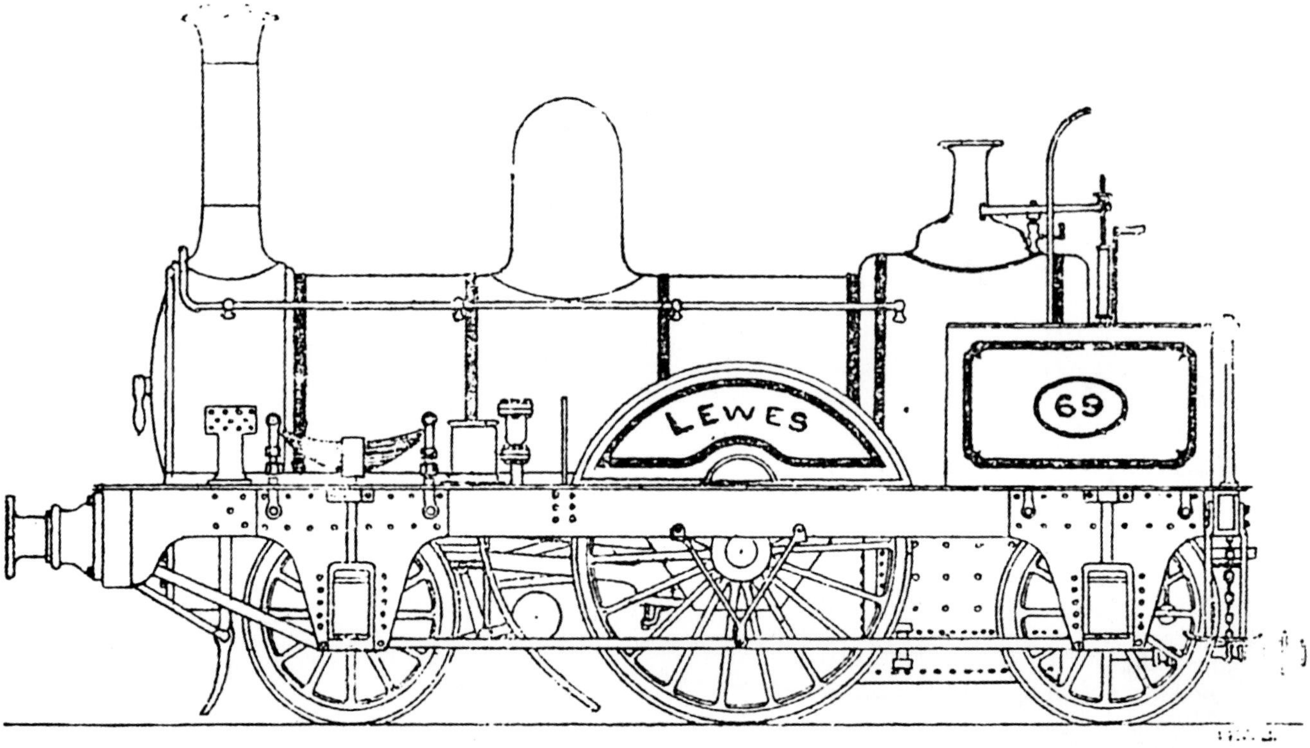

No. 69 was slightly different from the other members of the class built for the L. & B.S.C.R. as it was supplied with 6 ft. 3 in. driving wheels and a boiler with a firebox mid-feather (presumably longitudinal) increasing the overall heating surface to 1000 sq. ft. The position of the boiler feed pumps on the preceding locomotives had led to difficulties from exposure to the atmosphere, particularly in winter when they were liable to freeze up. They were repositioned between the inside and outside frames and driven from the crossheads on No. 69. Another difference when new between No. 69 and the others was that the former was fitted with a brass chimney cap in lieu of the copper caps of the latter. In this illustration, No. 69 is shown in Stroudley days when the mahogany cladding had given way to sheet iron cladding with conventional lagging, the 'classical' Wilson boiler mountings had been replaced and the engine had acquired the name *Lewes*. Entering service in August 1848, the locomotive was rebuilt under Craven's direction in 1857 and again by Stroudley in 1872, finally being withdrawn from service in March 1876 (*The Locomotive*).

> 'Cylinders and valves between with ordinary (then approved) link but slung only from one side. The steam dome on middle of the boiler, and two safety valves under a cover on the firebox. The fluted decoration of dome and valve covers came in afterwards and were a sort of combination of old London and South Western Railway domes and Gray's square boxes. So also, the radially barred splasher for driver was a mixture of a lot of various engines.'

Joy completed the preliminary design for the new locomotive during the Saturday evening and on the following Monday he took it to the Railway Foundry for approval after which he worked out the final details. These included a certain amount of 'thickening and strengthening' of various components, notably the boiler and firebox, resulting in an increase in weight of three tons over that originally envisaged. Joy then stated:

> 'This, then, was the origin of the engine afterwards called the "Jenny Lind", the type of the Leeds Railway Foundry engine, and I believe the first of the really steady fast runners and low coke burners.'

The final details for the new design were completed during the last weeks of 1846 but there was another pressing requirement for Joy to undertake at this time, namely the drawings for the new Smithy and Erecting Shop at the Railway Foundry. Despite the upheaval

This engraving of a side elevation view of one of the Midland Railway's Jenny Lind locomotives appeared in *The Engineer* for 10 January 1896. The class was introduced onto the Midland Railway in September 1847 and the general style of turnout, including the polished mahogany boiler lagging, was similar to its LB&SCR predecessors. Sadly, no makers' drawings appear to have survived of the tenders that initially accompanied these locomotives. (*The Engineer*)

that had occurred in the management structure during the preceding years, there had been an increase in activity on the Shop Floor resulting in a tenfold increase in the workforce from 40 to 400. The new shops were opened in May 1847 and by the end of the same month, the first of the new locomotives for the LB&SCR. was completed as that railway's No. 60 and it was given a test run from Leeds to Wakefield via Normanton. Joy recorded that on the return run, the locomotive lost steam and was nearly run into by the Manchester Mail. The loss of steam would appear to have been normal 'teething troubles' for Joy certainly believed that the use of 120lb/sqin boiler pressure, as opposed to the customary 80 or 90, was a major contributory factor to the design's subsequent success. He recalled:

> '... of course it was the steam pressure that did it. But who was to blame, or to credit, for this lift of pressure from 80 or 90 to 120 lbs.? I have no note, but doubt not it was Jimmy Fenton. Thus the engine came out a mixture of the good points of the Gray as first designed by Gray himself for the Brighton Railway, and the engine that had come of the long boiler, with its inside frame: from this type it got the elastic plate frame, for leading and trailing wheels, but not as rigid as Gray's design. So these engines at high speed always rolled softly and did not jump and kick at a curve. Another thing which I think came of my fancy was a very free exhaust. I always, from the first, saw the blast port cores made, and with my own hands passed over them, had them pared over to get a free passage.'

Delivery of the LB&SCR.'s ten singles was a protracted affair with Nos. 60-66 entering traffic prior to the end

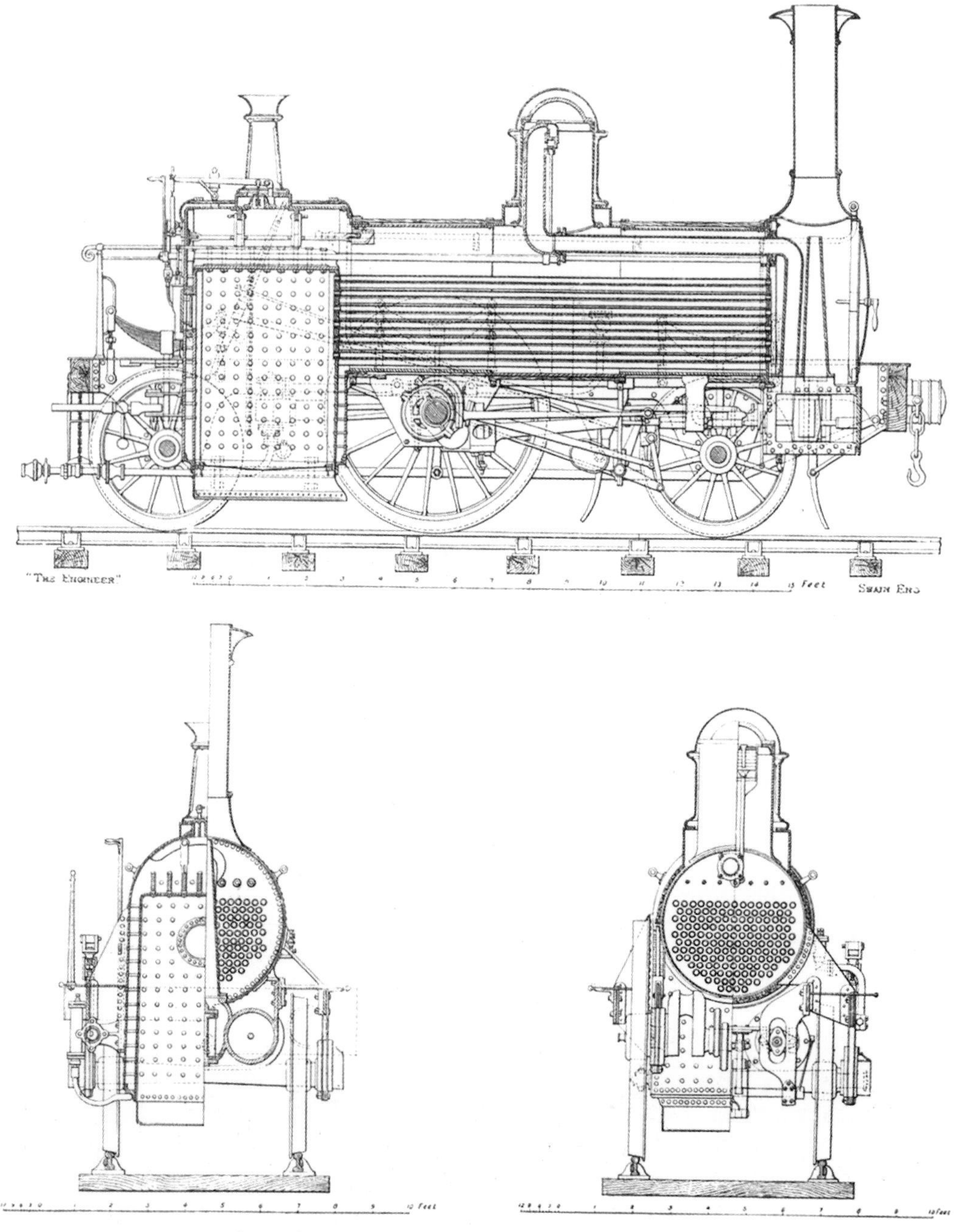

These longitudinal and lateral sections of the Midland Railway Jenny Lind appeared in *The Engineer* for 6 March 1896. Close study of these views reveals interesting constructional details, such as the combination of inside frames for the driving axle and outside frames for the carrying wheels and the 'underhung' weighshaft arrangement. The padded leather buffers, apparently favoured by Joy, are evident in these and the previous view and this constructional feature persisted on related locomotives built for the OW&WR in the 1850s. (*The Engineer*)

of 1847 and 67-69 following up to the end of August 1848. In the event, the pioneer engine was renumbered 70 owing to its original number having been previously allocated to one of the 'Hackworth' locomotives. According to Joy, when new the locomotive carried the Jenny Lind name, after the famous Swedish singer of the period. The main recorded dimensions for the earliest variety of the class, which (unlike later varieties) appears to have been equipped with a four-wheel tender, were as follows:

Cylinders	15in (Bore), 20in (Stroke)
Wheel Diameter	6ft (Driving), 4ft (Carrying)
Wheelbase	7ft + 6ft 6in
Boiler Barrel Length	10ft 6in.
Boiler Tubes	124, 2in diameter
Boiler Pressure	120lb/sq.in
Heating Surface	720sqft (Tubes)
	80sqft (Firebox)
Locomotive Weight (Working Order)	24.05 tons

The last engine, No. 69 differed from the others in having 6ft 3in driving wheels, a larger boiler and a double firebox. As recorded by Joy in May 1847, the boilers were lagged with mahogany which was polished when new but subsequently painted in alternate green and red strips before eventually being enclosed with conventional cladding. The Jenny Linds proved to be an instant success on the London-Brighton main line expresses and when displaced from these duties by more modern locomotives, they saw use on the company's secondary routes, such as on the Brighton-Portsmouth coastal trains. All received extensive reconstruction work during Craven's tenure of office, with two (Nos. 62-3) being renewed as double framed 0-4-2 side tanks, lasting until 1879-82. The largest locomotive, No. 69, was even rebuilt again under Stroudley but the last in service in recognizable form, No. 67 retained its Wilson-pattern dome cover until withdrawn in 1879. The influence exerted on the Brighton company's locomotive building policy by these engines continued into the 1860s as similar machines continued to be built in-house under Craven's auspices.

Back at the Railway Foundry, Joy stated that E.B. Wilson & Co. had:

> '... got lots of orders here and there for this engine and made at the rate of one per week-then a vast accomplishment. Now arranged same engine for a four-coupled.'

Close examination of the surviving drawings for both the Jenny Lind and the 'double frame standard goods' (to be described) reveal that, given the fact that the inside frames used for the coupled wheels on the 2-4-0 version of the Jenny flanked the firebox, the foundation ring and lower part of the firebox would have to have been 'waisted in' by approximately 2 inches

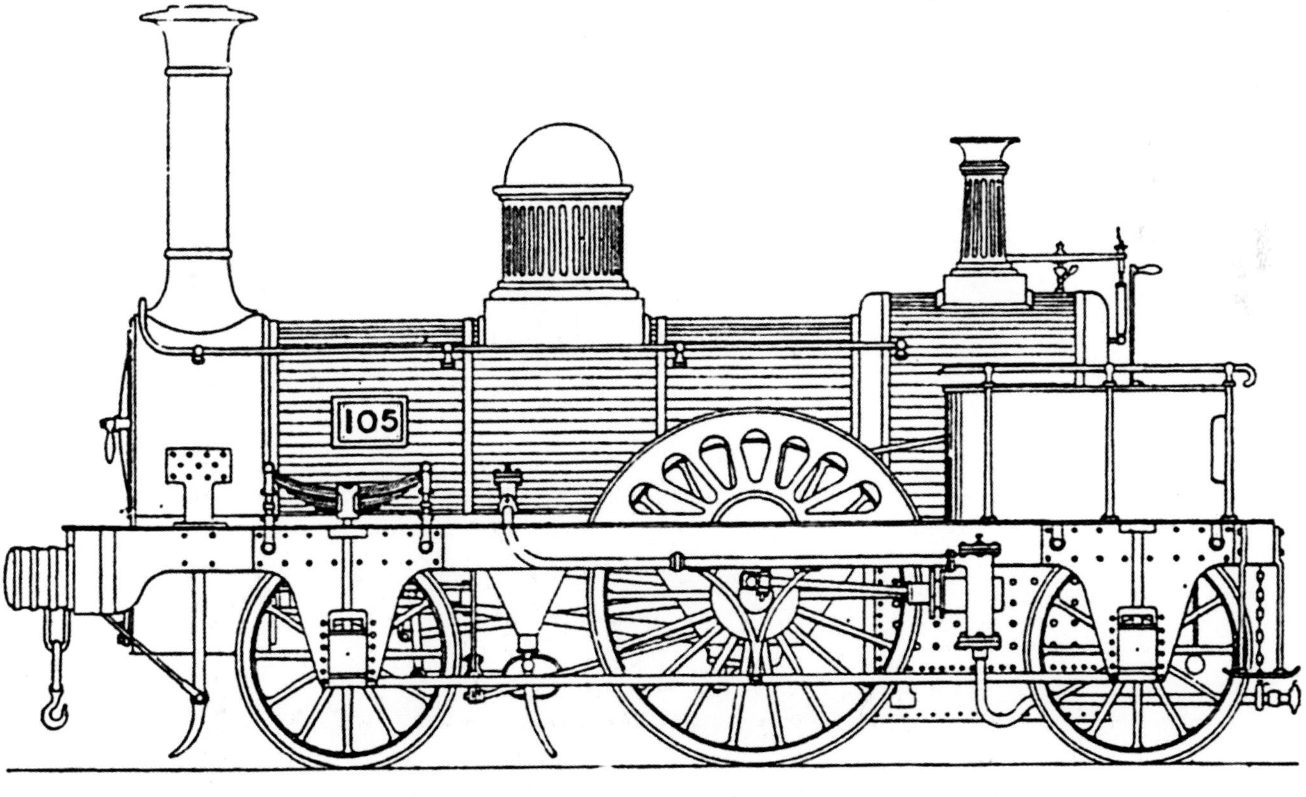

This illustration shows one of the second batch of Jenny Lind class locomotives delivered to the Eastern Counties Railway during the latter part of 1848. The longer overall locomotive wheelbase (14ft 7in as opposed to 13ft 6in) when compared with LB&SCR No. 61 is apparent and this allowed for a larger boiler. The change in the pattern of the spacing from the 14ft 6in wheelbase of Nos. 103-4 appears to have been brought about by a wish to get a better relationship between firebox and boiler barrel lengths. The feed pump situation with the ECR Jennies appears to have been the reverse of that experienced on the Brighton system as Nos. 103-4 were delivered with crosshead driven pumps and 105-7 with the axle driven 'exposed' variety as illustrated. (*The Locomotive*).

when compared with the former two classes. In any case, the basic Jenny pattern boiler, with its slightly raised casing and fluted dome and safety valve covers, formed the pattern of much of E.B. Wilson boiler design throughout the remainder of the company's existence, even persisting into the early days of the successor concern, Manning Wardle & Co. The new erecting shop facilities ensured that twelve pits were available for the erection of locomotives enabling a dozen to be built for stock at any one time to await suitable buyers. It was even recorded that a new locomotive would occasionally be sent to one of the main line stations and placed in a siding for inspection by the owning company as a marketing measure, with prices being quoted for either 'delivered under own steam or hauled dead'. During the same month that the first of the Brighton Jennies was delivered, the first Eastern Counties Railway example appeared. This locomotive was numbered 103 on that line and with its sister No. 104, delivered some three months later in September 1847, had a wheelbase lengthened by one foot at the leading end when compared with LB&SCR No. 60 at 8ft+6ft 6in. No. 103 was involved in a derailment in the Tottenham vicinity on 20 February 1860, resulting in the deaths of both crew members, along with four members of the public. Nonetheless, it proved to be the longest-lived of all of the Eastern Counties Jennies as it lasted until July 1874. Three further locomotives of the same general type were delivered to the Eastern Counties during the last quarter of 1848, being numbered 105-107. The quoted dimensions for these locomotives were as below:

Cylinders	15in (Bore), 20in (Stroke)
Wheel Diameter	6ft (Driving), 4ft (Carrying)
Wheelbase	7ft+7ft 1in
Boiler Barrel Length	11ft
Firebox Wrapper	4ft 6in (L) 4ft 2in (W)
Inner Firebox	3ft 9in (L) 3ft 6½in (W)
Total Heating Surface	1000sqft
Locomotive Weight (Working Order)	24.05 tons

Another interesting detail difference when compared with the earlier two locomotives was that these three reverted to the original arrangement of having their feed pumps driven by crank pins on the driving wheel centre bosses. As with No. 104, none of the later three survived into the 1870s. Eight members of the 2-4-0 variant class were also delivered to the Eastern Counties Railway between December 1848 and February 1850 as the Railway's 193-200. The quoted dimensions for these locomotives as built were rather different to locomotives of similar specification supplied to the Midland Railway and were:

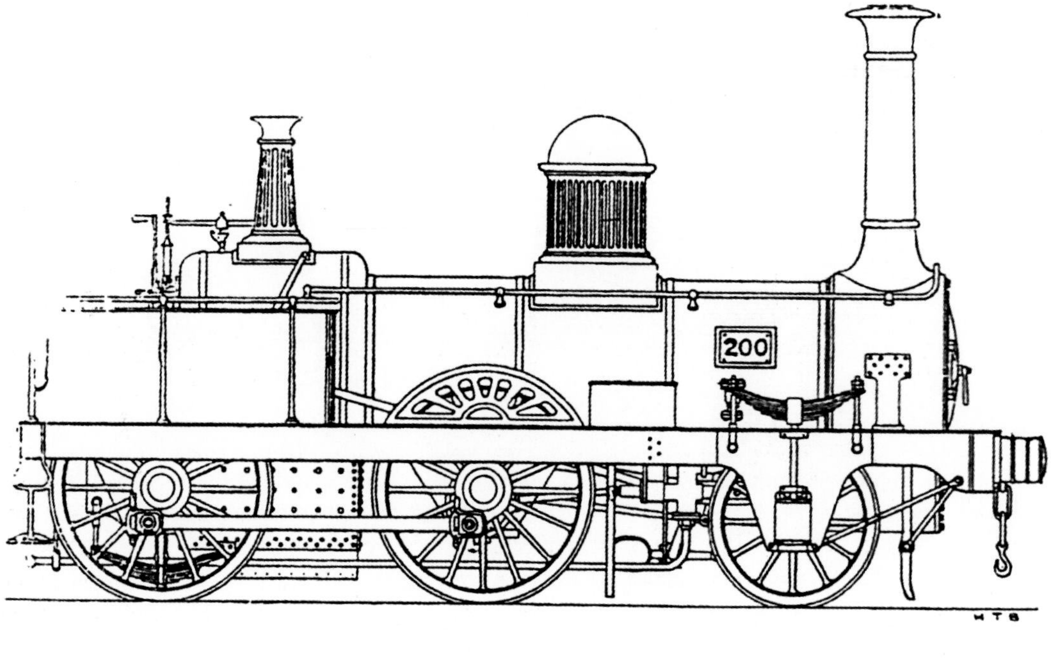

ECR Nos. 193-200 were 2-4-0 mixed traffic versions of the Jenny Lind class and the last member of the batch is illustrated in this drawing. The lateral position of the crosshead driven feed pumps can be deduced from the drawing as they are clearly inboard of the coupled wheels but outboard of the inside frames. (*The Locomotive*).

Cylinders	15in (Bore), 22in (Stroke), 2ft 5in Centre Spacing
Wheel Diameter	5ft (Driving), 3ft 8in (Leading)
Wheelbase	7ft 2½ in +7ft 6in
Boiler Barrel	10ft 10in Long (Lap Jointed) 3ft 6¾in (Internal Diameter)
Firebox Wrapper	4ft 2¾in. (L) 4ft 2in (W)
Inner Firebox	3ft 6¾in. (L) 3ft 6½in (W)
Boiler Tubes	1⅞in Diameter 11ft 3in. Long
Tube Heating Surface	863⅘sqft
Firebox Heating Surface	81⅓sqft
Grate Area	12⅗sqft
Locomotive Weight (Working Order)	24 tons 3½cwt (7.925+10.75+5.5)

Significantly, the boiler tubes were 1⅞in diameter rather than the normal Wilson standard of 2in, possibly in an attempt to gain better heat transference properties. It is also recorded that these locomotives (as with Nos. 105-7) were supplied with six-wheel tenders, probably of Wilson standard pattern, and that none were rebuilt. The class were withdrawn from service between November 1868 (Nos. 194-5) and February 1871 (Nos. 196 and 200).

Between the late summer of 1847 and June 1848 some eleven Jenny Linds were supplied to the York & North Midland Railway as this concern's Nos. 88, 90-96, 103-104 and 114. These locomotives were listed as having the 'as built dimensions': cylinders 15in by 20in; driving wheels 6ft diameter (5ft 6in for No. 103); carrying wheels 4ft diameter; wheelbase 7ft 8in+7ft 3 in; boiler 3ft 8in diameter, 11ft long with 124 boiler tubes of 2in diameter and total heating surface 800sqft, this latter figure apparently erroneous given the longer boiler barrel in relation to the Brighton locomotives. It was on this system that the class appeared to have had its greatest success, all coming into North Eastern Railway ownership with that company's absorption of the Y&MNR. on 31 July 1854. These locomotives saw service on express and mail trains from Normanton and Leeds to York and Hull and they underwent a number of improvements as train loads increased, including the increasing of the cylinder diameter to 16in, the replacement of the feed pumps with injectors and the fitting of Westinghouse brake equipment. One member of the class, allegedly the erstwhile No.96 renumbered 95 in 1849 (other accounts suggest No. 88), bore a brass nameplate 'Jenny Lind' on the boiler lagging below and parallel to the square base of the dome cover. In addition to these locomotives, two further Jenny Linds came into North Eastern Railway ownership, having been built at the Railway Foundry in 1853 for the York, Newcastle & Berwick Railway (YN&BR). The carrying wheel dimensions were the same as those for the ex-Y&NMR. locomotives, but the driving wheels were

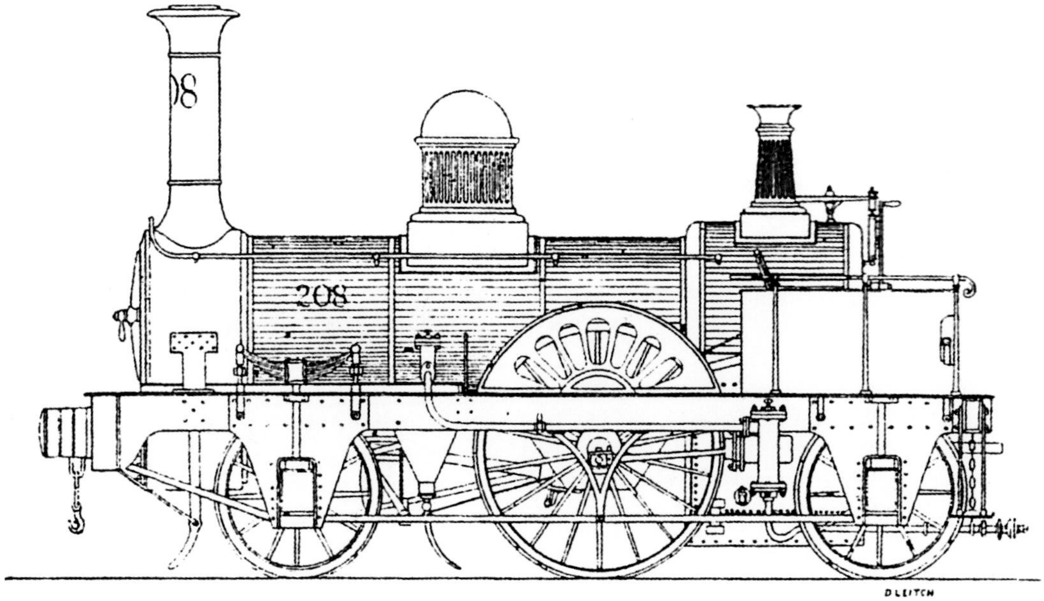

The L&NWR (Southern Division) purchased two Jenny Linds from the Railway Foundry in 1848 as its Nos. 208-9. The former is shown here, with its axle driven feed pump (and associated pipework) very much in evidence. (*The Locomotive*).

slightly larger at 6ft 3in diameter. The wheelbase was slightly shorter at 7ft 7in+7ft 1in, with the heating surface as built being quoted as 1006sqft, a figure closer to the true value for the ex-Y&NMR. locomotives. The two YN&BR Jennies (Nos. 27 and 212) passed into NER. ownership with the formation of that company in July 1854 and the former locomotive (renumbered 328 by the NER) was rebuilt at York in 1878, being 'Fletcherized' with a new boiler and cab and the leading wheels placed under the longitudinal centreline of smokebox. This locomotive, along with ex-Y&NMR No. 95, later NER 326 and finally 1709, ended their days working between Hull and Doncaster and survived into the 1880s, the last Jenny Linds in service on any British main line.

On 27 September 1847, the Midland Railway received the first of its Jenny Linds from the Railway Foundry at a cost of £2350 inclusive of tender, which may have been of the six-wheel variety as built. Some twenty-one further class members were supplied over a ten month period, the class initially bearing, in order of construction, the MR running numbers 45-52; 29-40; 78 and 80. Two more followed, 99 and 100 respectively in October 1851 and August 1850. These locomotives had 6ft driving wheels and 15in by 20in cylinders allied to a wheelbase 7ft 6in+7ft 0in Under another agreement with the Midland Railway and in pursuit of the latter's standardization policy directed by MR Locomotive Superintendent Matthew Kirtley, nine further locomotives were built jointly by E.B. Wilson and Derby Works (erected at the latter using components from the former) entering service between June 1852 and January 1854. All of these followed the basic Jenny Lind pattern, although MR Nos. 5, 12-3 and 101 possessed 5ft 6in driving wheels and 14in by 20in cylinders with No. 105 conforming to the class standard and Nos. 116-9 having 14½in by 20in cylinders and 6ft driving wheels. Nine further locomotives were officially 'reconstructed' at the Railway Foundry between June 1848 and June 1849 as Jenny Linds from R.B. Longridge-built 'long boiler' 2-4-0s of similar design to those built at the Railway Foundry. These units bore the MR Nos. 79 and 81-7 at the date of reconstruction. Three more, MR Nos. 88-90 'processed' at the Railway Foundry during 1849 were officially rebuilds of Tayleur & Co. 4-2-0s of 1846 taken over by the Midland Railway from the Bristol & Birmingham Joint Committee, whilst another, MR No. 1 offically began life as North Midland Railway Hawthorn 2-2-2 No. 22 in 1840 being 'reconstructed' in March 1848. It is questionable just how much of the original machines remained after these rebuilds had been carried out.

In May 1848, trials were carried out on the Midland Railway to determine the relative merits of the Jenny Lind and Sharp Brothers 2-2-2, known as the Jenny Sharp. The relevant comparative dimensions are detailed below:

OW&WR No. 42 is illustrated in this drawing running as GWR No. 207. The feed pumps at this stage appear to be crosshead driven and located between the inside mainframes. The engine was taken out of service by the GWR in March 1876. (*The Locomotive*).

	Jenny Lind	Jenny Sharp
Tubes	124: 2in dia. 11ft long	161: 2in dia. 10ft long
Tube H.S.	720sqft	847sqft
Firebox H.S.	80sqft	72sqft
Total H.S.	800sqft	919sqft
Cylinders	15in (Bore), 20in Stroke	16in (Bore), 20in Stroke
Driving Wheel Dia.	6ft	5ft 6in
Engine Weight (W.O.)	24tons 1cwt	21tons 9cwt
Tender Weight	15tons 13cwt	12tons 11cwt
Total Weight (W.O)	39tons 14cwt	34.0 tons
Payload (9 Coaches, 2 Vans)	64 tons	64 tons
Total Train Weight	103tons 14cwt	98.0 tons

The trials were carried out over a forty-mile stretch of track from Derby to Masbrough with an average upgrade of 1 in 330 for half the distance and a corresponding average downgrade of the same figure for the remainder. The first run, in the presence of MR Locomotive and Carriage Superintendent Matthew Kirtley, his assistants Marlow and Harland along with E.B. Wilson and James Fenton and Thomas Russell Crampton took place on 8 May behind the Jenny Sharp which managed an average speed of 49 miles per hour (43 on the 1 in 330 upgrade) with a consumption, including steam raising, of 16cwt of coke, or 44⅘lb/mile whilst the weight of water evaporated was 10,290lb, or 257lb/mile (5.7lb of water evaporated/lb of coke). The boiler pressure was 80psi whilst the time taken for the run was 50 min. 10½sec. On the following day and under the same conditions, the Jenny Lind managed an average speed of 52 miles per hour (47 on the 1 in 330 upgrade) with a total coke consumption of 13 tons, or 36⅖lb/mile. The steam pressure was 120psi during a run that lasted 46 min. 32 sec. with the highest speed reached being 59 m.p.h. The 50 per cent higher boiler pressure possessed by the Jenny Lind when compared with its Manchester-built rival had certainly proved its worth in giving the former the competitive edge during the trials. This was proved again with heavier loads: 139½ tons for the Jenny Lind and 133⅘ tons for the Jenny Sharp where the former managed 41mph on the 1 in 330 upgrade as opposed to 39mph for the latter, despite the slight disadvantage in loading.

The Midland-based Jenny Lind locomotives did not prove as long lived as their NER-based counterparts. The 'reconstructions' had all gone by May 1863, whilst the last two survivors of the 'officially new' pure-Wilson locomotives (the erstwhile MR Nos. 37 and 80 latterly running as 1014 and 1000 respectively) were officially rebuilt into double framed 0-6-0WT locomotives in April 1872. In reality, the latter contained only second hand Derby-built replacement boilers for the 2-2-2 locomotives, which must be regarded as being scrapped at this stage. Of the Wilson/Derby locomotives, once again the last survivor was officially a 0-6-0WT conversion, No. 105, latterly No. 1003, which was effectively scrapped in 1871. The MR also had six members of the 2-4-0 version of the Jenny Lind, all built entirely at the Railway Foundry and entering service between March and May 1848 as MR Nos. 131-6 at a cost of £2,350 each. These locomotives had cylinders and leading wheels of similar pattern to most of the Jenny Lind class with coupled wheels 5ft 6in diameter and a wheelbase of 6ft 9in+7ft 6in. The last survivor of this group was scrapped, as No. 2045, in January 1875 following a rebuild in December 1856. Finally, before leaving the subject of the Midland Railway Jenny Linds and related matters, it should be noted that seventeen more of the Longridge 'long boiler' 2-4-0's along with at least two similar MR locomotives built by Kitson, were reconstructed at the Railway Foundry between 1848 and the end of 1851. The rebuilt locomotives were inside cylinder 2-4-0s of double, rather than sandwich framed configuration and all had gone by May 1863.

In June and July 1848 E.B. Wilson & Co. completed an order for six locomotives for the Sheffield, Ashton-under-Lyme and Manchester Railway (SA-u-L&MR). Three of these were Jennies bearing the identities 58 *Niobe*, 59 *Tantalus*, and 61 *Jenny Lind*. These were larger than the original design with 16in by 22in cylinders and 206 boiler tubes (2in diameter) giving a heating surface of 1185sqft. which, when added to the figure of 149sqft, brought the total to 1334sqft. The loaded weight of the engine only was 27 tons 16cwt. The remaining three were of the outside cylinder Stephenson 'Long Boiler' 2-4-0 design, Nos. 55-7 respectively *Adonis*, *Jason*, and *Perseus*. The latter locomotive was converted to a 2-2-2 in the 1850s whilst No. 61 was also rebuilt under Manchester, Sheffield & Lincolnshire Railway auspices and all six locomotives appear to have lasted until the mid-1860s.

The Southern Division of the L&WNR purchased two Jenny Linds from the Railway Foundry in 1848 and these were numbered 208 and 209 as delivered. They both had respectable life spans by the standards of their contemporaries, with the former being scrapped in June 1868 and the latter in April 1873.

The success of the Jenny Linds encouraged E. B. Wilson to make his first purchase of freehold land to augment the Railway Foundry site and on 18 November 1847, a parcel of land was purchased from Joseph Oates and Albert Davy, the executors of the late John Pearson, wine merchant, who was deceased some years previously. The plot amounted to a trapezoidal entity, some 90ft by 297ft and 349ft, approximately 3170 square yards in area and bounded by Charlotte St. and Walker St.

During 1848, much optimism had been experienced at the Railway Foundry and it appears that the six SA-u-L&MR locomotives were intended to be part of a verbal order for ten. However, by December 1848, the effect of the collapse of the first 'Railway Mania' was being felt and verbal orders of this type were repudiated with the result, as Joy recorded, that about twenty locomotives in an advanced state of completion were left on the manufacturer's hands. Joy further records:

> 'No orders, so everything was to shut up, and I was to go in three months, that is, March 1849. Spent spring at the Railway Foundry finishing work just all under a cloud, and this was very dreary after the lively times we had had trying all sorts of engines. In March I left and looked after other work to no purpose, as everyone was reducing establishments. So got a holiday, and a tour to the English Lake district.'

David Joy's *Engine A* on the OW&WR was built at the Railway Foundry in 1849 for a contractor and purchased for £1,250 shortly before the opening of the line in 1852 following overhaul by E.B. Wilson & Co. and making its first trial trip on 29 April that year. As built the locomotive had 14in by 20in cylinders; leading wheels 4ft 2in; coupled wheels 5ft 6in; boiler barrel 11ft long and 3ft 8in internal diameter with ⅕149in tubes; firebox wrapper 4ft 5¼in long and 4ft 3in wide; firebox 3ft 9¼in long, 3ft 7in wide and 5ft 3in high. The heating surface was 939.6sqft. for the tubes and 85sqft for the firebox, giving a total of 1024.6sqft, whilst the grate area was 13.68sqft. This locomotive was numbered 31 by the OW&WR and the difference in wheelbase proportions from the ECR 2-4-0s, with the driving axle closer to the firebox, is readily apparent. (*E.L. Ahrons*).

As part of the aftermath of the 1848 crash, E. B. Wilson resolved to acquire the freehold elements of the site associated with Shepherd & Todd and raise finance by means of a mortgage. Even before achieving the former, steps were taken to accomplish the latter and the immediate consequence of this course of action was that a valuation of the whole Railway Foundry site was undertaken. This was carried out by James Tayor, acting as agent for the prospective mortgagee, Mr. Scholefield and was dated 29 December 1848. It was noted that generally the plant and buildings and were in 'as new' condition and that the whole site, freehold and leasehold, was worth in excess of £80,000. The freehold portion of the site amounted to approximately two acres upon which a total of £51,800 had been expended for fixtures, machinery and tools. Of this, given the prevailing economic climate, some £30,000 could be recovered during a possible sale within five years, or a total of £50,000 if the corresponding items on the leasehold portion were added. A note of caution was sounded, however, from the fact that without the leasehold portion, upon which there was a mere eleven years unexpired, the Railway Foundry would have been incomplete and unable to carry on its designated trade. In this instance, it appeared impossible to assess the value of the freehold portion in isolation. In order to remedy this difficulty, Mr. Taylor had been informed that a portion of land bounded by Jack Lane and the Midland Railway had been purchased by E. B. Wilson effectively as an 'insurance policy' should the lease have to be surrendered. In reality, no such conveyance was to take place during the manufacturer's existence as a going concern, although the lease (Fretwell's lease) was destined to run its course. At this stage, approximately 700 men were employed on site, although in a more normal economic climate, one would have expected to find 200 more.

Following the valuation, Wilson set about acquiring the title to the freehold portion and under an indenture dated 12 April 1849 he effected the transfer from John Shepherd, with Charles Todd and representatives of the late John Shepherd Sr. also as parties, for a consideration of £3,100. With effect from the same day, the freehold portion of the Railway Foundry was mortgaged to Robert Scholefield of London for £15,000. This sum was later increased by a further £5,000 in respect of the leasehold interest and with the due consent of Mr. Fretwell.

The economic climate of the period dealt a major blow to the Railway Foundry's fortunes and the most significant element was to the personal fortunes of E. B. Wilson himself. By the middle of 1849, Wilson's creditors included the Low Moor Iron Co.; the proprietors of Kirkstall Forge; Cammell & Co. of Sheffield; the Butterley Co.; the Patent Axletree Co. of Wednesbury; Thorneycroft & Co. of Wolverhampton and the Bowling Iron Co. of Bradford. It was clear that Wilson was unable to carry on running the business solely on his own account. Under an indenture dated 21 June 1849, Trustees, the principal, Joshua Pollard, of whom represented the Bowling Iron Co., were appointed to carry on the running of the business and so outwardly matters were able to proceed very much as before. In the spring of 1849, the Shrewsbury & Birmingham Railway (S&BR) took delivery of a Large Jenny. The engine, which was named *Salopian* was recorded as being built with the following dimensions:

Cylinders	15½in. (Bore), 22in Stroke
Wheel Diameter	6ft 6in (Driving)
	4ft (Carrying)
Wheelbase	7ft 3in by 7ft 3in
Boiler Barrel	10ft 6in Long
	4ft Internal Diameter
Firebox Wrapper	4ft 10in (L) 4ft 2½in. (W)
Inner Firebox	4ft 1½in. (L), 3ft 9½in. (W),
	5ft 6in (H)
Boiler Tubes	206, 2 in Diameter
Heating Surface	1141sqft (Tubes)
	130sqft (Firebox)
Grate Area	12.97sqft
Locomotive Weight	
(Working Order)	28 tons

The firebox was fitted with a longitudinal mid-feather as a means of obtaining a larger heating surface than would otherwise have been achieved. *Salopian* apparently gave satisfactory service, becoming Great Western Railway No. 54 on the absorption by that railway of the S&BR in 1854 and it was withdrawn from service in 1869. Two further Jenny Linds were to see Great Western ownership; these were both built for the Oxford, Worcester & Wolverhampton Railway (OW&WR). As will be dealt with later, David Joy was to take up an appointment as Locomotive Superintendent of the OW&WR in

April 1852 and towards the end of his tenure of office in 1856, the two engines, which had been built for stock as Works Nos. 558-9, were delivered as O.W. & W.R. Nos. 42 and 51, the latter engine being named *Will Shakespeare*. These possessed the following dimensions:

Cylinders	15in (Bore), 22in (Stroke),
Wheel Diameter	6ft 3in (Driving), 4ft 0in (Leading)
Wheelbase	7ft 7in+7ft 1in
Boiler Barrel	10ft 7in Long 3ft 10in (Internal Diameter)
Firebox Wrapper	4ft 4½in (L) 4ft 3in (W)
Inner Firebox	3ft 9in (L) 3ft 6in (W), 5ft 3in (H)
Boiler Tubes	162, 2in Diameter
Tube Heating Surface	891sqft
Firebox Heating Surface	82.83sqft

Their wheelbase and wheel dimensions appear to have been the same as those for the YN&BR, suggesting that the wheelsets and mainframes at least were constructed at the same time. Apart from an increase in driving wheel diameter by one inch to 6ft 4in, Nos. 42 and 51 remained largely unaltered throughout their working lives, being successively absorbed into West Midland Railway stock in 1860 and GWR stock (as Nos. 207-8) three years later. Mainly employed on the section of OW&WR south of Worcester, the pair survived into the latter part of the 1870s. Another OW&WR 2-2-2 began life in 1849 as a member of the 2-4-0 Jenny-derived class previously referred to, and it was supplied new to a Pontefract-based contractor, from which the engine was purchased by C.C. Williams in 1852, originally being designated A and later being renumbered 31 by the OW&WR. It was altered to a 2-2-2 at the Railway's workshops at Worcester in October 1855 but could always be distinguished from the true Jenny Linds by reason of the unequal diameters of its leading and trailing wheelsets as well as its leading dimensions.

OW&WR No.31 was altered by David Joy at Worcester Shops to a 2-2-2 with 5ft 8in driving wheels and 3ft 6in trailing wheels in 1855 and is recorded, despite its relatively small driving wheels, as putting in some fast running between Oxford and Worcester. The wheelbase as altered was described as being 8ft+7ft 1in which could hardly have altered from the original dimensions, given the nature of the conversion. Renumbered 206 by the G.W.R. in 1863, the converted locomotive was finally withdrawn from service in May 1876. (*E.L. Ahrons*).

Three Jenny Linds came into Great Northern Railway ownership: The first two were GNR. Nos. 201-2 and these were completed by November 1850 and originally delivered for trial, being purchased, after blastpipe modifications, for £2,000 apiece in July 1851. The dimensions given for these locomotives were as follows:

Cylinders	16in (Bore), 20in. (Stroke)
Wheel Diameter	6ft (Driving) 4ft. (Carrying)
Wheelbase	7ft 3in+7ft 3in
Boiler Barrel	10ft 4in (L) 4ft 2in (D)
Boiler Pitch	5ft 10in
Firebox Wrapper Length	5ft. 9in
Grate Area	15sqft
Boiler Tubes	206, 2in diameter
Boiler Pressure	120psi
Heating Surface	720sqft (Tubes) 80sqft (Firebox)
Tender (Six Wheels)	900 gallons (Water) 2½tons (Coke)

The quoted heating surface figures are clearly erroneous and appear to have been taken direct from those given for the earliest Jenny Linds. Following rebuilds in 1866 (moving the leading axle forward of the chimney centreline) and the fitting of Stirling domeless boilers during the following year, these locomotives spent their declining years on secondary express and branch line duties, being relegated to the G.N.R. Duplicate List in June 1882 and withdrawn in October 1889 (No. 202A) and November 1892 (No. 201A).

The remaining GNR specimen began life as Ambergate, Nottingham, Boston and East Junction Railway No. 5. This was a relatively late completion, appearing in 1855. This locomotive became G.N.R. No. 222, being rebuilt in 1867 and taken out of service during the following April.

In an era when the pace of passenger steam locomotive evolution was rapid, it is perhaps not surprising that the Jenny Linds and their 2-4-0 derivatives were not individually long-lived, but their influence was to be seen in locomotives of both wheel arrangements being constructed during the 1860s by Beyer Peacock, and a 2-2-2 exhibition specimen built in 1867 by Lilleshall & Co. The use of a higher boiler pressure than had hitherto been the norm was certainly one of the class's main strengths, along with a sensible wheelbase structure and corresponding good riding characteristics. The design's weak points were the fact that the inside frames terminated at the leading end of the cylinders and did not reach the front bufferbeam (with consequential detrimental effects for the rigidity of the forward part of the chassis), and that the rear of the inside frames were rigidly attached to the firebox wrapper at their trailing end. This would have meant insufficient provision for differential expansion between boiler and chassis during normal operation, a problem experienced with other early locomotive designs, including products of the Railway Foundry. Nonetheless, the Jenny Lind remains very much the design most associated by most commentators with E. B. Wilson & Co. and for this achievement alone deserves its place in history, although, as we shall see, it was to be other designs emanating from the Railway Foundry that were to have a longer lived influence on steam locomotive design generally. Before turning to these, however, it will be necessary to give details of E. B. Wilson's flirtation with the patents of Thomas Russell Crampton.

CHAPTER 5

CRAMPTON LOCOMOTIVES, OTHER ODDITIES AND EARLY OPERATING CONTRACTS

During the 1840s, Thomas Russell Crampton was busy putting his ideas on low centre of gravity locomotives with single rear axle drive into practice, advocating their benefits of dynamic stability, a relatively large heating surface and good use of weight transference when travelling under load in a forward direction. However, the low proportion of the locomotive's total weight devoted to adhesion militated against the last-mentioned of these advantages, whilst the largest of his locomotives, the L&NWR's *Liverpool*, is known to have caused damage to the permanent way with its 18ft 6in fixed wheelbase when operating services between London and Wolverton. His ideas gained credibility in Continental Europe, however, where examples remained in use into the early years of the twentieth century, with a particularly fine example, *Le Continent*, remaining in existence up to the present day. On the home front, Crampton's locomotives did not achieve lasting impact, but this did not prevent the Railway Foundry from entering the limited market that existed for them.

Crampton's first Patent (No. 9261) was taken out jointly with John Coope Haddan and was dated 15 February 1842. It amounted to some thirteen claims, the first ten of which related to locomotives. Of these, three related to expansive valve gears and two of these showed clear descent from the ideas of John Gray. It would seem that one of these later two was in reality Joy's apparent first attempt to arrive at such a gear previously referred to in Chapter Three. The Patent went on to detail a four-wheel locomotive with only the rear axle driven and located behind the firebox. In practice, it was necessary to have at least two leading carrying axles and this was envisaged in Crampton's Patent of 25 1846 (No.11349) which, amongst its sixteen claims, showed an inside frame 2-2-2-0 design with outside cylinders (as was normal Crampton practice), a firebox 'splayed out' longitudinally below the driving axle (to increase heating surface and grate area), and, crucially for subsequent events at the Railway Foundry, steam collection being accomplished by having a domeless boiler barrel allied to an 'inverted-U' shaped upper part of the firebox wrapper sharply raised above the top of the boiler. This latter feature would not have been lost on David Joy as it is certain from the general tenor of his writings that he would have studied Crampton's Patents as soon as they appeared in print. In reality, the first two locomotives built under this Patent, by Tulk & Ley of Whitehaven in 1846 for the Namur & Liege Railway, possessed the chassis arrangements envisaged in the Patent's drawing, but not the boiler design, which had a conventional barrel-mounted dome. One of the locomotives was tested on the former Grand Junction Railway with the result that the L&NWR built its first 'Crampton', *Courier*, in 1847 at Crewe Works. This locomotive employed a 'compromise' boiler design in which steam was collected both from a conventional dome and from an 'inverted-U' wrapper' raised to a height of 1ft 9in. above boiler barrel level.

From the point of view of E.B. Wilson's involvement in the Crampton story, three further sets of drawings from the 1846 Patent were relevant. One of these showed a locomotive with outside bearings for the carrying wheelsets, whilst the driving wheelset retained inside bearings. This drawing shows the eccentrics mounted on return cranks, as found on the Namur & Liege Railway locomotives but another drawing made provision for the mounting of the eccentrics laterally between the driving wheel and the crank web on an inside bearing axle. The third extra set of drawings covered what can only be described as a freak and before considering the more 'mainstream' 'Cramptons' constructed at the Railway Foundry, it is to this design that the first detailed consideration of the chapter will be given. The essential feature of this two axle double frame specification was that instead of the cylinders acting directly onto the driving crankpins via crossheads and connecting rods, inside cylinders drove onto bellcranks whose upper fulcra were outwardly projecting lateral shafts rigidly connected to rocking beams whose fulcra (the shafts) were longitudinally equidistant from, and vertically level with, the axle centres. At the upper ends of these beams, on each side of the locomotive, an intermediate connecting rod converted the rocking motion of the beam pin into rotary motion of the rear crankpin, whilst similar intermediate rods at the lower ends of the beams imparted rotary motion to the leading crankpins, the axle cranks being 'quartered' in the usual manner. In 1848, a locomotive was constructed to this design at the Railway Foundry for the Midland Railway, being named *Lablache*. As with other Crampton locomotives of the period, the firebox was located ahead of the rear driving axle, whilst it was claimed that better riding would result from the transmission loadings on the leading and trailing axles balancing one another (owing to the 180 degree differential). *Lablache* did not prove successful in operation, however and was soon converted to a more conventional unit, although little is known of its subsequent history.

Lablache, as events turned out, was not to be David Joy's only acquaintance with a locomotive employing the 'intermediate beam' method of power transmission. In 1841, John Jones of Bristol patented a system of drive in which a transverse drum, containing four 'vibrating vane' rectangular pistons, two of which were attached to each beam fulcrum, caused the beams to vibrate, with

Eight classic 'Crampton' 2-2-2-0 locomotives were constructed at the Railway Foundry, with the largest grouping, five examples, going to the Eastern Counties railway during the last quarter of 1848 as ECR Nos. 108-12, later renumbered 233-37. Never successful, these locomotives lasted only a few years in service until withdrawn in 1854-5. Their boilers were retrieved and used on the construction (at Stratford) of the '234' class double framed 0-6-0s. Their main constructional features, such as the mixed framing, regulator box (on the boiler barrel above the cylinders) and the large eccentrics (actuating Gooch 'stationary link' motion can be seen in this drawing) (*The Locomotive*)

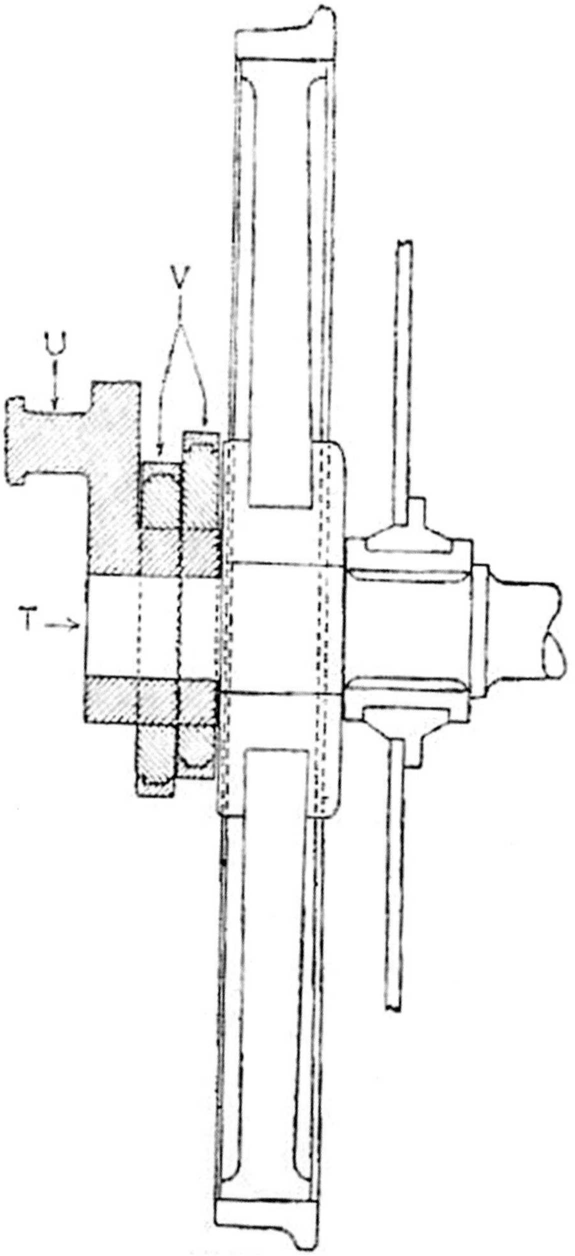

This cross-sectional drawing shows the arrangement of eccentrics used on the Wilson 'Crampton' singles. The large-diameter eccentrics were mounted outboard of the driving wheels which were equipped with bearings arranged for inside frames. (*The Locomotive*)

the final drive being obtained in the same manner as *Lablache*. As David Joy recorded in May 1847:

> 'We were asked at the Railway Foundry to build this engine, and I got out a set of drawings for her but when we got to the details of the vibrating pistons in their cylinders, the packings for these showed very slight chance of being made steam tight and E.B. Wilson & Co. gave it up after I had worked out the question to exhaustion and the manufacture was taken up by Messrs. Thwaites Bros. of Bradford.'

The builder was actually known as Thwaites & Carbutt at this stage, whose premises were Vulcan Works, Thornton Road in Bradford. This manufacturer was not primarily concerned with railway equipment, being better known for production of the 'Roots' blower for various applications. Be that as it may, the locomotive that eventually emerged from the Vulcan Works was a 0-4-2 tender engine for the South Yorkshire Railway. The adhesive wheels were 5ft 6in. diameter whilst the corresponding dimension for the trailing wheels was 3ft 9in. The boiler barrel was 12ft long with 149 tubes, whilst the wheelbase was 15ft 2in. (9ft 6in+5ft 8in) and the intermediate beam throw was 1ft 8in. The back-dome boiler, with its raised firebox wrapper, would appear to have been the result of David Joy's familiarity with the previously mentioned 2-2-2 design employed by the Manchester & Leeds Railway. *Albion* performed its first test run between Bradford and Skipton, and according to George Nokes in *The Evolution of the Steam Locomotive*, 'The speed attained and the low fuel consumption are stated to have satisfied the builders and others concerned.' Further tests were carried out on the Midland Railway between Derby and Birmingham and these were apparently successful with an alleged coke consumption of 5lb/mile less than conventional locomotives. *Albion* was purchased by the South Yorkshire Railway as that concern's No. 5 and survived to become Manchester, Sheffield & Lincolnshire Railway No. 156 in 1864, by which time the shortcomings of the basic design, exacerbated by wear on the drum and pistons must have been all too apparent. The engine had been replaced by 1870.

The first 'mainstream' 'Cramptons' produced at the Railway Foundry were built for the Eastern Counties Railway and were of the 2-2-2-0 variety with outside frames for the carrying wheelsets (the wheels of which were of unequal diameter to accommodate the cylinders) and inside bearings for the driving wheels. The boiler was of the domeless variety, with steam being taken via an internal pipe with an uppermost slit connected to a short internal 'T'-pipe which led into a double slide valve 'box' regulator and external steampipes supplying the cylinders individually. The driving wheels were

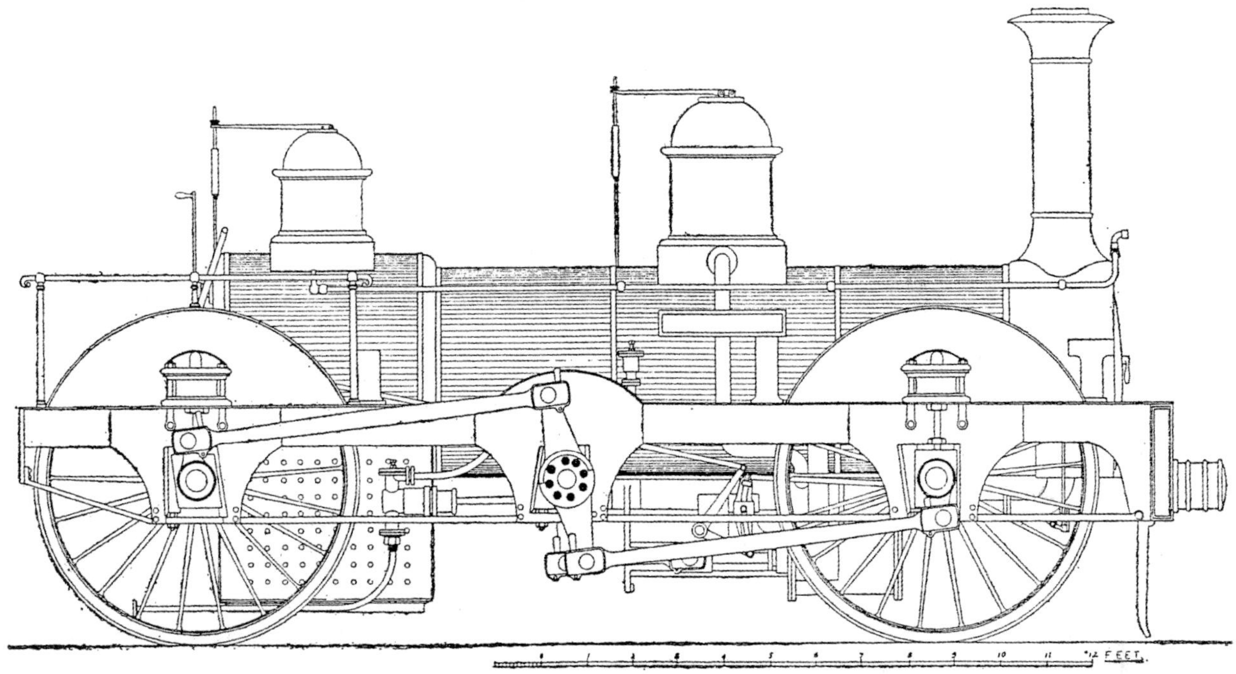

The side-lever 0-4-0 locomotive *Lablache* was described by Herbert T. Walker in *The Railway Gazette* for 4 September 1908. Its driving wheels were 6ft. diameter with a 16ft wheelbase and the cylinders measured 16in bore and 20in stroke. The 32 ton weight of the locomotive gave an axle loading of 16 tons which was considered excessive in an era when a 12½ ton loading would have been regarded as heavy. The boiler barrel was oval, being 3ft 9in wide and 4ft 1in high and it had to be made concave at its lower front end to clear the leading axle, which carried the eccentrics. The total heating surface was quoted as 1271.6sqft (96.6 for the firebox and 1.175 for the tubes). A double framed chassis was employed, but the wheel bearings were fitted on the outside frames only. The vibrating side levers, which transmitted the drive to the external connecting rods, were mounted on sleeves, each of which was carried by a bearing fixed to its adjacent pair of inside and outside frames. These sleeves surrounded a transverse fixed shaft and at their inner ends the sleeves were equipped with bellcranks onto which the internal connecting rods (actuated by the pistons) drove. The cylinders were mounted on a sub-frame fixed to the boiler. *Lablache* was designed as a consequence of Crampton's desire to balance the loadings generated by the use of conventional cylinder-and-connecting rod transmission in steam locomotives (in addition to equalizing weight distribution and reducing the vertical thrusts on the slide bars) and whilst much of his logic in this field appeared fine in theory, other weaknesses with the design, such as the axle loading; the poor shape of the boiler for a pressure vessel; the relatively complex motion design, and the poor design of the cylinder sub-frame, resulted in the early abandonment of this particular line of locomotive evolution. The accompanying side elevation, showing the leaf spring suspension originally envisaged, and schematic front view (the latter taken from an original tracing annotated 'Leeds, March 11th 1848') were originally published with Herbert Walker's Paper. (*The Late Herbert Walker*)

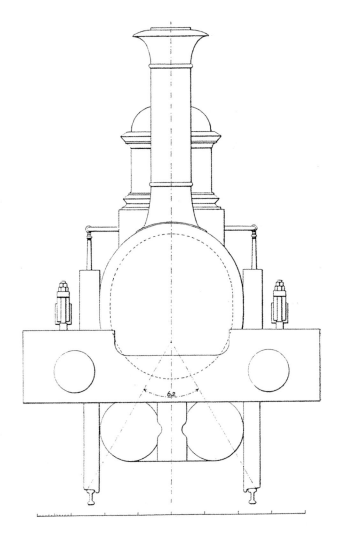

7ft diameter with the rear carrying wheels being 3ft 9in and the leading pair 4ft 6in diameter. The wheelbase was 15ft 3in (7ft 6in+7ft 9in) whilst the cylinder were 16in bore and 20in stroke. Gooch 'stationary link' valve motion was fitted, actuated by large eccentrics 'sandwiched' between wheel and crank web. The five locomotives were delivered between October and December 1848 and bore the E.C.R. running numbers when new 108-112. These locomotives did not prove satisfactory on the passenger duties for which they were intended and were soon relegated to coal workings, being renumbered 233-7 in 1852 and replaced in 1854-8. Their boilers were eventually re-used in the construction of new goods locomotives. Three similar locomotives are known to have been built at the Railway Foundry. The first of these, also completed in 1848, became No. 55 of the North British Railway and ran as a Crampton until 1863 when it was extensively rebuilt as a 2-2-2 still retaining the non-matching carrying wheelsets. The other two were advertised for sale in December 1849, described as having larger (16½in by 22in cylinders) and having been built new for a railway that had subsequently arranged for another company to work it. In the event, the locomotives were sold to the Aberdeen Railway during the following year where they became Nos.26-7. It is recorded that during their early careers the large eccentrics were replaced by smaller ones. Officially rebuilt as 2-2-2s during the 1860s and successively renumbered, these engines were broken up respectively as Caledonian Railway Nos. 563 and 562 in 1871.

Following his period on vacation, David Joy was recalled to the Railway Foundry on 1 November 1849 where he was detailed to take a batch of tracings for some iron work in connection with 'Baths and wash-houses' in Lambeth to London. Once this task was accomplished, he was to stay on in London as the London Agent of the Railway Foundry Company. Between this time and 5 March 1850, Joy was based at No. 19, Great George Street, Westminster, where he established his offices. He now had the chance to make the acquaintance of many of the country's leading railway engineers and it appears that Wilson made the weekly journey down from Leeds to accompany Joy every Tuesday evening to meetings of the Institution of Civil Engineers where, amongst others, they met John Fowler, Robert Stephenson and Cusack Patrick Rooney, Secretary of the Eastern Counties Railway (ECR). He went on to record:

> 'Wilson was a very energetic and daring man, and so we were all this winter full of schemes. One was for our taking over a section of the Eastern Counties Railway and working it by contract, finding all materials, coke, etc., and paying all wages, taking over a selected lot of the railway's engines. With this view, we had heaps of meetings with the chairman, Mr. Betts, and C.P. Rooney. And always these meetings had an appearance of secrecy, and were really one part of the Board working in opposition to the other.'

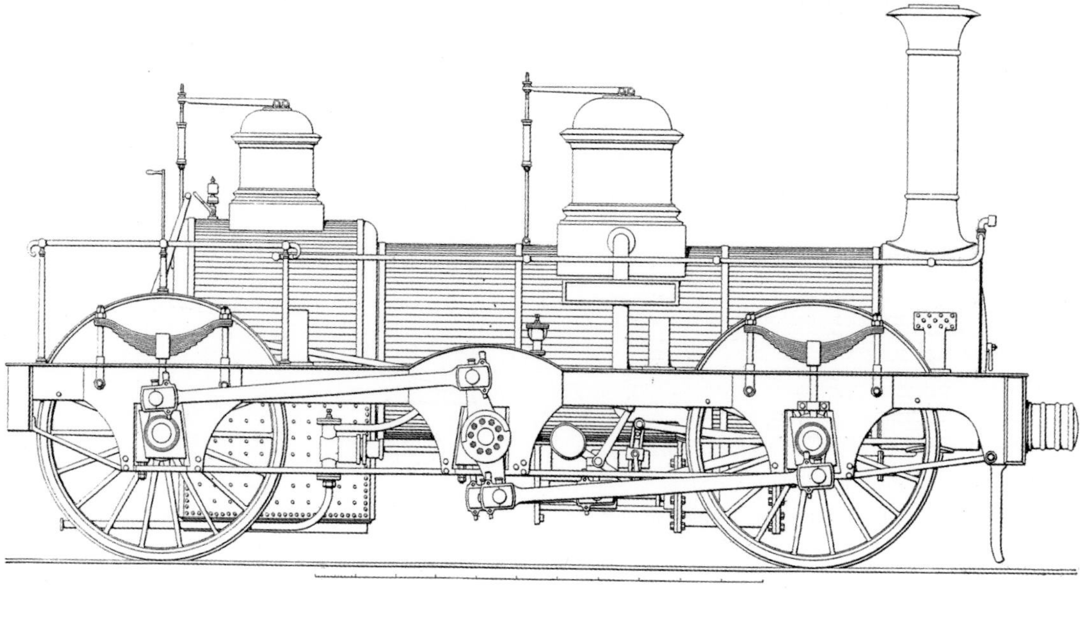

Lablache was eventually completed with India rubber springs, as evidenced by a surviving David Joy drawing, which formed the basis for this illustration. (*The Locomotive*)

Joy was thus able to inspect all parts of the ECR at this time, during which he was able to ride on the locomotives. He supervised the conversion of 'long boiler' locomotives into inside cylinder 'mixed frame' 2-4-0s and also took an interest in the fad of the period for light trains to carry the least possible weight following the 1848 financial crash. Joy goes on to record that James Samuel, the ECR Engineer, had 'two small engines running, the "Enfield" and the "Cambridge"'. A series of test runs were carried out with these locomotives and some notes were appended relating to these:

'"Enfield": December 10th 1849, 7 cwt. [0.35 ton] coke, 78 miles, 5 hours in steam = 10 lbs. per mile; at 45 miles per hour, sleet and mist, rails greasy.

One of the designs featured in Crampton's 1846 patent was a six-axle inside framed 'single' incorporating a domeless boiler with a firebox longitudinally 'splayed' at its base and with a wrapper raised in an inverted 'U' shape at its highest point to form a steam collecting space. Although the closest this patent came to practical application was the L&NWR locomotive *Courier* completed at Crewe Works in November 1847 (which in the event possessed an additional barrel-mounted dome), these drawings are clear evidence that the transition from back dome to domeless boiler and raised 'inverted-U' firebox had been envisaged at this early stage, although David Joy (who would have been familiar with the patent) did not immediately go down this particular road. (*The Locomotive*)

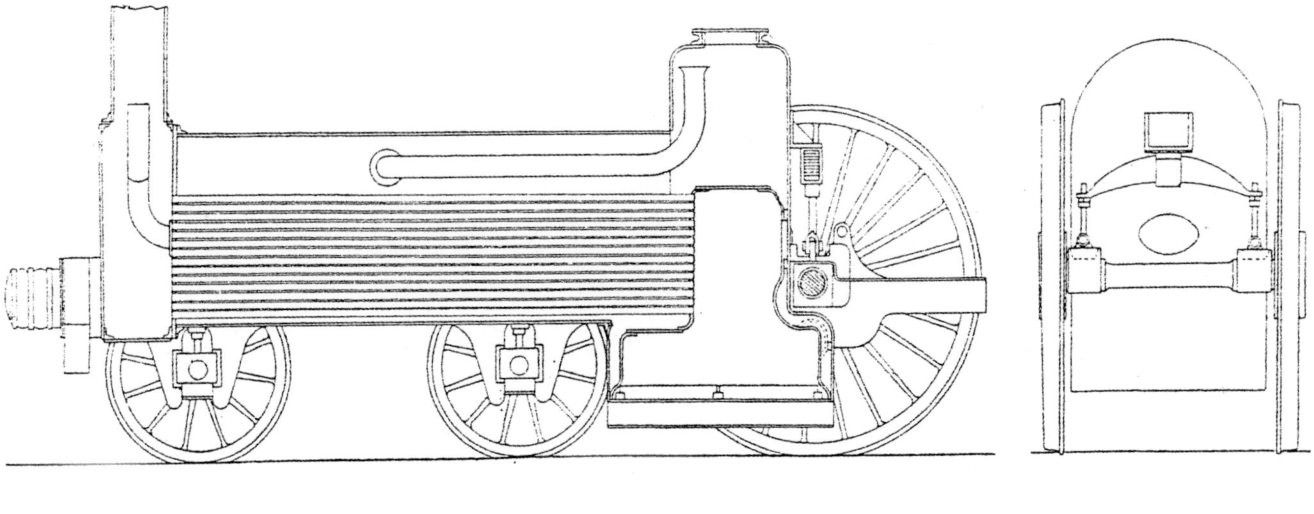

'December 11th, ran half miles in 45-44, 42-40 secs. = 45 miles per hour.

'"Cambridge" ran ½ mile in 34 secs. – 53 miles per hour.

'Cambridge to London, 57 ½ miles, 7 cwt. Coke = 13.6 lbs. per mile. Cylinders 8in. × 12in.; wheel 4ft. 9in., leading, 2ft. 6in.; boiler 6ft. 6in. × 2ft. 9in.; tubes, 112, 7ft. × 1 3/8in., outside cylinders, inside framed, Crampton's bearings [this entry referred to the locomotive Cambridge].'

As suggested by this entry, the chassis design of 2-2-0 back tank *Cambridge* was in some respects a scaled-down version of the inside framed 'Crampton', reverting to the 1842 concept of using only two axles. What was more significant for subsequent events at the Railway Foundry was that this locomotive, which had been built in August 1849 by W. Bridges Adams at Fairfield Works in Bow, utilized a domeless boiler barrel with full height 'inverted-U' firebox wrapper.

In response to his experiences with *Enfield* and *Cambridge*, Joy got hard to work at No. 19, Great George Street in January 1850 scheming out designs for light locomotives, being particularly attracted to the use of inside cylinders and the possibility of using boiler barrels that were concave in the region of the crankshaft in order to keep the centre of gravity as low as possible. He was also attracted to the idea of increasing boiler pressures so as to get more power out of a relatively small locomotive. It was at this time that he came up with his first design for a 'double boiler' locomotive (of the 2-2-2 tank configuration) that would use lighter, thinner plates for the barrel. This particular proposal never saw the light of day, but a drawing of it survives in the Institution of Mechanical Engineers Library in London.

The middle part of 1850 proved to be rather turbulent at the Railway Foundry, for the Shop Foreman, Bob Willis, received his marching orders and David Joy was detailed to replace him. Joy recounted:

'It was horrid hard work, back to 6 a.m. to 6 p.m., and not a moment's respite. Now we got another order from Great Northern Railway for 10 four-coupled passenger engines, 6ft, wheels. These … were the back stay for the running of the passenger trains, and all the specials of the Exhibition Time the following year.'

This drawing shows *Albion* completed by Thwaites & Carbutt for the South Yorkshire Railway in 1849. As mentioned in the text, Joy began design work on this locomotive, but did not complete work on the chassis portion, although he was probably responsible for the boiler configuration. The similarity of the locomotive's *modus operandi* to *Lablache* is readily apparent. (*The Engineer*)

The full story of these 2-4-0 locomotives rightfully belongs to the succeeding chapter, but one member of this class was to play its part in the proceedings discussed herewith. The turbulent climate persisted at the Railway Foundry into the summer and in June 1850, Joy wrote:

> 'Quarrelled with E.B. Wilson about forthcoming Exhibition for 1851, and went at a moment's notice, J.C. Wilson taking my place as shop foreman, and prigging [purloining] my books and papers in the shop foreman's office – all my John Gray's notes. Summer, again a holiday.'

Joy's presence at the Railway Foundry was soon sorely missed by the Wilsons and on 12 July (erroneously stated as August by Joy) 1850, E.B. Wilson fetched him and took him by cab to Arthington Hall, at Otley from whence he was to go on to open the Nottingham & Grantham Railway – the true title at this stage was the Ambergate, Nottingham, Boston & East Junction Railway (ANB&EJR), although the portion of railway built under the Act of Authorization only served Nottingham and Grantham at its extremities. Wilson had taken on a contract to work this line for a consideration of 2 shillings (10p) per mile run, but there were no locomotives or associated equipment ready. Joy stated in his Diary:

> 'To Nottingham early Saturday. Midland Railway supplied us with two old Bury singles [then MR Nos.107, originally Midland Counties Railway No. 16 *Cerberus* of 1840, and 115, originally Midland Counties Railway No. 36 *Vandal* of 1841: 2-2-0 tender locomotives with 5ft 6in diameter driving wheels, 13in by 18in cylinders and an engine weight in working order of about 8¾ tons] to be at Grantham Sunday Night. Saturday afternoon over the line with Underwood (engineer), Gough (secretary), and on the contractor's (G. Wythes) engine (ballast) went off the road, not very fast but a jolly tumble about. Water Tanks all to get ready by Monday. Then came

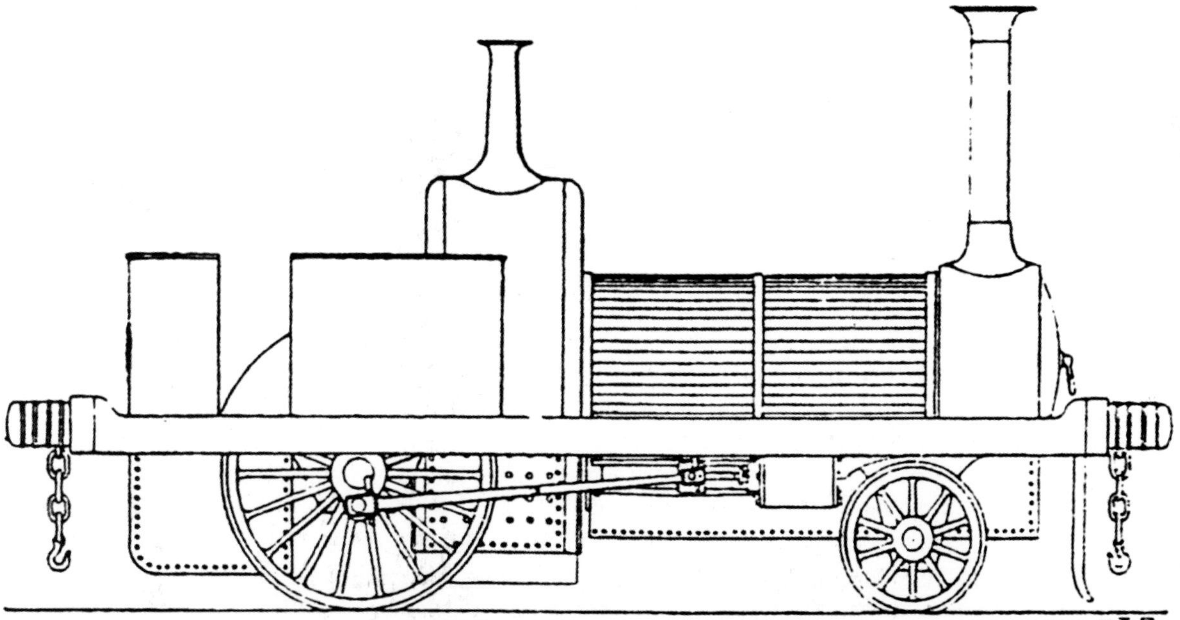

William Bridges Adams' light 2-2-0 well-tank locomotive *Cambridge* of August 1849 was illustrated in David Joy's Diaries and, given the 'Crampton' inspiration of some of its design, it appears that its upper firebox wrapper configuration may have owed its inspiration to the 1846 Crampton patent. It would appear that Joy's familiarity with this locomotive finally convinced him of the advantages, in relatively small locomotives, of adopting a domeless barrel and high inverted 'U' firebox wrapper, although his first thoughts in this direction were hardly conventional. *Cambridge* also appears from this drawing to have possessed both leading and trailing 'back' well tanks, a feature allowed by the use of outside cylinders, although no pipe is shown connecting them, nor any valve gear! (*The Locomotive*)

the opening. Started at 9 a.m. [Monday July 15] with first train – five or six carriages – part second and third – and a lot of low-sided wagons.'

During his time operating the ANB&EJR, Joy gained his first experience of steam locomotive driving, in the shape of the 'bar framer' No. 115. He also narrowly escaped death when, whilst on the footplate of the leading 'Bury' on a double header 'Special' working from Grantham to Nottingham, his train had been held at the junction with the Mansfield line (MR) line on the 'Down Main'. The Midland passenger working, consisting of twenty crammed carriages hauled by a 0-6-0 tender locomotive, was supposed to have been shunted onto the 'Up' line prior to reaching the next station, but instead was directed onto the down line. Fortunately Joy and his colleagues had seen the danger and jumped clear, reaching the comparative safety of the inside of the curve before the Midland engine smashed head-on into the leading 'Bury'. Both the latter and its trailing classmate were

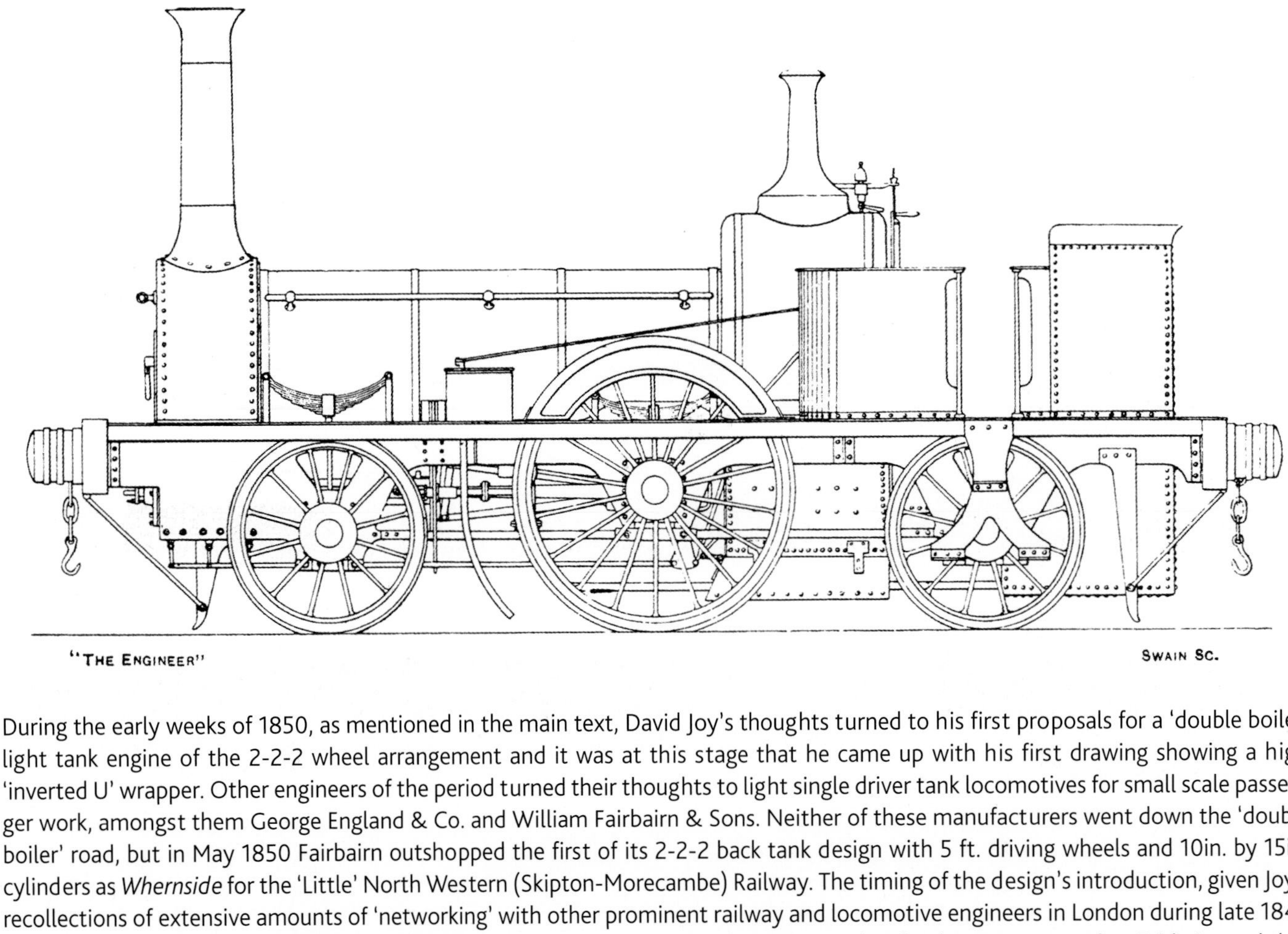

During the early weeks of 1850, as mentioned in the main text, David Joy's thoughts turned to his first proposals for a 'double boiler' light tank engine of the 2-2-2 wheel arrangement and it was at this stage that he came up with his first drawing showing a high 'inverted U' wrapper. Other engineers of the period turned their thoughts to light single driver tank locomotives for small scale passenger work, amongst them George England & Co. and William Fairbairn & Sons. Neither of these manufacturers went down the 'double boiler' road, but in May 1850 Fairbairn outshopped the first of its 2-2-2 back tank design with 5 ft. driving wheels and 10in. by 15in. cylinders as *Whernside* for the 'Little' North Western (Skipton-Morecambe) Railway. The timing of the design's introduction, given Joy's recollections of extensive amounts of 'networking' with other prominent railway and locomotive engineers in London during late 1849 and early 1850, does give weight to the suggestion that Joy may have 'compared notes' with relevant personnel at Fairbairn and that the latter concern (with which Joy was already well familiar) may then have gone on to build a locomotive with a *Cambridge* pattern boiler before the Railway Foundry got around to doing so. A connection with Fairbairn's and Wilson's work in this field is implied by E.L. Ahrons in the passage from *The British Steam Locomotive 1825-1925* quoted in the main text, but sadly there is no direct reference in Joy's Diaries. The Fairbairn 2-2-2 'back tank' in its original form is illustrated here, and it will be noted that the sole back tank (necessitated by the use of inside cylinders) was a feature also to be favoured by Wilson during the succeeding years. The three 'Little' North Western Railway 'Fairbairns' were rebuilt by the Midland Railway (who assumed ownership in June 1852) in 1864-5 as double framed 0-4-2WTs with 4ft 6in coupled wheels, 12in by 16in cylinders and small domes mounted above the raised firebox (presumably with the main steam pipe lengthened to suit). Further reboilered and altered, they were withdrawn from service during the 1890s. Their detailed history has been recorded elsewhere. (*The Engineer*)

badly damaged in the collision and Joy commented, 'It was an awful experience and none of us forgot it in a hurry.' The 'Burys' were returned to their owner and apparently repaired, being withdrawn and scrapped, as MR Nos. 137 and 145, in 1854-5. They were temporarily replaced by two more locomotives from the MR, one of which was a 'Sharpie' 2-2-2 before Wilson could supply more permanent replacements.

During his spell with the ANB&EJR, Joy felt constrained by the lack of ability on the part of locomotives of the period to generate adequate volumes of steam to cope with the work expected of them, especially on upgrades. He recalled:

'The Ratcliff Bank was a bother, as it started in 1 in 110 up, and went into a 1 in 130 and 1 in 176 – so we often

Today, two identifiable Fairbairn 'single driver' tank locomotives survive, both overseas, although one, the 5ft 6in gauge *02049*, preserved in the Portuguese National Collection and believed to date from 1854, has swapped its original pattern boiler for a back-dome variety (effectively reverting to the Hirst/Hawkshaw arrangement) and acquired a saddle tank. This photograph, taken at the Engenho de Dentro Railway Museum in Rio de Janeiro in February 2007, shows the older of the two survivors, *Baroneza* in its current home. Comparison with the previous illustration shows the cylinder arrangement to be convincingly 'original', indicating that the locomotive was built with a mainframe spacing standard with sister engines that were built to 5ft. 3in. gauge. The quoted dimensions for this locomotive are at variance with those given by Ahrons for the design, being: cylinders 11in by 15in; driving wheels 5ft; carrying wheels 3ft 6in; wheelbase 6ft+6ft; tube heating surface 300.6sqft; firebox heating surface 31.4sqft; weight in working order 16.75 tons (10.1 tons on driving axle); water capacity 400 gallons and fuel capacity 1 ton of coke. The boiler is described as possessing 87 tubes of 1½in diameter and 8ft 10in long, but this may not have been the original arrangement. (*Author*)

> had to stick on it with a load of goods even when we had taken a big run at it from the level at the bottom. Then the engine would puff out her last breath till she stuck dead. Then we put on the brake at the back and spragged the last two or three wagons, and then backed the engine close up with every buffer compressed or close and every drag chain slack; then at the given moment on went steam full and the engine would pluck wagon after wagon on till the last was caught up, and at a slow pace we would move on a bit to stick again, and repeat the dodge till we topped the hill, and then run merrily down to Bingham – 1 in 76.'

In September 1850, a special working to Matlock had necessitated the borrowing of MR No. 158, a double framed Wilson 0-6-0, but by the following month, 2-4-0 W/N 266 had arrived from the Railway Foundry. This locomotive possessed 5ft coupled wheels and was used for goods work and appears to have given complete satisfaction in service. For new small passenger locomotives, a less orthodox solution was adopted by the Railway Foundry. Crampton's Patent 12627 of 2 June 1849, taken out jointly with Henry Trewhitt covered the use of a dummy crankshaft (contained within the wheelbase) for the intermediate transmission of power. The advantage claimed for this idea was that no direct variable suspension loadings were transmitted to the crank axle, although the disadvantage in having no wheels on that axle would have been unnecessary increases in axle loading. This observation notwithstanding, at least six, and probably seven, inside cylinder 0-4-0 back tank locomotives were constructed by E.B. Wilson & Co. under this Patent. These 16 ton locomotives possessed 5ft diameter coupled wheels, 11in by 18in cylinders, water and coke capacities of 225 gallons and 1 ton respectively and a total heating surface of 576sqft. The boiler was 3ft by 9ft 3in and the boiler tubes were, unusually for Wilson practice, 1¾in diameter. The design was of vital importance as it appears to have been the first E.B. Wilson class to 'go the whole hog' and incorporate a boiler clearly inspired by the design of the ECR locomotive *Cambridge*. The implications of this decision were to be massive but despite this fact, and the fact that their use of the back tank configuration was also to influence subsequent Wilson practice, none of the locomotives were destined to have particularly long operating careers. Three went to the ANB&EJR

This view, taken on the same day as the previous one, emphasizes the raised firebox proportions. (*Author*)

as *Grantham* and *Rutland* in November 1850 with a third (unnamed) in January 1851. These locomotives were known as the 'Little Mails' on the ANB&EJR. Joy gave some details about the early operational career of the first two locomotives of the class. In relation to their being fitted with Stephenson's Link Motion, he said:

> 'What a mess the driver, old Pilkington, made of his first trip. I knew right enough about driving, with link gear and expansion, and told him after starting to pull her up on the link, but he would not believe she would pull and let her out, to stick fast at Elton three stations on. Then I made him link her up.
>
> 'These two little engines were known as "Grantham" and "Rutland" and were supposed to be alike, but "Grantham" had brass tubes and "Rutland" had steel tubes, and was somehow different, always giving more trouble, not so smart, and burning 1lb. more coke per mile.'

Joy further recounted that details of several runs with these locomotives were recorded, and that *Grantham* attained a maximum speed of 66 miles per hour with a two-coach train (net weight 11 tons) down the 1 in 165 bank near Bottesford.

The remaining Wilson locomotive delivered to the railway during David Joy's tenure of office as Locomotive Superintendent (which ended in October 1851) was a double framed 0-6-0 goods, of design to be described. During the autumn of 1851 the operating contract was taken over by Neal & Wilson of Grantham who added a Jenny Lind, a Hawthorn 2-2-2 and two more double framed Wilson 0-6-0s of more standard design. At some stage, probably in 1853, the locomotives were numbered, with the Little Mails becoming Nos. 1-3; the Hawthorn No. 4; the Jenny No. 5; the earliest 0-6-0 No. 6; the 2-4-0 No. 7 and the other 0-6-0s Nos. 8-9. They became respectively G.N.R. Nos. 218-22 and 391-4 in 1855, but sadly the Little Mails did not prove popular

Ambergate, Nottingham, Boston & East Junction Railway dummy-crankshaft 0-4-0WT *Grantham* was renumbered 218 by the Great Northern Railway in 1855 and was the first Wilson locomotive fitted with the *Cambridge* pattern boiler. Although the locomotive appears to have impressed Joy, the Great Northern Railway was not impressed with the 'dummy crankshaft' principle as it appeared to have little practical advantage and unnecessarily increased axle loading. All three ex-ANB&EJR class members were therefore converted to 0-4-2STs with the rear coupled axle taking the place of the 'dummy' one and the trailing axle taking the form of a carrying wheelset only. The trio were then assigned to the Stamford & Essendine Railway where they remained in service until the working of this line was taken over by the Marquis of Exeter from the GNR on 1 January 1865, after which they were withdrawn. The influence of their altered design was to live on during a seven year period after which the S&ER would once again come under full GNR control, however. (*The Locomotive*)

with their new owners all three were rebuilt as conventional 0-4-2STs (with the former 'dummy' axle being replaced by the relocated rear coupled axle and sundry mainframe and additional modifications carried out) during this latter year and were withdrawn between 1868 and 1874 in that form. All three of the 0-6-0 locomotives received Sturrock steam tenders in 1863, which were dispensed with after a short time in service. The last survivor of the A.N.B. & E.J.R. locomotives (No.9) was reboilered in 1892 and scrapped in 1901. At the same time as the first pair of Little Mails was delivered to the ANB&EJR, a sister engine was supplied to the North Eastern Railway at Darlington as No. 273. This engine was destined to be the longest lived of the class in main line service and was even exhibited at Darlington in 1875, featuring in an engraving in *The Engineer*. It was replaced three years later. The remaining known members of the class were *Langdale* and *Windermere* supplied in late 1850 to the Kendal & Windermere Railway. Taken over by the Lancaster & Carlisle Railway in May 1857, where they were numbered 66-7 respectively, they came into L&NWR stock in December 1859 and, after each had been renumbered three times, they were sold out of stock, in all probability for stationary use, in 1865. It may be that a seventh locomotive of Little Mail class was constructed in 1851 as W/N 301 and was not sold in its original form. This possibility will be considered further in Chapter Seven.

The Hawkshaw 2-2-2 design for the Manchester & Leeds Railway may have pushed another builder in the direction of adopting the full-blown domeless barrel/fully raised 'inverted-U' firebox wrapper method of boiler construction. William Fairbairn & Sons constructed twenty-one 'Hawkshaw' locomotives for the Lancashire & Yorkshire Railway (the M&LR's successor) in 1848-9 and during May the following year, a full half year before the Little Mails, produced the first of its 2-2-2WTs *Whernside*

The North Eastern Railway's sole Wilson 'dummy crankshaft' locomotive was illustrated by this engraving made at the time of the engine being exhibited at Darlington in 1875, probably after withdrawal from service. At this stage, it had been the last member of the class in normal service. Comparison of this illustration with the previous one shows little difference between the two and it is interesting to notice that both views show the same type of ungainly tapered chimney, despite the fact that the maker's drawings *held by the Institution of Mechanical Engineers* show a much more attractive design, more in keeping with Railway Foundry practice. The boiler design; 'back tank'; 'wiggly' footplate steps; dummy crankshaft; crosshead-driven feed pump and cylinders set below axle level are all evident in this illustration, as is the additional pair of 'block' buffers, for handling colliery wagons, fitted by the N.E.R. and still attached at the leading end. (*The Engineer*)

for the 'Little' North Western Railway (Skipton to Morecambe). This inside framed locomotive, which had 10in by15in cylinders and 5ft driving wheels, was followed in June 1850 by *Penyghent* and in October 1851 by *Competitor*. There is no reference to these locomotives in David Joy's Diaries and this fact is prima facie evidence that Joy was not involved at the design stage. Against this, it has to be argued that Joy had a wide circle of contacts in the engineering world, and that as will be noted later, E.B. Wilson did build locomotives to a similar design, albeit after the Fairbairn class had appeared. Be that as it may, Fairbairn built several locomotives of this design to standard gauge for home use and 5ft 3in and 5ft 6in gauges for export. One specimen of slightly greater than the latter gauge was delivered (apparently with three classmates) to Brazil's first railway, the Estrada de Ferro Maua, in 1852 and hauled Brazil's inaugural train on 30 April 1854. The engine, which is named *Baroneza* was taken over by the Estrada de Ferro Dom Pedro II in 1883 at which point it was re-gauged to 5ft 3in. This suggests that Fairbairn 'Single Well Tanks' of 5ft 3in and 5ft 6in gauges at least possessed the same mainframe spacing and that the variation was accounted for by the design of wheel centres, possibly axle bearings and difference in axle lengths. Remaining in use until the early years of the twentieth century, *Baroneza* is displayed today in the Engenho de Dentro Railway Museum in Rio de Janeiro, still with its original pattern of boiler. It is the earliest extant locomotive in the world to have always carried a boiler of this design. Another locomotive, CCeP. No. 02049, built by Fairbairn in 1854 to a similar specification, but to 5ft 6in gauge survives at Braga Depot in Portugal. This locomotive was converted to a saddle tank with a back-dome boiler at a relatively early stage in its career, however, and is preserved in this condition.

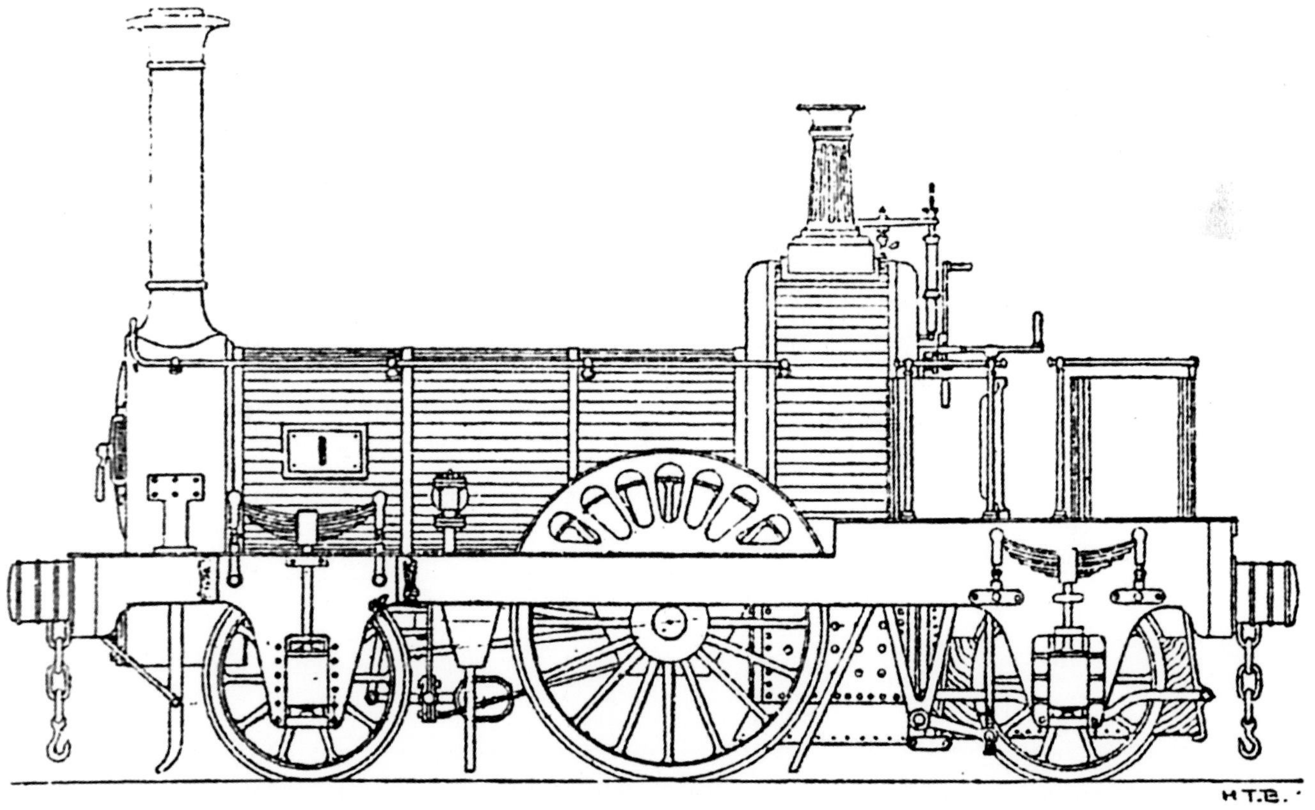

The original drawing purporting to be 2-2-2WT Nos. 1-3 of the Norfolk Railway conformed to the description for Wilson locomotives of this configuration given by Ahrons, although these particular locomotives were not constructed to the design specified. As mentioned in the main text, however, there is evidence to suggest that *Oberon* and *Titania* of the Whitehaven & Furness Junction Railway were built to this design. (*The Locomotive*)

E.L. Ahrons in *The British Steam Railway Locomotive From 1825 to 1925* states:

> 'E.B. Wilson's 2-2-2 tank locomotives were somewhat similar to those of Fairbairn but the bearings of the carrying wheels were outside, as in the "Jenny Linds". The cylinders were 10in. by 17in., and the driving wheels 5ft. 6in. The weight in working order was 19 ½ tons. In place of the dome, the firebox casing was raised 1ft. above the barrel to provide a steam space, though the steam was taken from a perforated pipe at the end of the barrel. The raised flat ends of the casing were stayed by means of short longitudinal stays secured to angle irons. This form of raised casing was used for many years by Manning Wardle and Co. in tank engines built by them.'

The implications of the last sentence of this quote will, rightfully, be considered in subsequent chapters, but its general tenor raises an interesting question when taken in conjunction with other published evidence. In May 1851, the Norfolk Railway (which was being worked by the Eastern Counties Railway) came to an agreement whereby it could work some of its branch line trains under its own auspices. In order to undertake this task, three 2-2-2WT locomotives were purchased from the Railway Foundry, and their dimensions were given as follows: driving wheels 5ft 6in; carrying wheels 3ft 6in; wheelbase 13ft 7in (6ft 5in+7ft 2in); cylinders 10in by 17in; length of boiler barrel 9ft 3in and that of the firebox 2ft 10in. The weight in working order was 19.525 tons (5.8 + 6.875+6.85). *The Locomotive* for 15 April 1905 illustrated a design that conformed very much to Ahrons' description, adding that the locomotives became E.C.R. Nos. 1-3 in March 1852. The difficulty arises from the fact that in the 15 August 1907 issue of the same journal, this authenticity of this drawing was repudiated in favour of a replacement that depicted an inside framed design not unlike its Fairbairn counterpart. This amendment was confirmed in the issue of exactly thirty-one years later, which for good measure added that they were altered at Norwich to a 'mixed frame' configuration under a drawing made during the month in which the ECR took possession of them. Assuming that all of the amended information was correct and that the three Norfolk Railway locomotives were built as 'inside framers', then why was the design that Ahrons appears to have 'latched on' to apparently rejected? This is especially ironic, given the modifications made subsequently by the Eastern Counties Railway. Evidence that the Railway Foundry did construct a 'mixed frame' 2-2-2WT class comes from the fact that two locomotives of this configuration were supplied in 1851 as *Oberon* and *Titania* to the Whitehaven & Furness Junction Railway. The former appears to have been somewhat accident-prone, being involved in incidents at Broughton in 1857 and

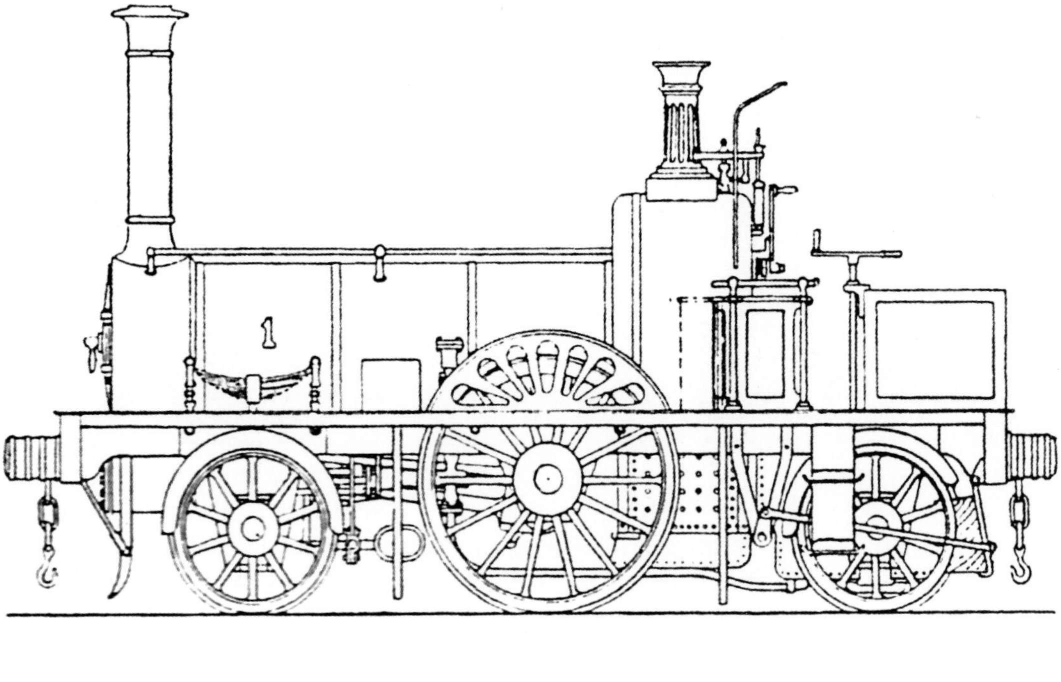

As built, the Norfolk Railway locomotives bore a greater resemblance to their Fairbairn contemporaries, being inside (single) framed throughout, although there were detail differences between the three class members. (*The Locomotive*)

in Whitehaven Tunnel in 1866, the year in which both locomotives became Furness Railway property respectively as Nos. 47 and 48. Crucially, *The Locomotive* for 15 October 1942 states that another engine acquired from the W&FJR, *Queen Mab*, built by R. & W. Hawthorn in 1860, later Furness Railway No. 46 was 'of the same general design'. This locomotive is known from an accompanying sketch to have had larger cylinders (14in by 20in) and outside bearings on all axles, but this latter feature suggests that the author was aware that the Wilson locomotive did possess outside bearings, albeit only for the carrying wheelsets. They were withdrawn by the Furness Railway in 1872 and the erstwhile *Titania* is recorded as having 5ft 6in driving wheels, 11in by 17in cylinders (the originals 'bored out' by ½in or replacements?) and wrought iron wheels with steel tyres when it was in the hands of Whitehaven locomotive builder Fletcher, Jennings & Co. two years later. *The Locomotive* for 15 January 1948 further records:

> 'At any rate this locomotive was rebuilt as an [sic] 0-6-0 saddle tank with wheels 3ft. 6in. diameter. New side rods, crankpins and coal boxes were fitted, also one No. 7 Giffard injector, 130 brass tubes, a weather-board and a new dome close to the funnel. In her rebuilt form this engine was sold to the Winder Iron Ore Company, near Frizington, in February 1875. A new crank axle and tyres were supplied in 1879.'

The mention of the fitting of a dome authenticates the fact that domeless barrel was originally fitted, whilst the choice of 3ft 6in diameter for the (presumably new) coupled wheels indicated that the old carrying wheel diameter was used as the 'datum' for the layout of this rebuild. In the apparent absence of the fitting of new frames, sadly no mention was made as to whether the inside frames were strengthened and fitted with horncheeks for the leading and trailing wheels (with the outside frames being discarded) or whether the outside frames were fitted with additional horncheeks for the middle wheelset and the engine thus acquired full 'double-framed' status. No photograph has come to light at the time of writing to settle this argument, but the former proposition would appear to be the more feasible one as double framed locomotives with coupled wheels of less than 4ft 2in diameter were extremely rare in British locomotive practice.

The next locomotive to be considered is the one double-boiler design that came to fruition. Returning to January 1850, Joy recalled that he was called upon

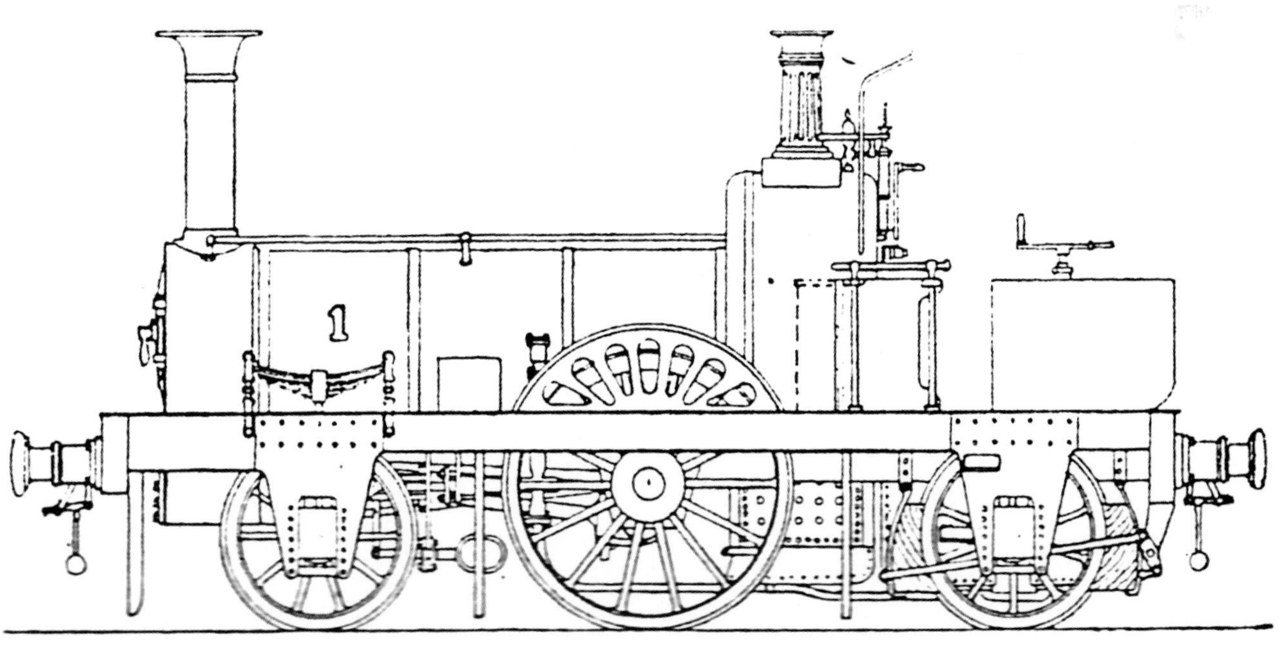

The final irony in the story of the Norfolk Railway 2-2-2WTs is the fact that they were *altered* to a mixed frame configuration, allegedly at Norwich with the first conversion being carried out in 1852. They were withdrawn from traffic twenty years later with at least one class member subsequently being put to stationary duties. (*The Locomotive*)

to speak in public for the first time (at the Royal Society of Arts) and that he:

> '... worked on at double boiler in a new form as a coupled engine. This tracing I lent to someone and lost [a copy now survives in the Institution of Mechanical Engineers] but I remember it well enough, with the particulars from my note-book to reproduce it.

The locomotive had been completed by April 1851 as a 2-4-0 back tank and initially underwent trials at Leeds and Bradford against a standard Jenny working trains of ten ordinary carriages giving a net load of about 60 tons. It was found that the weight (initially 19.65 tons in working order) was very unevenly distributed wheel-against-wheel, and this was altered so that there was an approximate load of 3¼ tons on each wheel. As altered to its final known form it had the following dimensions:

Cylinders	12.5in (Bore), 18in Stroke
Wheel Diameter	5ft (Coupled), 3ft 6in (Leading)
Wheelbase	6ft + 6ft 6in
Boiler Barrels	10ft 6in (L), 1ft 9in (D)
Boiler Pitch	4ft 9½in
Firebox Wrapper	2ft 9in (L) 4ft 4in (W)
Water Spaces	3in (Front and Back) 2.5in (Sides), 3½in Between Inner Fireboxes
Boiler Tubes	136, 1.75in Diameter, 289sqft Total Cross-section
Heating Surface	694sqft (Tubes), 61sqft (Firebox)
Grate Area	7.5sqft
Water Capacity	520 gallons
Coke Capacity	0.75 tons (42cu.ft)
Height of Locomotive	13ft 6in
Width Over Crankpins	8ft 3in
Buffers	5ft 8in Centres, 3ft 3in Pitch
Weights: Empty	16.0 tons
Working Order	19.85

By 1 May 1851, it had been moved to London for the Great Exhibition where, painted in blue livery, it was a companion to the Great Western Railway's *Lord of the Isles* and the L&NWR's *Lady of the Lake* in the Exhibition. E.L. Ahrons considered the double-boiler arrangement unnecessary for coke burning, but also felt that it was doubtful that coal burning was under consideration at the time of its construction. Its subsequent history is unknown.

At this stage one important observation needs to be made: of the 'dummy crankshaft' locomotives, Joy stated, 'They were credited to W. E. Carrett as his design as the double boilers had been to me'. Whilst Joy was preoccupied with his work on the ANB&EJR, his design responsibilities passed to William Elliot Carrett (1828-1870) who remained at the Railway Foundry until his departure in 1852, as recorded in the *Leeds Mercury* for 4 September that year. He was later a partner in Carrett, Marshall & Co., successors at the Sun Foundry, the premises formerly occupied by Charles Todd following the latter's departure from Shepherd & Todd. This was principally a general engineering concern making products such as stationary engines and boilers, but its solitary locomotive, 1860-built *Natal* survives in reconstructed form in South Africa.

A design that stands alone in the general scheme of E.B. Wilson product practice was represented by a pair of double framed 2-2-2s built for the Southern Division of the L&NWR. This class was known as the McConnell Patent or 300 class. It consisted of a dozen members, ten built by Fairbairn and the Wilson pair, Southern Division Nos. 298-9 supplied respectively in in 1852 and 1853. These locomotives possessed the following dimensions:

Cylinders	18in (Bore), 24in Stroke
Wheel Diameter	4ft 6in (Leading), 7ft 6in (Driving), 4ft 0in (Trailing)
Wheelbase	8ft 4in+8ft 6in
Boiler Barrel	11ft 9in (L), 4ft 3¼in (D)
Tubes	305, 1¾in
Total Heating Surface	1163sqft

The most distinctive feature of these locomotives was the use of the McConnell patent boiler with longitudinal mid-feather and leading combustion chamber. The boiler and combustion chamber had to be recessed to accommodate the crankshaft, onto which the axis of drive was inclined upwards from the leading end despite the fact that the cylinders sat above the leading axle.

Although David Joy's first attempt at designing a 'double boiler' tank locomotive proved abortive, the 'coupled' version materialised as this double framed 2-4-0WT and appeared at the Great Exhibition of 1851. This drawing was prepared using the still-extant Joy original and was similar to the illustration in the Exhibition Catalogue. It reveals two interesting additional features, namely the additional ducts taking steam generated in the barrels to the steam space within the common firebox wrapper, and the fact that wooden lagging was arranged to follow the 'joint' contour of the smokebox rather than the contours of the individual barrels. (*The Locomotive*)

The 300 class, which was used on passenger workings between London and Birmingham, achieved some initial popularity with the locomotive crews, but their boiler design proved to be their weak point; its structural complexity made it a poor shape for a pressure vessel, necessitating more frequent repairs than with a conventional boiler, whilst the relatively short length of the boiler tubes led to overheating of the smokebox. Southern Division Nos. 298-9 were renumbered 37-8 respectively in April 1856, becoming L&NWR 637-8 and finally 1187-9 on the Duplicate List in 1862, being scrapped shortly afterwards.

CHAPTER 6

THE STURROCK INFLUENCE AND ANOTHER OPERATING CONTRACT

In 1850 Archibald Sturrock (1816-1909) took over as Locomotive Superintendent of the Great Northern Railway from Edward Bury and one legacy with which he had been left was an order, placed on 26 March 1850, for a batch of 2-4-0 tender locomotives, apparently of the bar framed pattern favoured by Bury. Sturrock had very different ideas on locomotive design, having previously served as Manager of Swindon Works under Daniel Gooch. He was therefore much more at home with the 'Sandwich Framed' (composite iron and timber for the outside and iron for the inside frames) method of construction used for Gooch's broad gauge 'singles' than with Bury's methods of construction. In the *Railway Magazine* in 1907, Sturrock recorded:

> 'In July 1850 I was appointed locomotive engineer to the Great Northern Railway with its narrow gauge [the ordinary standard gauge which he was comparing the Great Western broad gauge] and of course resigned my appointment on the Great Western Railway. Mr. Geo. Stephenson had given evidence before the Parliamentary Committee that it was no use granting the Great Northern Railway Bill as the gradients on the proposed line were so bad that if the Bill were granted, the line could not be worked.'

Noting that what Stephenson really meant was the GNR could not be worked in competition with the L&NWR on whose behalf he was giving evidence, Sturrock went on to record:

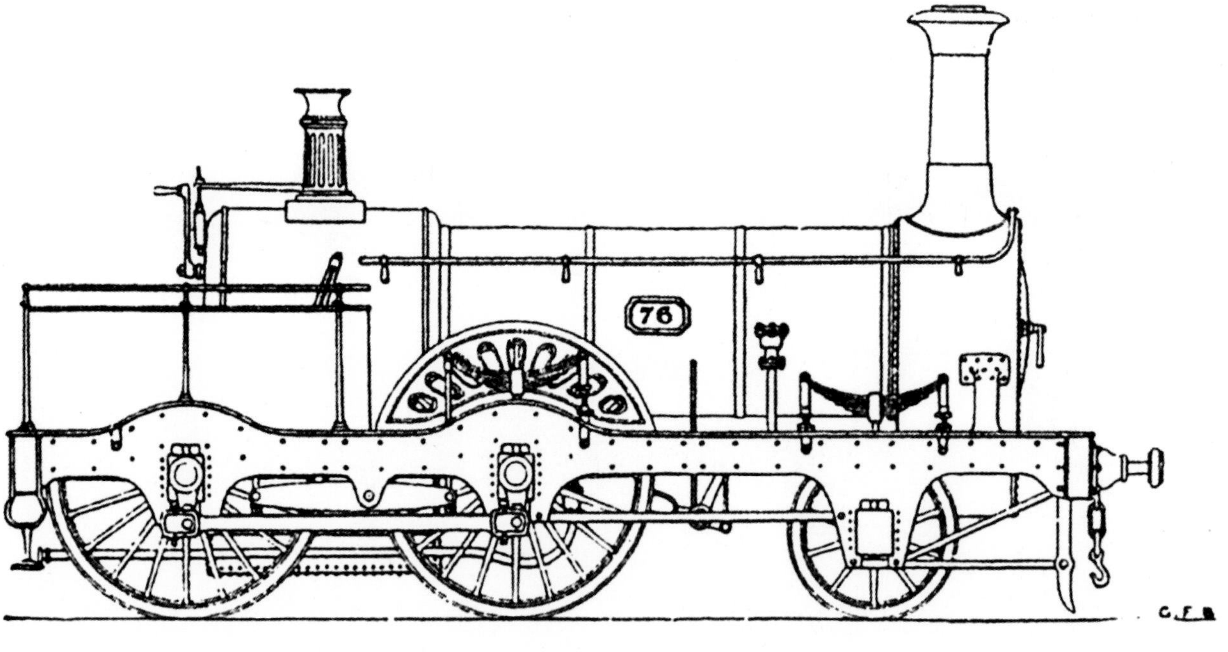

This was the first E.B. Wilson-built member of the Great Northern Railway '71' class sandwich framed 2-4-0 to enter the railway's running stock (on 28 April 1851). Although not the first Railway Foundry product to combine the sandwich framed chassis arrangement with a coupled wheel arrangement, this design was very much 'the shape of things to come' for E.B. Wilson locomotive design, although the domeless boiler was not generally retained on subsequent variants. The inside frames would have run, Jenny Lind-fashion, from the leading ends of the cylinders back to the throatplate. (*G.F. Bird*)

> 'Through correspondence with Mr. Ramsbottom, the locomotive engineer of the London and North-Western Railway, I learnt that his engines had only 50 sq.ft of firebox surface and used 80 lbs. steam pressure. My experience told me that 50 sq.ft of firebox could not supply sufficient steam to large cylinders to run continuously at high speed, so I determined to adopt 100 sq.ft of fire box surface. To obtain power to climb the bad gradients, stated by Mr. Stephenson to be insurmountable, I determined to increase the pressure from 80 to 150 lbs.'

Bury's order was therefore reviewed and the locomotives totally redesigned. The original order quantity of ten locomotives from the Railway Foundry was increased to fifteen (five further similar locomotives were ordered from R. & W. Hawthorn & Co.) and the design that eventually emerged was double framed with 'sandwich' outer frames and inner frames of Jenny Lind pattern extending from the front of the cylinders to the firebox wrapper. The outer mainframes incorporated curved portions above the coupled axles (to 'back' the flycranks), with the smokebox and firebox wrapper being secured to these frames by means of palm stays. The boilers were of the domeless variety with slightly raised firebox wrapper and classic Wilson fluted safety valve cover. Compensating lever suspension (unequally spaced) between the coupled axles was employed and the splashers incorporated ornamental frets. The leading dimensions of the locomotives were as follows:

Wheel Diameter	6ft. 0in (Coupled) 4ft 0in (Leading)
Cylinders	16in (Bore), 22in (Stroke)
Wheelbase	7ft 9in+7ft 3in
Boiler Barrel Length	10ft 0in
Boiler Barrel Diameter	3ft 11in
Pitch	6ft 3in
Firebox Wrapper	5ft 2½in (L) 4ft 0in (W)
Internal Firebox	4ft 6in. (L), 3ft 3½in (W)
Heating Surface	802sqft (Tubes) 102sqft (Firebox)
Grate Area	13.2sqft
Number of Boiler Tubes	157, 2in Diameter
Locomotive Weight	27.9 Tons (10.45+9.35+8.1)
Water Capacity	1300 Gallons
Coal Capacity	5 Tons

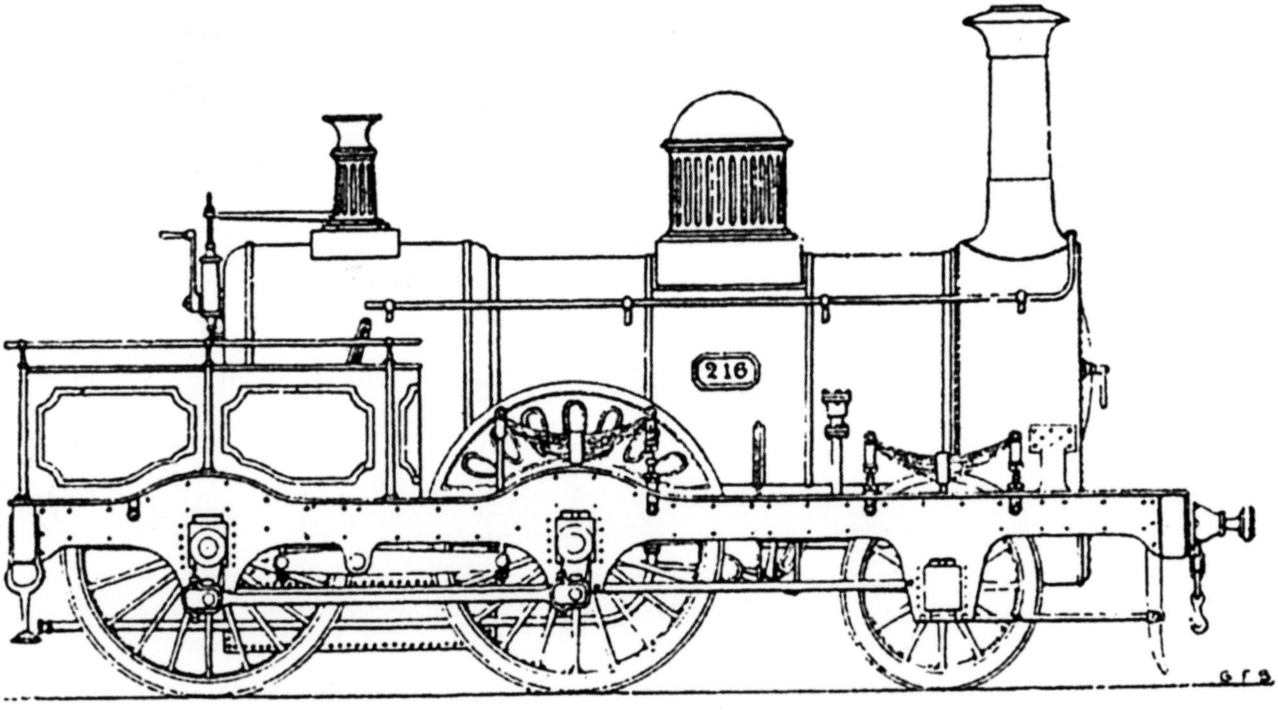

One of two Wilson sandwich framed 2-4-0 locomotives originally purchased and later re-sold by Charles Cave Williams is illustrated in this drawing. This particular locomotive eventually became Great Northern Railway No. 216 (as shown) and was withdrawn from service in April 1887. The domed boiler is shown to advantage, contrasting with the previous illustration. (*G.F. Bird*)

Apart from the domeless boiler, this new design was to have a profound influence upon subsequent passenger locomotive development at the Railway Foundry and similar locomotives were to be constructed for other customers. On the G.N.R. the class was known as the '71' class with the Hawthorn locomotives (Nos. 71-5) being taken into stock between 17 May and 10 July 1851 and the Wilson batch (Nos. 76-90) between 28 April and 21 September of the same year. The class originally saw service on the Great Exhibition traffic of 1851 and then gravitated to secondary passenger working, receiving extensive overhauls (some officially regarded as rebuilds) during the period from 1864-7. Four were fitted with Stirling boilers during 1875-6, of which three, Nos. 78, 87 and 88 were later placed on the Duplicate List and finally withdrawn respectively in October 1898, December 1897 and November 1899. In the case of the first and last of these, it is certainly questionable as to how much of the original locomotive actually remained as both had received new mainframes during Patrick Stirling's tenure of office.

Concurrently with the order for the passenger locomotives, the GNR was in need of goods locomotives and on the same day that Bury placed his order for the 2-4-0s, 0-6-0s were also put on order. Once again, Sturrock reviewed the order in July 1850 following his formal appointment and applied the principles of firebox design that he recounted to the *Railway Magazine* over half a century later, causing £100 to be added to the unit cost for the firebox redesign. The Railway Foundry had already produced at least a dozen 0-6-0s with outside sandwich and inside plate mainframes during the late 1840s, with underhung cylinders and piston rods beneath the leading axles (six for the Midland Railway as Nos. 207-8 and 223-6 in 1849-50, later 218-23 and finally 290-5, scrapped between January 1858 and May 1868 respectively; two built for the L&YR as Nos. 202-3, re-numbered respectively 220-1 and withdrawn in 1870 and 1869; two for the Sheffield & Manchester Railway as Nos. 91-2; one for the South Yorkshire Railway as *No. 4*, later MS&LR No. 155, and one (believed to be W/N 158) which eventually became Ambergate,

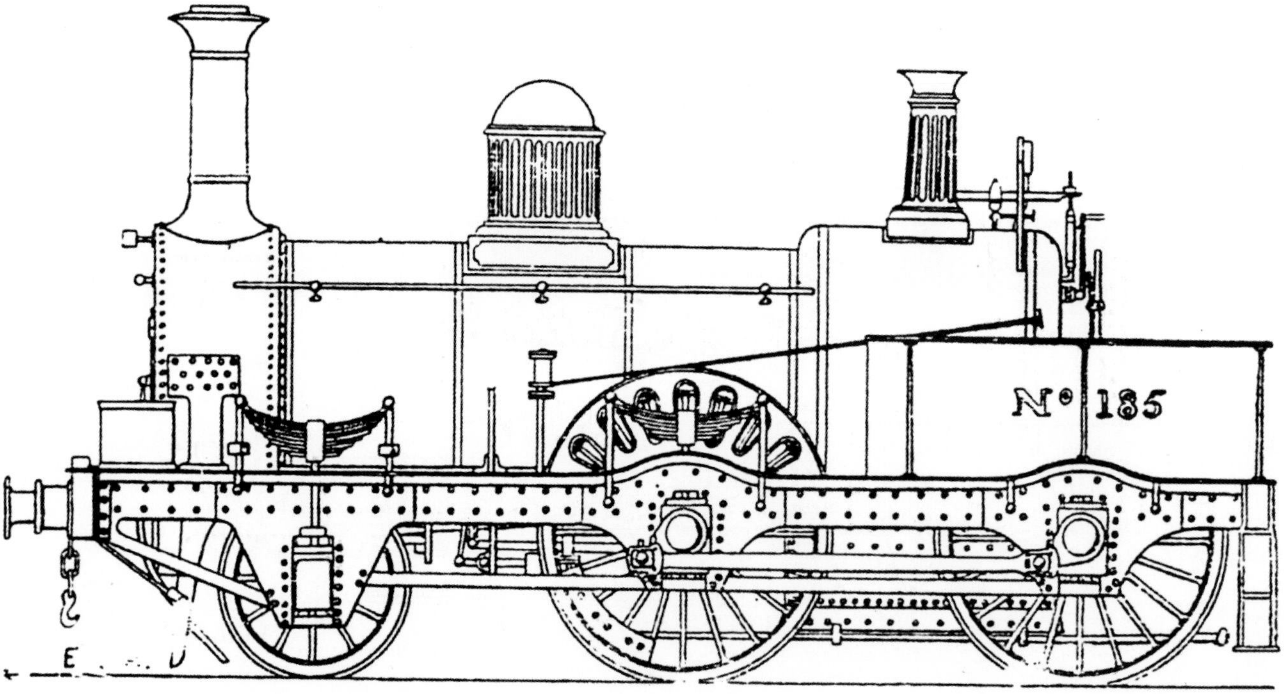

This OW&WR 2-4-0 (E. B. Wilson W/N 333 of 1853) began life as its original owner's No. 24, being renumbered 185 by the G.W.R. in 1863. Unlike the locomotives shown in the two previous illustrations, the plate-work for the sandwich frames was 'built up' rather than 'one piece'. Reboilered in June 1870 and March 1887 by the G.W.R. and receiving new inside frames on the former occasion, this locomotive was finally taken out of service and scrapped in 1899. Note the fact that the smaller leading wheelsets found on this variant when compared with the previous two illustrations did not require splashers. (*E.L. Ahrons*)

Nottingham, Boston & East Junction Railway No. 6) but, as recorded in *The Engineer* in 1920, this design proved troublesome in service owing to the tendency of the cylinders to work loose and the difficulty in dismantling for maintenance purposes caused by the position of the piston rods. Nonetheless, E.B. Wilson got the order for sixteen locomotives (at £1,900 apiece) with cylinders mounted in a more conventional position. These became the GNR '116' class. Numbered 144-158 and 167 in the G.N.R. list, the locomotives (E.B. Wilson Works Nos. 215-30, apparently in order of GNR numbering) entered service between 25 October 1850 and 10 February 1851 and their leading dimensions were as follows:

Wheel Diameter	5ft 0in
Cylinders	16in (Bore), 22in (Stroke)
Wheelbase	7ft 0in + 7ft 6in
Boiler Barrel	10ft 0in (L) 3ft 10in (D)
Internal Firebox	3ft 10½in (L) 3ft 3½in (W)
Heating Surface	815sqft (Tubes) 78sqft (Firebox)
Number of Boiler Tubes	158, 2in Diameter
Tender Water Capacity	1300 Gallons

This class were put to work on a variety of goods duties, with coal train workings from Yorkshire to London playing a large part in their employment. During the period 1864-7 all were extensively altered under Sturrock's direction, receiving new boilers, cylinders and with the wheelbase shortened to 14ft equally divided. The three later survivors, (GNR Nos. 144A, 149A and 155) all received new mainframes and Stirling pattern domeless boilers (again being effectively renewals) with 144A being the last to be withdrawn, in December 1898.

Further Wilson 0-6-0 goods locomotives of generally similar design were added to GNR stock during the ensuring few years, the first being two bearing the GNR Nos. 164-5 for £2000 apiece respectively in October and November 1850. These retained the same cylinder

The large-wheeled O.W. & W.R. 2-4-0s, Nos. 40-1 (W/Ns 466-7) were, as with the locomotives in the previous illustration, equipped with 'built up' sandwich frames as opposed to the one-piece variety (i.e. in line with NER rather than GNR practice). They became GWR Nos. 188-9 in 1863 but never achieved the success of their smaller wheeled sisters. This drawing shows No. 41 as renumbered 189 by the GWR but before it (and its sister) were fitted with 4ft leading wheels in 1873. No. 188 was withdrawn without further alteration in July 1878 but, as stated in the main text, No. 189 was further rebuilt, at Worcester in 1882, remaining in service in this form until March 1886. (*E.L. Ahrons*)

bore and coupled wheel diameter as the '116' class but the cylinder stroke was increased to 24in and the water capacity to 1350 gallons. No. 164 was withdrawn in May 1874, apparently without radical alteration but No. 165 was rebuilt with a Stirling boiler in December 1888 and was withdrawn from Ardsley Sheds in February 1900. The next batch of 0-6-0 locomotives were the first thirty members of the '168' class (the remaining ten being built by Fairbairn), being taken into stock as GNR Nos. 168-197 (E.B. Wilson Works Nos. 267-86 and 309-18) between 24 October 1851 and 15 July 1853. They were built with the following dimensions:

Wheel Diameter	5ft. 0in
Cylinders	16in (Bore), 24 in, (Stroke)
Wheelbase	7ft 9in+7ft. 9in
Boiler Barrel Length	10ft 6in
Boiler Barrel Diameter	4ft 3in (Vertical) 4ft 1in (Horizontal)
Firebox Wrapper	5ft 2in (L) 4ft 3in (W)
Internal Firebox (Inside)	4ft 5¼in (L) 3ft 7in (W) 5ft 2in (Above Grate Bars)
Number of Boiler Tubes	187, 2in Diameter
Locomotive Weight	29.5 Tons (10.5+11½+7.5)
Tender Wheels (Locos. 167-88)	3ft. 6in
Water Capacity	1400 Gallons
Coal Capacity	1½ Tons

The General Arrangement Drawings were published in D.K. Clark's *Railway Machinery* for these locomotives soon after construction and reveal, as would be expected, that their basic design followed the same principles as the '71' class 2-4-0s with composite iron and saplin ash outside 'sandwich' frames (3⅝in thick and 23ft 9in long) and 3/16in thick iron plate inside frames, once again of Jenny Lind pattern. The vertical

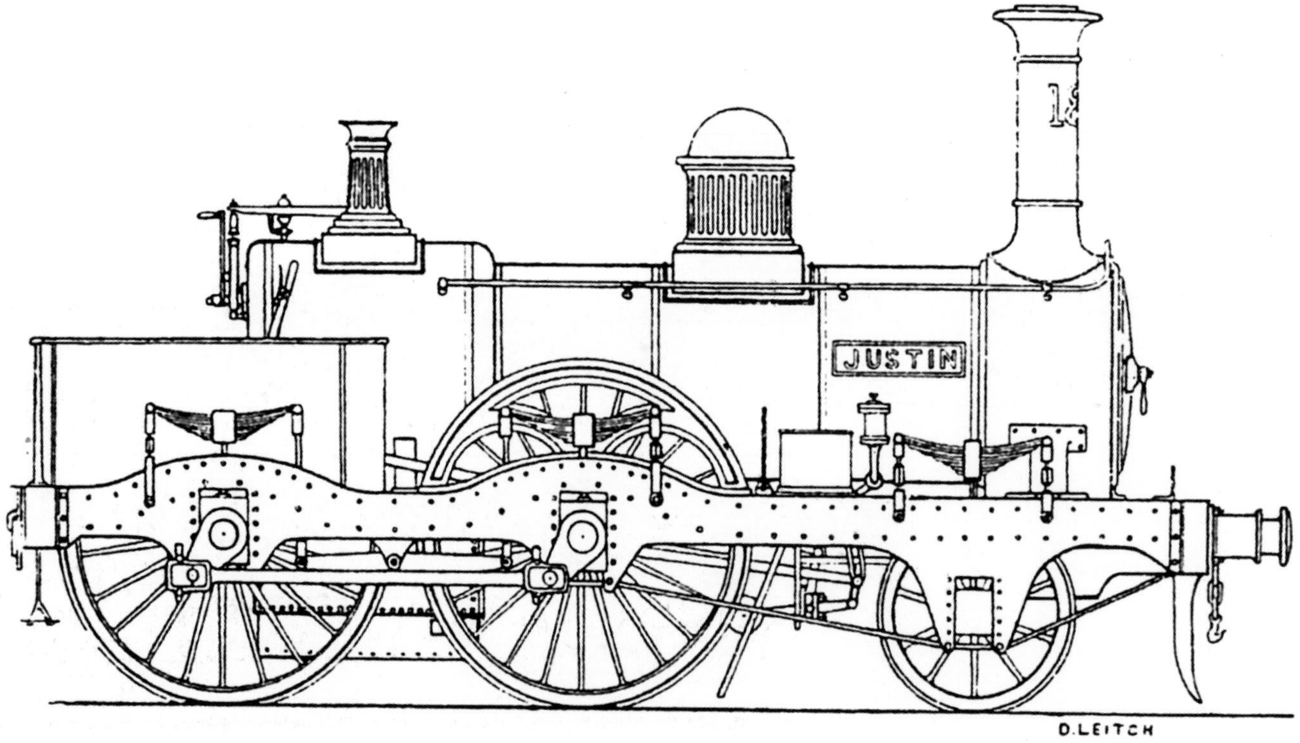

Continuing with the 'high stepper' theme, this is *Justin*, originally No. 19 of the South Staffordshire Railway. An interesting feature of this design variant was that the palm stays securing the firebox wrapper to the sandwich frames were not concealed by the waist sheets. The pattern of frets in the splashers appear to have been peculiar to this class. More significantly from the structural point of view, the inside mainframes extended to the rear of the front bufferbeam, contrary to the normal pattern of evolution of related E.B. Wilson locomotives. (*D. Leitch*)

major axis elliptical boiler barrel cross-section, seen on *Lablache*, made a reappearance (it was not present on the Fairbairn-built class members) and the inner firebox was divided for about two-thirds of its height by a mid-feather (five inches long) in order to increase the available heating surface, which was not specified on the Drawings. The careers of these locomotives followed a similar pattern to the '116' and 164' class locomotives, with extensive late Sturrock and early Stirling-era overhauls taking place during the 1862-67 period and the later survivors being fitted with Stirling domeless boilers, in this case between 1882 and 1890. Eight of these locomotives became part of Sturrock's unsuccessful 'steam tender' experiment during the mid-1860s, whilst the last survivor in service with its original mainframes was No. 177A (withdrawn in May 1902) with No. 192A (which received new frames in July 1871 and had once received a steam tender) lingering on until withdrawn in January 1909.

A further 21 'Wilson Goods' 0-6-0s of similar pattern, but not with elliptical section boilers, were supplied to the G.N.R. as part of the eventually 63-strong '308' class at a price of £2,575 each. These locomotives entered GNR stock between 8 February 1854 and 7 November 1855. Their leading dimensions were:

Wheel Diameter	5ft. 0in
Cylinders	16in (Bore), 24 in, (Stroke)
Wheelbase	7ft 9in + 7ft. 9in
Boiler Barrel Length	10ft 7in
Boiler Barrel Diameter	4ft 3in
Number of Boiler Tubes	209, 2in Diameter
Heating Surface	1146.45sqft (Tubes) 122.75sqft (Firebox)
Locomotive Weight	33½ Tons
Water Capacity	1400 Gallons 1½ Tons

Essentially, these locomotives were an updated version of the '168' class in which a normal pattern boiler barrel was substituted for the oval one, using the latter's maximum diameter so as to obtain a higher number of tubes and greater heating surface. So far as is known, the firebox mid-feather was dispensed with. The tenders appear to have been of the same design as those

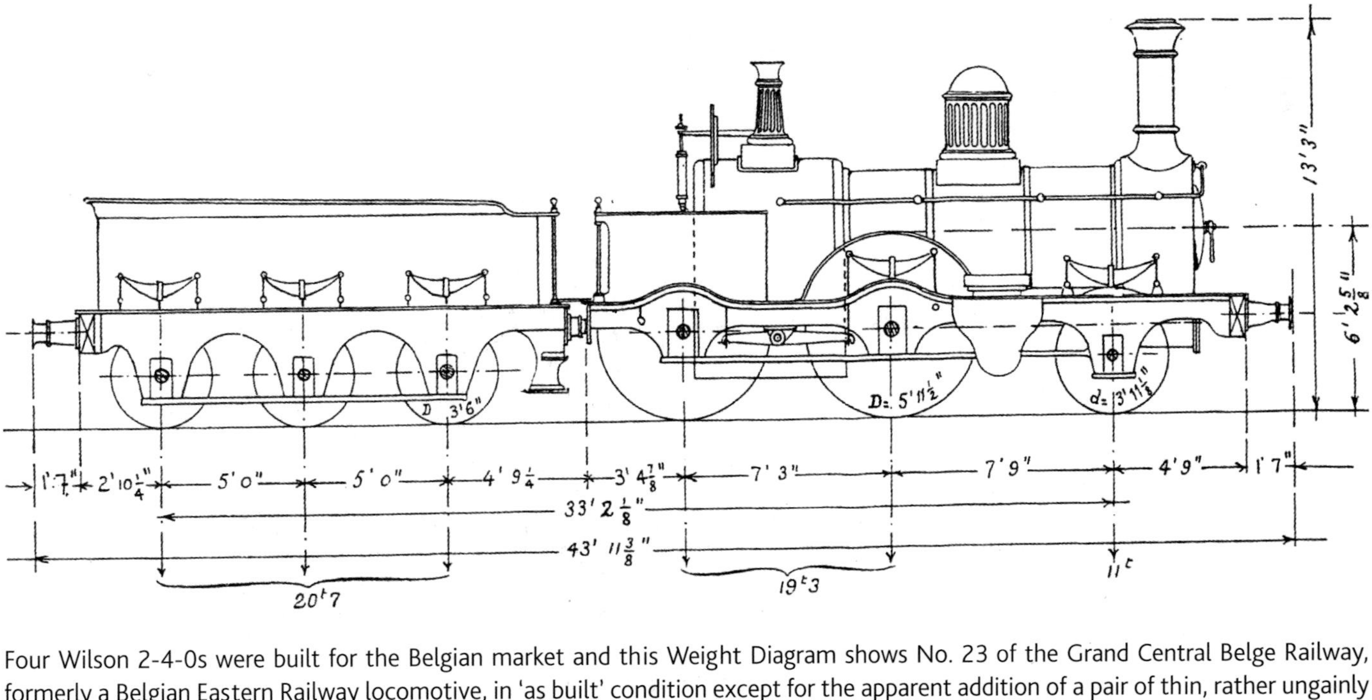

Four Wilson 2-4-0s were built for the Belgian market and this Weight Diagram shows No. 23 of the Grand Central Belge Railway, formerly a Belgian Eastern Railway locomotive, in 'as built' condition except for the apparent addition of a pair of thin, rather ungainly hopper-style sand boxes on the outside of the sandwich frames below running board level ahead of the leading coupled wheels. The basic design was very similar to GNR Nos. 216-7 and OW&WR Nos.21-26 and although from the information to hand, it is not possible to tell whether BER Nos. 23-5 possessed the 'one-piece' outer frames of the former or the 'built-up' arrangement of the latter, the general frame profile is more suggestive of the former. (*The Locomotive*)

originally supplied with locomotives 167-88 and the chassis design also appears to have been virtually identical, retaining the compensating levers between the leading and intermediate axles. The Wilson-built class members bore the GNR Nos. 338-47 and 370-80 and their careers once again followed a familiar pattern, with extensive overhauls being undertaken during the 1864-7 period, three locomotives receiving steam tenders around this time and eight locomotives eventually receiving Stirling domeless boilers. The last survivor with a domed boiler was No. 338, withdrawn in November 1901, but No.343 (latterly hardly recognizable as a standard 'Wilson Goods') which had sported a steam tender in the 1860s, received new frames in September 1870 and a Stirling boiler in December 1887, lasted in service until November 1905.

Given the adoption by the Great Northern Railway of Wilson 'Standard Goods' 0-6-0s, it was hardly surprising that the constituents of the neighbouring North Eastern Railway would follow suit. Shortly after the delivery of GNR No. 338, a similar locomotive appeared in March 1854 on the York, Newcastle & Berwick Railway. One important design difference was that whereas the horncheek bearing portions of the side mainframes were integral with iron portions of the sandwich frames on the GNR locomotives, they were separate fabrications on the YN&BR ones. In all, fifteen such locomotives were ordered by the YN&BR prior to the July Amalgamation to form the NER, of which six (E.B. Wilson Works Nos. 386-91) were numbered 230-5 in the YN&BR list, initially retaining these numbers under NER ownership. The remaining nine (Works Nos. 392-400) were delivered to the NER between September and November 1854 as Nos. 236-41 and January-March 1855 as Nos. 242-4. The last three survivors, Nos. 233, 237 and 243 were rebuilt at York in the 1880s and replaced respectively in 1905, 1902 and 1904. The first and last of these locomotives are known to have ended their careers with 17in cylinders. Six similar locomotives were ordered by the North Eastern Railway in 1855, being delivered as E.B. Wilson Works Nos. 459-64 between August and December that year bearing the NER Nos. 399-404. As with Nos. 230-41, these locomotives were built with 5ft diameter wheels and 16in by 24in cylinders although No. 402 may have acquired 17in cylinders during its first major rebuild at York in December 1880. This locomotive proved to be the last survivor of the batch and, following a second rebuild in 1889, it was replaced in 1902.

Another NER 'constituent', the Leeds Northern Railway, ordered in total nine 'Wilson Goods' 0-6-0s that were delivered to the N.E.R. during 1856. These were E.B. Wilson works Nos. 484-92 and were

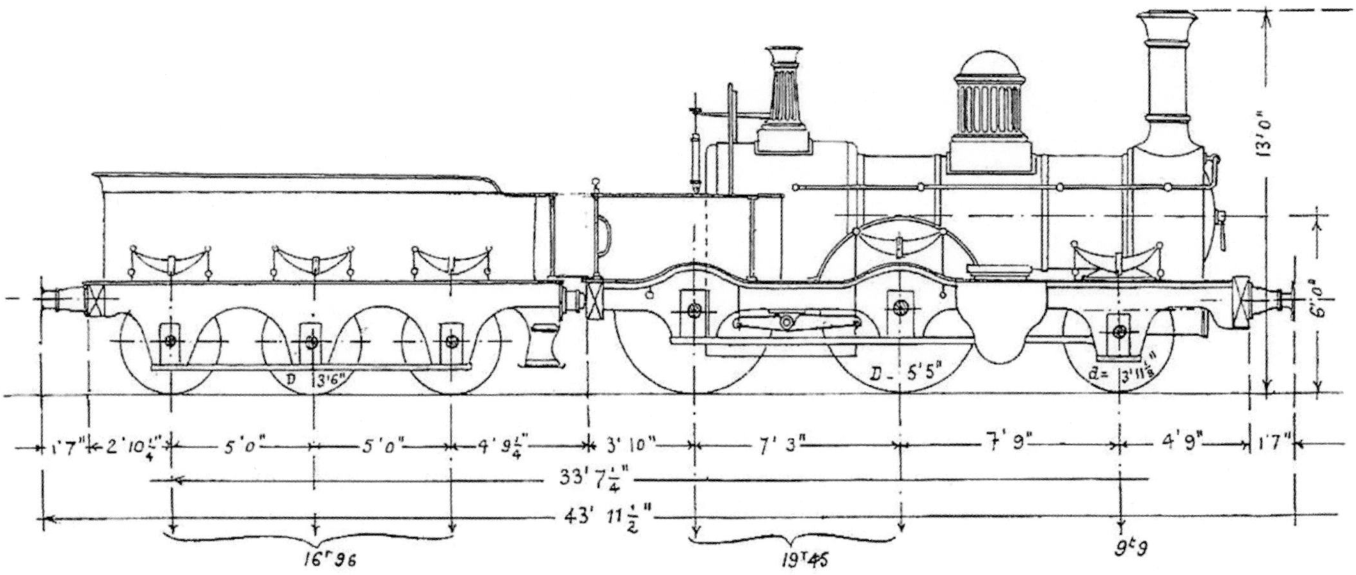

This Weight Diagram shows BER (later Grand Central Belge) E.B. Wilson 2-4-0 locomotive Nos. 24-5, built with smaller coupled wheels than the preceding locomotive. This and the preceding illustration are significant in that they give a guide to the longitudinal appearance and dimensions a typical later pattern E.B. Wilson tender, information that is sadly lacking from other sources. (*The Locomotive*)

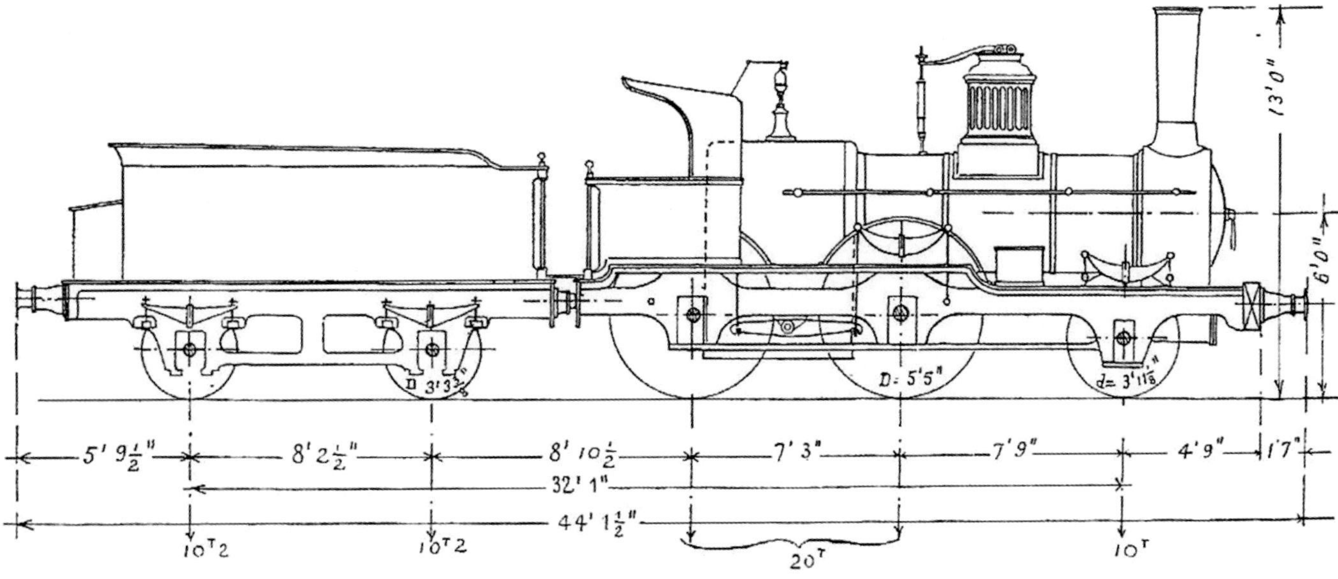

As mentioned in the main text, the ex-BER 2-4-0s were modified in the 1870s and this Weight Diagram shows Nos. 24-5 in later condition. It appears that the upper portions of their classic fluted dome covers were modified to a bell-mouthed profile to take the Salter safety valves. (*The Locomotive*)

numbered 379-87 by the NER. The first five differed from the remaining four by having 4ft 6in as opposed to 5ft 0in wheels as built. As with other Wilson 0-6-0s of the same general type owned by the NER, rebuilds were carried out at York and Leeds. The last survivor, No. 384, was rebuilt at York in 1889, placed on the Duplicate List in 1900 and scrapped in 1901.

The final two batches of 'Wilson Goods' 0-6-0s built for the North Eastern Railway retained the 5ft coupled wheels and 16in by 24in cylinders as built. E.B. Wilson Works Nos. 459-64 were turned out between August and December 1855 and Works Nos 589-98 were delivered between June and August 1857, bearing the NER Nos. 399-414. At least four of these locomotives are known to have received 17in cylinders during subsequent rebuildings and one of these, NER No. 408 (renumbered 2281 in the Duplicate List in 1901) was only replaced in 1920.

The York, Newcastle & Berwick Railway purchased six Wilson 'sandwich framed' 2-4-0s in 1853 and these were given the Nos. 213-8, initially retaining them in NER ownership. Nos. 215 and 218 possessed 16in by 22in cylinders, 6ft coupled wheels and cost £2,800 each when new, whilst the remaining four were built with 15in by 22in cylinders, 5ft 6in coupled wheels and cost £2,375 each when new. All were rebuilt during the 1869-78 period (No. 218 after a boiler explosion at Holbeck, Leeds on 23 July 1876) and in their final years sported Fletcher cabs and boilers. Nos. 215 and 218 are recorded as putting in nearly three decades of service working between Leeds Holbeck and Thirsk. The last survivor in service was No. 216 (renumbered 1821 in 1889 and 1796 in 1894) withdrawn shortly after its final renumbering.

A surviving map of 1850 shows that at this stage the Railway Foundry was still reliant upon its original connection to the main railway network, but shortly afterwards, a new connection from Hunslet Junction was made, giving a much more direct route. In much later years, Manning Wardle, Hunslet and Hudswell Clarke would all benefit from this refinement.

Returning to the subject of David Joy, following his spell with the Nottingham and Grantham Railway, his Diaries record that after 1851 he was on the lookout for another appointment and in January the following year he was in Glasgow in what turned out to be the unsuccessful pursuit of the post of Locomotive Superintendent to the North British Railway. Shortly afterwards he was to be similarly disappointed after his application for the equivalent post with the Lancaster and Carlisle Railway which eventually opted instead for locomotive working by the L&NWR, to whom it was leased in 1859 and by whom it was absorbed two decades later. In the spring of 1852, Joy's luck changed as he recorded:

'At [the] Railway Foundry, where I sometimes called, [I] heard that C.C. Williams of London was going to work Oxford, Worcester and Wolverhampton Railway, just now to be opened. [I] got [a] big geological map, and spotted it all out, very sanguine to get into such a nice neighbourhood. Saw E. B. Wilson and worked up for it. Still it hung fire till I got very low about it, till one Monday morning I had dreamed that there was a letter for me, and there was one from E. B. W.-, telling me to meet him at C. C. Williams' office next morning in London. I was off like a shot that afternoon at 4 o'clock by Great Northern Railway – April 18th.'

Joy's experience in connection with the operation of the Nottingham and Grantham Railway impressed Charles Cave Williams to such an extent that Joy was immediately detailed to procure the requisite locomotives, rolling stock and operating personnel to enable the line to open on 1 May. Joy recorded that he:

'Went to Welwyn – Great Northern Railway and got "Mudlark", a contractor's engine, to Offord [again Great Northern territory] – got a big six-coupled

This drawing illustrates of the six 2-4-0s supplied by E.B. Wilson in 1857 to the specification of James Cudworth of the South Eastern Railway. (*The Locomotive*)

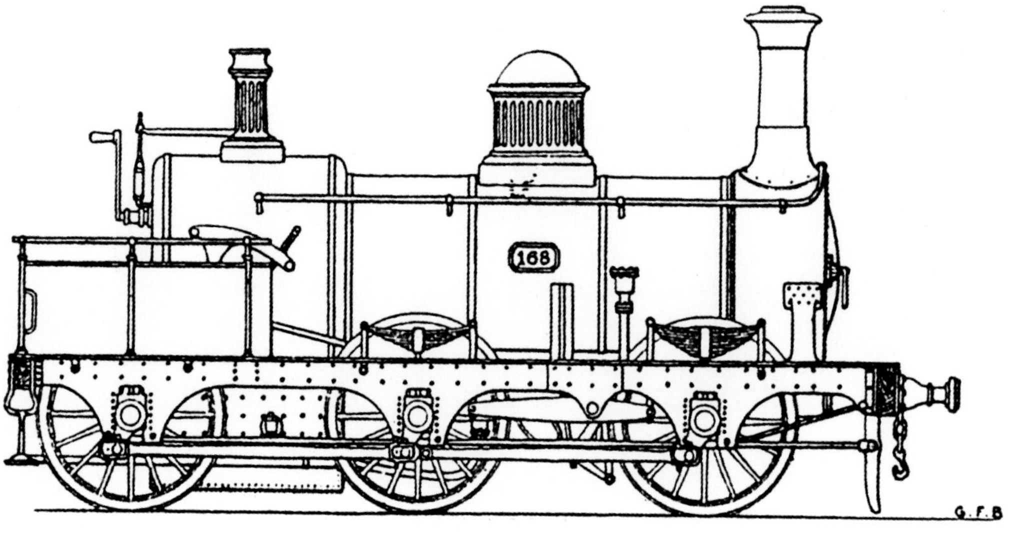

A representative of the second group of 0-6-0s built at the railway Foundry for the G.N.R. is depicted in this drawing. This is the group that were provided with slightly oval boilers (the major axis being vertical) when new. (*G.F. Bird*)

long boiler engine by Stephenson, in good condition. Then next day to Shrewsbury to hire Shrewsbury and Hereford engines. Had to see Jeffrey before breakfast, but he could spare none. On to Leeds and Pontefract after a four-coupled "Jenny", a contractor's engine, just put in fine order at [the] Railway Foundry with the cheque (£1250) to pay for it. Then to Leeds to see a little engine in the shops at [the] Railway Foundry – called "Canary"; she was a little mite. Arranged for all three to go to Worcester.'

Mudlark was a 0-4-0 tender engine, whilst the six-coupled locomotive was a classic Stephenson 'Long Boiler' inside cylinder 0-6-0 tender locomotive of the 1840s period with a Gothic Firebox. The four-coupled Jenny and its subsequent career have been dealt with in Chapter Four, whilst *Canary* with its 14in by 18in cylinders appears to have been a mystery. The sketchy illustration published in the *Railway Magazine* suggests that the words 'in the shops' may have been of key importance in that *Canary* was probably a rebuild rather than a new locomotive. The locomotive's design as depicted suggests a construction date of around 1840, whilst no evidence has ever been found of the existence of a Wilson standard 0-4-2 tender design with 14in by 18in cylinders. In addition to these locomotives, two long boiler 2-4-0s were hired from the North Staffordshire Railway. These latter locomotives were designated D and E, the 2-4-0 (as previously mentioned being labelled A, *Mudlark* being F, the 'long boiler' locomotive B and *Canary* C).

A detailed history of the events surrounding the protracted construction of the OW&WR is outside the scope of this book, but suffice to say that the Act of Authorisation was passed on 4 August 1845 for a line linking Wolvercote Junction, (a short distance north of Oxford where the Oxford to Rugby Railway via Banbury branched off) to Wolverhampton via Evesham, Worcester, Kidderminster, Stourbridge and Dudley. The Great Western Railway oversaw the project, taking a shareholding, and the Civil Engineer was Isambard Kingdom Brunel, whose underestimation of the construction costs, together with the GWR's early insistence on the provision of broad gauge track, were to usher in over a decade of delays and legal disputes which also involved the L&NWR, the MR and

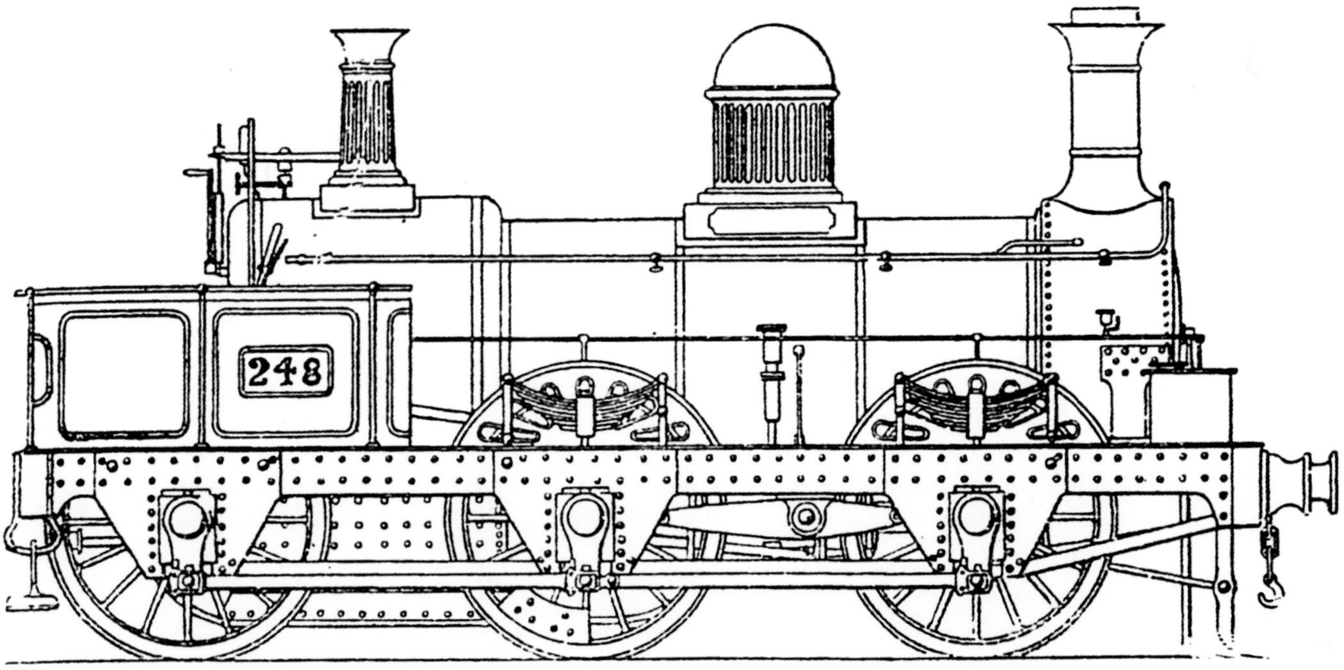

OW&WR Nos.27-30 and 34 were the first 'Wilson Goods' locomotives owned by the railway and were delivered in 1854-5. This drawing shows the first member of the class running as G.W.R. No. 248. The 'built-up' mainframes favoured by the OW&WR are much in evidence. (*E.L. Ahrons*)

the family of the contractor, Francis Tredwell. The upshot of all these difficulties was that the first section of the line, four miles long southwards, linking Worcester with Abbotswood Junction on the Midland Railway's Birmingham and Gloucester line was only opened on 5 October 1850, being worked as a branch line by the latter company. At the time of Williams' assumption of operating responsibilities, only this line, extended northwards to another junction (a little way north of Droitwich) with the MR Stoke Works line on 18 February 1852 was operational with all of the previous day-to-day running being undertaken by the MR. On the first day of Williams' take-over of responsibilities, the lines between Droitwich and Stourbridge to the north and Norton Halt (between Worcester and Abbotswood) and Evesham were opened. David Joy's diaries record that following a derailment on the opening day of the Evesham-Stourbridge portion of the line, 1 May 1852, a locomotive was borrowed from the Tredwells to assist with the working of the line following a derailment at Stourbridge:

> '... then in running back round my carriages the station master himself turned the wrong points, and shot me off the road on the bridge over the canal—tender first. Somehow, I had not a thought of my own personal danger, though the whole lot of us might have gone over into the canal. My only idea was my engine, for the train was fast—she was badly off the road, so I at once got hold of the contractor's engine, "Jack of Newbury "—an old "White Horse of Kent" type—and got to Kidderminster as fast as I could, to fetch my directors, etc. Utterly done up, I got to Worcester, and to bed.'

A six-mile northward extension from Stourbridge to Dudley followed on 20 December with the official opening of the stretch of line from Evesham to Oxford taking place on 4 June 1853, with Wolverhampton finally being reached for an official opening on 1 July 1854. The motley collection of locomotives with which Williams had commenced his operations soon proved inadequate for day-to-day needs and the first twenty numbered locomotives (twelve passenger 2-4-0s and eight goods 0-6-0s) were delivered from R. & W. Hawthorn during 1852-3. Apart from the fact that the 2-4-0s had domed boilers and the 0-6-0s sandwich frames with curved portions above the flycranks,

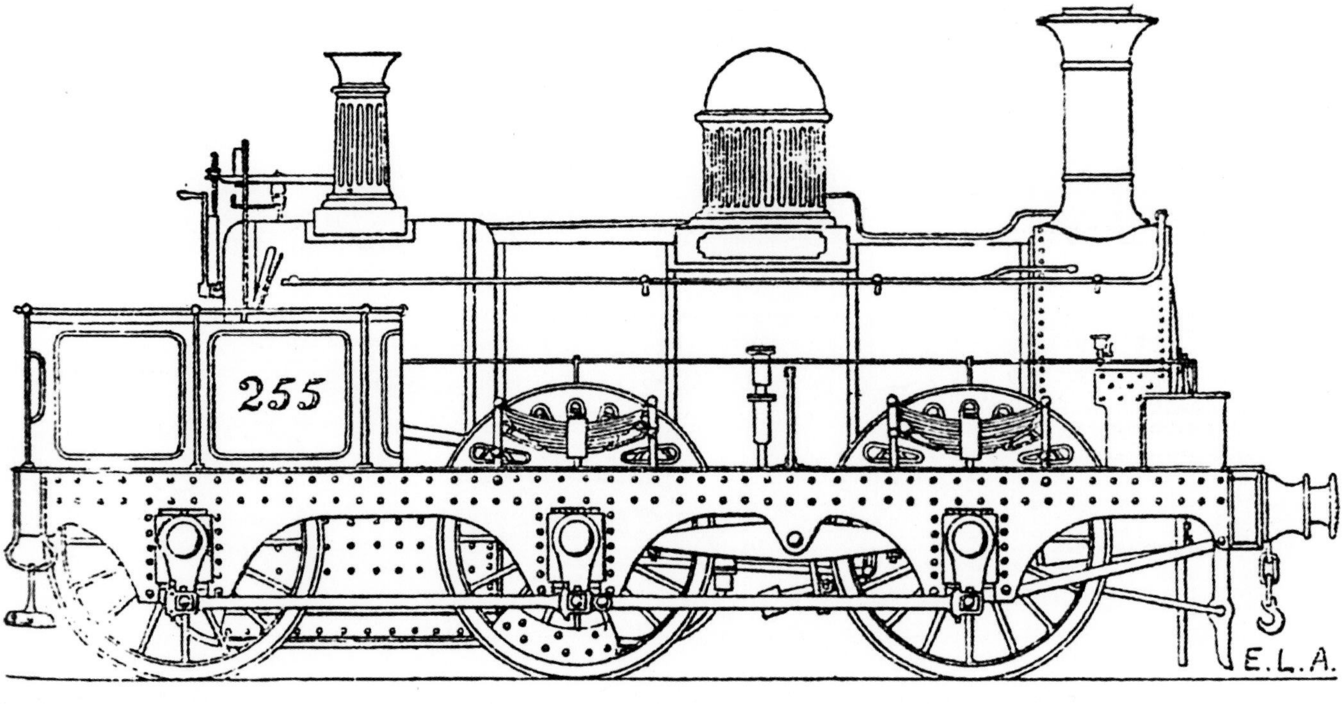

By way of comparison, former NA&HR No. 3, seen here as GWR No. 255 was fitted with one-piece iron portions to its sandwich frames. Unlike the OW&WR Wilson 0-6-0s, none of their seventeen NA&HR counterparts was ever radically altered by the GWR. (*E.L. Ahrons*)

Archibald Sturrock's design influence was clearly evident. What is not clear is that given Joy's association with the Railway Foundry, the orders for these locomotives were not given to E.B. Wilson & Co. It is only to be assumed that either fortunes at the Railway Foundry had recovered sufficiently from the 1848 Crash to ensure that the Leeds factory was once again working at something approaching full capacity, or that R. & W. Hawthorn – as we have seen, another manufacturer apparently favoured by Sturrock – offered a more competitive price. The Hawthorn locomotives became OW&WR Nos. 1-20 and all except No. 13 (2-4-0) and 7 and 19 (0-6-0) survived to be taken into GWR stock, with the surviving 2-4-0s becoming GWR Nos. 171-81 and the 0-6-0s 239, 241-3, 245 and 247. The last survivor of the 2-4-0s (178) was withdrawn in June 1902 with the last of the 0-6-0s (245) following suit six months later, both after rebuilding by the GWR.

The first Railway Foundry products to be ordered under the Williams regime were six 2-4-0s of generally similar design to the Hawthorns, (curved sandwich frames and compensating levers between coupled axles) but with the classic Wilson boiler mountings. They were numbered 21-26 and possessed the following dimensions:

Wheel Diameter	5ft. 9in (Coupled) 3ft 9in (Leading)
Cylinders	16in (Bore), 22 in, (Stroke) 15.5in (Bore) for No. 25
Wheelbase	7ft 6in + 8ft 0in
Boiler Barrel Length	10ft 6in (10ft 11in between tubeplates)
Boiler Barrel Diameter	4ft 1in
Firebox Wrapper	5ft 2in (L) 4ft 1in (W)
Internal Firebox	4ft 6in. (L), 3ft 6.5in (W) 5ft. 5in (H)
Heating Surface	1136 sq.ft (Tubes) 112¾sqft (Firebox)
Grate Area	15sqft
Number of Boiler Tubes	199, 2in Diameter
Locomotive Weight	29 Tons 3 cwt

These locomotives, two of which were E.B. Wilson works Nos. 330 and 335 and all of which were equipped, as with the Hawthorn 2-4-0s, with a transverse firebox mid-feather, created a good impression with Joy, who apparently preferred them to their Hawthorn-built counterparts, and following successive absorption into West Midland Railway stock in 1860 and G.W.R. stock in 1863, they became the latter concern's Nos. 182-7 in the order

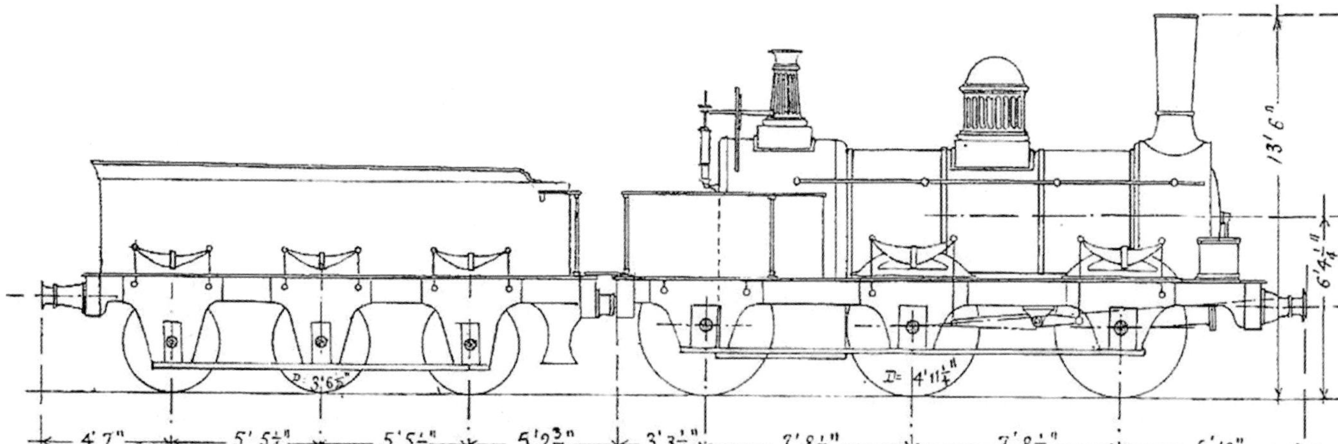

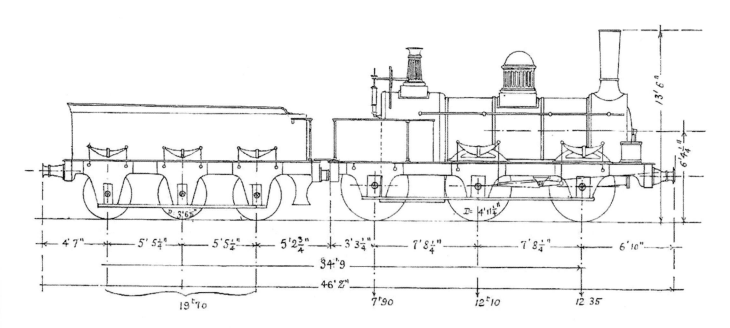

This Weight Diagram shows the two E B. Wilson 0-6-0s supplied to the Belgian Eastern Railway as the latter concern's Nos. 62-3 as running in GCB. days with stovepipe chimneys. Unlike the probable situation with Nos. 23-5, these locomotives clearly had 'built-up' outside mainframes. (*The Locomotive*)

of their previous running numbers. Normally based at Worcester, all received new boilers on rebuilding and Nos. 182 and 186 new inside frames. The last survivor was No. 183, which was scrapped in March 1904 having been reboilered in December 1870 and June 1887.

Four more Wilson-built locomotives of Sturrock-pattern were purchased by Williams for the OW&WR in 1853, but they were not destined to stay long on the system. Two were 2-4-0s with dimensions generally similar to OW&WR Nos. 21-6 as built but with coupled and leading wheel diameters reduced respectively to 5ft 6in and 3ft 6in and cylinder bore increased to 16½in, the stroke remaining the same. The boiler barrel was slightly longer at 10ft 8in. As with the first six 'Wilsons', the firebox mid-feather was retained. The remaining locomotives were typical Wilson sandwich-framed 'Standard Goods' 0-6-0 specimens, generally similar to the '308' class of the Great Northern Railway but with nearly 20sqft of extra firebox heating surface and the rear portion of the wheelbase increased correspondingly from 7ft 9in to 8ft 6in. These four locomotives would appear to have been allocated the running Nos. 27-30 on the OW&WR but during the following year they were sold to the Great Northern Railway, entering that system's running stock on 30 March. The 2-4-0s became GNR Nos. 216-7, being rebuilt with Stirling boilers and withdrawn respectively in April 1887 and March 1886. The 0-6-0s became GNR Nos. 368-9, the latter being an early withdrawal from service in August 1869, but the former lingering on, after receiving a Stirling boiler in September 1886, until August 1899.

The next batch of Wilson 0-6-0s for use on the OW&WR were ordered by the Railway Company rather than Williams and delivered in 1854-5 as OW&WR Nos. 27-30 and 34, becoming GWR Nos. 248-52 in 1863. They were built with the following dimensions:

Wheel Diameter	5ft. 3in (5ft. 0in for No. 28)
Cylinders	16in (Bore), 24 in, (Stroke)
Wheelbase	7ft 9in+7ft. 9in
Boiler Barrel Length	10ft 9in
Boiler Barrel Diameter	4ft 3in
Number of Boiler Tubes	198, 2in Diameter
Inner Firebox	4ft 6¾in (L), 3ft 7½in (W), 5ft 8½in (H)
Heating Surface	1130sqft (Tubes) 104sqft (Firebox)
Grate Area	16⅕sqft

These locomotives were very similar to YN&BR Nos. 230-5 as built, especially No. 28 with its 5ft wheels which appears to have been identical. Two class members, GWR Nos. 248-9 (the latter being the erstwhile No. 28 fitted with 5ft 5in wheels in 1864) were withdrawn with their original boilers in 1877 and 1886 respectively, whereas the remaining three all had their wheelbases lengthened at the rear by 4in and carried

As with their Wilson 2-4-0s, the South Staffordshire Railway's Wilson 0-6-0s deviated from the norm in that their inside mainframes extended to the rear of the leading bufferbeam, a feature displayed by *Viper* in this drawing. (*D. Leitch*)

Great Western boilers. They also received new 17in bore cylinders. All three survived into the twentieth century, with the last of the class in ordinary service, No. 250 being withdrawn in May 1907. It was, however, No. 252 (withdrawn in August 1904) that was destined for immortality. The leading two thirds or so of its chassis (with the cylinders suitably sectioned) were used for many years as an instructional model at Wolverhampton and today this model survives at the Armley Mills Industrial Museum at Leeds. The 'sandwich frame' method of construction is still evident in this item, which is also the largest substantial surviving domestically-based relic of the once numerous typical British 'double framed goods' 0-6-0.

Two further 'sandwich framed' Wilson 2-4-0s were supplied in 1855 (Works Nos. 466-7). These were built with the following dimensions:

Wheel Diameter	6ft. 6in (Coupled) 4ft. 6in (Leading)
Cylinders	15.5in (Bore), 22in (Stroke)
Wheelbase	7ft. 2in + 7ft 6in
Boiler Barrel Length	11ft 0in
Boiler Barrel Diameter	4ft 1in
Firebox Wrapper	4ft. 6in (L), 4ft 3in (W)
Inner Firebox	3ft 9¾in (L), 3ft 6½in (W), 5ft 0in (H)
No. of Tubes	162, 2in
Heating Surface	891sqft (Tubes) 83.95sqft (Firebox)
Grate Area	12.95sqft
Locomotive Weight	31 Tons 11cwt (10.15 + 12.0 + 9.4)

Despite the fact that two Wilson 2-4-0s with larger coupled wheels had proved successful on the NER, this pair were not popular with the locomotive crews who said that they 'would not "run"'. Initially numbered 40-1 in the OW&WR list, they became respectively GWR. Nos. 188-9. Both were fitted with replacement 4ft leading wheels in August 1873; No. 189 having received new 16in bore cylinders at Hereford in 1864, No. 188 was withdrawn in largely original condition in July 1878 but No. 189 was rebuilt at Worcester in July 1882 with new 5ft 9in coupled wheels, Wolverhampton- pattern cab and boiler mountings and closed-in splashers. In this form it remained in service until March 1886.

The final batch of Wilson 0-6-0s ordered by the OW&WR were taken into stock in 1856. They were built to the following dimensions:

Wheel Diameter	5ft. 0in
Cylinders	16in (Bore), 24 in, (Stroke)
Wheelbase	7ft 8½in+7ft. 8½in
Boiler Barrel Length	10ft 5½in
Boiler Barrel Diameter	4ft 1in
Firebox Wrapper	5ft 1½in (L) 4ft 7in (W)
Number of Boiler Tubes	189, 2in Diameter
Inner Firebox	4ft 6.in (L), 3ft 6½in (W), 5ft 5in (H)
Heating Surface	1039½sqft (Tubes) 96.53sqft (Firebox)
Grate Area	15¾sqft

The reason for the shortening of the wheelbase by one inch when compared with Nos. 27-30 and 34 is not clear. The new locomotives were numbered 43-6 in the OW&WR list with the first of these known to have borne the Works No. 516. They were renumbered 264-267 by the Great Western and 265-7 were early withdrawals in 1878-9. No. 264 was rebuilt on similar lines in 1875 to the first rebuild of Nos. 250-2 – even to the extent of having the same revised wheelbase dimensions – and carried three further GWR pattern boilers, respectively in 1889 (when it was renumbered 49), 1909 and 1914, the latter of Belpaire pattern prior to eventual withdrawal in 1921 by which time virtually nothing of the original locomotive would have remained.

The final Wilson design to make its appearance on the OW&WR was an inside framed 0-6-0 back tank design and this, and a pair of 0-4-2STs, will be dealt with in the appropriate chapter.

On 1 February 1856, Williams' operating contract with the OW&WR came to an end. One of the consequences of the responsibility from the ordering of locomotives passing from Williams to the OW&WR was that Joy's responsibilities gradually passed to the first OW&WR employed Locomotive Superintendent, Frederic Hayward. Despite this development, as we have seen, E.B. Wilson locomotives had remained a major part of the OW&WR's locomotive practice during the later Williams years and Joy's Diaries record that he was involved with the line's working right up to the final settlement of the terms of the contract in March 1856. As part of this process, the transfer value of the locomotives and rolling stock from Williams to the OW&WR needed to be determined by arbitration with one of the arbitrators appointed by Williams being none other than Archibald Sturrock. Williams had invoiced the OW&WR for £160,296 in respect of the transfer, but the arbitrators actually awarded him £183,205, a surplus of £22,909. David Joy could justly be proud of his efforts in relation to the contract, but it was to be of no avail in obtaining him further direct association with the OW&WR. As he recorded in his Diaries: 'once again I was on the world'. He returned to the Railway Foundry briefly, during which time he undertook work on the Willis Road locomotive, but soon passed on to pastures new. After a varied and fruitful career, he died at Hampstead, London on 14 March 1903.

The Sturrock-influenced 'sandwich framed' school of locomotive design was very much the dominant influence on E.B. Wilson's locomotive product policy during the 1850s. As with the OW&WR, the Newport, Abergavenny and Hereford Railway (NA&HR) was to become part of the West Midland Railway in 1860 and products of the Railway Foundry found their way onto this system. The first seven locomotives (NA&HR Nos. 1-6 and 10, Nos. 1,3 and 4 being respectively E.B. Wilson W/Ns 445, 449 and 451) were delivered in 1854-5 with GNR-pattern sandwich mainframes to the following dimensions:

Wheel Diameter	5ft. 3in
Cylinders	16in (Bore), 24 in, (Stroke), 16.5in (Bore) for Nos. 5 & 6
Wheelbase	7ft 9in + 7ft. 9in
Boiler Barrel Length	10ft 6in
Boiler Barrel Diameter	4ft 2in
Firebox Wrapper	5ft 1in (L) 4ft 2in (W)
Internal Firebox	4ft 6in (L) 3ft 6.5in (W) 5ft 5in (H)
Number of Boiler Tubes	208, 2in Diameter
Heating Surface	1198sqft (Tubes) 120sqft (Firebox)
Grate Area	15sqft
Locomotive Weight	34 Tons 6cwt (12.75+12.75+8.8)

Ten further 0-6-0s followed as NA&HR Nos. 9 & 11 in 1856; 12 and 13 in 1857 and 14-19 in 1858, the latter being the last locomotives built by E.B. Wilson for an English Railway as Works Nos. 628-33. Their variant dimensions when compared with Nos. 1-4 and 10 as built were: wheels 5ft diameter; boiler 4ft diameter; 188 2-inch tubes giving a tube heating surface of 1083sqft (firebox as before) and weight 32 tons 4cwt (12.0+12.0+8.2). All of these locomotives were renumbered by the WMR and GWR respectively in 1860 and 1863 as follows: 1-6: 71-6 and 253-8; 9: 79 and 259; 10: 80 and 268, and 11-19: 81-9 and 269-77. None of these locomotives was radically rebuilt by the GWR although No. 255 had its bore increased to 17in and 275 reduced to 15½in It is recorded that Nos. 253-9 were mostly stationed at Hereford (Barton) and the others at Pontypool Road and Newport. They were withdrawn from service between 1879 and 1881, the last survivors being Nos. 256 and 258, going in July that year.

Two further six coupled locomotives had been supplied from the Railway Foundry in 1856 (W/Ns 512-3) as NA&HR Nos. 7-8 to a unique sandwich framed back tank design for banking work on the Llanhilleth branch. Apart from the change from tender to tank configuration, their basic chassis design differed from that found on Nos. 1-6 and 9-19 in two other important respects. Firstly, there were no compensating beams between the leading and intermediate wheelsets. Secondly, the inside frames, instead of terminating to the rear at the throatplate, would have continued through to the rear bufferbeam in order to support the back tank. Further evidence for this latter design modification can be gleaned from the relatively slim dimension given for the firebox wrapper in the table of dimensions below:

Wheel Diameter	5ft. 0in
Cylinders	18in (Bore), 24 in, (Stroke)
Wheelbase	7ft 3in+8ft 3in
Boiler Barrel Length	10ft 0in
Boiler Barrel Diameter	4ft 2in
Firebox Wrapper	5ft 2in (L) 4ft 0in (W)
Internal Firebox	4ft 6½in (L) 3ft 5in (W) 5ft 7.5in (H)
Number of Boiler Tubes	189, 2in Diameter
Heating Surface	1045sqft (Tubes) 122sqft (Firebox)
Grate Area	15½sqft
Locomotive Weight	40.06 Tons (11.5+15.5+13.06)

The firebox wrapper width given would appear to be the minimum dimension (i.e. between the inside main-frames) as the boiler barrel dimension would have necessitated 'waisting-in'. The early use of a cylinder diameter of 18 inches was also a notable feature. Both locomotives were withdrawn by the GWR without major alteration in October 1877, latterly working out of Pontypool Road.

The remaining four E.B. Wilson locomotives owned by the NA&HR were Nos. 27-30 later respectively WMR 93-6 and GWR 190-3. They were classic sandwich framed 2-4-0s with fluted dome boilers and were respectively E.B. Wilson W/Ns 491, 490 and 501 of 1855 and 545 of 1856. Their leading dimensions were as below:

Wheel Diameter	6ft. 0in (coupled), 4ft. 0in (leading)
Cylinders	16in (Bore), 22 in, (Stroke
Wheelbase	7ft 9in+7ft. 4in
Boiler Barrel Length	10ft 0in
Boiler Barrel Diameter	3ft 9in
Firebox Wrapper	5ft 3in (L)
Internal Firebox	4ft 6in (L) 3ft 6.5in (W) 5ft 5in (H)
Number of Boiler Tubes	157, 2in Diameter
Heating Surface	824¼sqft (Tubes) 97.85sqft (Firebox)
Grate Area	15¾sqft
Locomotive Weight	29 Tons 3cwt (9.45+11.7+8.0)

These locomotives proved to be rather more to the Great Western Railway's liking than the other Wilson specimens on the NA&HR and Nos. 190-3 were all rebuilt twice (with coupled wheelbase lengthened by 5in and GW-pattern boilers) with last survivor, No.192, being withdrawn in March 1903.

The Sturrock-influenced school of Wilson locomotive design was represented on the South Staffordshire Railway (later absorbed into the L&NWR). Two 0-6-0s with 5ft diameter wheels and 16in cylinders were turned out of the Railway Foundry in December 1852 and January 1853 respectively as No. 16 *Stag* and No. 17 *Viper*. They were respectively renumbered 301-2 by the Southern Division and 901-2 by the unified L&NWR before being broken up, probably in January 1864. This railway also possessed two Wilson 2-4-0s which entered service in May 1853 as No. 18 *Eske* and No. 19 *Justin*. These had the customary 16in by 22in cylinders and 4ft leading wheels and compensating levers associated with the classic Wilson sandwich framed configuration, but the coupled wheels were, in line with W/Ns 466-7, larger than normal at 6ft 6in diameter. These locomotives were slightly longer lived than their goods counterparts, with *Eske* receiving an early rebuild in 1857, being renumbered 160 by the Southern Division and successively 760, 1205 and 1935 by the unified L&NWR (in May 1862, September 1863 and December 1871) before scrapping in April 1876. *Justin* became 181 in the Southern Division list and bore the numbers 781, 1207 and 1936 under the L&NWR (the respective re-numberings being carried out at the same times as its sister) and was scrapped in October 1874.

A 5ft 3in gauge version of the 2-4-0 specification was supplied in 1857 as W/N 578 to the Kilkenny Junction Railway as No. 2, being renumbered 22 by the Waterford and Limerick Railway in 1864 and 1 by the Waterford and Kilkenny in 1867. From the point of view of the 0-6-0 specification with 5ft wheels and 16in by 24in cylinders, one example entered service on the Maryport and Carlisle Railway in 1855 as this concern's No. 13, being withdrawn in 1873 and scrapped the following year. Four similar locomotives (W/Ns 504-7) were supplied to the Scottish North Eastern Railway during the same year as S.N.R. Nos. 49-52. These were converted to 0-4-2s with 3ft 7¼in trailing wheels in 1861-6 and the latter three were taken into Caledonian Railway stock as Nos. 489-92 being renumbered in 1874 as C.R. Nos. 661-3 in the order of their previous numbers. They were further renumbered 459-61 in 1877 and withdrawn in 1880-1, the last survivor being the latter locomotive. Six further locomotives of the same specification were built for the South Yorkshire Railway as Nos. 10-12 and 14-16 in 1856, later coming into MS&LR stock respectively as Nos. 161-3 and 165-7. Withdrawal of these locomotives from service by their new owner commenced in 1887 but two class members, Nos. 162 and 167 survived until 1901, latterly as Nos. 95 and 100 respectively.

One part of the world where the Wilson 'sandwich framed' 2-4-0s and 0-6-0s found a small measure of favour was Belgium. In 1853, one of the former type as

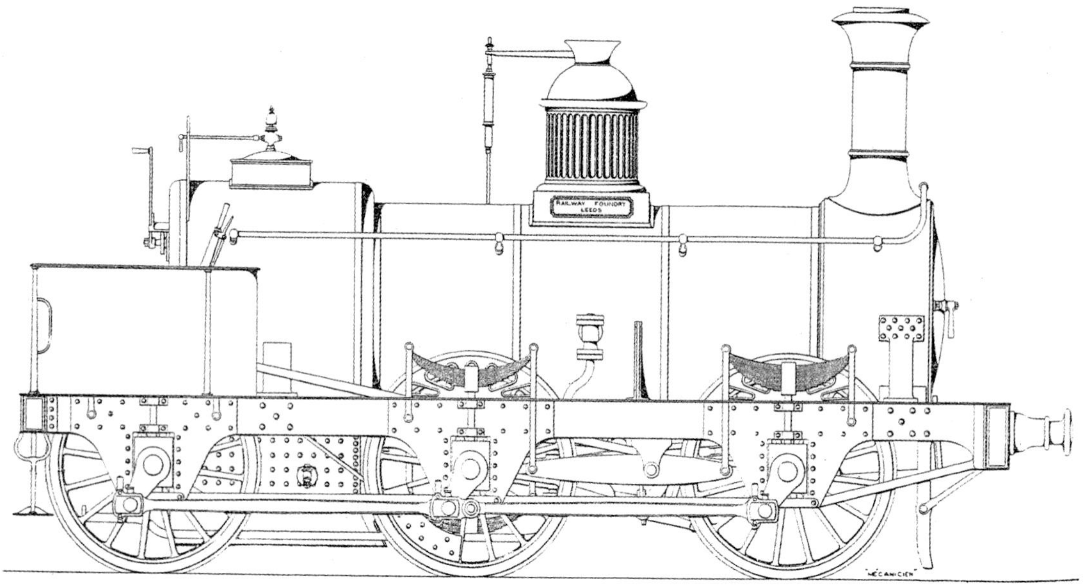

The Maryport and Carlisle Railway possessed a solitary 'Wilson Goods' with 'built-up' outer mainframes. This was No. 13 in the railway's running stock and it was depicted in this fine line drawing. (*The Locomotive*)

exported to the West Flanders Railway as E. B. Wilson W/N 342 becoming No. 27 *Britannia* on the Belgian system. Despite its wheel arrangement, it was apparently supplied for use on the line's heavier goods trains and when featured in *The Locomotive* magazine for 15 October 1910 a photograph taken at Bruges in August 1906 showed that, apart from the fitting of a cab, the replacement of its crosshead-driven feed pumps by injectors and the addition of a boiler mounted sandbox, little external alteration had taken place. The appended dimensions for the locomotive were:

Wheel Diameter	5ft 6in (coupled), (leading not specified)
Cylinders	16in (Bore), 22 in, (Stroke)
Boiler Barrel	
Between Tubeplates	10ft 0.5in
Number of Boiler Tubes	184, 1¾in Diameter
Heating Surface	856.59sqft (Tubes) 68.64sqft (Firebox)
Working Pressure	124 lb/sq.in
Locomotive Weight (Empty)	20.07 Tons

These dimensions applied at the time of the feature and the boiler would have been a replacement, the probable reason for the given dimension for the tube diameter. Even at the time of the feature, the locomotive was a unique survival and it is a tragedy that its historic value was not sufficiently appreciated to warrant preservation. Sadly, in a Europe living under the shadow of gathering storm clouds, this was not to be and by September 1913, the engine's nameplates, which had been specially replaced for the 1906 photograph, were noted on the wall of the Foreman's Office in Bruges.

Further Wilson 2-4-0s were supplied to the Belgian Eastern Railway. B.E.R. *No. 23* entered service in 1855 with the following stated dimensions:

Wheel Diameter	5ft.11.5in (coupled), 3ft. 11.125in (leading)
Cylinders	16in (Bore), 22in, (Stroke)
Wheelbase	7ft 9in + 7ft 3in
Boiler Barrel	
Between Tubeplates	10ft 4in
Boiler Barrel Diameter	3ft 9in
Number of Boiler Tubes	156, 2in Diameter
Heating Surface	795.1sqft (Tubes) 82.7sqft (Firebox)
Grate Area	14.7sqft
Locomotive Weight	30.15 Tons (19.15 Adhesive) 28 Tons (empty)
Tender Water Capacity	1680 Gallons
Tender Coal Capacity	1 Ton
Tender Weight	20.35 Tons 11.1 Tons (empty)

In 1856 two similar locomotives with the following variant dimensions followed as B.E.R. Nos. 24-5:

Wheel Diameter	5ft. 5 in (coupled), 3ft. 11.125in (leading)
Cylinders	16.25in (Bore), 22 in, (Stroke
Wheelbase	7ft 9in+7ft. 3in
Boiler Barrel	
Between Tubeplates	10ft 4.625in
Boiler Barrel Diameter	3ft 9in
Number of Boiler Tubes	156, 2in Diameter
Heating Surface	801.4sqft (Tubes) 78.0sqft (Firebox)
Grate Area	13.8sqft
Locomotive Weight	29.4 Tons (19.15 Adhesive) 26.5 Tons (empty)
Tender Water Capacity	1204 Gallons
Tender Coal Capacity	1.6 Tons
Tender Weight	16.9 Tons 9.9 Tons (empty)

All three of these locomotives were taken over by the Grand Central Belge (GCB) and rebuilt in the Central Shops at Leuven in the 1870s with cabs, raised running boards over the coupled wheelsets, repositioned safety valves and replacement tenders with four wheels instead of six (20.4 tons loaded and 10.4 tons empty: 1600 gallons of water and 2.7 tons of coal). They were still performing useful service in 1899, based at Walcourt Depot and hauling light local trains. By this stage, the GCB had been nationalized and the locomotives were scrapped shortly afterwards.

Two sandwich framed 0-6-0s, with 'built up' horn-cheek bearings of the type found on the N.E.R.-based locomotives, were supplied to the Belgian Eastern Railway as Nos. 62-3 in 1856 to the following dimensions:

Wheel Diameter	4ft. 11.25in
Cylinders	16.0625in (Bore), 24 in, (Stroke
Wheelbase	7ft 8.25in + 7ft. 8.25in
Boiler Barrel	
Between Tubeplates	11ft 2in
Boiler Barrel Diameter	4ft 2in
Number of Boiler Tubes	185, 2in Diameter
Heating Surface	1022.5sqft (Tubes) 85.3sqft (Firebox)
Grate Area	14.4sqft

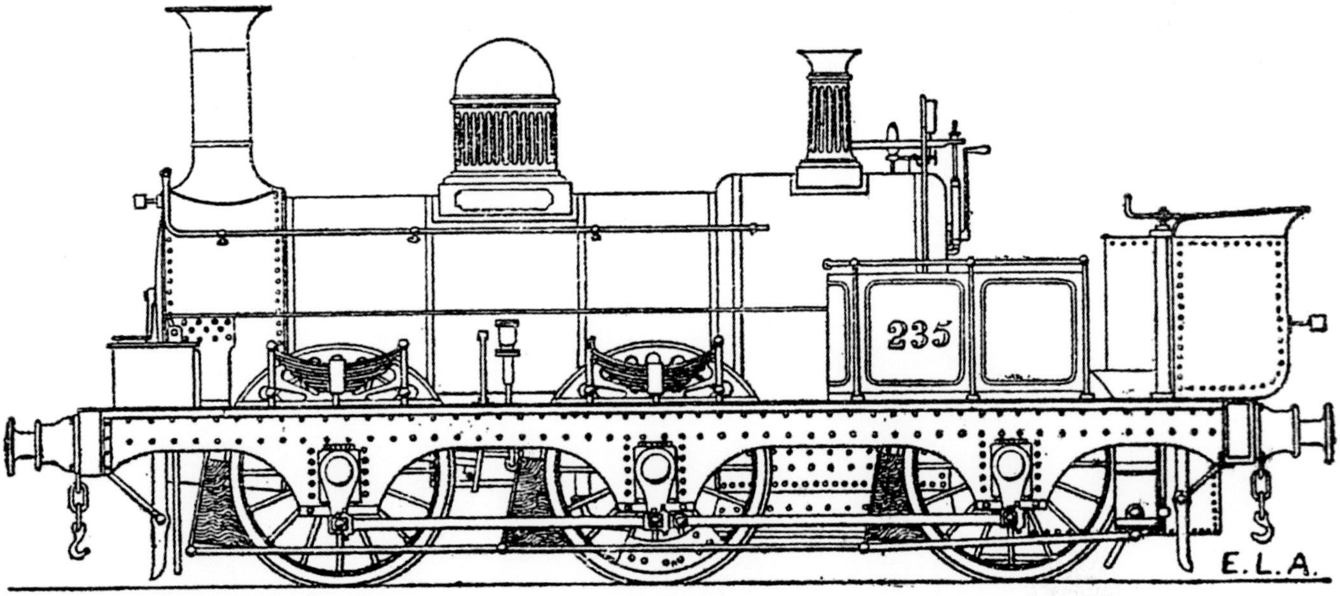

NA&HR No. 7 is depicted here as GWR No. 235. Rather sadly the asymmetrical arrangement of the bunker and waist sheets is not shown completely (this could only be accomplished if a right hand view were available), nor is the arrangement of the rear part of the inside mainframes, which, against normal practice for Wilson sandwich framed locomotives, would have extended to the leading face of the rear bufferbeam in order to carry the water tank. (*E. L. Ahrons*)

Locomotive Weight	32.15 Tons
	28.7 Tons (empty)
Tender Water Capacity	1528 Gallons
Tender Coal Capacity	1.8 Tons
Tender Weight	18.35 Tons
	11.0 Tons (empty)

These locomotives spent much of the careers hauling goods traffic on the Leuven-Charleroi line and they were still in existence at the time of the Nationalization of the GCB in 1897-8, but, as with the 2-4-0s, they were scrapped shortly afterwards.

In 1857, a class of six 2-4-0s was built at the Railway Foundry to the specification of James Cudworth, Locomotive Superintendent of the South Eastern Railway. These differed significantly from the mainstream 1850s Wilson 2-4-0 designs in having conventional plate (as opposed to sandwich) outside frames and plainer domes, although they did have firebox lateral mid-feathers. They were built to the following dimensions as SER. Nos. 179-84:

Wheel Diameter	6ft. 0in (Coupled)
	4ft. 6in (Leading)
Cylinders	16in (Bore), 24in (Stroke)

The remains of OW&WR. No. 34 are seen at Armley Mills Industrial Museum, Leeds on 23 May 2015. The engine became GWR No. 252 in 1863 and was later rebuilt with new boiler and cylinders and a rear wheelbase lengthened by 4 inches. Note that the inside frames reach the leading bufferbeam, contrary to the prevailing Wilson practice for locomotives of this general type (the Ahrons' drawing is rather 'ambiguous' regarding the initial state of affairs for this class). Nonetheless, the original 'built-up' pattern of construction of the outside 'sandwich' frames is still evident. (*Author*)

Wheelbase	7ft. 3in + 7ft 7in
Boiler Barrel Length	10ft 0in
Boiler Barrel Diameter	3ft 10.375in
Firebox Wrapper Length	5ft. 1.375in
No. of Tubes	185, 2in
Total Heating Surface	1115sqft
Locomotive Weight	29.5 Tons

These locomotives were supplied at a cost of £2,495 each and were the maker's W/Ns 583-8 (in SER No. order), the first four entering service in May 1857 and the other two in June. They were fitted with inwardly tapered axle bearings to prevent lateral oscillation in motion and were initially used on London-Ramsgate stopping services. In 1870-1, all were fitted with coal-burning 'double firebox' (longitudinal mid-feather) boilers and latterly they found employment on the Reading-Redhill route. The first withdrawal was No. 179 in July 1880, with the last to go, No. 183 lingering on until July 1884.

One point that needs to be made at this stage is that although the Railway Foundry made great reliance on three basic locomotive types, namely the Jenny Lind (including its 2-4-0 counterpart) and the two sandwich framed specifications: the 2-4-0 ostensibly intended for passenger or at least mixed traffic work and the 0-6-0 goods variety, and there was a great deal of standardization of components such as wheels, axles, bearings and other chassis parts, there was also a fair amount of variation to cope with customer requirements, particularly in relation to boiler and firebox dimensions. The fact that individual customer requirements could be accommodated within a strategy that placed a great deal of reliance upon building components for stock was a major testament to the way in which locomotive building was undertaken at the Railway Foundry. The influence of these core designs upon the products of other manufacturers, both private and the railway companies themselves has already been noted in relation to the Jenny Lind specification and it was no less true in the case of the sandwich framed locomotives. Eventually, increasingly divergent customer requirements would be one of the factors that would bring about the demise of E.B. Wilson & Co., but before discussing those events in detail, it will be important to consider further development of inside framed locomotives at the Railway Foundry and the unforeseen legacy that three of these designs in particular was destined to leave.

CHAPTER 7

THE LATER 'INSIDE FRAMERS' AND THE EMERGENCE OF A NEW LOCOMOTIVE DYNASTY

Despite the commercial success of the Jenny Linds and their Sturrock-influenced successors, the Railway Foundry did not refrain completely from producing purely inside framed locomotives and the next two designs to be considered were both constructed to Brunel's 7ft 0¼in gauge although neither was constructed for the Great Western Railway. In 1851, three 2-2-2 well tank locomotives were built for the Bristol and Exeter Railway to the design of Locomotive Superintendent James Pearson for use on branch line services. These locomotives were built to the following dimensions:

Wheel Diameter	5ft. 6in (Coupled) 3ft. 6in (Leading & Trailing)
Cylinders	12.5in (Bore), 18in (Stroke)
Wheelbase	7ft. 3in+7ft 3in
Boiler Barrel Length	9ft 6in
Boiler Barrel Diameter	3ft 1in
Firebox Wrapper	3ft. 2in (L), 3ft 10in (W)
Inner Firebox	3ft 7in (L), 3ft 3in (W), 3ft 10in (H)
No. of Tubes	131, 1¾in
Water Capacity	480 Gallons

The boiler barrel was domeless and the firebox wrapper was of the raised variety. The locomotives were numbered 32-4 in the Bristol and Exeter Railway's stock, with the two preceding locomotives, Nos. 30-1 being constructed to the same design by the Bedlington manufacturer, R.B. Longridge & Co. The only Wilson-built member of the class still extant at the time the B&ER was absorbed by the GWR in 1876 was No.32 which became 2055 in the Great Western list but only remained in service until June 1878.

The second group of locomotives built at the Railway Foundry to Brunel's 'seven foot' were not built for mainline use at all, but for construction work on Portland Breakwater in Dorset, which began in 1849. Once again, Longridge & Co. was aiming for the same market as this manufacturer also came up with a locomotive design for use on 'breakwater' railways which, as with the Wilson locomotive possessed a sharply raised firebox wrapper allied to a domeless barrel. One of these remained in use until 1913 at Holyhead, and is believed to have survived derelict for a further three decades. In *The Chronicles of Boulton's Siding*, A.R. Bennet states that:

> 'In 1853, a year after Longridges had supplied their engines to Holyhead, Messrs E. B Wilson & Co. built several of substantially the same design, but of greater comeliness and finish, for use on the Portland Breakwater.'

Bennett appears to have suggested that the Longridge design preceded the Wilson one, an assertion that appears to be founded on the fact that the published maker's drawing for the Wilson design, supplied by Manning Wardle to *The Locomotive* magazine in 1908, is dated December 1853, a year of construction which the magazine feature ascribes to all of the class members. There are, however, difficulties with this assertion. Given that there was ample evidence that Wilson and Hawthorn as manufacturers were well familiar with each other's work, and also Wilson and Fairbairn, it is a tempting, though unproven, assertion that Longridge and Wilson would have become familiar with each other's work at the time of construction of the B&ER 2-2-2 WT locomotives in 1851. Given that the Wilson 'dummy crankshaft' 0-4-0WT was already in existence at this time, the obvious inference is that the 'inverted U' firebox wrapper principle was transmitted to Longridge at this time. A second question is therefore posed; had the first Wilson 'breakwater' 0-4-0WT been constructed, or at least designed by 1851? The date on the maker's drawing would appear to preclude such a proposition, but it should be remembered here that it was not unusual for a General Arrangement drawing to be retrospective, and also that such drawings could often be prepared as a consequence of relatively minor updating of a design. In the Industrial Locomotive Society's journal *The Industrial Locomotive* (No. 125) it is stated that Admiralty Records confirm that the Railway Foundry supplied two locomotives for the Portland Breakwater works in 1851, followed by one each in 1854, 1855 and 1857. Taken at face value, this would appear to strongly support the theory that there was some 'comparing of notes' (whether officially sanctioned or not) between employees at Wilson and Longridge at or immediately following the time of construction of the Bristol & Exeter Railway locomotives. The problem here is that photographic evidence shows that one member of the class was completed in 1852 as Works No. 329, probably the last Railway Foundry product to be out-shopped during that year. This locomotive was acquired by the Torbay and Brixham Railway in 1868 as *Queen*, passing into South Devon Railway stock two years later and being taken over (and immediately withdrawn from service) by

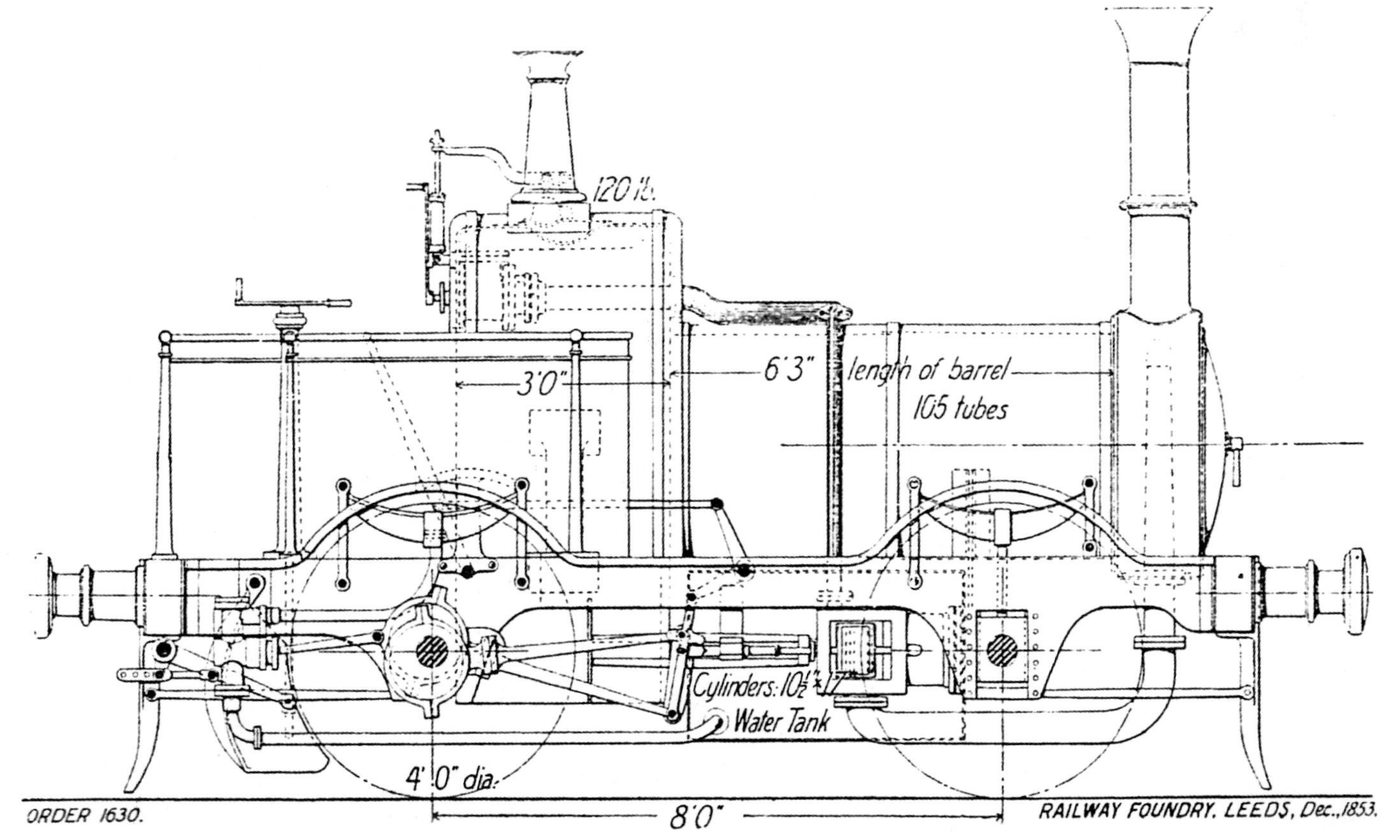

This maker's drawing of the Wilson 'breakwater' locomotives as built from 1854 onwards was first published in *The Locomotive* for 15 January 1908, having been supplied by Manning Wardle. It shows a number of important details, notably the structure of the boiler, with its domeless barrel, inverted 'U' shaped wrapper and main steam pipe passing from an internal regulator, above the barrel and, after division, each part down each side of the barrel to its respective steam chest. The boiler was fixed to the mainframes by means of a bracket immediately behind the leading axle and a pair of palm stays slightly ahead of the trailing one. Sadly, the drawing is rather scant on detail in relation to the manner in which the slide bar bracket and cylinder castings were fixed to the mainframes, although it is apparent that four slide bars per cylinder were used. The 'trailing arm' configuration of the secondary weighshaft bellcranks, a feature transmitted to the Manning Wardle Old 'I' and 'K' classes is also apparent. (*The Locomotive*)

the GWR on 1 January 1883, being noted later in a scrap road by E.L. Ahrons. Its dimensions were:

Wheel Diameter	4ft. 0 in
Cylinders	10.5in (Bore), 17in (Stroke)
Wheelbase	8ft 0in
Bolier Pressure	120 lbs/sq.in
Boiler Barrel Length	6ft 4.5in
Boiler Barrel Diameter	3ft 1in
Firebox Wrapper	3ft 0in (L), 3ft 3in (W)
Heating Surface	280sqft (Tubes), 49sqft (Firebox)
No. of Tubes	94, 2in
Water Capacity	150 Gallons

The inside mainframes on this design were of the sandwich variety, whilst the cylinders were mounted horizontally and level with the pitch of the axles. On so broad a gauge it was possible for the long coupled wheelbase to be accommodated by locating the driving cranks either side of the firebox, with each pair of eccentrics placed between the outer face of a crank web and its associated axlebox. The steam chest on each side was located outboard of its cylinder whilst water feed was accomplished by means of a feed pump driven from the forward eccentric. Close examination of the two published drawings of the Wilson 'breakwater' design suggest that the cylinder/steam chest assemblies on each side were supported by two means;

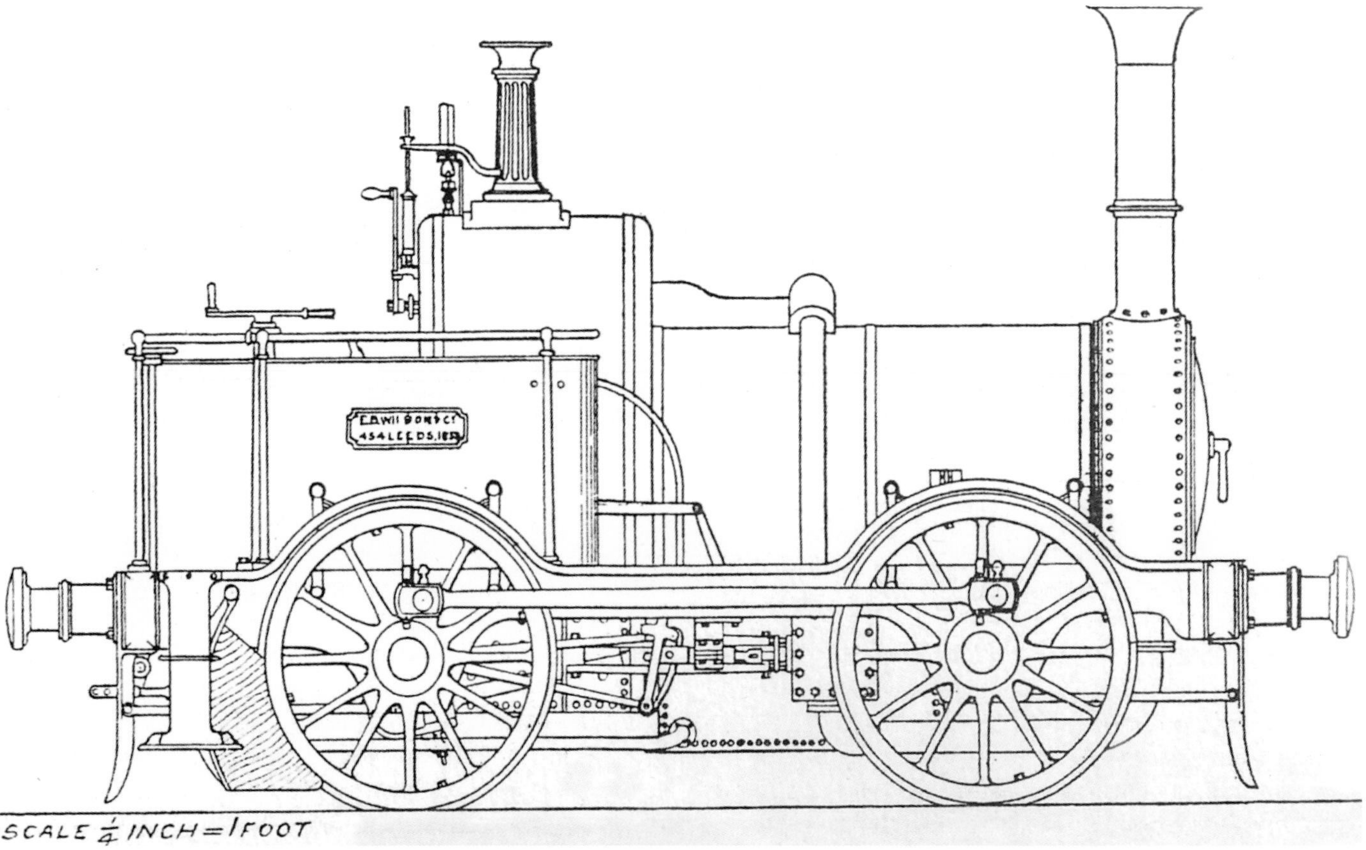

This drawing originally accompanied A.R. Bennett's description of the 'breakwater' locomotives that passed through Isaac Watt Boulton's hands and depicts W/N 454 of 1855, later *Henry B. Loch* at Port Erin. This shows the external detail to advantage, including the arrangement of the steam chests and valve gear. Unlike the previous drawing, the support for the valve spindle bearing is shown correctly, i.e. wholly outboard of the slide bars and this component appears to be attached to adjacent sandwich frame by means of *vertical* bolts passing through the wooden (ash) layer and retained by a special iron at the lower end and the running board at the upper end. A feature of note is that the footplate was entered on the right hand side only, the corresponding area on the left hand side being required for coal, although whether there was a dedicated coal bunker (or 'coke box' as it was later to be termed by Manning Wardle) or whether sacks of fuel were merely carried on the footplate is not known. (*The Locomotive*)

firstly, a bracket would have been fitted on each side to the inside of the sandwich frames mounted level with the steam chests, possibly allied to some form of cross tie linking the cylinder castings and passing through the water tank. Secondly, the lower portion of the boiler bracket/frame stretcher close to the leading axle would have carried pedestals to which the leading end of the cylinder castings would have been attached. The cylinder castings themselves were of a peculiar pattern and appear to have incorporated a lengthened leading portion so as to meet the boiler stretcher, the leading end of the functional part of the cylinder presumably being cast 'blind'. An important design feature from the point of view of future developments was the fact that the bellcranks linking the weighshaft to the drop-links trailed the weighshaft. The significance of this fact will be discussed in detail at a later stage. The boiler and firebox were of the classic domeless barrel/'inverted U' wrapper pattern but differed from the pattern used on the 'dummy crankshaft' locomotives in two respects: the main steam pipe passed from the regulator out through the front of the wrapper and *above* the barrel before dividing to feed the steam chests. Secondly, the boiler tube diameter was the effective Railway Foundry standard of 2in rather than 1¾in.

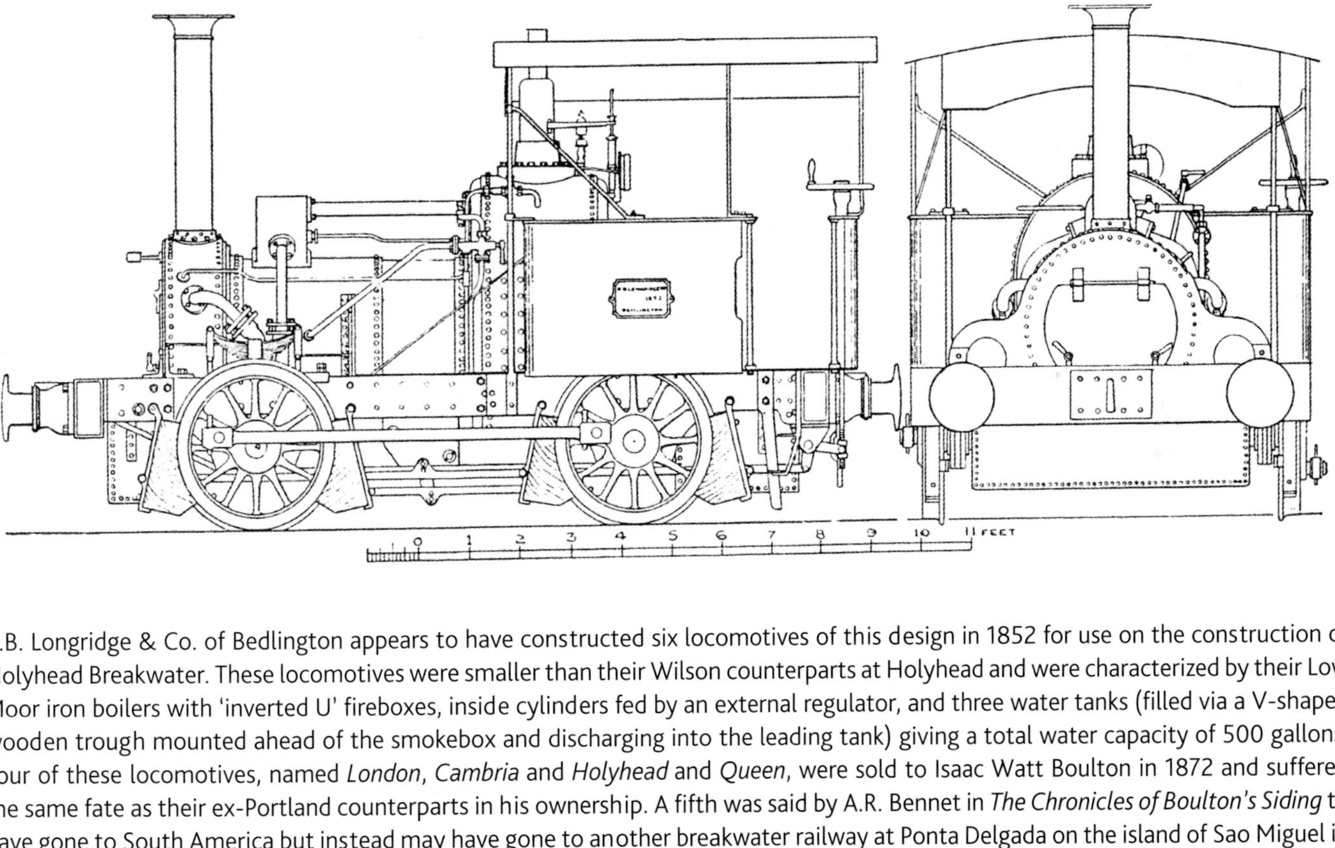

R.B. Longridge & Co. of Bedlington appears to have constructed six locomotives of this design in 1852 for use on the construction of Holyhead Breakwater. These locomotives were smaller than their Wilson counterparts at Holyhead and were characterized by their Low Moor iron boilers with 'inverted U' fireboxes, inside cylinders fed by an external regulator, and three water tanks (filled via a V-shaped wooden trough mounted ahead of the smokebox and discharging into the leading tank) giving a total water capacity of 500 gallons. Four of these locomotives, named *London*, *Cambria* and *Holyhead* and *Queen*, were sold to Isaac Watt Boulton in 1872 and suffered the same fate as their ex-Portland counterparts in his ownership. A fifth was said by A.R. Bennet in *The Chronicles of Boulton's Siding* to have gone to South America but instead may have gone to another breakwater railway at Ponta Delgada on the island of Sao Miguel in the Azores (traces of which, including two locomotives built in 1882 and 1888 still survive at the time of writing). The remaining locomotive, named *Prince Albert*, was retained by the Board of Trade after the contractors had completed their work and was employed for repair work until 1901. It was then sold to William Wild & Sons Ltd. who operated 1¼ miles of the broad gauge track at Holyhead to link the company's silica works with the quay. At this stage, the original boiler was replaced, the original 10-spoke wheels replaced by new components with twelve spokes and the sanding gear and guard irons were removed along with a spark arrester that the engine carried in the late nineteenth century. In 1913, the remaining broad gauge line at Holyhead was converted to standard gauge and *Prince Albert* was withdrawn from service. Sadly, a suggestion made by Mr. Bennett to Messrs W. Wild & Sons (and mentioned in *The Railway Gazette* for 16 May 1913) that the locomotive, and a companion open carriage used during a visit by the Prince of Wales in 1873 still extant at that stage, should be presented to the Science Museum fell on deaf ears and *Prince Albert* was scrapped after about three decades of dereliction during the early 1940s. The drawing shows the locomotive in its post-1901 condition. (*The Locomotive*)

It is difficult to reconcile the '1851' date given in Admiralty records with the known Works No. for *Queen* and the question also remains as to when the other locomotive attributed to that year was actually delivered. The known dimensions for the Wilson 2-2-2WTs of 1851 (described in Chapter Five) do not offer any help on this matter as the boiler tube diameter is not given, hence a date cannot be ascribed to the changeover at the Railway Foundry from 1¾in to 2in tubes for 'inverted U' pattern boilers. If one assumes the *Queen* had a sister engine built in 1851, then to all intents and purposes, any theory that the Wilson design preceded the Longridge one is effectively home and dry. If *Queen* was in fact one of a pair produced at the same time, then one possibility is that Bennett was correct in his assertion that the Longridge design came first, but close examination of the dimensions published for the last domestic survivor of the Longridge design as shown below reveals an intriguing possibility, assuming that its 1901 replacement boiler was identical in all material respects to the original:

Wheel Diameter	3ft 2 in
Cylinders	10¼in (Bore), 18in (Stroke)
Wheelbase	7ft 6in
Boiler Pressure	120 lb/sq.in
Boiler Barrel Length	5ft 5in
Boiler Barrel Diameter	3ft 0in
Firebox Heating Surface	32sqft
No. of Tubes	80, 1¾in
Water Capacity	500 Gallons

Given what has already been stated regarding the Railway Foundry policy on boiler tube diameter and boilers of the type used on these 'breakwater' locomotives, could a Longridge employee in late 1851 or early 1852 have somehow become aware that the Admiralty had contacted Wilsons during the former year in pursuit of a 'breakwater' locomotive, seen a basic scheme for the design in Leeds, along with the design for the 'dummy crankshaft' locomotives and then produced the design for Holyhead leading to the appearance of

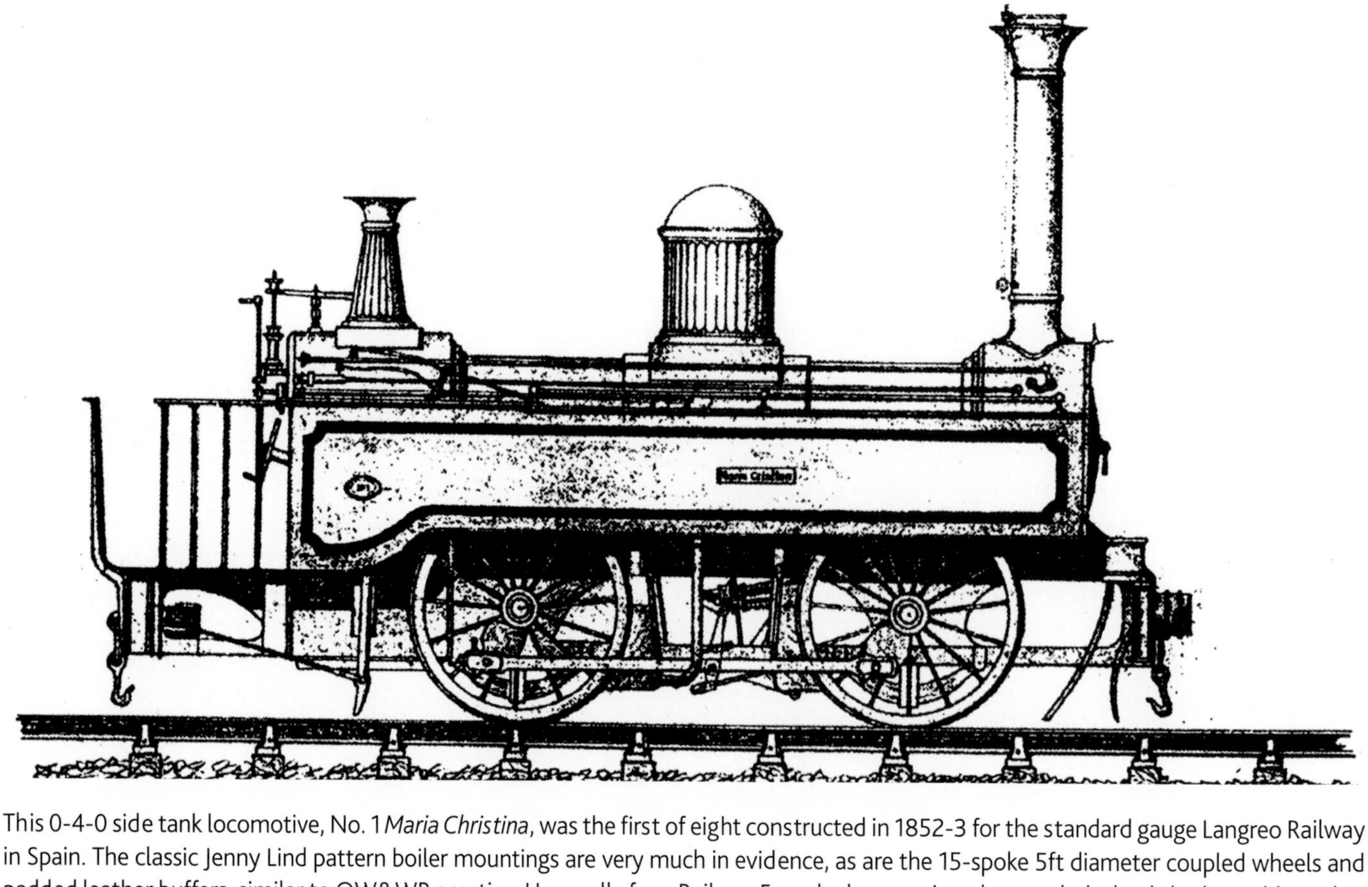

This 0-4-0 side tank locomotive, No. 1 *Maria Christina*, was the first of eight constructed in 1852-3 for the standard gauge Langreo Railway in Spain. The classic Jenny Lind pattern boiler mountings are very much in evidence, as are the 15-spoke 5ft diameter coupled wheels and padded leather buffers, similar to OW&WR practice. Unusually for a Railway Foundry locomotive, the coupled wheels had an odd number of spokes. At this early stage, E.E. Wilson tank locomotive design had yet to assume settled pattern of evolution. (*Derek Brown*)

these locomotives slightly in advance of the Portland ones? The true answer may probably never be known.

The December 1853 drawing for the Wilson locomotives gives the variant dimensions of 105 tubes (again 2in diameter) and 6ft 3in boiler barrel length. It would appear that the three later Wilson locomotives for the Portland works were built to this specification. By 1864, one of these locomotives, W/N 454 of 1855 (presumably the penultimate Portland locomotive) had found its way to the Isle of Man, working as *Henry B. Loch* on the breakwater at Port Erin. It returned to England approximately a decade later where it joined the three remaining ex-Portland Wilson locomotives in the ownership of Isaac Watt Boulton at Ashton-under-Lyme. There being no domestic market for broad gauge 'breakwater' locomotives by the mid-1870s, and with no easy prospect of their conversion to standard gauge, they were converted to portable and winding engines. Bennett records that one was sold to a Mr. A.P. Bell for £350 and another to Denton Colliery Co.

The following part of this chapter has had to be reconstructed from a variety of documentary sources, but it is important in that it proved to herald the most enduring part of the legacy of the Railway Foundry. If one moves forward a few months from the 'Williams' period in David Joy's Diaries, there is an entry dated 8 October 1856 which reads, 'To Leeds – arranged with B & H to sell little engine for tipping.' The entry is accompanied by a sketch showing a tiny inside cylinder 0-4-0ST with 9in by 14in cylinders, 5ft wheelbase and 3ft wheel diameter. For some peculiar reason, the sketch implies that the engine was double framed, which in practice could never have been the case as it was simply not, as has been noted, normal practice to build double framed locomotives with coupled wheels of less than 4ft 2in diameter. The one major design grouping that contravened this rule, a 0-6-0T specification for Mauritius with coupled wheels of 3ft 10in and in later cases 3ft 7in., actually remained in use for nearly a century and at the time of their demise, with that of the Mauritius Government Railways system, were the last traditional British six-coupled 'double framers' in ordinary service anywhere in the world. The apparent 'double framed' configuration of the 0-4-0ST seems to have been a quirk of Joy's sketching style, which may, as will later be seen, have been repeated. What is more important is that the sketch showed a domeless boiler, 'inverted-U' wrapper, classic Wilson-pattern chimney, shallow saddle tank not covering either firebox or smokebox and lack of an entry point to the footplate on the left hand side. The precise meaning of the 8 October entry is unclear – was the locomotive already in David Joy's ownership, having possibly been used in some way during the construction of the OW&WR without ever becoming the latter's property, or had it been on hire to Joy who would have been in a position to advise any future buyer as to its capabilities? The term 'tipping' to certainly applies to contractors' work. At the time of writing no evidence has come to light to suggest that the Railway Foundry ever supplied such a *new* locomotive in the latter part of 1856 of the early part of 1857. What can be said is that the design, as a 'single framer', certainly existed and originated somewhat earlier that the entry in Joy's Diaries. In 1855, construction work began on the Dursley and Midland Junction Railway, opened for goods on 26 August 1856 and for passengers on the 18 September), which linked Coaley on the MR Bristol-Gloucester line with Dursley. Following authorization in the Dursley & Midland Junction Railway's minutes, shortly after opening, a 0-4-0ST with cylinder, wheel and wheelbase dimensions identical to those quoted by Joy for the Leeds-built little engine was purchased from an unspecified commercial railway operator, possibly the person or entity to whom the 'David Joy' locomotive was sold following the diary entry. Close examination of both the two known surviving photographs of the Dursley locomotive, and Official MR Diagram D1318 of 12 December 1879, albeit made after the engine was rebuilt at Derby in the late 1870s, reveals that it had a domeless boiler, 'inverted-U' firebox, classic Wilson chimney (as built), lift-up smokebox door, cotter pin coupling rod bearings and 'double crank boss' wheel centres. These are of course, all features that were to find their way into the early standard Manning Wardle 0-6-0STs, but the Dursley locomotive still possessed two features that did not, namely the relatively shallow and narrow 'box' tank and entry to the footplate from the right hand side only, both found on the Joy sketch. The former feature, one can argue, was a transitional point of evolution, given that earlier Wilson standard gauge tank locomotives had carried their water supply in 'back' well tanks. The latter was necessitated by the need to allow for sufficient coal space, given that a rear mounted coal bunker (as found on the standard Manning Wardle 0-6-0STs) would have

This photograph, apparently a reproduction of a newspaper illustration, shows the E.B. Wilson 0-4-0ST locomotive at work on the Dursley Branch during the early 1860's, having been sold by, or at least under the direction of, David Joy from Leeds in 1856 and apparently re-sold to the Dursley company in 1858. The injector (apparently of Giffard pattern and mounted horizontally), weatherboard and safety valve cover appear to have been Midland Railway alterations probably fitted when the locomotive was taken over in 1861. (*Author's Collection*)

been precluded by the need to keep the rear overhang within reasonable limits. Other inside cylinder 0-4-0ST designs of the period were affected by the same need to mount the rear axle sufficiently clear of the firebox to allow free movement of the connecting rods and 'single side' footplate entry could also be found on early standard Beyer Peacock and Sharp, Stewart designs of this configuration.

The evidence so far presented clearly tends to throw out previous assertions that the Dursley locomotive was a Bristol product of the 1840s and instead strongly suggests that it emanated from the Railway Foundry in the early 1850s. This view was envisaged in the *Stephenson Locomotive Society Journal* in 1952 which asked (on page 72), 'Would it have been one of Manning Wardle's earliest products?' which could not in fact have been the case given its date of construction. Can the point be proved beyond reasonable doubt? The engine was absorbed into Midland Railway stock in 1861and is recorded as bearing no less than six different numbers (one twice) under its new owner: 156 (on takeover); 203 (May 1866); 1020 (September 1868); 2020 (February 1872); 1411 (December 1878); 1411A (January 1879), and finally 2020 again in July 1879. It was hired out to no less than nine different industrial users during the period between November 1875 and April 1883. More importantly, it received a new boiler in June 1878 which was described as having 50 tubes each of 2in diameter with a 2ft long grate and a total heating surface of 203sq.ft. As has already been noted, 2in was the preferred tube diameter for Wilson locomotives, even with boilers of this type by 1852 (as evidenced by *Queen* and its sisters), the flirtation with 1¾in tubes exhibited by the Little Mails apparently being largely over by this stage. A main line company, such as the Midland, would have regarded this dimension excessive on such a small engine had it been designing a new boiler. The inference from all of this evidence is that it was not considered worthwhile redesigning the engine's boiler and that the new boiler was simply a 'like for like' replacement of the original. This being the case, it would finally appear certain that the Dursley engine was a Railway Foundry product, with its relatively crude design of tank and its cylinder dimensions placing its date of construction towards the end of 1852 or the early to mid-part of 1853. Possibly fitted with new 9in by 16in cylinders (the relevant figure on MR Diagram D1318 is 'ambiguous': it could be a '4' or a '6') and thicker tyres to increase the wheel diameter by 2in at the same time as its new boiler, the locomotive was eventually sold by the Midland Railway to Bridgewater Navigation Co Ltd. of Runcorn in Cheshire for £400 in December 1883.

The next evolutionary stage in the genesis of the first of the Manning Wardle standard designs came in November 1853 with the delivery of two 0-4-2STs (W/Ns 387-8) to the O.W. & W.R. as its Nos. 34-5. Their dimensions were as follows:

Wheel Diameter	3ft 5 in (Coupled), 3ft 0in (Trailing)
Cylinders	9.25in (Bore), 14in (Stroke)
Wheelbase	5ft 6in+4ft 9in
Boiler Barrel	7ft 0in (L), 2ft 9in (D)
Firebox Wrapper	3ft 0in (L)
Firebox	2ft 5in (L), 2ft 9in (W), 3ft 4.5in (H)
Heating Surface	224.7sqft (Tubes), 38.58sqft (Firebox)
No. of Tubes	79, 2in
Weight (W.O)	13 tons 16cwt (4.7+4.9+4.2)

Although sadly of indifferent quality, this illustration is of vital historical importance as it shows the Dursley Branch E.B. Wilson locomotive at work for Bridgwater Navigation Co. Ltd. at Runcorn Docks after sale by the Midland Railway in 1883. The smokebox and chimney are clearly non-original, dating at the earliest from the rebuild at Derby in the late 1870's, but original features, such as the mainframes (modified), wheel centres and boiler design (although not actual construction) remain, as does the distinctive coal bunker, whose side sheeting (unlike early Beyer Peacock and Sharp Stewart inside cylinder 0-4-0STs) did not reach the rear of the footplate, a feature present on Joy's 1856 sketch. Note also the lack of any steps on the 'bunker' side of the footplate and the drain cock lever passing between the rear suspension and the boiler cladding. The wheel centres and coupling rods have a definite Manning Wardle 'look' about them, underlining the importance of this design. The opening of the Manchester Ship Canal in 1894 caused the Bridgwater Navigation to be linked to the MSC rather than to the Mersey and this historic locomotive appears to have been withdrawn as redundant in consequence. (*John Ryan Collection*)

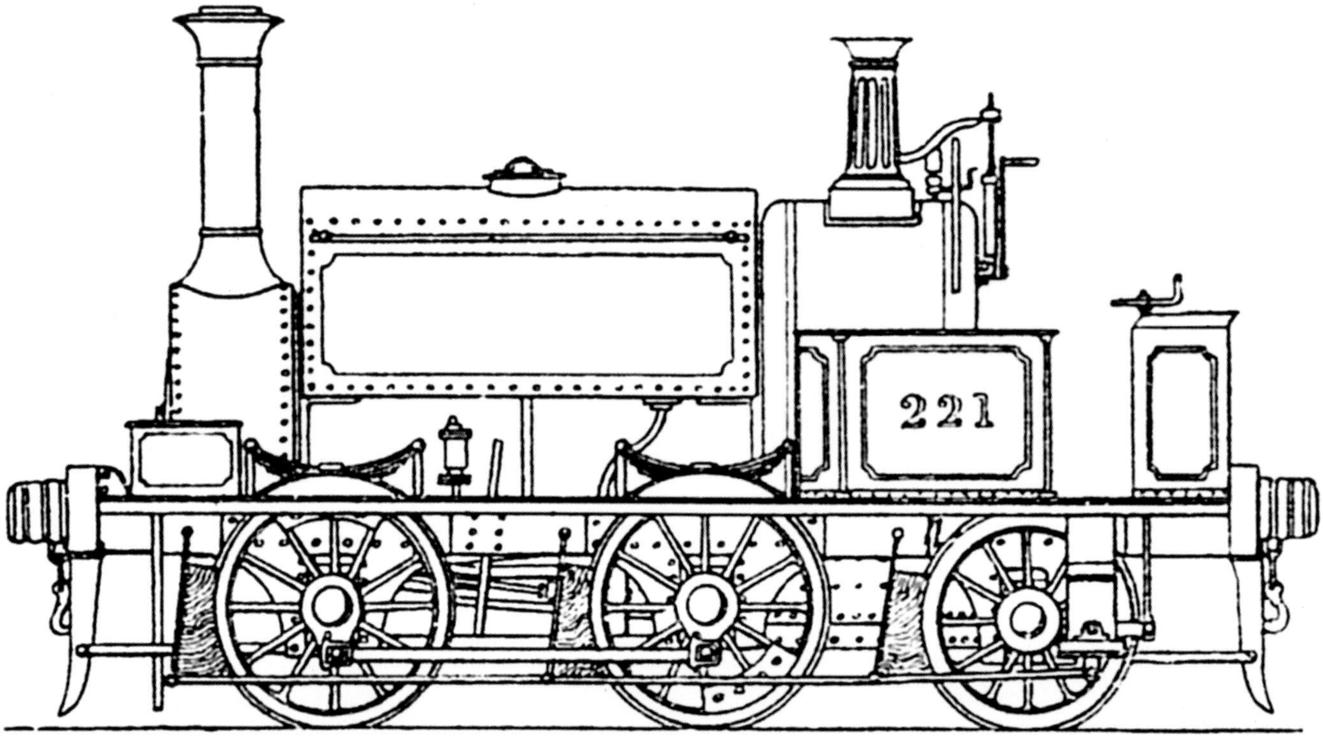

The important design features of E.B. Wilson W/Ns 387-8 of 1853, the two 0-4-2STs for the OW&WR are illustrated well in this drawing and show clearly how the evolutionary path to the Manning Wardle Old 'I' class was well established by this stage. Early features that were later to be discarded, namely the relatively small cylinder dimensions and the stays linking the mainframes to the adjacent guard-irons, were still present at this stage however. (*E.L. Ahrons*)

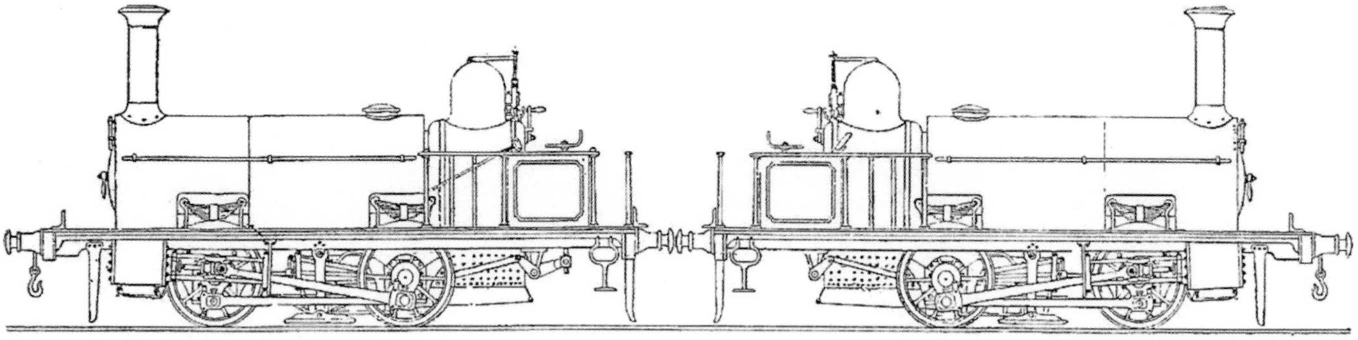

This drawing shows the design of the 14 outside cylindered 0-4-0STs delivered to the Great Indian Peninsular Railway in 1857 for use on the railway crossing the Bore Ghat with a ruling gradient of 1-in-37. The locomotives bore the Works Nos. 530-43 and the running numbers 95-108, not in corresponding order, however, as the first four to enter service, Nos. 95-8 were Works Nos. 534-7. This quartet did not enter service until July 1858 and the first train to run over the Bore Ghat, two locomotives and three brake vans, did not do so until March 1863. As shown in the drawing, these locomotives were originally designed for back-to-back working and as built they were equipped with back dome boilers with only slightly raised firebox wrappers, saddle tanks covering both boiler barrel and smokebox, extending down to the running boards, and 'sledge brakes' acting directly on the rails. In the grand scheme of E.B. Wilson locomotive evolution, the design was very much a 'stand-alone' one although it can be argued that the method of attachment of the cylinders to a relatively shallow leading portion of the mainframe, together with the coupled wheel arrangement, transmitted to the line of evolution that became the standard Manning Wardle 0-4-0ST designs. It has been suggested that these locomotives were built with a footplate mounted Giffard injector in addition to and eccentric driven feed pump (4in bore by 6¼in stroke) and if this is correct, the use of the former component predated its adoption on British main line railways. (*The Locomotive*)

Although it is unlikely to be conclusively proved today one suggestion to be made is that the cylinders of these locomotives were cast from the same patterns as used for the Dursley locomotive and simply bored out a further quarter of an inch in order to increase the available tractive effort. The basic boiler and wheelbase dimensions were to be of major significance for future events, along with the now deeper saddle tank, but some design features were still present that were not to last in the grand scheme of evolution, namely the padded leather buffers (a relic of earlier OW&WR practice) and the tie rods linking the mainframes with the lower parts of the guard-irons. At this stage in the proceedings, it should be noted that the manufacturer was not willing to use the 'double boss' wheel centre for a wheel as large as 3ft 5in and that, as with *Queen*, it would appear that both the Dursley 0-4-0ST and the OW&WR 0-4-2ST designs would have had trailing weighshaft-to-drop link bellcranks as part of their valve gear configurations. A diagram reputedly existed apparently showing these locomotives as double framed and this may have come into being as a consequence of Joy's sketching style, as has been referred to previously.

OW&WR Nos. 34-5 were not renumbered by the West Midland Railway but became respectively 221-2 under Great Western control in 1863. Both apparently ceased work with the GWR in June 1872 but No. 222 was not officially withdrawn until October the following year. No. 221 was sold to Woodall & Co. of Tansley Green near Dudley, after which all trace appears to have been lost, whilst No. 222 went to Bryndu Colliery Co. as *Bryndu No. 3*. It was seen under repair at Swindon by E.L. Ahrons in 1885 and is believed to have been owned by Cefn & Pyle Branch Railway at the time of this line's acquisition by the Port Talbot Railway in January 1897, being advertised for sale and scrapped soon afterwards.

At some point during 1854 or 1855, the final major stage in the evolution of what was to become Manning Wardle's 'Old I' class 0-6-0ST took place. During the first week of the latter year, construction work began, led by the contractor Samuel Morton Peto and his associates Edward Betts and Thomas Brassey, on the world's first known military railway. This was in pursuance of the Siege of Sevastopol during the Crimean War. This was initially constructed to convey armaments and supplies from the harbour at Balaclava, via the town of Kadikoi and up (via some very steep

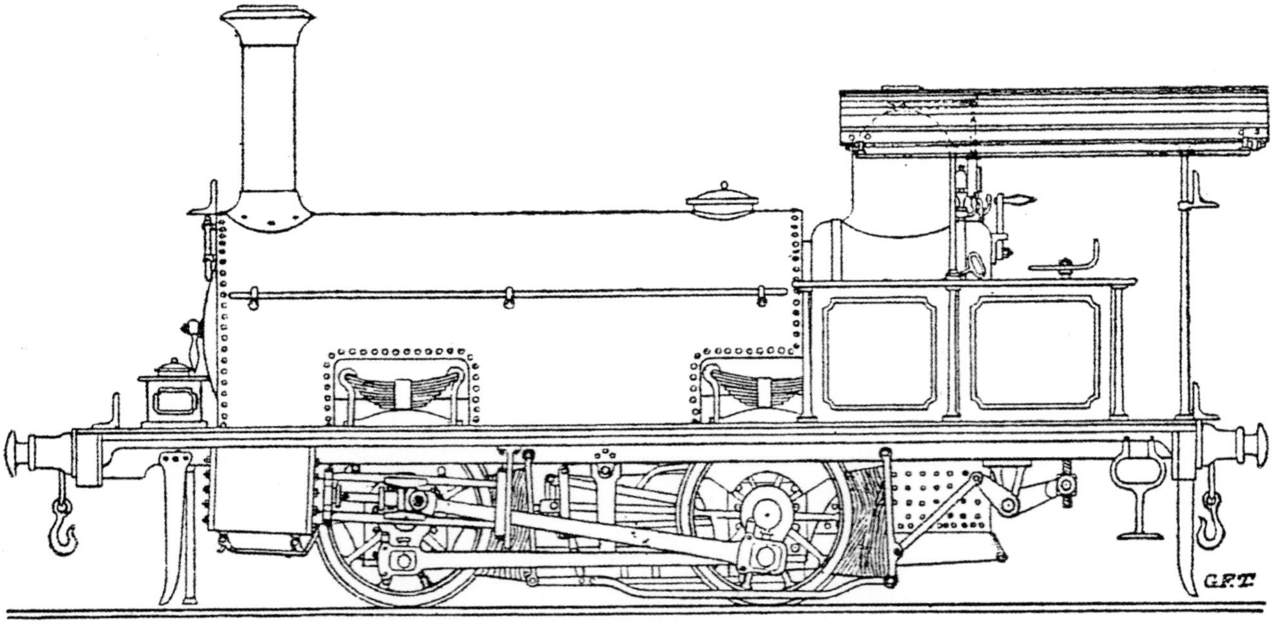

The Wilson 0-4-0STs did not prove satisfactory in their original duties, being replaced on the Ghat system successively by locomotives of the 4-6-0ST and 0-8-0ST configuration. They were soon assigned to other work and 'separated', with conventional brake blocks being substituted for the original brakes and a roof provided for the enginemen. This drawing shows the engines after these modifications had been carried out. (*The Locomotive*)

gradients worked by stationary winding engines) onto the plateau approaching Sevastopol from where bombardments and assaults were to be launched. After two 'Bury' pattern 2-2-0 locomotives from the L&NWR had been tried on the flatter section, together with another engine, *Swan* from the St. Helens Railway & Canal Co., the Grand Crimean Central Railway, as the undertaking had become known, turned to the Railway Foundry in the pursuit of more suitable motive power. On Saturday 8 November 1855, nearly a month after the end of the siege as events turned out, important reports appeared in the Leeds press. The *Leeds Mercury* recorded on that day:

> 'The Government have decided to send out another locomotive engine of a make suitable for the heavy gradients on the above line…'

The same journal further recorded:

> 'The engine which leaves here for Southampton to-day has had a thorough renovation and repainted at the Railway Foundry. Her "iron sides" are adorned with the English, French, Sardinian, and Turkish war flags, conspicuously painted thereon, and she is called the "Alliance"…'

The *Leeds Intelligencer* added further:

> 'We understand that a small locomotive engine, called "The Alliance" was yesterday forwarded from the Railway Foundry, Leeds, to Balaclava. The engine is what is called a tank engine with 11-inch cylinders, 17 inches stroke, six wheels of three feet diameter, all coupled. The engine was originally made for Messrs Leather, coal owners, for use on the tramway to and from their pits, and was purchased on Saturday last by a government agent. During the interval the words, "The Alliance", and the national flags of England, France, turkey and Sardinia have been painted on it.'

Three days later the *Leeds Intelligencer* observed:

> 'On Saturday morning a telegraphic message was received at the Railway Foundry, Leeds, ordering a second locomotive tank engine for the Crimean Railway, similar to the one purchased a few days previously. The engine had been made for Sir John L. Kaye, and at the time the order was received, was working at Sir John's collieries. It was brought down to the Railway Foundry on Saturday night, and after being overhauled will be forwarded to its destination.'

It was further recorded by the *Leeds Mercury* (as quoted in the *Sheffield Telegraph*) that the Wilson locomotives weighed no more than 12 tons in working order. When one scrutinises these contemporary reports and compares them with the known dimensions of the Manning Wardle 'Old I' class, it is clear that by November 1855, the Railway Foundry had taken the basic boiler, tank and wheelbase specification (with the crank axle moved one inch forwards) of OW&WR Nos. 34-5, fitted larger 11in by 17in cylinders and smaller 3ft. coupled wheels (probably) of the 'double boss' type following on from the Dursley engine, and again probably compensating beams. For better adhesion properties, all of the three axles were now coupled. Apart from the fact that no injectors would have been fitted, water feed being accomplished by means of crosshead driven pumps (as with OW&WR Nos. 34-5), and that tie bars linking the lower 'horncheek' areas of the mainframes with guard irons placed at their extreme ends may still have been employed, the 'Old I' class had evolved in all its significant essentials. The reference to 'iron sides' has been taken in some quarters to suggest that the locomotives were armoured, but in all probability, they were simply the flat sides of their saddle tanks. The second locomotive was named *Victory* and both were used to move supplies along part of a system that now served the headquarters of the Sardinian and French forces as well as the British, some fourteen miles of 'main line' in addition to several sidings and loops. Following the cessation of hostilities on 29 February 1856 and the signing of the Treaty of Paris on the 30th of the following month, the track fell into the hands of the Russians who sold it to the Turks, but the fate of the locomotives apparently goes unrecorded. Nonetheless *Alliance* and *Victory*, as the two Railway Foundry products became, had won their place, not only in military but also in industrial railway history. Sir John L. Kaye is later recorded as owning a locomotive of Wilson origin called *Balaclava* that appears to have been of similar design to *Victory*. This locomotive later passed through

Manning Wardle's hands for rebuilding and appears to have end up in the hands of Isaac Watt Boulton.

Despite the evolution of the design of locomotive represented by *Alliance* and *Victory*, tank locomotives with the more conventional, for the want of a better term, Jenny Lind, pattern boiler continued to be built, and an interesting design of 0-4-0 side tank appeared in 1852 for the (British) standard gauge Cia del Ferrocarril de Langreo en Asturias ('the Langreo Railway'). This design had 15in by 22in inside cylinders and 5ft coupled wheels. The first four locomotives are known to have been Works Nos. 296-99 of 1852, whilst the remaining four are believed to have been Works Nos. 325-28 of 1853, although all eight were intended to be ordered as one batch for the opening of the railway in 1852.

At least 12 0-6-0 inside framed back tank locomotives were constructed to the following dimensions:

Wheel Diameter	4ft 8in
Cylinders	15in. (Bore), 20in (Stroke)
Wheelbase	6ft 5in + 7ft 7in
Boiler Barrel	9ft 6in (L), 3ft 8½in (D)
Firebox Wrapper	3ft 8in (L), 3ft 6in (W)
Firebox	3ft 1.5in (L), 3ft 0in (W), 4ft 8in (H)
Heating Surface	752.6sqft (Tubes), 58.0sqft (Firebox)
Grate Area	9.3sqft
No. of Tubes	150, 2in
Weight (W.O)	29 tons 1cwt (9.05+9.5+10.5)

These locomotives were fitted with the classic Jenny Lind pattern ornate boiler mountings although they did have conventional plate-work over the boiler cladding as befitted their date of construction. Four were supplied in 1856 to the OW&WR as Nos. 47-50, later GWR 231-4, the latter two being E.B. Wilson & Co. W/Ns 546-7. These were all withdrawn from service between March 1877 and November 1880 in un-rebuilt state, the last to go being No. 48. Six were built for stock as W/Ns 552-7, whilst two known locomotives of this general design went to the Belgian Eastern Railway in

By 1867 the class had been rebuilt with mainframes lengthened at the rear end and an additional coupled axle added. The saddle tank was foreshortened to just behind the leading wheelset, whilst additional water capacity was provided at the rear, in some cases above and in others below the footplate. The newly 'exposed' portion of boiler barrel now carried a 2in Naylor's safety valve, although the original dome-mounted twin 4½in diameter Salter valves were retained. The locomotives at this stage were mainly used for shunting purposes although they saw main line goods service, equipped with tenders, during the 1877 famine. Some also saw use, after the removal of the trailing couple rods, on secondary passenger workings between Bombay and Thana. Subsequent rebuilds of the class are detailed in the main text. (*The Locomotive*)

1855 as Nos. 94-5. These were built to the slightly variant dimensions:

Wheel Diameter	4ft 6.125in
Cylinders	15in. (Bore), 20in (Stroke)
Wheelbase	6ft 5in + 7ft 7¼in
Boiler Barrel	9ft 4in (Between Tubeplates), 3ft 9in (Diameter)
Boiler Pressure	114 lb/sq.in
Heating Surface	748.9sqft (Tubes), 56.5sqft (Firebox)
Grate Area	9.05sqft
No. of Tubes	150, 2in
Water Capacity	700 Gallons
Coal Capacity	1.3 Tons
Weights	30.2 tons (Working Order), 23.8 Tons (Empty)

They were rebuilt at the Leuven Central Shops of the Grand Central Belge system under the direction of Chief Engineer Maurice Urban in the mid-1870s receiving *inter alia* safety valves relocated from the firebox wrapper to the dome, along with associated alteration to the upper portion of the dome cover. They were eventually scrapped under Belgian State Railways ownership in 1903. Two others, known to be W/Ns 560-1 were supplied by the agents Dickenson Bros. to Sweden where they became respectively *Thor* and *Loki*. The latter was withdrawn in 1869 whilst the former survived at least until 1902 and both may have been converted to 2-4-0WTs during their careers.

Between 1854 and 1857, at least four inside framed 0-6-0 'ballast locomotives' were produced at the Railway Foundry. The earliest pair were OW&WR Nos. 32 and 33 completed respectively in 1854 and 1855 (Order

The Sociedas del Camino de Herro de Buenos Aires al Oueste line linking Plaza del Parque to Floresta, a mere six miles long, was the first railway in Argentina and its first two locomotives were 2-2-0ST built at the Railway Foundry. This view shows the still extant No. 1 *La Portena* after its right hand eccentric driven feed pump had been replaced by an injector. The domeless boiler, flat sided saddle tank and lift-up smokebox door were features found on many Manning Wardle products built in the years following the appearance of *La Portena* and in many ways, despite its uncoupled wheels of relatively large diameter, this locomotive can be regarded as an important direct ancestor of the standard outside cylindered Manning Wardle 0-4-0ST classes. (*Author's Collection*)

Nos. 1738 and 2246, W/Ns not known). Their known dimensions were as follows:

Wheel Diameter	4ft 6in
Cylinders	16in. (Bore), 22in (Stroke)
Wheelbase	7ft 1in + 7ft 2.125in
Boiler Barrel	9ft 10.5in (L), 3ft 9in (D)
Firebox Wrapper Length	4ft 8in
Inner Firebox	3ft 10.75in (L), 3ft 1.5in (W), 4ft 6in (H)
Grate Area	12.09sqft
Heating Surface	734.0sqft (Tubes), 70.84sqft (Firebox)
No. of Tubes	144, 1.875in
Weight (W.O)	25.6 tons (10.6+7.5+7.5)

In 1863, these locomotives became GWR Nos. 278-9 in previous order, being withdrawn in September 1878 and August 1885 respectively. The second pair of locomotives constructed to this basic design were completed for the Blyth and Tyne Railway in 1857 as Nos. 15 and 22 (E.B. Wilson Order No. 2387, W/Ns 579-80).

A significant proportion of inside framed E.B. Wilson products were built to 5ft 6in gauge, not only for the Indian market, but also for Argentina and Spain. In 1855, a batch of ten 2-2-2s with 6ft 6in driving wheels and 15in by 22in outside cylinders were supplied to the East Indian Railways as EIR Nos. 80, 83-88, 90-1 and 94. These bore the E.B. Wilson works Nos. 430-9. These locomotives were built as part of a shared order with Beyer Peacock and a similar policy was followed in relation to an order for twenty-five inside cylinder 0-4-2s with 16in by 22in cylinders, 5ft coupled wheels and 3ft 9in trailing wheels completed during the previous year for the same customer, with other class members being built by Stothert & Slaughter, Vulcan Foundry, Kitson and R. & W. Hawthorn. The Railway Foundry products bore the Works Numbers 405-29 and 18 of these became EIR. Nos. 106-9, 121-3, 134, 315-7, 322-5, 327, 329, and 330. Three of these locomotives suffered the indignity of being used as motive power for steamboats, never receiving EIR numbers, whilst four further units were lost at sea along with the same number of Kitson-built classmates. Four further Wilson locomotives were supplied to the same design and customer in 1856 as W/Ns 562-5 (EIR Nos. 332-5), presumably as replacements for the lost locomotives. Railway Foundry-built members of the 0-4-2 class remained in use into the 1890's, but this class as a whole became extinct in 1898.

The next design of locomotive produced at the Railway Foundry for the Indian market appeared in 1856 and this time the customer was the Great Indian Peninsular Railway. The fourteen locomotives concerned (W/Ns 530-43) became GIPR Nos. 95-108 were outside cylinder 0-4-0STs built for back-to-back working on the Ghat inclines, which had a ruling gradient of 1-in-37. Their leading dimensions were as below:

Wheel Diameter	4ft 0in
Cylinders	15in. (Bore), 22in (Stroke)
Wheelbase	8ft 6in
Boiler Barrel	11ft 6in (L), 4ft 0in, 4ft. 1in and 4ft 0in (D) (3 Rings)
Number of Tubes	149, 2in Diameter
Inner Firebox	4ft 0in (L), 4ft 3in (W), 4ft Below Centre Line
Grate Area	13.0sqft
Heating Surface	904.5sqft (Tubes), 66.5sqft (Firebox)
Water Capacity	900 Gallons
Coal Capacity	0.75 Tons
Weights	22.5 tons (Empty) 29 Tons (W.O.)

Further 'as built' details recorded were that the cylinders were inclined (presumably on a tangential measure) at 5 in 96 with a lateral spacing of their centres of 7ft 2½in. The axle journals were laterally spaced at 4ft. 7in centres, being 7½in diameter and 8in long. The eccentric sheaves were forged solid on the driving axle. The driving crank pin was 3⅛in diameter and 3in long, whilst the blast pipe orifice was 4in diameter. Unfortunately, these locomotives, which did not enter service until July 1858, did not prove successful for their intended purpose and were soon assigned to other work. By 1867 they had been rebuilt as 0-6-0STs, shifting their centre of gravity rearwards. The wheelbase was now 14ft 3in on some class members and 14ft 7in on others, whilst the overall water capacity was increased to 1100 gallons. During the period 1889-94 the class was rebuilt again as 0-4-2STs with standard GIPR 'Z' class boilers incorporating two firebox mounted 3in Ramsbottom safety valves, being classified Z44 and their leading dimensions were as below:

Wheel Diameter	4ft 0in Coupled, 3ft 6in Trailing
Cylinders	15in. (Bore), 22in (Stroke)
Wheelbase	8ft 6in + 5ft 9in or 6ft 1in
Boiler Barrel	10ft 6in (L), 4ft 2in, 4ft. 3in and 4ft 4in (D) (3 Rings, ½in Plate)
Number of Tubes	194, 1.75in Diameter
Firebox Wrapper	4ft 4in (L), 4ft 3in (W), 4ft 10in Below Centre Line
Grate Area	14.0sqft
Heating Surface	971sqft (Tubes), 81.68sqft (Firebox)
Water Capacity	1100 Gallons
Coal Capacity	Not Stated
Weight (W.O.)	41 Tons, 28 Adhesive

Many of the class had working lives of half a century or so, some retaining their original cylinder castings to the end. One solitary example, G.I.P.R. No. 107 was converted to a side tank in 1905, equipped with liners to reduce the cylinder diameter to 11in and used with a single trailer carriage on 'railmotor' workings on the Bhopal-Ujjian line, later being transferred to the Balharshar Colliery branch. It remained in existence into the latter half of the 1920s. Whilst the 'Ghat' 0-4-0STs could hardly have been described as a success in their original capacity, the GIPR certainly got its money's worth out of them!

The final E.B. Wilson locomotives for India were two small 2-4-0WTs with 11in. by 17in cylinders and 4ft coupled wheels (W/Ns 568-9) of 1856, which became Bombay, Baroda and Central India Railway Nos. 1 and 2.

In August 1857, the first railway in Argentina was opened and this 5ft. 6in gauge line linked Parque terminus in Buenos Aires with Floresta. The first two locomotives to see service on this section were built by E.B. Wilson as Works Nos. 570 and 571, respectively *La Portena* and *La Argentina*, and they were given the running numbers 1 and 2. Despite having all wheels of equal 4ft diameter, they were 'single drivers' of the 2-2-0 configuration (having insufficient space between the wheels and the slide bars for coupling rods) with 10in by 15in cylinders. Above running board level, the classic Wilson features that would have been found on the 'Crimea' 0-6-0STs were present. No injectors being fitted as built, a preheater connection for the water tank (known as a 'warming valve') was taken from the firebox wrapper, although it is not

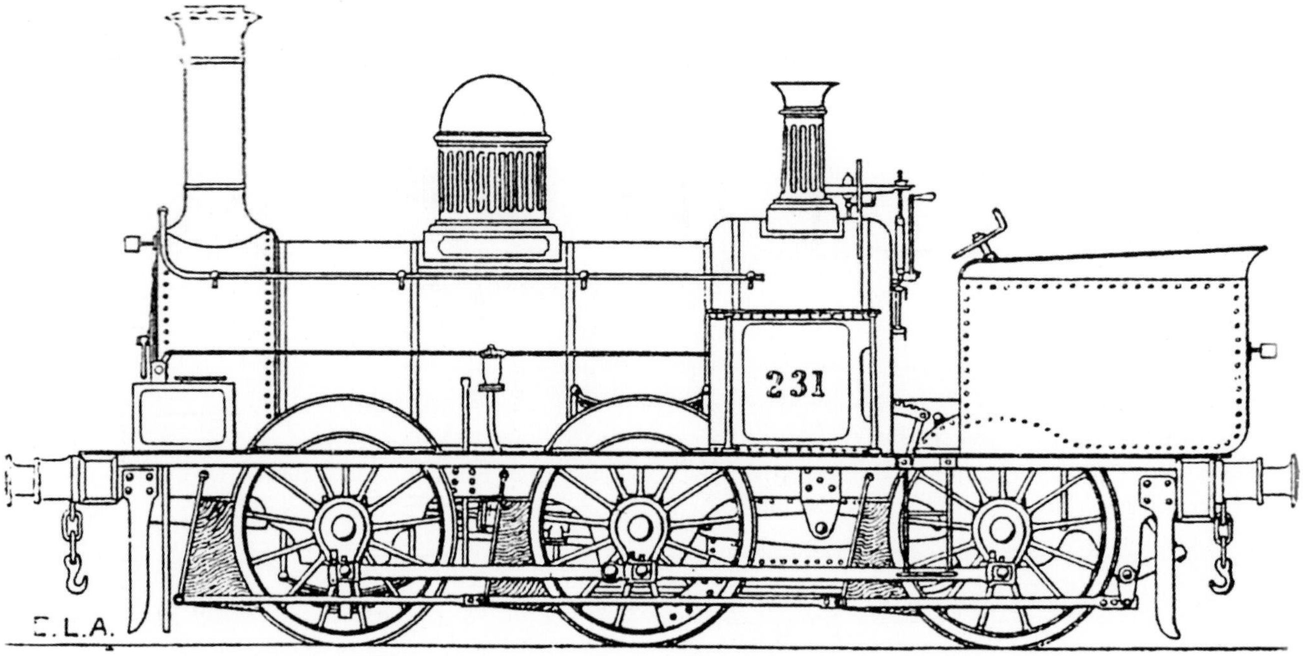

One of the 0-6-0 inside framed 'back tanks', OW&WR No. 47 is seen here in G.W.R. days as No. 231. The 'back tank' configuration was perpetuated in a relatively small number of locomotives by Manning Wardle, notably in addition to side tanks in the West Yorkshire class. These Manning Wardle locomotives are outside the scope of this volume, however. (*E.L. Ahrons*)

clear whether the 'Crimea' locomotives had this feature. *La Argentina* was transferred to Paraguay in 1863 or 1864 and soon faded into obscurity, but *La Portena* survived to be taken into Buenos Aires Western Railway stock in 1890, finishing its working life on shunting duties. Today, the engine is preserved in the Colonial Museum in Lujan, a unique and priceless relic, not only of Argentine railway history, but also of Leeds locomotive evolution.

Other export orders known to have been fulfilled by the Railway Foundry included six 0-6-0s with 17in by 25in cylinders in 1853 for Hanover State Railways; three 2-2-2s for Sweden in the mid-1850s, and four 2-4-0WTs with 5ft 6in coupled wheels and 14in by 18in cylinders of 5ft 6in gauge (W/Ns 572-3 and 603-4) in 1857 for Portugal.

One of the most elusive Wilson locomotives to obtain precise technical details of is W/N 601 *Enterprise*. This locomotive was supplied in 1858 to the contractor Davies & Savin for working on the Llanidloes & Newtown Railway, later seeing use circa 1864 on the construction of part of the Afonwen-Caernarfon line (eventually part of the L&NWR system) prior to becoming Cambrian Railway No. 1 and eventually being authorised for disposal, after an eight year period of stationary use, in July 1894. The engine is recorded as being a 0-6-0 *side tank* with 11in by 18in. cylinders and it is claimed by some sources that its true identity was W/N 301 of 1851. If this latter assertion is correct, then one is left with an intriguing possibility. A building date of 1851 is simply too early in the history of the Railway Foundry for the construction of a 0-6-0 side tank locomotive. This fact, coupled with the 18in cylinder stroke suggests that W/N 301 as built would have been a sister to the Little Mail locomotives discussed in Chapter Five, and was probably left on the maker's hands as a stock item. Even by 1858, its basic design appears to have fallen out of favour with potential customers and the Railway Foundry's best option during what were then its dying weeks, would have been to somehow adapt W/N 301 for the resurgent contractors' market and re-brand it as a new locomotive, hence the revised Maker's No. Close inspection of the surviving Little Mail drawings in the Institution of Mechanical Engineers' Library shows that whilst the locomotives' cylinders were underhung when they possessed (originally four) 5ft coupled wheels, fitting 3ft wheels to all three axles would have required re-positioning of the cylinder/steam chest assembly (with associated valve gear modifications) in the more conventional location above the axle centreline. Such a conversion would have raised the boiler quite considerably in relation to the mainframes, but this would have been mitigated to the tune of 1ft as a consequence of the smaller

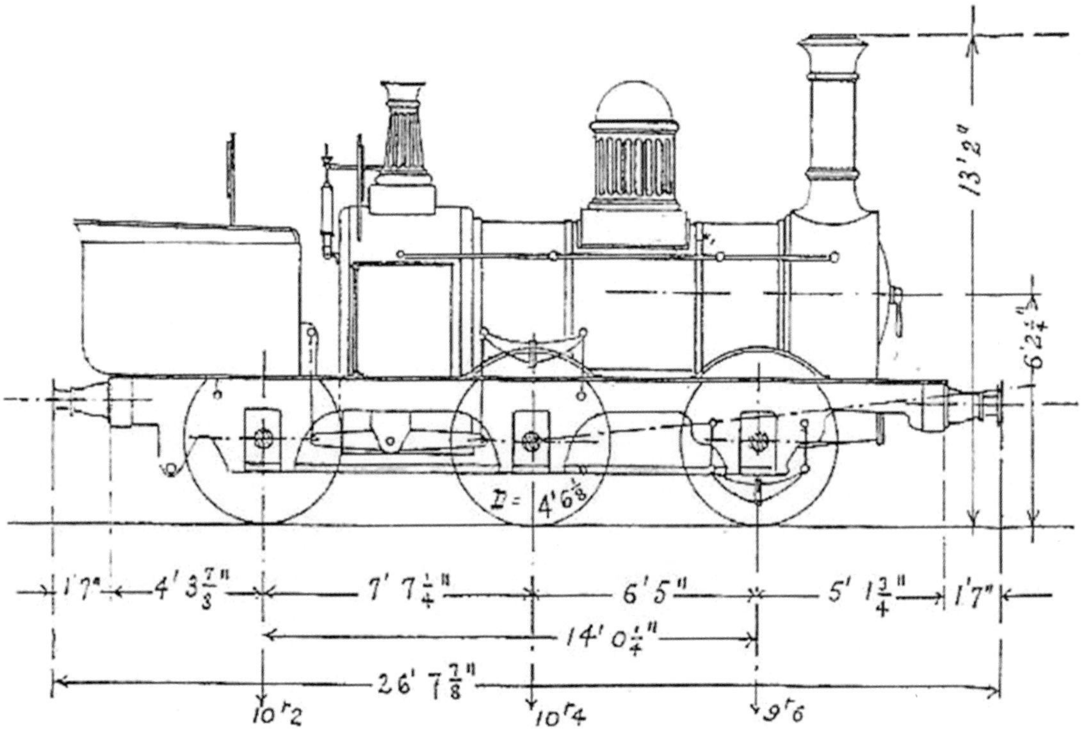

As mentioned in the text. E.B. Wilson & Co. also constructed two of the 0-6-0BT design for the Belgian Eastern Railway in 1855 (BER Nos. 94-5). This weight diagram shows the two locomotives in original state. (*The Locomotive*)

wheels, which would have lowered the frames in relation to the rails, reducing the depth provision for a back tank and hence necessitating the side tanks. Upward extensions of the mainframes would also have been necessary to cater for re-positioning of the buffers to as to ensure that they remained at the correct vertical pitch. Tragically, no illustrations have survived of *Enterprise* to show whether its origins were as detailed here.

Works No. 602 of 1858 was a 0-4-0WT with 12in by 15in outside cylinders and 4ft wheels built for the Alyth Railway (later absorbed into the Caledonian Railway), which was sold to Thomas Wheatley in 1883. A 0-6-0WT *Devonshire* was built at the Railway Foundry in 1857 for Dunstan & Barlow of Sheepbridge Ironworks. The known dimensions of this locomotive were:

Wheel Diameter	3ft 6in
Wheelbase	5ft 10in + 6ft 11in
Cylinders	13in. (Bore), 18in. (Stroke)
Number of Tubes	122, 2in Diameter
Boiler Barrel	3ft 6in (D), 8ft 5in (L)
Firebox Wrapper	3ft 9in (L)
Heating Surface	610sq.ft (Total)
Overall Length	25ft 8in

This locomotive was taken into Midland Railway stock on 1st November 1870 as MR 1065, renumbered 2065 in March 1872 and reboilered in October 1879. It was finally broken up in April 1891.

The largest Spanish order was for twenty inside cylindered 5 ft. 6 in. gauge 'long boiler' 0-6-0 locomotives with four wheeled tenders for the Madrid, Zaragoza and Alicante Railway. These locomotives, which were given M.Z.A. running numbers 246-65, were Works Nos. 607-26 in the Railway Foundry list and were built with the following leading dimensions:

Wheel Diameter	4ft 8in
Cylinders	17.25in. (Bore), 23½in (Stroke)
Working Pressure	120 lb/sq.in
Number of Tubes	168, 2in (D) 13ft 8¾in (L)
Grate Area	14.5sqft
Heating Surface	1196sqft (Total)
Water Capacity	1450 Gallons
Coal Capacity	3 Tons 10cwt
Locomotive Weight (W.O.)	28 Tons 5cwt
Tender Weight (W.O.)	21.0 Tons

These locomotives were part of an order shared equally with Kitson & Co., whose products of the same design bore the MZA running numbers 266-285. Originally supplied for mixed traffic use, the class proved successful and versatile in service and examples remained in use into the RENFE era, well past their centenaries. MZA Nos. 246 and 248-252 were renumbered as RENFE 030-2013-2018. It is pleasing to record that the first member of the class, MZA No. 246

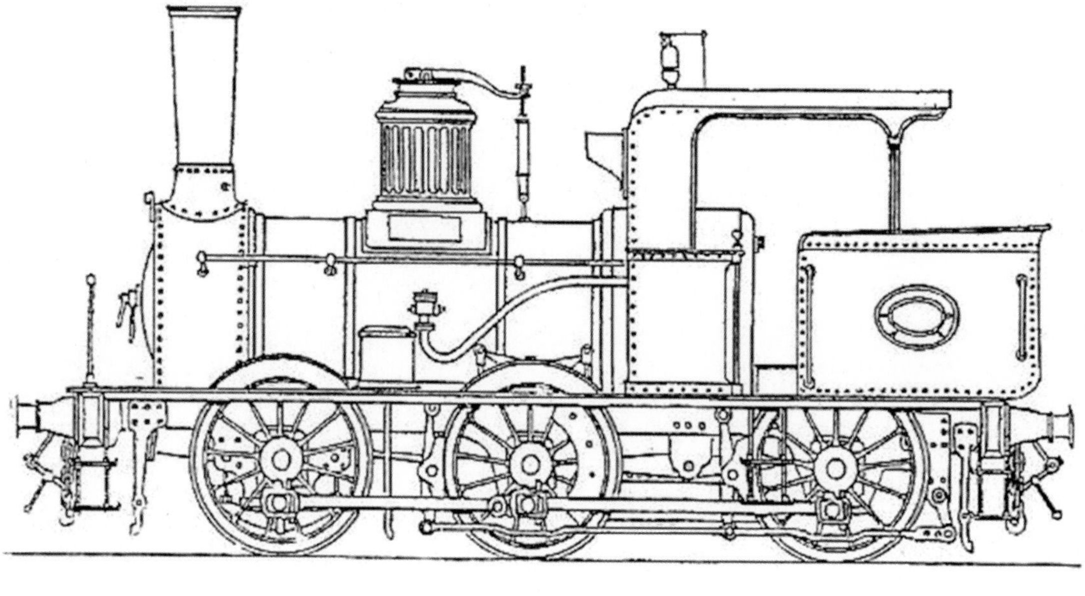

This drawing shows BER Nos. 94-5 after rebuilding in the 1870's. The original fluted dome covers appear to have been retained, albeit modified to take dome-mounted safety valves. (*The Locomotive*)

is preserved today at in the Railway museum at Vilanova i la Geltru in Catalonia.

In *The Chronicles of Boulton's Siding*, Chapter 13, there is an obscure reference the acquisition by I.W. Boulton in July 1883 from a Miss Lister Kay (sic) of Wakefield of:

> 'two old locomotives, an 0-4-0 by Wilson and an 0-6-0 by Manning Wardle ... the former was a saddle tank called *Solferino* which had 12in by 18in cylinders, 3ft coupled wheels and weighed 14 tons in working order.'

A. R. Bennett then went on to speculate incorrectly that this locomotive had originally been built to 5ft 6in gauge and had seen service in the Crimea, an impossibility given that the Balaclava railway was built to standard gauge. There are numerous inaccuracies in *The Chronicles of Boulton's Siding* – for instance, on the same page as his speculation, Bennett refers to another Manning Wardle '0-6-0 box tank' with 10in by 20in cylinders and 2ft 9in wheels, which was acquired by Boulton in 1867; there is no known 'match' for this description. Assuming that the description of *Solferino* was correct, and given that the battle commemorated by the name took place on 24 June 1859 as the last battle of the Second War of Italian Independence, the engine would appear to have dated from the last months of locomotive construction at the old Railway Foundry and would, given the configuration of the Ghat Incline 0-4-0STs, *La Portena*, *La Argentina* and W/N 602, have had outside cylinders. In all probability, *Solferino* was the direct ancestor of the Manning Wardle standard 0-4-0ST designs although, as will be seen later, early Manning Wardle locomotives of this type were constructed to smaller dimensions. The 0-6-0 Manning Wardle acquired with *Solferino* and mentioned by Bennett appears to have been an 1864 Manning Wardle rebuild of the Wilson locomotive *Balaclava* owned by Sir John L. Kaye mentioned previously.

Two 'single driver' locomotives were built for New South Wales in 1858 and these were to be the last new locomotives sold by E.B. Wilson & Co. as a going concern. The first of these was a 'Crewe-Allan' pattern 2-2-2 tender engine with 15in by 22in cylinders, 5ft 9in driving wheels weighing 20.6 tons in working order. Numbered 9 in the NSW list, it was originally put to work in December 1858 on the Campbelltown extension of the Sydney-based railway system, it remained in top-link service until displaced by the arrival of newer locomotives in 1865-6 when it was transferred to secondary duties, being scrapped nearly two decades later. The other Railway Foundry product for NSW could best be described as an outside cylindered inside framed 2-2-2 well tank with reinforced running board valences and 5ft 6in driving wheels. This was not put into service until January 1859, becoming No. 8 in the NSW list and initially employed on suburban duties in the environs of Sydney. This locomotive was transferred to Darling Harbour for working coal traffic in 1869, becoming Sydney yard shunter a few years later, taking up similar duties at Goulburn in 1878. Withdrawn from service during the following year, it was scrapped in 1884.

OW&WR No. 32 is shown in this diagram as G.W.R. 279. Officially described as a 'ballast' engine' this locomotive, and its three known sisters (two of which were built for the Blyth & Tyne Railway) were once again prototypes for some similar locomotives built by Manning Wardle.

CHAPTER 8

THE END OF THE SECOND RAILWAY FOUNDRY

Despite the success that E.B. Wilson & Co. had enjoyed in the market for railway locomotives and other products, such as stationary and marine engines, the reign of the Railway Foundry as a leading light in the development of main line products was destined to be a short one. External factors, such as the competition from west of the Pennines in the form of Fairbairn, Sharp, Roberts & Co., Beyer Peacock and Vulcan Foundry, or in Leeds itself from Kitsons were significant in bringing about the Railway Foundry's fall, but the main problem was discord amongst the key players themselves. The latter difficulty was evident by 1856 by which time conflict between Wilson and the Trustees had reached the Court of Chancery. Wilson appears to have quit the Railway Foundry at this stage. By 1858, Edward Brown Wilson was recorded in the register of the Institution of Mechanical Engineers as being based at 36, Parliament Street, Westminster, apparently working on his own account on various projects. In the 1861 census, he was recorded as lodging at 6, Great Ryder Street, Westminster and he died in Tonbridge, Kent thirteen years later. The *Leeds Times* of 12 June 1858 recorded an incident that typified the climate of disharmony that prevailed during the final years of the Railway Foundry:

> 'It is now five years [in reality this was nine years] since the Railway Foundry passed into the hands of trustees. The original merits of the question do not concern us; it is simply with the facts we have to deal. Since that time the "hands" in the establishment have been systematically reduced from 1,300 men down to 240, and then next to none at all. The place may now be considered closed to all intents and purposes, and when the operations of the house can be again resumed is one of those glorious uncertainties of the law known only to the Court of Chancery. One peculiar question has already arisen out of the mechanical chaos which there prevails, and to the details of this matter we now purpose shortly to address ourselves.
>
> 'Mr. Robert Savage, who has been attached to the establishment for the last dozen years, was brought up at the Leeds Court House on Wednesday, charged with having maliciously destroyed certain templates and gauges, the property of his employers. The complainants in the case were Messrs. Joshua Pollard and Wm. Singleton – Trustees for the benefit of the creditors of Mr. E. B. Wilson – and they were represented by the barrister Mr. Blanshard. Mr. Savage was defended by Mr. P. W. Roberts of Manchester, an attorney who is generally known as "the Miners' Attorney-General".
>
> 'According to the opening of Mr. Blanchard it appeared that a number of men, amongst whom was Mr. Savage, received notice to leave in May. Their time expired on 3rd of June. Mr Savage was then the foreman of the boiler department, and Mr. Alexander Campbell the general foreman of the works. On the 26th of May Mr. Campbell received certain intelligence which led him to visit the boiler shed and he there found two of the sons of Mr. Savage, in company with a third youth named Scatcherd, busily engaged in cutting up the templates and gauges which served as templates and models in that part of the establishment. The articles in question had apparently been removed from the walls from which they were generally suspended, and were being cut into scrap iron by the large shears fixed in the boiler shed. Mr. Campbell inquired of the lads who had authorised them to cut up the models and they replied that it was Mr. Savage himself. Mr. Campbell thereupon proceeded to Mr. Savage's office, and said to him, "Robert, you must not cut up these templates". Mr. Savage replied that he was not cutting up any

that were of use. Mr. Campbell rejoined, "Of use or of no use, you must not cut them up, even to the value of a penny". Those plates that are of no use you had better label to that effect and place on one side, but if you cut them up you may bring both yourself and me into serious trouble by doing so at the present time". Upon that, Mr. Savage went to the lads, who were all under him, and told him to leave off their work which they at once did. Here the matter ended for the time, and Mr. Savage left when his notice expired on the 3rd of June. It was further contended by the complainants that Mr. Savage had no business to cut up any plates without the authorisation either of Mr. Campbell or Mr. Wardell [sic], the engineer of the establishment; that no such incident was remembered, and had certainly not been sanctioned either by the managers or the trustees; that the plates themselves were always useful as models of pattern or of size; that by the said destruction several repairs had been prevented either temporarily or until the missing models had been replaced; that the whole business was a malicious proceeding dictated either by some person outside or by the spite and malice of a man whose term of service was just expiring; and that the cutting up of the models came within the meaning of the statute 7 and 8 Geo. IV., c.30,s.24, which laid down that such a destruction of valuable property was a malicious action, and one punishable either by a fine or imprisonment. To support the argument of the learned counsel, the following witnesses were called: - Mr. Alexander Campbell, general foreman of the Railway Foundry; Mr. Chas. Henry Wardell [sic] , engineer to the establishment; Dobson Stones, engine tenter; William Bland, turner; and Charles Hall, boiler maker. Mr Hall, who was the last witness, proved something on the other side. It had been affirmed by Mr. Campbell that none of the models in question had, within his knowledge, been previously broken up, that there was no necessity for such a Vandalistic work, and that the firm would suffer by an action of this kind in so far as the loss of valuable models and patterns was concerned; but Mr. Hall proved, on the other hand, that he had frequently cut up, by order of his foreman, Mr. Savage, templates which were obsolete in design, that it was a greater trouble to find old templates and gauges than to make new ones, inasmuch as, it old models were easily found, they were generally out of radii from being knocked against each other; and that it would require more labour to rectify these than to make new ones for actual and immediate service.-This was the case for the complainants.

'Mr. Roberts then addressed the court in defence of Mr. Savage. He took several preliminary objections, principally on the ground of the court's having no jurisdiction to deal with the case. In the first place, what had been done by the defendant had been done by him in the belief that he was right and perfectly warranted in breaking up the plates and gauges. He was told by Mr. Campbell on the day in question, for the first time, that he must not break up the templates, and he immediately went and stopped the boys. In the second place, the limit of what could be recovered as damages was placed by the act at £5, whereas the complainants had assessed the damage done at considerably more than that sum-an assessment which has certainly deprived the court of the power of action under the present information as if it had been a trial for £100 in the County Court. In the third place, the tenor of the evidence was that there was no malice at all between complainants, defendant, or the workpeople; and that the defendant did not gain anything at all by the act with which he was charged. Lastly, Mr. Roberts contended that there was no proof of ownership, a proof that was certainly required by the act of Parliament under which the present proceedings were taken.

The court having decided against the defendant on these preliminary objections, and declared that the case was within their jurisdiction.

'Mr. Roberts continued his remarks in defence. He dwelt largely upon the absence of motive on the part of the defendant, showed that there was not a farthing of advantage to him in the breaking up of the metal, and at great length and with some vigour characterised the prosecution as one dictated by malicious and jealous motives. The trustees, he insinuated, knew that they were losing a good man, and to prevent him from hampering them by opposition, they had taken the present proceedings against him. Mr. Roberts' address was frequently cheered from the body of the court.

'The magistrates, after a brief deliberation, came into court and announced their decision as follows:- We are of the opinion that the charge set forth in the information against Robert Savage has not been sufficiently proved; and the defendant is therefore acquitted.

'The decision of the court was loudly applauded by the defendant's brother-workmen who crowded the gallery.'

It was clear by this stage that the writing was on the wall for E.B. Wilson & Co., despite the efforts of the Trustees over nearly a decade to keep the firm in business. Despite the fact that the Railway Foundry had posted a £12,000 profit in its final year of trading, the *Leeds Intelligencer* for 2 December 1865 recorded that in 1858 it was discovered that the debts of the business were some £100,000 greater than had previously been anticipated and this proved to be the final straw. During the same year, the firm's Engineer and Outdoor Representative, Charles Wardle and the Works Manager, Alexander Campbell (both of whom appear to have held their senior posts following Wilson's departure) 'jumped ship' and together with a Mr. John Dickenson and a Mr. Robert Boddy purchased a plot of land from Viscount Gustavus Frederick Boyne in Jack Lane to establish a new concern. Manufacturing work ceased at the Railway Foundry in the second half of 1858, and on 16 March 1859, Vice-Chancellor Wood at Chambers recorded:

'It is ordered that all of the property comprised in or subject to the trusts of the indenture of June 21st 1849 in the pleadings in these causes mentioned or so much thereof as is unrealized be sold with the approbation of the judge to whose court these causes are attached and it is ordered that the money to arise by the said sale be paid into the Bank [of England] ....to the credit of these causes subject to further order of this court.'

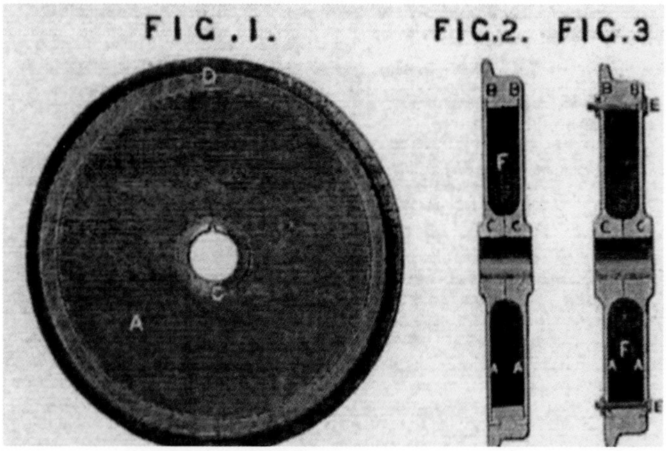

Following his disappearance from the Railway Foundry in 1856, Edward Brown Wilson was recorded as working from 36, Parliament St., London by the Institution of Mechanical Engineers, apparently on a consultancy basis. During the period from December 1862 to December 1864, Wilson published engravings relating to his ideas in *The Engineer*. Most of these related to the manufacture and pressing of steel; one even related to the design of domestic fireplaces, but the feature reproduced here, from the 17 July 1863 issue, shows a proposal for a design of composite railway wheel (the cavities in the drawing being filled with wood, India rubber or some other sound-deadening material). Despite these efforts, he was never to achieve the lofty heights of success associated with the early 'Jenny Lind' era and he died in 1874.

The most immediate impact of this order was that on Wednesday 20 July 1859, the realizable assets of the Railway Foundry, (for sale as an entity or divided into seven Lots), were put up for auction by Messrs. Hardwicks & Best at the Scarborough Hotel, Bishopsgate St. in Leeds. *The Leeds Intelligencer* for 23 July 1859 recorded that only the first Lot ("The Foundry", adjoining Pearson Street) received any interest from bidders, the best bid being from a Mr. Newsam for £1,100 but this was rejected. The disposal of the site was not destined to be a swift process, particularly as the leasehold portion was nearly time-expired and not excluded in the auction. In order to make the site more attractive to potential bidders, the 1845 mortgage was redeemed by the Trustees Joshua Pollard and William Singleton by the payment of £5,854 18s. on 15 April 1861, whilst the plot of land described as acquired by Wilson in the 1848 valuation bordering the southern side of Jack Lane, opposite Manning Wardle & Co., and the Midland Railway siding was also purchased in attempt to make good the loss of the value of the site resulting from the expiry of Fretwell's lease. It did not prove possible, even with these measures having been implemented, to sell the site as one entity and Lot Six, described as 'a plot of valuable Building Land, adjoining Jack Lane, comprising 7283 square yards, more or less, abutting upon Jack Lane North-East, upon the said [Midland] Branch Railway North-West, upon Jack Lane New Pottery, and property of Charles Grosvenor and others South East' was eventually destined to become the site of Hudswell Clarke & Co. which took the Railway Foundry name. By 1864, more of the site, although sadly by this stage without usable buildings, was acquired by J.T. Leather and this became the home of Hunslet Engine Co. This was not the end of the story from the legal point of view as the *Leeds Intelligencer* feature of 2 December 1865 recorded that further proceedings in Chancery concerning liability for the additional debt of £100,000 had taken place between the Trustees and general creditors (with judgement and costs being awarded in favour of the latter, apart from the costs incurred by the Bowling Iron Co.) during the preceding November and that these were likely to be the subject of appeal. Nonetheless, with two manufacturers destined to become leading lights in the production of industrial locomotives newly established on former E.B. Wilson premises, and a third on adjacent land using ex-Wilson personnel, the stage was set for one of the most important periods in the commercial history of the city of Leeds. It is the impact made by the latter concern, Manning Wardle & Co. to which attention must now be paid.

CHAPTER 9

THE MANNING WARDLE STANDARD CLASSES AND THEIR DERIVATIVES

For approximately one year, Charles Wardle, Alexander Campbell, John Dickenson and Robert Boddy carried on their business as general engineers on the land formerly owned by Viscount Boyne, but 1859 was to see two events that were to define the future of the new entity. The first of these was that Messrs Dickenson and Boddy were to sell their interests and a new partner, John Manning, was to appear on the scene. The second major event was that following the attempts to sell the Railway Foundry's real estate in July, its chattels were auctioned shortly afterwards. Two standard gauge Sturrock-pattern 2-4-0s were auctioned on 22 August 1859 following the demise of E.B. Wilson for £1,900 apiece as Lots 1121 and 1121A and these passed to the Leeds and Bradford Railway. Lot 1119, which sold for £260 to a Mr. Brundell of Doncaster was described as a 0-4-0 with 3ft wheels, 9in by 12in cylinder (sic), 54 boiler tubes and a tank 8ft by 1ft. The description is puzzling in attempting to identify the locomotive as it does not at first sight appear to correspond with anything that had been produced before at the Railway Foundry. One possibility is that the engine was not built on-site at all, but purchased from another manufacturer. Taking the apparent single cylinder configuration of the engine at face value it should be noted that such locomotives were rare in the 1850s (the 'traction engine' type locomotives produced by makers such as Aveling & Porter, John Fowler and Stephen Lewin had yet to make their appearance), but one such design, with a non-depending firebox, was produced by Neilson. Far more likely is the fact that this description, as with the cylinder stroke, is an error (i.e. the '12in' was in reality 1ft 2in or 14in). In this connection, it should be noted that a locomotive bearing a very close resemblance to the Dursley engine, but with a full length tank and running boards raised over the wheels in lieu of splashers (the latter possibly a subsequent modification necessitated by damage sustained 'in the field') turned up in the ownership of the contractors Isaac White and Sebastian Meyer (or at least one of them) and was photographed in Epworth Cutting during construction of the Axholme Joint Railway. If one extends the tank found on the Dursley engine to cover the smokebox, as was the case with the Epworth locomotive, then it would be approximately 8ft long, whilst the quoted depth of 1ft corresponds with the known surviving Midland Railway diagram for the Dursley locomotive. If this suggestion is correct, then the locomotive covered by Lot 1119 would probably have been of similar age to the Dursley locomotive, rather than being a latter-day Wilson product.

On Friday 2 September 1859, Manning Wardle & Co. purchased Lots 3370-3407 which consisted of drawings for seventeen types of locomotive and others for boilers, tenders and other components. Sadly, the particulars of sale did not specifically identify these. The only Wilson drawing to survive today in the Hunslet Archive at Statfold Barn depicts a Sturrock-pattern 0-6-0 goods locomotive. This drawing appears to have been used as the basis for eight locomotives supplied to the North Eastern Railway as W/Ns 24-7 of 1861, 120-1 of 1865 and 183-4 of 1866. In addition to continuing to construct non-locomotive products (thereby carrying on a Railway Foundry tradition), other locomotives of Wilson design continued to be turned out during the early years of the Boyne Engine Works, as the new factory was named.

The new concern of Manning Wardle & Co. had only limited success in marketing the Wilson tender and well-tank designs that it had inherited, and it was to be another Wilson specification that was destined to have a far greater impact on the fortunes of Boyne Engine Works. The then-buoyant coal and iron-related industries, together with a growth in demand from

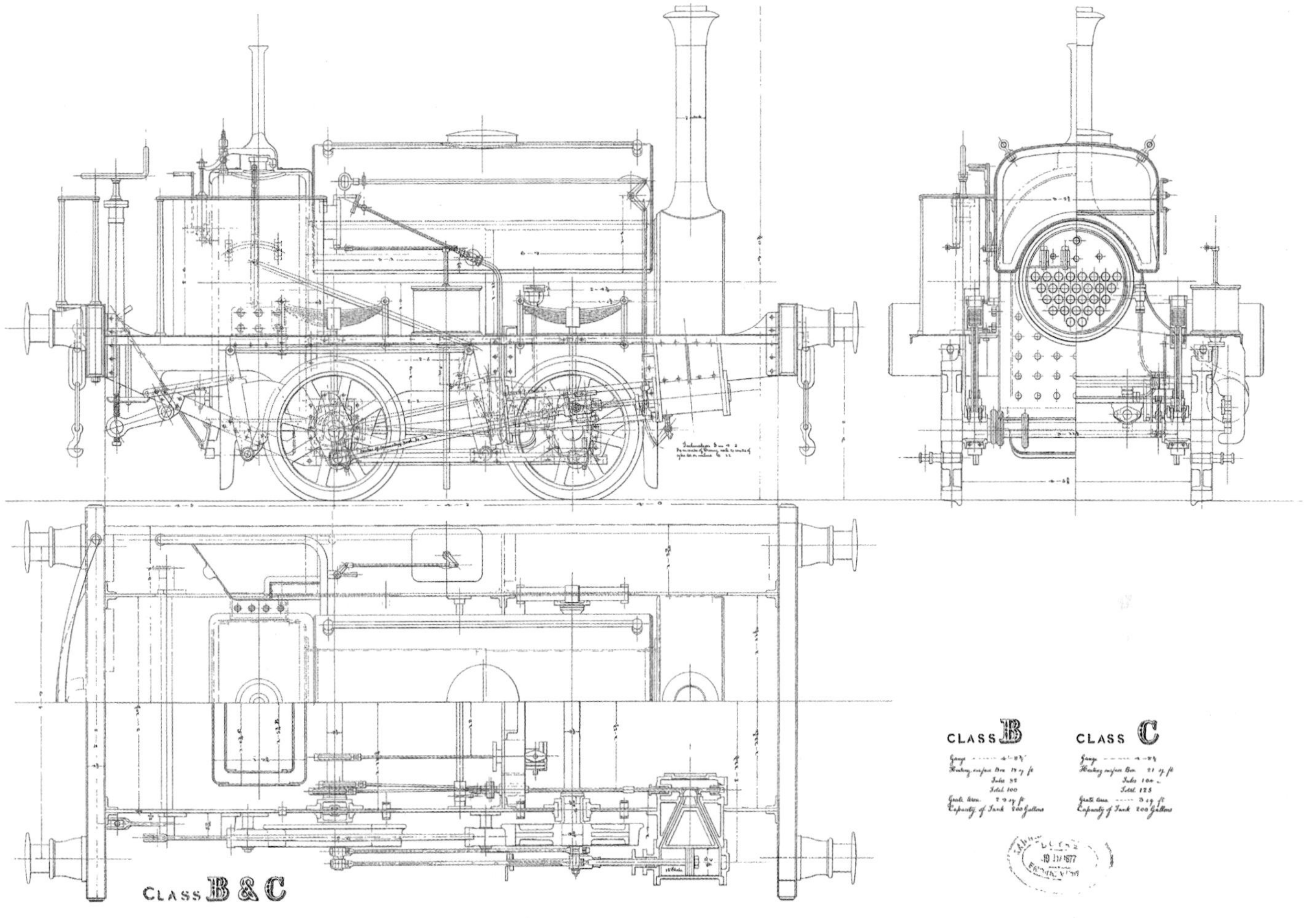

This Manning Wardle drawing, dated 19 November 1877 shows the 'B' and 'C' class 0-4-0ST standard design and emphasizes its diminutive proportions when compared with the normal standard gauge. The last known extant survivor, on domestic soil at least (W/N 97, delivered 3 November 1863) was converted to 3ft gauge before being scrapped in 1948. The detailed features shown, including the round cornered tank, are (as to be expected) consistent with the date of the drawing.

contractors spurred on by the arrival of the second 'Railway Mania', proved to be a ready market for a simple robust little tank engine design that had already proved itself and the Wilson 'Crimea' pattern saddle tank locomotive turned out to be the answer to these customers' requirements. With little or no significant modification when compared to the Crimea locomotives, the first member of the Manning Wardle 'Old I' class appeared as W/N 4 under Order No. 22 on 16 September 1859 for the contractor Brassey & Ballard and delivered to Colwell, Great Malvern for work on the Worcester-Hereford section of the West Midland Railway. The notes in the Engine Book for this locomotive, which were written up nearly two decades after its completion read:

'This is the first engine made of "K" class pattern. Cylinders 11" by 17", boiler barrel 7'3" by 2'9". The firebox is 3in deeper than present "K", in all other respects the same. The leading and trailing axle journals are 3 ¾" diameter and the driving axle journals 4 ¼". The leading and trailing crankpins are ¼" less in diameter than the present day "K" in the part that fits in the wheel centre, whilst the driving crankpin is the same as now (July 1878). The coupling rods have no wrought iron packing behind the brasses. The eccentric straps are made of brass and the leading and trailing axle boxes are the same as present day 'E' class (leading). The driving axle boxes are the same as the present day 'K' (leading and trailing). The expansion brackets

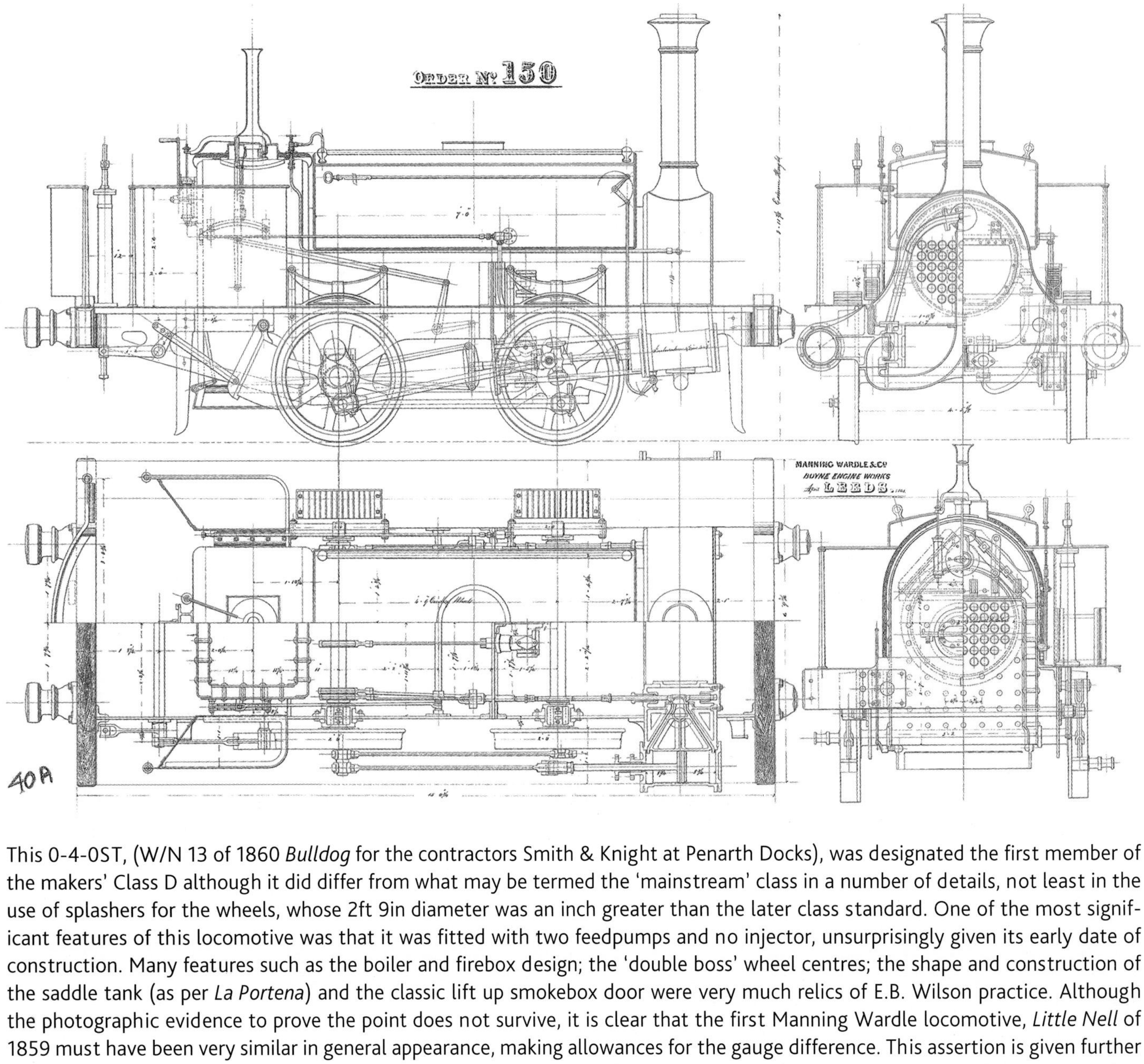

This 0-4-0ST, (W/N 13 of 1860 *Bulldog* for the contractors Smith & Knight at Penarth Docks), was designated the first member of the makers' Class D although it did differ from what may be termed the 'mainstream' class in a number of details, not least in the use of splashers for the wheels, whose 2ft 9in diameter was an inch greater than the later class standard. One of the most significant features of this locomotive was that it was fitted with two feedpumps and no injector, unsurprisingly given its early date of construction. Many features such as the boiler and firebox design; the 'double boss' wheel centres; the shape and construction of the saddle tank (as per *La Portena*) and the classic lift up smokebox door were very much relics of E.B. Wilson practice. Although the photographic evidence to prove the point does not survive, it is clear that the first Manning Wardle locomotive, *Little Nell* of 1859 must have been very similar in general appearance, making allowances for the gauge difference. This assertion is given further weight by the fact that a contemporary description of the Manning Wardle 0-4-0ST at the London Exhibition of 1862 states that locomotives of the general type could be constructed to a gauge as low as 3ft. (*Hunslet Archive*)

> are of the old style fixed to the corners of the firebox shell. The reversing handle had the old style of catch.'

The description of the locomotive, which was named *Rutland*, raises interesting points, not least of which is what constitutes the main difference between the 'Old I' class and its eventual successor, the 'K'. An attempt to answer this question and put it in its historical context will be made later; at this stage it will be noted how constructional details and customer base changed over the years. As a perfect illustration of the development of the customer base at this time the next locomotive produced under Order No. 39 (W/N 5 of 5 October 1859) went to the Middlesbrough iron founders Messrs. Bolckow & Vaughan as the first of several Manning Wardle products for this customer. As confidence grew at the Boyne Engine Works,

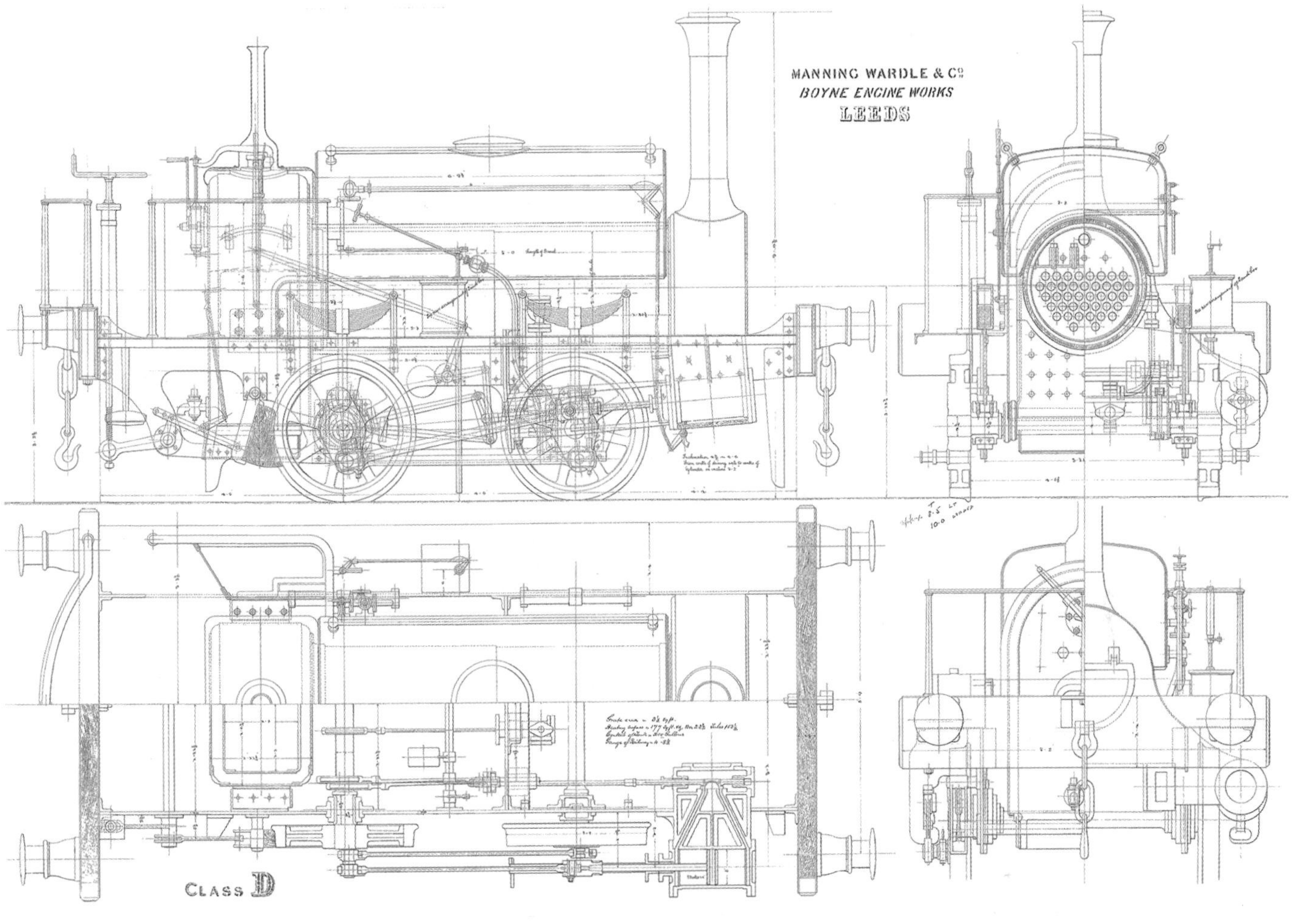

By way of comparison with the preceding illustration, this undated drawing shows the 'D' class in its mature form as reached by the mid-1870s. The saddle tank now has a 'softer' less angular cross-section and the right hand feedpump has been replaced by an injector (sadly this item is only shown in plan view in the drawing). The buffer height from the rail has also been raised when compared to W/N 13, resulting in the need for higher pitched bufferbeams and upward extensions of the mainframes to accommodate them. (*Hunslet Archive*)

locomotives of the 'Old I' class were typically built in small batches for different customers, usually two or four, effectively a small-scale form of the building for stock that had been so much a part of E.B. Wilson & Co.'s strategy. This is illustrated well by the fact that the next 'Old I' class locomotives to appear were all built under Order No. 200. These four locomotives were identical as built to W/N 4 save for incorporating the type of reversing lever that was still in production (presumably on the 'K' class) in 1878. Construction of the class continued steadily throughout most of the 1860s, with W/N 30 proving to be the 'odd one out' of the '11 inch' 'Old I' class in one important respect. This locomotive was subsequently in the ownership of the contractor Benton & Woodiwiss and was recorded in the Engine Book as 'rebuilt by Messrs Benton & Woodiwiss and numbered 543, there [sic] 33. New boiler [short 'K'] put in, angle iron shell [wrapper] joints.' It is not clear what is meant here: should the note not begin: 'rebuilt to the order of…'? In any case, the rebuilt locomotive became W/N 543 of 1875 under Order No. 8509, significantly not regarded as a new locomotive as the Order No. did not end in a zero, which was standard practice for new locomotives by this stage, although given the extent of the rebuilds undertaken by the makers on other locomotives, it is not clear why a new works number was allocated to this particular specimen. After various other spares were supplied, the last spares were supplied for this locomotive under Order No. 42966 of 22 July 1898.

This 'D' class locomotive, W/N 799 (July 1st 1881) began its working life with the contractor Lucas & Aird Ltd. (as did many others of the makers' products) at Cudworth in Yorkshire, but is seen here in later life at the Quarries of P. W. Spencer Ltd., Thornton-in-Craven. (*J. Peden*)

W/N 1318 started life as *Bolton Abbey*, being delivered to the contractor J. Green & Sons at Bolton Abbey Station in Yorkshire. Apparently undersized for customer needs, it was returned to the makers (being replaced by 'H' class W/N 1283 of 1895) and re-sold to London County Council for use on a contractor's railway linking Abbey Wood Station with Crossness (Southern Sewage Outfall) pumping station, where it is seen here as *Belvedere*. Following the end of its time at this site, the locomotive migrated across the Thames Estuary to Rainham Rubbish Shoot where it was scrapped in 1939. The original tank-mounted take-off for the feed pump water inlet (and its associated piping) has been removed, and it is not clear from this view where the relevant components have been replaced, although the piping for the pump 'flood' valve is still visible. (*Greenwich Heritage Centre*)

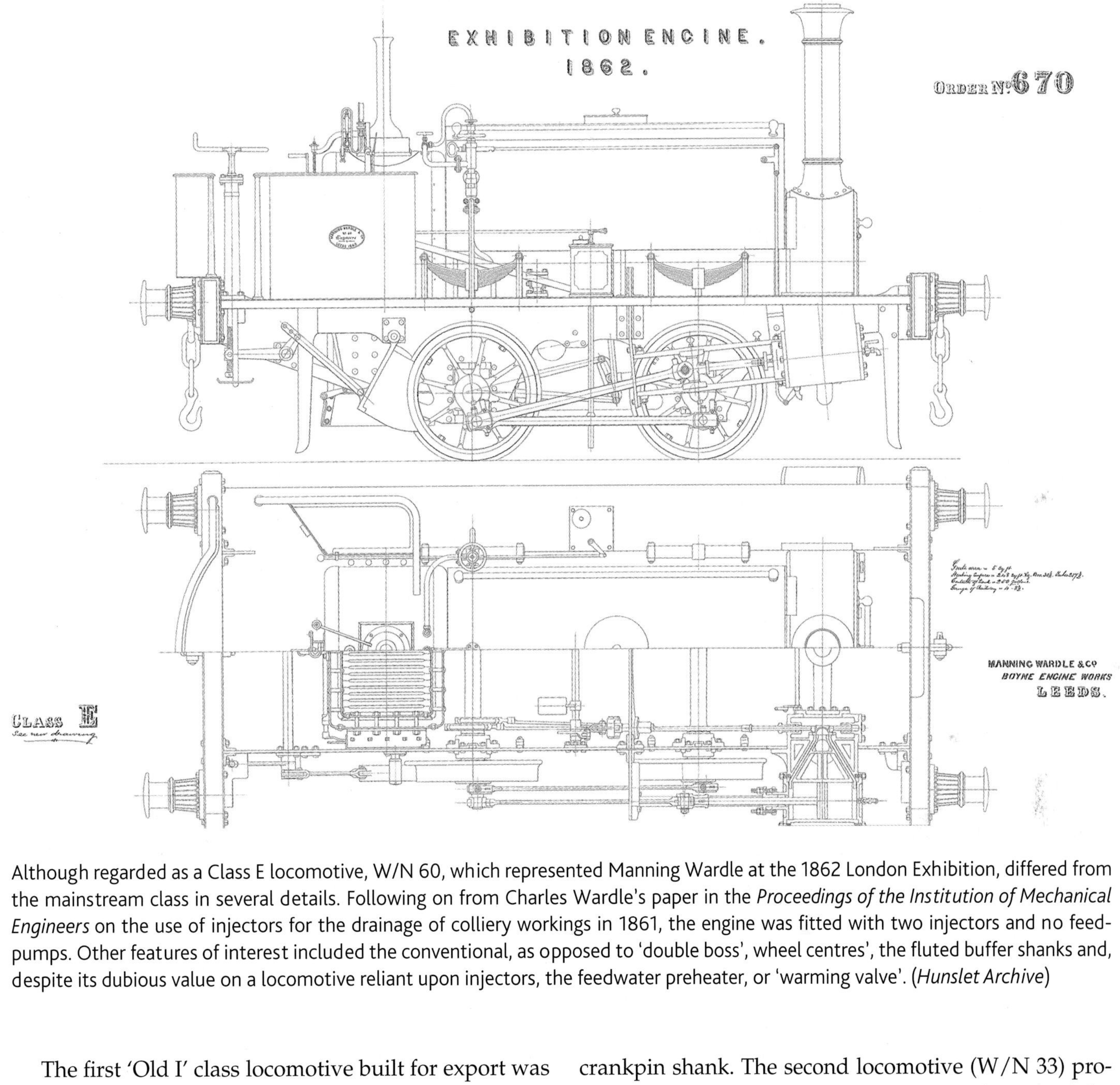

Although regarded as a Class E locomotive, W/N 60, which represented Manning Wardle at the 1862 London Exhibition, differed from the mainstream class in several details. Following on from Charles Wardle's paper in the *Proceedings of the Institution of Mechanical Engineers* on the use of injectors for the drainage of colliery workings in 1861, the engine was fitted with two injectors and no feed-pumps. Other features of interest included the conventional, as opposed to 'double boss', wheel centres', the fluted buffer shanks and, despite its dubious value on a locomotive reliant upon injectors, the feedwater preheater, or 'warming valve'. (*Hunslet Archive*)

The first 'Old I' class locomotive built for export was one of a pair constructed under Order No. 530 of W/N 32 *Pioneer*. This engine was 'sent away' on 20 September 1861 and was shipped all the way to Sydney to the order of the contractor Brassey & Ballard. Significant design modifications were made at this stage. It is not clear why wrought iron wheel centres were preferred for this locomotive over the standard pattern: it may be that they offered better ventilation in the New South Wales climate against overheating axleboxes but this would have been restricted by the enlargement of the 'thickening up' necessitated by the enlargement of the area around the crankpin shank. The second locomotive (W/N 33) produced under Order No. 530 incorporated some of the modifications found on W/N 32, but not the wrought iron wheels, or (apparently) the cast iron eccentric straps. Two of the four locomotives built under Order No. 920 were described as 'same as No. 35' but possessed 11in diameter cylinders. These were W/Ns 65 & 67 and apart from their cylinder dimensions, they incorporated certain refinements found on the first class member to be built with '12 inch' cylinders (to be described). The third locomotive built under Order No. 1320 marked an interesting departure in the 'Old I' story in that it retained the

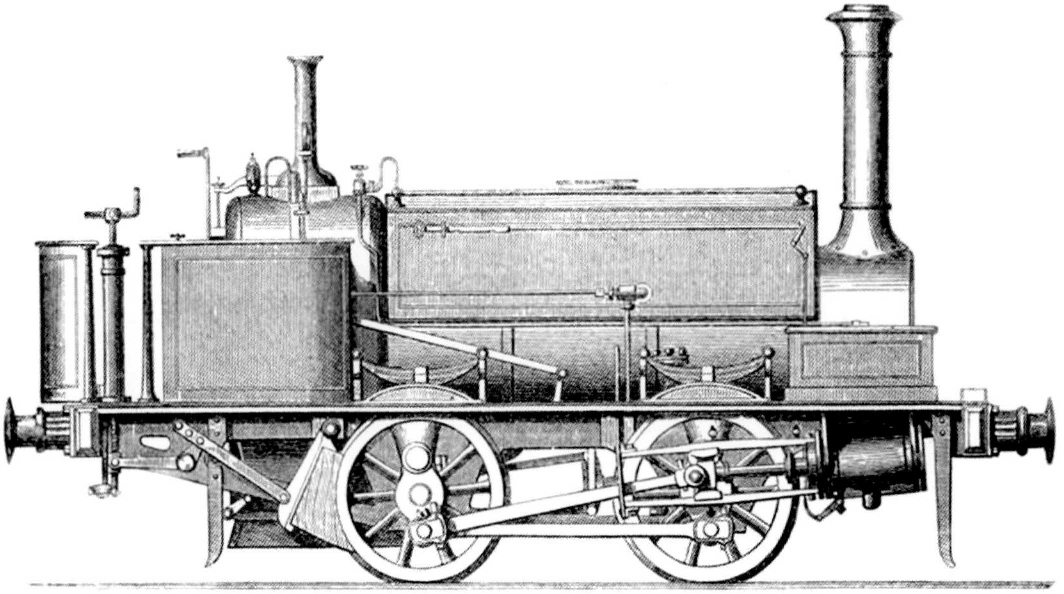

This engraving shows the 'E' class as depicted in the 1862 Exhibition Catalogue and shows important differences from the General Arrangement Drawing of W/N 60, notably in the use of shallower mainframes and bufferbeams, and also the need for splashers. (*Author's Collection*)

This Works Photograph of W/N 226 of 1867 illustrates the characteristics of the early 'E' class locomotive well, including the angular corners to the tank; the 'warming valve'; 'double boss' wheel centres with circular section spokes; 'shovel'-pattern rear steps and a single pair of sandboxes located between the axles. Note also the fire-iron support brackets on the top of the tank and the 'stovepipe' chimney. This locomotive was very long-lived, surviving until 1951, although it spent all of its working life in the North West of England. (*Hunslet Archive*)

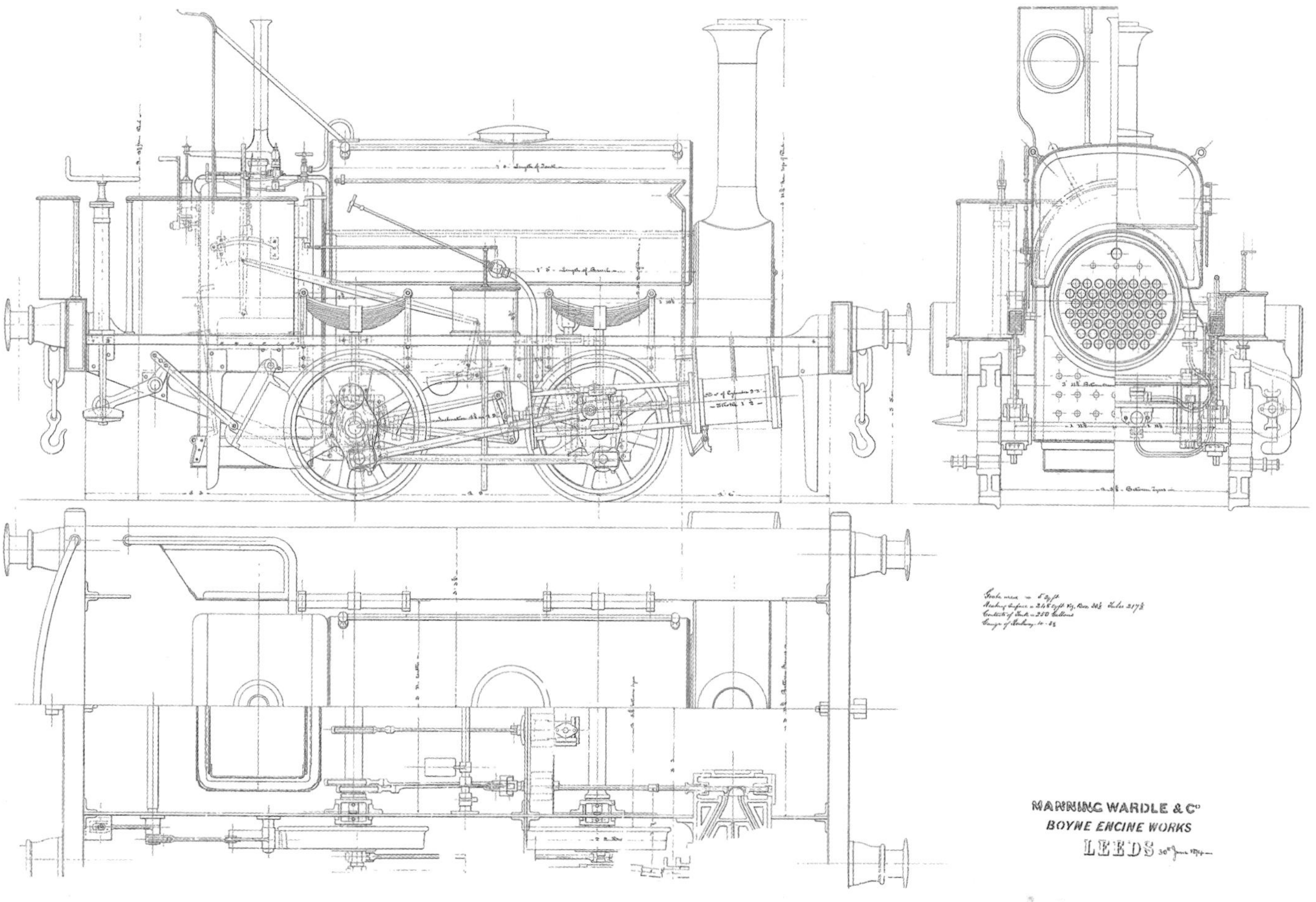

The mainstream Class 'E' specification is depicted in this drawing dated 30 June 1874 which sadly has suffered considerable damage over time, particularly in the vicinity of the right hand cylinder and associated external motion. (*Hunslet Archive*)

original '11 inch' cylinder dimension but was built to the Russian standard gauge of 5ft and supplied to Messrs Peto & Betts in Riga (Latvia), bearing the No. 1 and leaving the Boyne Engine Works on 9 March 1864 as W/N 117. It, and the seven succeeding locomotives supplied by Manning Wardle to this destination, were used in the construction of the Dunaberg & Witespek Railway. Sister engine W/N 105 was described by the makers as:

> 'Old Class I Alt. Same as No. 33 but with alterations necessary for 5ft gauge viz: frames, footplating; spring links; hornblocks; wheels and axles; compensating beam brackets & brake arrangement; wheel centre boss thickened on inside. Leading and trailing axles 4 ¼in diameter in journals. 4in in the middle; driving axle 4 ¾in diameter in journals with crank bearing and axle middle diameter 5in (the standard adopted, as with the design of eccentrics and connecting rods, for the 'K' class as at May 1878). Firebox depth reduced to 3ft 5in from crown plate to base on all class members henceforth.'

Work on this railway must have proceeded fairly speedily as Beyer, Peacock & Co. was to supply 0-6-0 goods locomotives for its day-to-day operation during the following year. On 4 May 1865, W/N 162 *Driver* was despatched under Order No. 1940 for shipment to the Auckland & Drury Railway Co. in New Zealand. This locomotive was put into storage after approximately eighteen months' work when construction work on the A&DR ceased and sold in 1871 to the Bay of Islands Coal Co. at Kawakawa, where it was put to stationary use in 1877 following conversion of the Coal Co.'s railway to 3ft 6in gauge in 1875. It was last noted at Kawakawa Colliery in this capacity circa 1893, although its boiler and saddle tank *may* have crossed the Tasman Sea for use in a stationary engine at Wallarah Colliery, Catherine

This 'E' class locomotive was despatched new to the contractor R.T. Relf at Okehampton on 15 March 1876 as W/N 594 *Pioneer*. It ultimately came into L&SWR ownership as *No.* 407 later 0407 on the Duplicate List. It is seen here, exhibiting the alterations made by its final owner, awaiting scrapping at Eastleigh Works in 1921. (*Real Photographs Ltd.*)

Hill Bay in NSW. A sister engine to *Driver*, *Auckland* was supplied to the Auckland & Drury Railway Co. on 9 October 1866 as W/N 201 with wrought iron wheels, two Giffard injectors, a special canopy and the general design modifications associated with W/N 192 (to be described) and this engine was used by the successor contractor Brogden & Sons to complete the line to 3ft 6in gauge in 1872-4, having arrived too late for the first phase of construction. It then followed *Driver* to Kawakawa for a mere year's ordinary service thereafter being converted to a stationary engine for use by Scotty's Hauraki Gold Mining Co., Coromandel District, NZ, where it was reported idle until 1909. If one takes the maker's Engine Book details at face value, then the next locomotive to be described basically as the 'same as No. 33', but presumably with the 3ft 5in firebox, is of vital importance. W/N 165 was supplied on 22 June 1865 under Order No. 1990 as *Yaxley* to Messrs Brassey & Ballard at Ampthill in Bedfordshire for construction work on the 'Midland Main Line' from St. Pancras. This locomotive was described by the makers as, 'the same as No. 33 but with one injector and one pump, brake on four wheels, two dampers to ashpan and four washout plugs in smokebox.' This observation is important for two reasons; firstly early surviving illustrations of '11 inch' locomotives W/Ns 16 18, and 57 and '12 inch' locomotive W/N 52 show that these locomotives were built with brakes acting on the rear axle only, and this would appear to have been the early standard for the class, a 'throwback' to the Wilson 0-4-0ST locomotive supplied to Dursley! Secondly, and taken at face value, *Yaxley* would appear to have been the first 'Old I' class locomotive to have been built with an injector, which would have replaced the left hand feed pump that would otherwise have been fitted. Authenticated photographic evidence appears to back this proposition up, but given that injectors had made their first appearance on a Manning Wardle locomotive well before this date, it is perhaps surprising that *Yaxley* was the first 'Old I' so fitted from new. W/Ns 172, 174, 177 and 178 (respectively built under Order Nos. 2150, 2130 and two under Order No. 2200) were all built for contractors and the first two of these were fitted with block buffers for earth wagons – these were normally fitted in addition to conventional buffers. W/N 192 of 22 March 1866, *Christiana* incorporated certain detail alterations, namely:

> '… first engine with corner irons in firebox shell rather than flanging the plates. Firebox shell and smokebox standard with 'K' (April 1878). Tubes 78, 2″ diameter [the 'Old I' standard]. Axle boxes same as present 'K'. Driving journals same as leading and trailing; wheels, crankpins, coupling rods and motion same as present 'K' (April 1878).'

This 'E' class locomotive, Works No. 962, was built in 1885 for the abortive Suakin-Berber Railway Campaign in Sudan under General Sir Gerald Graham. This was commenced following the assassination of General Gordon in Khartoum on 28 January 1885 and it was intended to construct a railway of approximately 280 miles (including non-linear portions and sidings) from the Red Sea Port of Suakin to the Nile Port of Berber, some 220 miles distant. In the event, the project ran into severe difficulties owing to the hostility of the terrain and the local rebel forces and the Secretary of State For War, Lord Hartington, decided to withdraw from conflict In the Sudan on 20 April, ordering General Graham to cease work on the railway at Otao, approximately 20 miles from Suakin, five days later. On 29 May, the staff of the contractors, Lucas & Aird Ltd. (a major customer of Manning Wardle at this stage) set sail for England. No. 962 was returned from Suakin and was initially stored at a depot within the Royal Arsenal's territory on Plumstead Marshes. From here, it was transferred to the Chattenden & Upnor Military Railway in Kent where this photograph was taken, probably at Upnor during the early 1890s. The improvised passenger train appears to contain a mixture of uniformed military personnel and munitions workers in protective clothing. At this stage, two gauges were in use on the Chattenden & Upnor Railway, but by the time of 'handover' from the Royal Engineers to the Admiralty (officially in 1906), the C. & U. was a solely 2ft 6in gauge railway. No. 962 may have played a constructional role in the Chattenden Naval Tramway from Chattenden Barracks to Sharnal Street Station on the SE&CR's Hundred of Hoo Branch (opened in 1901), but by 1907 the locomotive was part of Royal Arsenal Railways' stock, being named *Lord Roberts*. It was scrapped within the Arsenal in 1916.

Some details were of a 'retro', nature, however as the description continued, 'eccentrics, connecting rods, crossheads old '11 inch' style same as Engine No. 4, also two pumps'; by this stage a non-standard feature: presumably no injector was fitted. After passing into the heads of another contractor, J. Mackay in the early 1870s as *Christopher*, this locomotive ended up as Rumanian State Railways 04. The longest-lived 'Old I'

E' class 0-4-0ST W/N 1135 *Annie* (21 April 1890) was another contractor's locomotive, the original customer being J. Mackay at Maidenhead. The engine is seen here the worse for wear with S. Pearson & Sons Ltd. at this company's East London warehouse, Walthamstow, having previously been owned by another contractor, Penthink Bros. Features to note include the leading ends of the mainframes, which extend above running board level between the leading bufferbeam and the leading spring hanger (necessitating modifications to the smokebox design); the rail washing gear Actuated by the rod behind the injector steam feed); the Roscoe pattern lubricators; the brackets on the tank for the fire irons; the valences over the upper parts of the leading wheelsets; the brake linkage with the brake hangers pivoted about their lower ends; the weatherboard braced by struts fixed to the tank and the dual block and conventional buffers. Damage to the locomotive caused by 'rough handling' is visible to the cylinder cladding, waist sheets, step and head and tail lamps. (*J. A. Peden Collection*)

class locomotive of any description was W/N 241 supplied under Order No. 3270 on 4 January 1868 *Thorncliffe* to Newton Chambers & Co., Thorncliffe Ironworks in Yorkshire. This locomotive kept Boyne Engine Works busy with a string of spares orders including no less than three for new cylinders (No. 26899 of April 1888, customer's design; No. 58428 of 9 December 1905, and No. 80424 of 6 March 1920), no less than five for new axles: No. 38285 of 10 March 1896 - complete set; 55071 of 11 August 1904 – crank axle only; No. 63921 of 8 March 1909 – leading and trailing plus associated crankpins; No. 82980 of 1 December 1922 – crank axle plus special eccentric and straps, and finally a complete leading wheelset, wheel diameter 3ft 0¾in on tread, by Kitson & Co on 21 February 1928. In Addition to these, a new Best Yorkshire Iron boiler with copper firebox and brass tubes was fitted under Order No. 66291 of 26 January 1911 and new motion parts (contemporary class 'K' pattern) under Order No. 55579 of 13 May 1904. In the event, *Thorncliffe* became the only true 'Old I' to survive into the 1950s, albeit only briefly and much modified following a rebuild by Hudswell Clarke in 1932.

As early as 1861, an important dichotomy emerges in the 'Old I' story: in order to increase the power output of these locomotives, it was decided to increase the cylinder diameter to 12in on the two class members, produced under Order No. 590. These locomotives, W/Ns 35 of 14 December 1861 *Pioneer* and 36 *Whixall* of 29 January

W/N 1369 of 1897 *Princess* was supplied new to the contractor William Mousley in North Walsham, Norfolk and when sold by this user passed to Thomas Wrigley, who hired the locomotive out to various industrial users. Being a relatively late member of the class, the design has undergone several modifications when compared with W/N 226 including a weatherscreen; stronger mainframes; steel plate bufferbeams; Ramsbottom safety valves; brakes to all wheels (with cast iron blocks); rail washing gear, and 'oval' section wheel spokes. The fitting of cabs to the class did not become a standard feature until 1902, whilst circular smokebox doors were never fitted from new as standard for this class.

1862 were both built for the contractor Thomas Savin, the former going to Merthyr Tydfil for construction work on the Brecon & Merthyr Railway and the latter to Whitchurch for similar duties in relation to the Oswestry, Ellesmere and Whitchurch Railway. Savin's motivation in requesting the increased cylinder diameter would appear to have been a requirement for greater tractive effort as this would have increased, theoretically at least, by a factor of 144/121 or approximately 1.19 over the locomotives with 11 inch cylinders. Further examples of what may be termed the 'pure' 'Old I class' with 12 inch cylinders soon followed, with the last example, W/N 155 *Stoneyway* was supplied to Brassey and Ballard at Dunstable on 28 February 1865. Amongst the '12 inch' 'Old I' class locomotives, perhaps the best-known example was W/N 50 originally delivered to J.T. Leather (Waterloo Main Colliery) on 20 June 1862. This locomotive was sold in February 1872 to the contractor Robert T. Relf for work on the construction of the Okehampton-Lydford contract of the L&SWR, passing into the ownership of the latter company at the end of 1879. Under L&SWR ownership, *Lady Portsmouth* as the engine became, received the number 392 and was engaged on several miscellaneous duties, including a short period on the Bodmin & Wadebridge Railway, and spells on loan to the Lee-on-Solent Light Railway between 1897 and the latter line's takeover by the L&SWR in 1909. *Lady Portsmouth* was renumbered 0392 in the Duplicate List during the early years of the twentieth century and around this time appears to have received disc wheels. It was withdrawn by the L&SWR in December 1913 and sold to Bute Works Supply Co. Ltd. two months later, being re-sold in May 1914 to Lt. Col.

This 'F' class 0-4-0ST was supplied in May 1881 to the South Eastern Railway for shunting at Folkstone. It underwent several sundry alterations over the years, including the fitting of a cab during a 1904 rebuild and it ended its days working at the Southern Railway's Meldon Quarry prior to withdrawal for scrapping in 1938. This photograph was taken at Meldon close to the end of the engine's career. (*John Scott-Morgan Collection*)

Works Number 1057 of 1888 was an 'F' originally built for the contractor T.A. Walker as *Massey* for construction work on the Manchester Ship Canal. Upon completion of this work, the locomotive was sold to the Wantage Tramway as its No.7. This view, taken at Wantage circa 1900 shows several details well, such as the relatively good standard of turn-out when compared with later photographs, the 'dished' lift-up smokebox door, the lamp-irons, the tie-rod for the sandbox linkage, the rail washing gear and the original additions made to the skimpy weatherboard. (*John Scott-Morgan Collection*)

W.T. Co. No.7 is seen here at Wantage circa 1920 as evidenced by the 'post-First World War' standard of turnout and the fact that the passenger service appears to still be operating – it was discontinued in 1925. By way of contrast with the previous photograph, the right hand side of the locomotive is shown, enabling further details to be discerned, such as the reversing lever, rear sanding control, steam take-offs for whistle and blower, water cock and clack valve for the feed pump, and, in clearer resolution that the pervious view, the brake linkage. (*John Scott-Morgan Collection*)

Holman F. Stephens, according to the Order Book, for use on the Shropshire & Montgomeryshire Railway. The Order Book then shows (unsurprisingly given the unsuitability of the S&MR for tank locomotives) its next home to have been another Stephens line, the Weston, Clevedon & Portishead Railway. At this stage, it is worth referring to the Maker's Engine Book:

> 'When repaired under Order No. 72440 [January 1916] this engine had a new best mild steel boiler complete flanged plates instead of corner irons. New steel fire box riveted in with steel rivets. New smoke box with door and fittings complete. The boiler was raised 6in higher than original. New steel tubes, 70 of these were supplied by them and 7 taken from stock … New Ramsbottom safety valves with cast steel seating and cast iron casing. New steel plate chimney. Steel plate motion bracket, steel plate stay in front of fire box shell. Stiffening plate at leading end of frames. New leading rail guards. There is a vacuum brake on this engine not fitted by us. We fitted a new hand brake, with cast steel hangers and cast iron blocks. Fitted with new leading and trailing sandboxes…cock gear details altered … There is an Avonside Co. injector on the left hand side and a Gresham & Cravens No. 8 injector on the right hand side. These injectors were not supplied by us … The following parts of the engine are not of our make and are different to ours. Wheels, axles, axleboxes, coupling rods, crank pins, buffers, injectors, footsteps, and cab. The clack boxes are our oldest style. The springs are class 'K' 10-plate kind. The coupling rods have round eyes.'

By the late 1930s further additions to the cab of W.T. Co. No.7 had been made as evidenced by this view of the locomotive outside the Locomotive Shed at Wantage. The final 21 years of operation were freight only and after closure the engine passed to the dealer T. Adams of Newport in South Wales. (*John Scott-Morgan Collection*)

T. Adams re-sold Works Number 1057 to a local customer, Cordes Steel Mills of Newport where it is seen circa 1960 in this view. Little modification appeared to have taken place since the sale, although the front left hand buffer appears to have sustained damage. In 1962, the engine was offered to the Kent & East Sussex Railway for the princely sum of £80, but sadly the offer was declined, a tragic decision not only in the light of the locomotive's 'celebrity' status, but also in the fact that a sister engine ran on a Colonel Stephens Railway. (*John Scott-Morgan Collection*)

At this stage, the former *Lady Portsmouth* became *Hecate* and received a royal blue livery with black and white lining but whatever Stephens' plans for this engine on the WC&PR, they were to be in vain and shortly afterwards, it was sold to the War Department for use at Tidworth Camp. Spares continued to be supplied from Leeds until Order No. 86157 (18 October 1926 – a new copper steam pipe, 6in longer than old class 'K' to cater for the raised boiler pitch), which would have been made by Kitson & Co. This case history illustrates the challenges faced by the maker in overhauling a relatively old locomotive that had received alterations elsewhere. *Hecate* was noted out of use at Tidworth Station in April 1929 and again at George Cohen & Sons depot at Neath in December 1933, being advertised for sale and disappearing shortly afterwards.

In all, there were thirty-nine 'official' standard gauge '11 inch' 'Old I' class locomotives built basically to the same pattern as W/N 4 with relatively small detail differences. To this must be added W/N 543, the rebuilt W/N 30 as previously described and the eight 5ft gauge examples.

The '12 inch' locomotives amounted to twenty-four officially new units, all standard gauge, to which must be added W/N 709, a renewal of W/N 80 carried out under Order No. 13950 and delivered on 15 November 1882 to contractor J.T. Capell, later becoming L&SWR No. 458 *Jumbo* but only lasting until scrapped in April 1897. At this point is should be observed that '11 inch' and '12 inch' 'Old I' class members were sometimes built under the same Order Nos., also specimens of standard and 5ft gauge, and, as will be seen later, locomotives with differing wheelbase dimensions.

This head-on view of Works Number 1057 emphasizes the diminutive proportions of the locomotive in relation to the track gauge and also shows up details of the leading tank handrail, smokebox door and cylinder/steam chest assemblies well. The poor weather conditions in Newport on that day will also be noted! (*John Scott-Morgan Collection*)

An offshoot from the 'Old I' class was created by the fitting of 3ft 6in rather than 3ft coupled wheels and this first occurred with W/N 235 *General Flores*. This was described as: 'same as 192 [i.e. with 11in by 17in cylinders] with the following alterations: wrought iron wheels 3ft 6in diameter, canopy, new brake arrangement, footplate, bufferbeams and rail guards.' This locomotive was built for the first railway in Uruguay and was sent away on 23 June 1867. It was to be the first of seven locomotives built to the same set of ruling dimensions for one country and effectively represented a 'withered arm' of 'Old I' class evolution that lived on as part of the makers' product policy for over two decades after the cessation of construction of officially new class members for other customers. A repeat of W/N 235 was supplied under Order No. 4970 as W/N 300 *Canelones*, differing from its precursor by virtue of being provided with a canopy weather-screen at the leading end. W/N 1045 was despatched on 12 December 1887 under Order No. 26200 via Liverpool to become North East of Uruguay Railway No. 1 and was described by the makers thus:

> 'Special inside cylinder locomotive similar to Engine No. 300 but with the latest improvements requested by the customer ... Engine in many

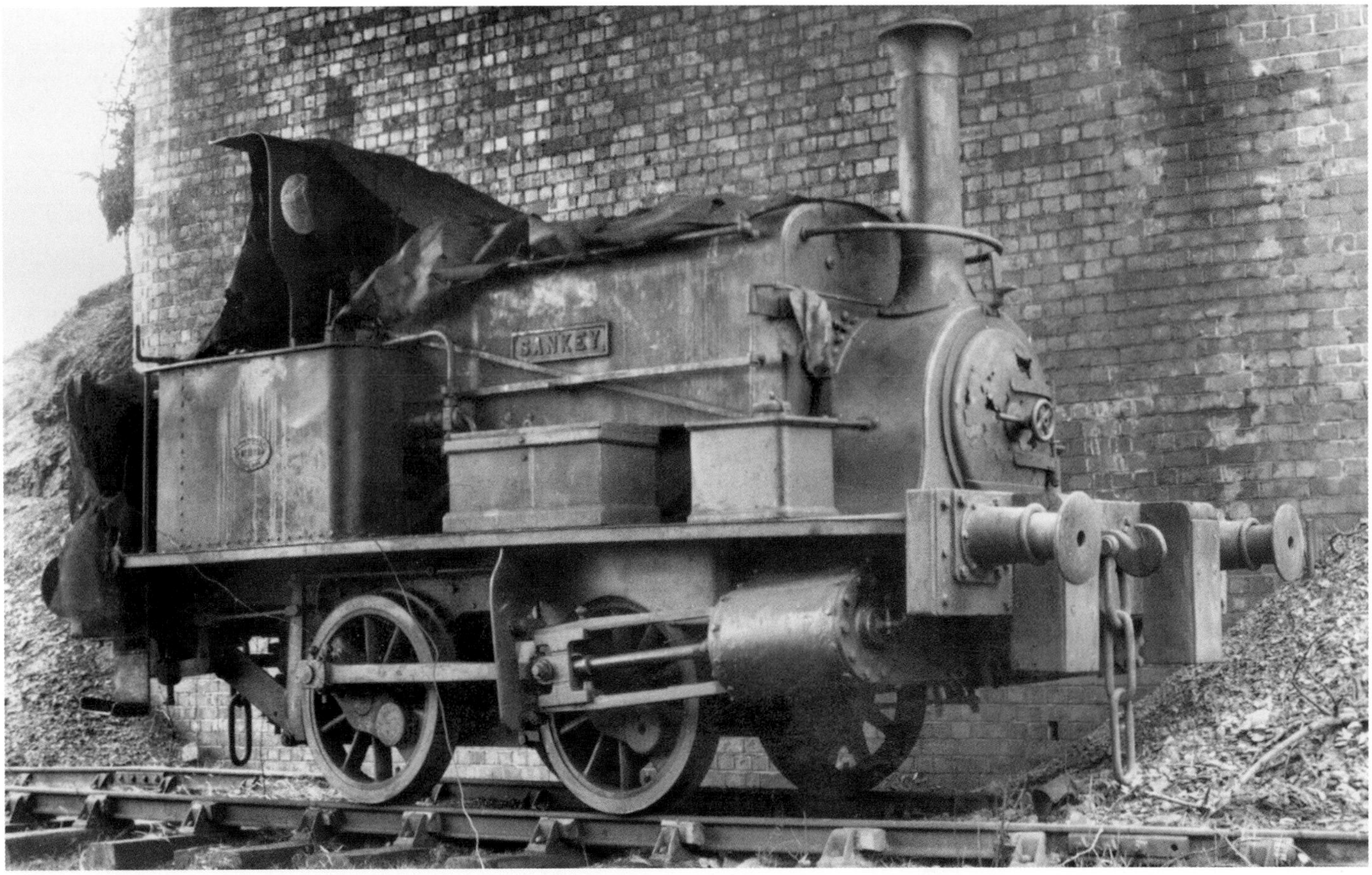

Massey's sister engine, *Sankey* (Works Number 1088 of 1888) was another T.A. Walker locomotive built for work on the Manchester Ship Canal and it passed through the hands of the contractors S. Pearson & Son and Topham, Jones and Railton before being acquired in 1919 by the Edge Hill Light Railway in Warwickshire. This line, engineered by Lt. Col. Holman F. Stephens, only saw operation between 1922 and 1925 but *Sankey* remained stored out of use under a bridge until scrapped by James Friswell & Co. of Banbury in 1946. Certain detail differences from *Massey* are visible in the photograph, notably the circular side-hinged smokebox door fitted in 1915 (suffering from corrosion in this view) and the additional block buffers for moving earth wagons. Today, only a nameplate from the engine survives, preserved in the Colonel Stephens Museum at Tenterden. (*John Scott-Morgan Collection*)

respects like ordinary class 'K': short 'K' boiler, also crankpins, coupling rod brasses, motion, springs and spring gear: axle boxes all 6½in length, 4¼in diameter [bore]; frames, smoke box, chimney barrel and tank corners all steel, slide valves 7in long; cow catchers, special wrought iron spring buffers, special wrought iron spring buffers, special drawgear. Roscoe lubricator connected to steam pipe and one Furniss lubricator on each side of smoke box connected to cylinders. Large American headlamp and two tail lamps, two [water] gauge and one hand lamp – all lamps except head lamp to be of Central Uruguayan pattern (supplied by Linley & Co. of Birmingham), headlamp as Order No. 16100 [makers' pattern].'

What had evolved was a specification with its dimensional characteristics basically from the 'Old I' class, its constructional characteristics based on the 'K' class as per late 1880s, and its details, including wheel diameter, dictated by customer requirements. Two locomotives built under Order No. 28420 (W/Ns 1148-9 sent away on 29 October 1889) again via Liverpool but by this stage the North Eastern Railway of Uruguay had been formally leased by the Central Railway and was regarded as an extension of the latter. The locomotives thus assumed the identities E7N and E8N. They differed from W/N 1045 mainly by means of the fitting of a vacuum brake for passenger working, although other detail differences were present. The final pair of locomotives belonging to this group were W/Ns 1197-8. These were

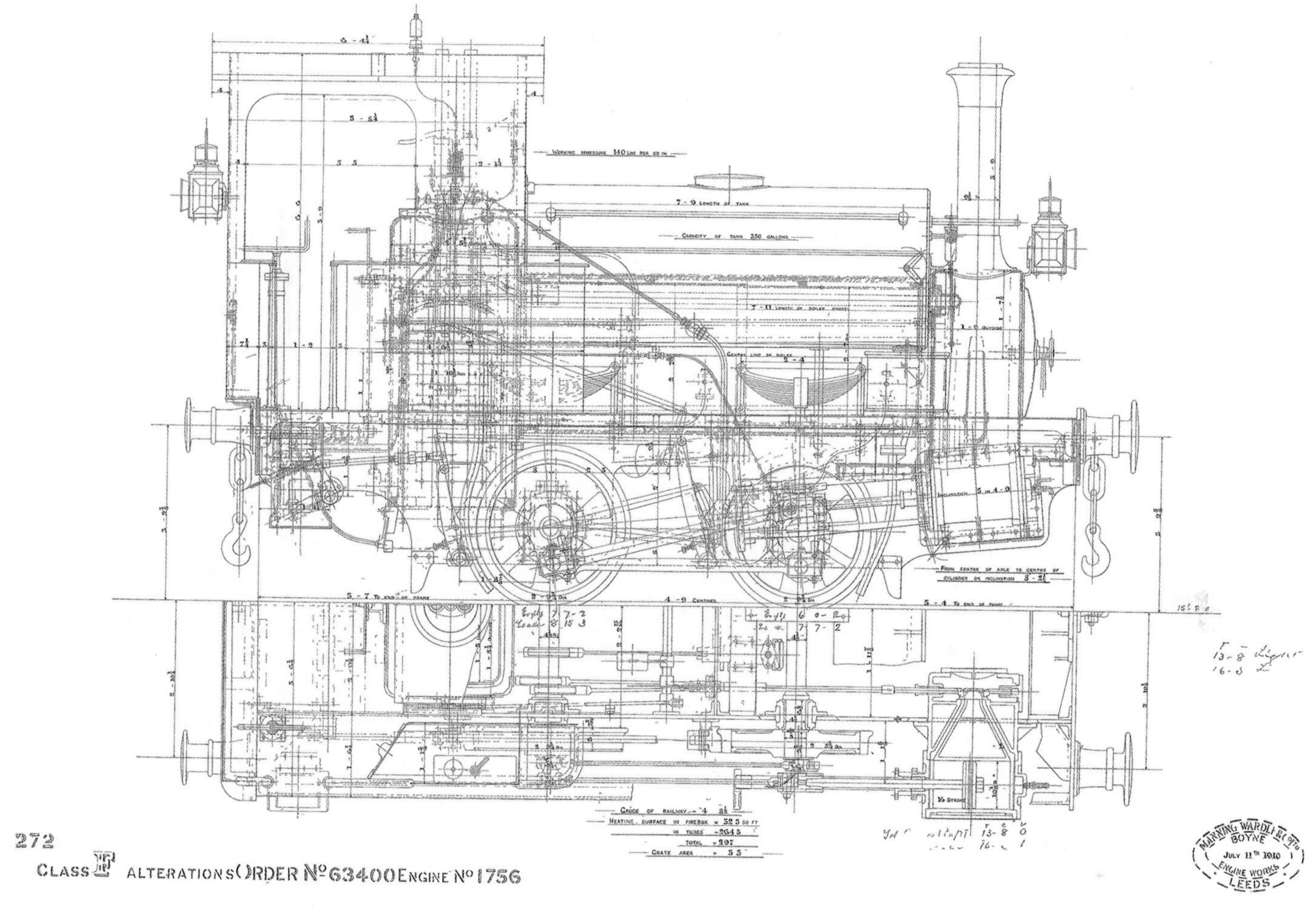

This drawing of W/N 1756 of 1912 shows the 'F' class in relatively late form with standard cab; re-designed mainframes; one-piece cast iron chimney; circular smokebox door with reinforcing strip on smokebox front and cylinders with aprons top and bottom. (*Hunslet Archive*)

sent away respectively on 22 September and 22 October 1890 being shipped via Liverpool and Buenos Aires to Montevideo. W/N 1197 carried the legend 'No. 1 Mercado Central de Frutos Del Uruguay'. With W/N 1198 being similarly adorned with the '1' replaced by a '2'. These locomotives were similar to W/Ns 1148-9 save for the fact that their crank axle wheelsets were flangeless, a new pattern of axlebox was provided and other minor detail alterations were made. More significantly certain materials tests were demanded by James Livesey & Son (who were possibly acting as agents), with the required test pieces being from the boiler (one from the barrel; one each from the wrapper and the leading tubeplate); the mainframes (one from each plate); two from steel plates (one ¼in thick and one ⅛in thick); copper plates (one piece for tensile strength and two bent pieces), whilst the springs and wheel centres had to be tested by the makers. It is pleasant to record that of the seven Uruguayan members of the wider 'Old I' dynasty, two are still extant, with W/N 1045 (latterly No. A.42 on the North Eastern section) on static display at Penarol Diesel Works, Montevideo and W/N 1198, which ended its operational career as No. 3 *La Mancera* with the National Port Authority in Montevideo being preserved in working order in the city.

The 'Old I' was succeeded in Manning Wardle product policy by the makers' most prolific standard class, the 'K'. Before further consideration of the mainstream class members in detail, the process that drove this transition needs to be outlined. Whilst the adoption of a 12in rather than 11in cylinder diameter on the mainstream (or 'Ordinary', as the makers termed it) 'K' class would seem an obvious move, the lengthening of the rear portion of the wheelbase by 6in with a corresponding

The last 'F' class locomotive built at the Boyne Engine Works was W/N 2044, originally supplied on 8 February 1926 for use at what became R. Leggot Ltd.'s Chalk Quarries near Barton-on-Humber. The engine ended its days with W.R. Cunis Ltd. at Rainham where it is seen here out of use on 26 October 1957 prior to scrapping during the following year. In common with an earlier class member, W/N 1962, it was built with mainframes of rectangular profile and block buffers only. It also exhibits many of the later constructional features associated with the class including the smokebox reinforcing strap supporting the final pattern of circular door; the cylinders with aprons both above and below, and the brake blocks acting on all wheels, which have conventional 'single boss' centres. A World War One-pattern 'Austerity' cab has also been fitted. (*John Scott-Morgan Collection*)

increase in boiler barrel length, the defining difference between the two classes, would not. In order to understand why this happened, one must refer to the makers' description of the first of the 'transition' locomotives, W/N 72, produced under Order No. 1020 and exported on 18 March 1863 to Sydney to the order of the contractor Tooth & Mort. The description of this engine as built stated:

> 'Same as No. 35 but stroke increased to 19in, boiler barrel 7ft 9in long, [also 84 tubes 1⅞in diameter but this fact confirmed by the entry under W/N 163]; wheelbase 5ft 5in plus 5ft 4in; special frames; smoke box, cylinders, feed pumps, tank, compensating beams, boiler brackets and footplates.'

The significant point to note here is that by early 1863, the manufacturer's attention had turned seriously towards getting a better performance from locomotives built to the basic 'Crimea' specification (the appearance of the 'M' class was but a few weeks away). The question of the ideal boiler tube diameter for getting the best compromise between heat transmission and draughting (which, as we have seen, had made its presence felt at the Railway Foundry over a decade before) had resurfaced, and it was clearly felt that heat could be extracted more efficiently from the tubes by lengthening them, slightly reducing their diameter and in the process increasing the boiler water capacity. As a by-product of this process, the throatplate was moved further away from the middle axle allowing for an increased

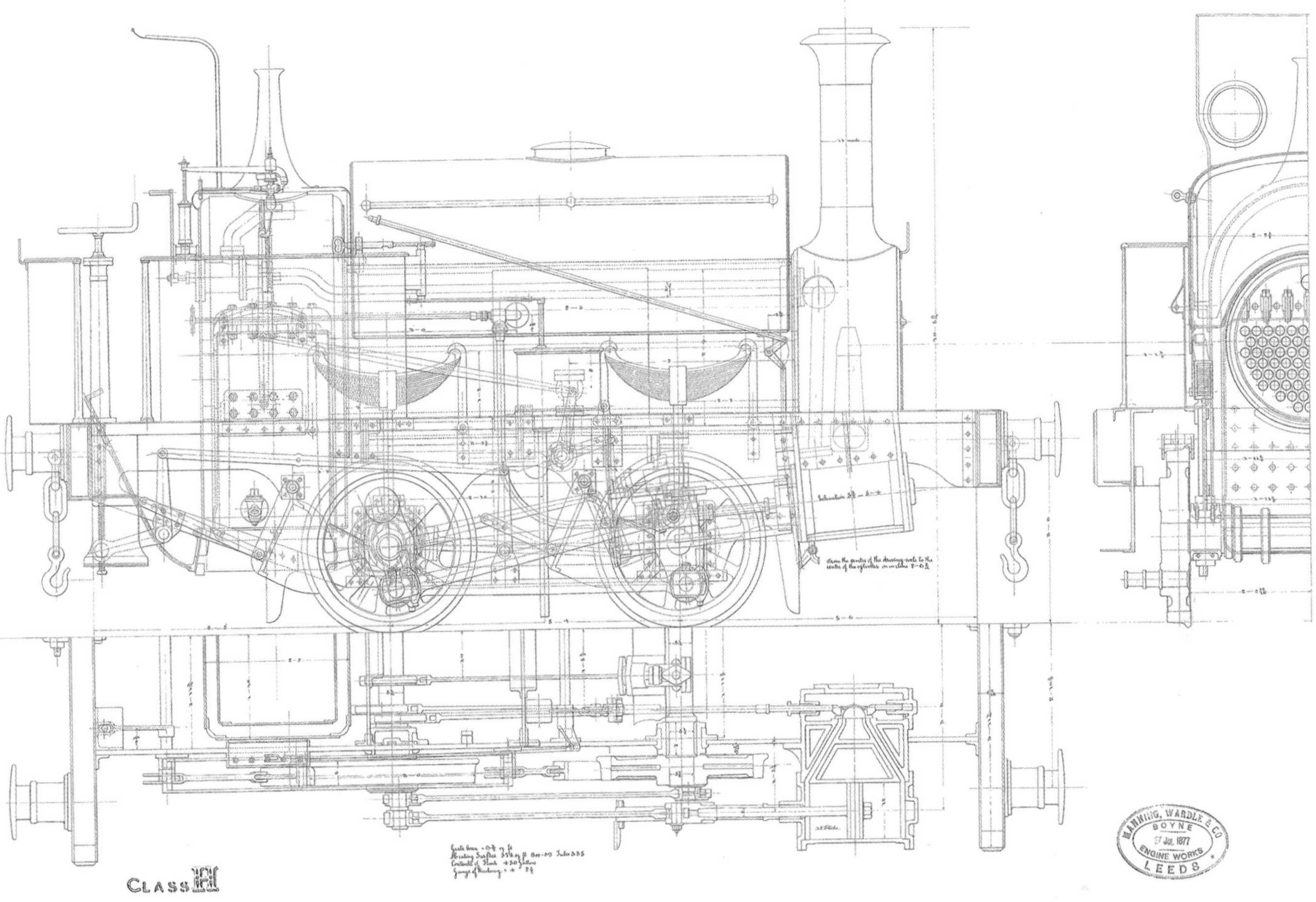

7

The design of the early standard 'H' class is illustrated to advantage in this drawing dated 27 July 1877 and it makes an interesting comparison with late surviving 'celebrity' W/N 345 of 1871. The side elevation indicates the presence at this stage of the early lift-up pattern of smokebox door but sadly the injector (on the right hand side) is not shown. (*Hunslet Archive*)

cylinder stroke, hence the increase of this dimension to 19 inches. A sister engine was constructed under order No. 1950 as W/N 163, departing from Leeds on 8 July 1865, once again to the order of Tooth & Mort. Identical to the earlier locomotive in all respects, save for the fact that it was described as 'the first 'K' with 78 2in tubes', it was still in substance a transitional locomotive with its non-standard cylinder stroke. The next stage in the story was something of a backward step in that the three locomotives concerned were described as, 'Same as No. 33 except boiler barrel 7ft 9in long, same as present class "K"; 84 tubes 1⅞in diameter. Brass feed pumps.' A reversion to 11in by 17in cylinders had therefore taken place. These locomotives were all exported to New South Wales initially for use on the Government Railway's Blacktown-Richmond branch under Order No. 1180 as W/Ns 88 *Windsor* and 89 *Richmond* (sent away 29 August 1863 and arriving in March 1864) and 109 *Sydney*, which was sent away on 23 February 1864 and commenced service with the opening of the branch line on 29 November 1864. *Windsor* and *Richmond* were originally numbered 15 and 16 in the NSW list, but the latter locomotive was renumbered 14 around the time of *Sydney's* entry into service, with the new arrival becoming No. 16. In 1865, the locomotives became (in order of the W/Ns) 29, 31 and 30. A photograph exists of the former with wrought iron wheel centres having conventional spokes but these are not referred to in the maker's records and it appears that they were fitted in NSW as sister engine No. 31 had 'double boss' wheel centres throughout its life. All three class members later moved away from their original place of work and No. 30 was a

'H' class 0-4-0ST W/N 345 (3 March 1871) *Holmes* remained in iron industry-related employment throughout its long life, being originally supplied to Parkgate Ironstone Co. of Rotherham and passing the company's Charwelton Quarries circa 1930 and eventually to Pitsford Ironstone Co., Northamptonshire around five years later as No. 2. The locomotive is shown here out of use in 25 September 1962, still retaining its lift-up smokebox door. When taken out of service in 1959 it was the oldest Manning Wardle locomotive in existence in the United Kingdom, if not the entire world, and its scrapping in January 1964 was an unforgivable act, particularly as the former Wantage Tramway Co. No. 7 (originally *Massey*) had been similarly lost a matter of weeks before. (*B. Webb*)

Parkgate Iron Co. No. 6 (W/N 740 of 1879) was another relatively long-lived locomotive still in service at its Rotherham base some seven decades after delivery. Although delivered substantially as an ordinary 'H' class locomotive, it had been adapted for a cut-down loading gauge by the time that this picture was taken. (*John Scott-Morgan Collection*).

relatively early casualty, being scrapped in 1890, whilst Nos. 29 and 31 became respectively Nos. 18 and 19 in the Public Works Department list and both were scrapped in 1923. Their design, amended to incorporate cast iron pumps and a special weather-screen, appeared on the home market under Order No. 1200 as W/N 92 *Earl Carlisle* on 27 October 1863 for the contractor T. Nelson on the Castleton & Grosmont Railway. Another variant of the design represented by W/Ns 88-9 and 109 was built under Order No. 1200 as W/N 90 and this was despatched on 22 September 1863 to J.T. Leather, Waterloo Main Colliery where it became No. 3. This unit had cast iron pumps, but unlike the NSWGR locomotives it had 12in by 17in cylinders. A similar locomotive was built under the same Order No. as W/N 93 *Black Park Colliery* No. 1 for Stott, Milne & Co. of Chirk, being despatched on the same day as W/N 92. A *short* boiler with 78 tubes of 2 in diameter was supplied under Order No. 20264, apparently in 1883. This would have required certain detail modifications, for instance a shorter water tank, but given that there was no difference between the leading portion of the wheelbase of the 'Old I' and 'K' classes, the fitting of a boiler of the former dimensions to a chassis of the latter ones would have been perfectly feasible, although the same would not have been true for the reverse course of action.

The next stage in the transitional phase between the 'Old I' and 'K' classes came with W/N 110 supplied under

On 2 January 1871, Gjers, Mills & Co. of Ayresome Ironworks, Middlesbrough took delivery of the first of its six 'H' class locomotives. This locomotive, *Ayresome* No. 2, was soon returned to the makers, being re-sold to Topham, Jones & Railton before ending its career at Round Oak Steelworks, by whom it was renamed *Langland*, rebuilt in 1899 and scrapped at some stage after October 1922. This variation of the 'H' class was built with 3ft. 6 in. wheels and various detail differences from the class 'norm'. The photograph shows W/N 777 of 1881 *Ayresome* No. 5 at Aycliffe Line & Limestone Co. and apart from the larger-than-standard wheels, points to note are the canopy supported by a leading weatherboard and rear stanchions (an arrangement common on four coupled Manning Wardle designs between the 1880s and the First World War) and the special cast steel 'oblique oblong' dumb buffers, which were also found on the maker's 3ft 10in gauge products for the Low Moor Iron Co. (*The late Ken Cooper*)

This locomotive, W/N 905 of 1884, spent its known working life in London's Docklands prior to being put up for sale by the Port of London Authority in 1920. Despite receiving spares from the makers in that year, no further revenue-earning service is known for the engine. (*John Scott-Morgan Collection*)

This 'H' class 0-4-0ST (W/N 1413 of 1 September 1898) was supplied to John Aird & Co. being intended for work in Egypt. Instead, it is put to work at the rather less exotic location of Millom in Cumberland (now Cumbria) and it is believed to have been photographed here at this location. The engine is seen here surrounded by all of the paraphernalia associated with its contractor's duties, namely the earth wagons, the temporary track on which it is standing, and, of course, the navvies and their tools. The simple 'wrap over' weather-board, although not unusual for a locomotive of this particular era, may have been fitted with the engine's original planned destination in mind. (*Author's Collection*)

This locomotive began life as W/N 1619 of 1904 *Mornington* and was built for service on Purfleet Wharf in Essex. This concern had also purchased a similar but slightly older locomotive, W/N 1442 *Denmark* second-hand and when this latter locomotive was scrapped in 1934, it bequeathed its identity and some of its components to W/N 1619. As the new *Denmark*, this locomotive remained in use for over two further decades. (*John Scott-Morgan Collection*)

Order No. 1400 on9 March 1864 as Hucknall Colliery No. 1 to a Nottinghamshire colliery. The makers recorded:

> 'This is the first class 'K' engine. 12 inch by 17 inch cylinders; boiler barrel 7ft 9in by 2ft 9in Firebox 3ft 5in deep (as 106), axles, connecting rods, eccentrics as 105. Coupling rods and crankpins as 32 – same as present class 'K' [May 1878 – the first part of this latter assertion was of course subject to the rear wheelbase difference between the two classes].'

Although officially a 'K' class locomotive, it should be remembered that W/N 110 was still constructed with an 84-tube boiler with 1⅞in tubes as were W/Ns 126-7; 134; 140 (confusingly classified 'Old I' despite being 'same as No. 110');146-7 and 154, which was described as:

> '… boiler 'K' size 84 tubes 1 7/8in diameter; cylinders 11in by 17in; axles and coupling rods class 'K' pattern; ashpan with front and rear dampers; full set of cylinder cocks; special frames and brake arrangement; splashers, footplate and buffer beams; weather-screens front and back.'

Taking into account the descriptions of these locomotives, and the fact that W/N 163, although fitted with a 78 tube boiler, possessed non-standard 12in by 19in cylinders, W/Ns 72, 88-90, 92-3, 109-110, 126-7, 134, 140, 146-7,154 and 163, 16 units in all, can all be regarded as transitional locomotives between the 'Old I' and 'K' classes, being 'united' by a common 10ft 9in wheelbase and corresponding boiler length (as built), but not by boiler tube configuration or cylinder dimensions.

The first truly standard 'K' class locomotive was W/N 166 Shut End Works delivered under Order No. 1990 on 19 June 1865 to John Bradley & Co., Shut End Colliery where it was later renamed *Prince of Wales*. Despite not originally built for a contractor, the maker's records state that it was built with block buffers for earth wagons. Be that as it may, W/N 165 was sold to Braddock & Matthews for construction work on the L. & N.W.R. Dallow Lane Branch at Burton-On-Trent by 1880, for in March that year a new boiler 'same as present class "K"' was fitted, also a Diamond Canopy. This was the maker's term for the familiar sheet iron 'wrap-over' arrangement (first used on W/N 253 when new and much simpler in construction than the pillar-supported 'special canopy' found on other Manning Wardle products) that provided the cover for enginemen on many of its products, particularly during the last three decades of the nineteenth century. W/N 165 received new round cornered sandboxes on 19 February 1886 and another new boiler (Best Yorkshire Iron) in April 1897. After seeing service on the Bolton-Kenyon

This view shows the latter day domestically-based 'H' class locomotive W/N 1846 (29 April 1914) *Felspar* originally built for Shap Granite Co., Cumberland. This locomotive earned the distinction of twice passing through the hands of the dealer G. Cohen of Canning Town: firstly to British Portland Cement Co.'s works at West Thurrock in Essex, and then to Associated Portland Cement Co.'s works at Holborough, Kent circa 1939. The engine is seen in this view at Holborough on 24 March 1946 exhibiting features typical of one of the makers' standard 0-4-0STs of such a late date of construction, including later pattern (more substantial) mainframes with a leading stay (visible beneath the cylinders); circular smokebox door; flanged saddle tank with countersunk rivets; 'modern' pattern wheel centres, and what may be termed an 'austerity' pattern cab (here showing signs of damage on the left hand side) with no radiuses on the upper parts of the cutouts (a measure introduced during the build up to the First World War and persisting on some locomotives right up to the end of the company's existence). *Felspar* was unique amongst 'H' class locomotives in being built with Isaacson's valve gear. The railway system at Holborough fell out of use around 1971 and tragically, a late attempt to save this locomotive from the scrap man's torch failed: it became the last of a trio of important late surviving standard Manning Wardle 0-4-0STs to end its days this way. (*The late B. Roberts*)

Junction widening contract in Lancashire, the engine became *Messenger* with Cannock & Rugely Colliery Co., passing to West Cannock No. 5 Colliery in 1914, where, after a period on loan to the War Department (Cannock Chase Military Railway) during the First World war, it was scrapped in 1922.

As previously mentioned, the 'K' class proved to be the most successful of the Boyne Engine Works products when measured in terms of its numerical strength. Some 246 class members were built to standard gauge; with one additional locomotive (the last class member) produced as a rebuild of an earlier machine, whilst there were four examples modified for 5ft gauge and five for 5ft 6in. As was to be expected, several modifications appeared over the years, some dictated by general design or manufacturing techniques, and others by specialist customer requirements. Locomotives built for contractors were normally provided with 'block buffers for earth waggons [sic]'. Mostly these were fitted in addition to conventional spring buffers and located between the latter. To illustrate how

I' class 0-4-0ST W/N 1254 (31 March 1897) was the last of three 0-4-0STs (the previous pair being of the 'H' class) built by Manning Wardle for the Aberford Railway (Garforth Colliery Co. Ltd) and was named *Empress* in honour of the Diamond Jubilee of Queen Victoria. Although still equipped with a 'wrap over' roof (subsequently widened), the engine incorporated certain refinements in boiler and smokebox design, including a circular smokebox door and the fitting of Roscoe cylinder lubricators. *Empress* received a new boiler in 1920 but is not believed to have lasted much longer, not being on the railway at the time of its closure in March 1924, the last of the collieries that it served lasting barely longer.

the design had 'matured' it was also recorded of W/N 182 in 1878 that 'the boiler, also axleboxes, crankpins, coupling rods, connecting rods, crossheads, motion and brake gear same as present class "K"'. 5ft gauge W/Ns 206-7 were for built for Messrs Peto & Betts, being sent away on 27 April 1866, presumably to a destination within the Russian sphere of influence. They were described as being 'as far as possible' duplicates of the 'Old I' locomotives of the same gauge supplied to this contractor, but they would have incorporated the differences necessary to define them as 'K' class locomotives. W/N 212 *Meltham*, originally supplied under Order No. 2700 to the contractor Barnes & Beckett at Netherton near Huddersfield, proved to be a class 'celebrity' by virtue of its longevity. It received several spares orders from the makers including a new firebox and smokebox with circular door (Order No. 40036 of 3 February 1899); new smokebox, door and cast iron chimney (Order 84635 of 8 August 1924), and new cylinders under Order No. 84706 of 26 September 1924. The replacement components were of 'updated' specification at the time of their fitting to be in line with then current practice for the class. Be that as it may, W/N 212 passed through the hands of another contractor, Messrs Briar & Son & Wilson as *Stanza* before coming into Air Ministry ownership as RAF No. 103. It was last noted, out of use, in the yard of T.W. Ward Ltd., Grays, Essex in June 1949. W/N 243 was described as 'same as No. 193' [which, in turn, was the same as W/N 182 except for being fitted with block buffers] but it was 'the first class "K" with trailing sandboxes in the coke boxes' reflecting the need for greater sanding capability. Sister locomotive W/N 244 was described as, 'same as No. 182 except wrought iron wheels, 3ft 0in

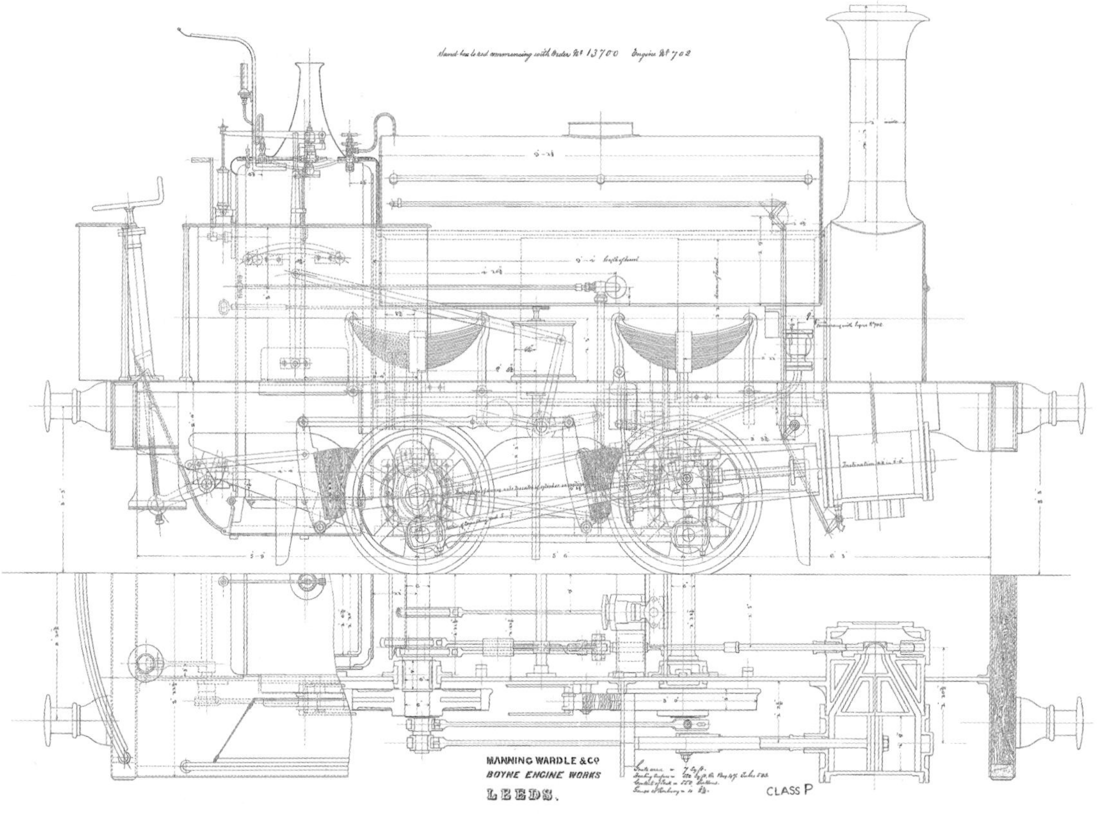

This early Makers' General Arrangement Drawing of the 'P' class shows the design in its original form, with weather screen, lift-up smokebox door and vertical sandpipes. (*Hunslet Archive*)

diameter'. This locomotive earned two important historical distinctions. The first of these was that it was fitted with a new boiler by the makers on no less than three separate occasions: Order No. 37999 (18 January 1896) - new boiler, smokebox and circular door; Order Nos. 69485 & 69618 (6 February 1913) – new boiler, firebox, smokebox, door and tubeplate (arranged for 1⅞in tubes); and Order No. 83991 (1 January 1924) – new boiler and smokebox, retaining old door. The second was that it was the oldest 'K' class locomotive definitely known to have survived into the 1950s. Never straying from its original workplace during its active career, *Conduit No. 1* passed into the ownership of NCB West Midlands Division Area 2 on 1 January 1947 and was scrapped at Cannock Central Workshops in 1952.

W/N 253 (sent to J. Ashwell, contractor on the Settle & Carlisle Railway on 14 July 1868, again under Order No. 3400) was historically significant in that the makers recorded: 'Same as No. 182. This is the engine "Diamond", afterwards fitted with an overhead canopy. The same kind as now put on a "K" but higher.' This is the 'wrap-over' pattern of shelter for the crew referred to earlier. The engine received several spares from the makers, the last being new wheelsets under Order 78187 on 1 July 1918. W/N 266, the last engine produced under the same Order No., was a 5ft 6in gauge version supplied on 1 December 1868 to F.R. Eltaye in Calcutta. In order to suit the Indian customer's requirements, new drawings were made for the canopy; footplating, bufferbeams; expansion and motion brackets; smokebox and feed pump fastening; wheels; crankpins; axleboxes; hornblocks; eccentrics; connecting and coupling rods. More significantly from the point of view of the 'K' class generally, the makers stated, 'This is the first engine on which we put the round edged tank [i.e. dispensing with the angle iron upper corners but retaining the flat sides].' After the appearance of this engine, there was a run of class members basically similar to W/Ns 182 or 193, with the only entry of note being made against W/N 369 (exported to Humphrey Davy in Berlin). The entry stated:

'This engine is the same as ordinary "K" but with block buffers. Spring balances and regulator quadrant

Moira Colliery in Leicestershire possessed four specimens of the 'P' class 0-4-0ST, modified from the standard specification by reason of a shorter wheelbase for negotiating sharp curves. The oldest of these locomotives, *Rawdon*, was Works No. 546 and, importantly in the light of another modification, it fell chronologically between the first two standard gauge locomotives built for internal use at the Royal Arsenal, Woolwich ('H' class W/N 515 of 1875 *Driver* originally *The Gunner* and 'Special' W/N 581 of 1876 *Gunner*). These two locomotives both possessed what were described by the makers when referring to the earlier one as 'special wrought iron bufferbeams for going round sharp curves'. In reality these were the classic 'Woolwich' pattern full width 'composite' (i.e. timber and iron) bufferbeam, found on all 'purpose-built' nineteenth century standard gauge Royal Arsenal locomotives (as opposed to those acquired second hand) but rarely elsewhere. Nonetheless, the makers repeated their description of the buffers for *Rawdon* and Moira Colliery must therefore count as a rare non-Woolwich application of the 'composite buffer' principle. *Rawdon* was rebuilt by the makers in 1901 and later acquired a home-made cab, loosely copied from the maker's 'Austerity' pattern in 1922. (*Author's Collection formerly Robert Price*)

> marked in German. Safety valve levers and boiler plates conform to Russian Government regulations. Fitted with Diamond canopy.'

One matter about which the makers' records are contradictory concerns the fitting of the first crank axle forged at the Boyne Engine Works, which was fitted to a 'K' class locomotive during a repair. This is credited both to W/N 180 under Order 13256 of November 1877 and to W/N 453, with no Order No. specified but once again a date of 1877 stated. The year of the event would therefore appear not to be in doubt, but there would appear to be no way today of resolving which of the two locomotives achieved the all-important distinction. The next important stage in the evolution of the 'K' class came with the appearance of W/N 488. This engine, supplied on 3 August 1874 to the contractor Logan & Hemingway at Newport, was described as:

> 'Ordinary class "K" except straight weather screen, brake on all wheels, special arrangement of mountings [take-offs from the firebox wrapper], two whistles, two wet and two dry sandboxes. First "K" with brass steam funnel [i.e. the E. B. Wilson cast-iron pattern safety valve bonnet was dispensed with].'

This locomotive, No. 7 in the customer's list, effectively set the pattern for future members of the 'K' and 'L' classes supplied to Logan & Hemingway, which was destined to be an important Manning Wardle customer during the succeeding years. Contractors such as Logan & Hemingway and T.A. Walker tended to evolve certain specific requirements for their locomotives in relation to such items as buffers; drawgear; rail-washing gear; sanding arrangements and lamps. Logan & Hemingway appear to have detested the use of cabs when they became common fitments, instead tending to prefer the old E.B. Wilson-pattern straight weather screen (as modified to take a pressure gauge). The preserved W/N 1210 retains this feature today.

The makers' details for W/N 556 are interesting in that they show certain alterations made to 'update' the locomotive in line with then-current practice. The notes describe the engine as being:

> '... altered in 1884, sandboxes moved to front of engine, two mud plugs on wrapper, right and left above firebox for washing roof .... Pump removed and replaced by extra [Giffard] No. 5 Injector on right hand side – steam valve taken off from site of warming valve.'

The reference to a 'warming valve' is significant; the Wilson-era preheater valve and associated pipe leading from the wrapper to the rear of the saddle tank remained a standard feature of many early Manning Wardle products, and would have been used to pre-heat the feed water when the engine was in motion and relying on its feed pump rather than the injector (if fitted).

By way of contrast, W/N 627 *Medway* (supplied under 11510 on 13 November 1876 to Burham Brick, Lime & Cement Co. Ltd., Burham in Kent) was never a contractors' locomotive but it was clearly intended for working on sharply curved track, being fitted with

Works Nos. 884 and 885 were built new for the Manchester, Sheffield & Lincolnshire Railway, being delivered respectively on 26 February and 1 March 1883 as MS&LR Nos. 511-2, renumbered 62-3 in 1893. The former is illustrated here after becoming Great Central Railway No. 62B in 1909. These locomotives spent most of their lives as dock shunters at Grimsby and Immingham. Few alterations have been made since the locomotive was built, save for the fitting of a Robinson chimney and Ramsbottom safety valves. Original details, such as the bent weatherboard; the fire-iron brackets; the backward sloping handbrake column and the sandbox located between the wheelsets, primarily serving the rear pair are visible, as is the drain cock arrangement connected to the steam chests rather than the cylinders. Nos. 62B and 63B became respectively L&NER Nos. 6431 and 6430 in 1924 following the Grouping, the latter having received a new boiler in October 1921. Both were withdrawn from service in 1931. (*John Scott-Morgan Collection*)

Jessie (Works No. 1231) is a fine representative of the 'P' class of late nineteenth century vintage. The engine was dispatched by the makers on 29 June 1891 to Shireoaks Colliery Co. Ltd., near Worksop in Nottinghamshire, where it worked all of its life, during which it was rebuilt by the makers in 1907. The 'plain' (as opposed to fringed) canopy, supported by two rear pillars and a leading weatherboard, is much in evidence in this right hand view, whilst the 'double boss' pattern of wheel centre was still a standard fitment at this stage, along with steam chest drain cocks. The pipes leading from the central sandbox appear to be vertical, whilst additional sanding for the rear wheels when reversing is provided by two rear sandboxes. The water inlet for the feed pump can be seen mounted on the side of the saddle tank whilst the right hand Roscoe lubricator for the cylinder is visible on the front of the tank. (*John Scott-Morgan Collection*)

translation slides above the leading axles, the leading splashers being ¾in wider than standard to suit and the flanges on the intermediate wheelset being ⅞in thinner than the other two pairs. The use of translation slides was normal practice when sharper than normal curves were being negotiated. In addition, it was recorded that this locomotive was built to a height restriction of 9ft 2in and that its buffers were set at 5ft 8¾in lateral centres and 3ft 1¼ in pitch, with wrought iron cases and heads 1ft 4in diameter. Absorbed into the Associated Portland Cement Manufacturers' empire in 1900, *Medway* appears to have been disposed of by 1903 as a replacement locomotive bearing the same name arrived on site during that year, but its ultimate scrapping date is unknown.

The 'K' class was to remain in production until 1914, although, as previously noted, its last-built member, W/N 1820 was a rebuild of an earlier specimen, W/N 1212. Over the years, its details underwent a considerable amount of updating; the weather screens and canopies (normally of the 'Diamond' wrap-over variety as first fitted to W/N 253) of early members progressively gave way to cabs, initially of with the four-radius cut-out as found on W/N 1232, which was replaced on class members built from the late 1890's onwards by the more familiar type with only two radii situated in the upper part of the cut-out (non-standard cab types evolved for Russian and Scandinavian customers). Chimney construction went from the early fabricated varieties to sheet iron barrels with cast caps and ultimately to

The variant of the 'P' class design supplied to Carron & Co. Ltd. of Grahamstone near Falkirk in 1889-90 (W/Ns 1158 and 1182-4) possessed several variations from the class 'norm', including their distinctive cabs and 3ft 7in 'disc' wheels. These locomotives also introduced the circular smokebox door to the class as a standard fitment, albeit of the earlier pattern without the stiffening support ring on the smokebox itself. Although precise scrapping dates for these locomotives do not appear to have survived, they were all gone by the end of the 1950s. This view shows class pioneer *Carron* No. 9 (1158 of 1889). (*John Scott-Morgan Collection*).

the one-piece cast-iron variety. Manning Wardle injectors (normally used in conjunction with feed pumps) became standard fittings from 1877 onwards, although there was a flirtation with injectors from other suppliers during the Edwardian period. Mainframes and attendant components were generally strengthened, whilst the familiar 'double-boss' wheel centres of early years (which themselves had been redesigned from having circular section spokes in favour of oval section spokes in the mid-1870's) disappeared on new locomotives from 1898 onwards in favour of the more conventional variety. In addition, it must be noted that circular smokebox doors were the norm from 1890 onwards, some earlier class members receiving them when fitted with new boilers and the design of 'circular door' smokebox was later altered to incorporate a stiffening strip, the door design also being altered to suit. Salter safety valves gave way to Ramsbottom and the cylinders were redesigned, incorporating aprons top and bottom after 1906. Unlike the 'Old I' class, the 'K' class made the transition from Manning Wardle's formative years into a period well into the manufacturer's existence as a limited company, although it was not produced during the final years of manufacture at the Boyne Engine Works. Before turning to the next class for consideration, mention has to be made of solitary W/N 1253 of 1897. This was built to a bespoke order for 5ft 6in gauge for a Chilean customer to a non-standard ('special') design with 16in cylinder stroke and features including centre couplers and a large American- pattern headlamp.

By the time of the build-up to the First World War, the 'K' had little advantage to offer over the 'L' class and it is to that class that consideration must turn. The original intention with the 'L' class was to create a slightly

The prototype of what may be termed the 'Super P' 0-4-0ST design with 14in by 20in cylinders, W/N 1773 of 1912 built for Ellison & Mitchell Ltd. of Kilnhurst, Yorkshire, is illustrated in this works photograph. The photograph has been retouched to remove the background, a common practice with 'official' views of this type! (*Author's Collection*)

W/N 1773's classmate, W/N 1795 of 1912 is seen under restoration on the Middleton Railway during the line's Bicentenary Celebrations on 24 June 2012, coincidentally a century to the day after it was delivered new to T.W. Ward Ltd. in Sheffield. Shortly afterwards, the engine was moved to covered accommodation at Barrow Hill Roundhouse, near Staveley. The cab being fitted is not of the original design, being in effect a modern take on the 'Austerity' cab (which, as it happens, would not have been fitted to a 1912-built locomotive when new) in which no part of the leading spectacles is obscured by the tank. (*Author*)

The largest 0-4-0ST design built at the Boyne Engine Works was represented by a four-strong class with 16in by 24in cylinders, of which the prototype, W/N 1802 of 1912 (originally *Cyclops*), still survives at Eskbank House, Lithgow in New South Wales, having been exported to Australia in 1919 and re-named *Possum*. It is seen here on display at this location in March 2002. (*Author*)

smaller version of the 'M' class (to be described) retaining the latter's '13 inch' cylinders and to this end, some four locomotives (W/Ns 504-5; 731 & 908) were built to standard gauge, with a fifth, W/N 769, being constructed to 5ft gauge. This 'Old L' class as it may loosely be termed, was characterized by its 3ft 2in diameter boiler and 11ft 3in wheelbase but was far from uniform in its design; W/Ns 504-5 were fitted with wheel splashers, curved weather screens and tank warming valves whereas W/N 731 had higher-pitched running boards and a diamond canopy, and only two of its members were built for the domestic market. The class 'celebrity' was W/N 731 which in altered form ended its days on the Weston, Clevedon & Portishead Railway where it worked until the line's closure in 1940. With a wheelbase only 3 in shorter than the 'M' class, the 'Old L' class would have had little advantage over the former and it is perhaps significant to note that the first customer for what became the mainstream 'L' class was the contractor T.A. Walker, a major customer for the 'M' class albeit in several cases in a mutated form. The locomotive concerned was W/N 1034 and the concept was changed from a baby 'M' to a souped-up 'K' in which the latter's wheelbase; barrel length and cylinder diameter were retained, but the boiler diameter and cylinder stroke were increased. The revised 'L' class was to number some ninety-nine locomotives that were given the official classification, to which must be added six de facto class members in all but name in the Loco Details (one of which, W/N 1970, received the 'L' classification in the Order Book), two further Kitson-built de facto examples and, possibly, W/N 1612, a crane locomotive built to 5ft 6in gauge for India using many 'L' components. As with the 'K' class, there was a considerable amount of detail revision over the years and generally the observations that apply to the 'K' class between 1887 and 1914 also apply to the 'L' class. There were, however, three important differences. The earlier of these concerned valve gears. In 1905 W/N 1034 was fitted with Marshall's valve gear under Order No. 558900. Following Manning Wardle & Co. Ltd.'s incorporation and flotation in 1905, three of the directors of the company were also directors of Marshall's Valve Gear Co Ltd. and several Manning Wardle locomotives were built using the gear. In 1906 Marshall sued Manning Wardle for misappropriation of his patent and succeeded in his action. Although some further Manning Wardle locomotives continued to be built with the gear (including 'L' class W/N 1690), the Leeds company was eventually forced to turn to another specialist valve gear and on 13 August 1908 Rupert John Isaacson's valve gear, a variant of Walschaert's, was patented jointly with Edwin Wardle; John Edwin

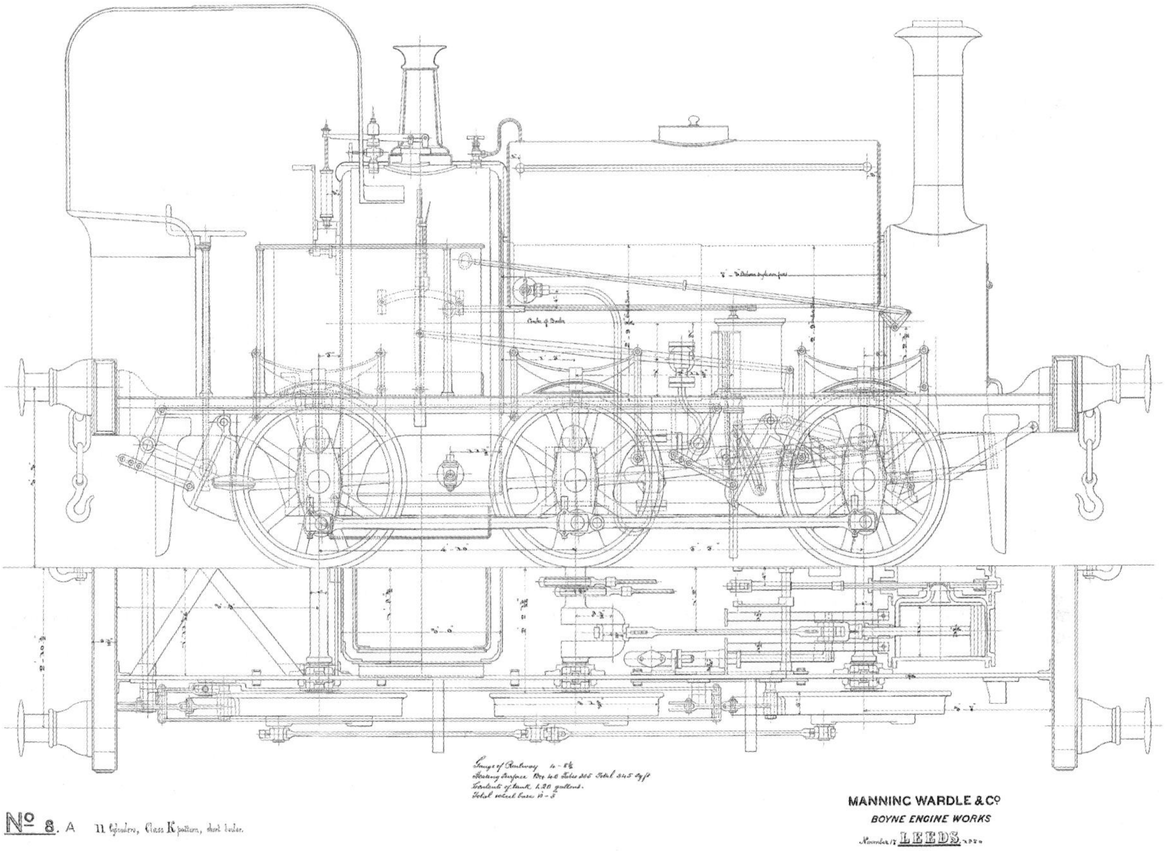

Manning Wardle's major initial commercial breakthrough came with the 'Old I' class and although in production since 1859 and effectively copied from the E.B. Wilson locomotives sent out to Crimea in 1855, it was not until 17 November 1870 that this side elevation and half plan view of the class was completed at the Boyne Engine Works. All of the classic Wilson-derived features, including the fluted safety valve bonnet, are present except for the early pattern weatherboard (found today in modified form to accommodate a pressure gauge on the preserved W/N 1210 of 1891 *Sir Berkeley*). The crosshead driven feedpump on the left hand side is shown to advantage and the Wilson 'Crimea' locomotives would simply have had a second similar fitting 'mirror imaged' on the right hand side (similar arrangements being employed on the 'Dursley' locomotive and OW&WR Nos. 34-5). By the time the drawing was made, an injector was the order of the day on the left hand side although this is not shown. Another notable feature is the valve gear which is arranged so that the reversing drop link bellcranks trail the weighshaft (with their balance weights leading). This arrangement was inherited from the Wilson 'breakwater' locomotives and would also have been found on the 'Dursley' specimen and OW&WR Nos. 34-5. (*Hunslet Archive*)

Firth; Charles Ernest Charlesworth; Horace Sanderson and Henry St. John Sanderson (No. 27899, applied for 18 December 1907)). Horace Sanderson was at this time the company's Commercial Director, whilst Henry St. John Sanderson was also a shareholder and having these people as signatories to the patent, it was hoped that the difficulties experienced with Marshall would not recur. Charles Ernest Charlesworth of Conyingham Hall was a colliery owner and Manning Wardle customer. The design and modus operandi of this valve gear is shown in one of the accompanying illustrations. This gear was applied to 'L' class W/Ns 1745 and 1805-6.

The second major difference between the development paths of the 'K' and 'L' classes lay in the fact that by 1916 (W/Ns 1894-5 and de facto locomotives), it had become standard practice to use two injectors on the 'L' class rather than one injector and one pump. Finally, whereas only four members of the 'K' class were fitted with steam braking apparatus, seven officially classified 'L' class locomotives were so equipped from new and it became a standard fitment for the de facto members of the class constructed from 1917 onwards, and was also applied to the two Kitson-built members of this group, W/Ns 5457-8 of 1931-2.

Works Number 21 of 1861 was originally supplied to the contractors J. & J. Charlesworth as *Henrietta*. Passing to the East & West Yorkshire Union Railway, in January 1894, the locomotive was sold to Hawthorn Leslie who carried out a major overhaul and re-sold the engine to the contractors Meakin & Dean. After working on contracts at Birkenhead and Blagdon Reservoir, the locomotive which had acquired a non-standard conical safety valve casing and a 'stovepipe chimney' was acquired in 1907 by the Hundred of Manhood and Selsey Tramways, part of the Colonel Stephens empire, from Herbert Weldon, being named Sidlesham at that stage. In this early view on that line, the conical casing (sitting on the original square pedestal) is visible, but a more ornate chimney has been fitted by 1907 a non-original canopy and brake blocks had also been fitted. (*John Scott Morgan Collection*)

Sidlesham is seen here circa 1931 having acquired the rear cab sheet from the derelict Neilson 0-4-2ST locomotive *Hesperus* circa 1930 along with a more respectable 'trumpet' for the safety valve in 1908. Other later details included a tool box on the rear spectacle plate (inside); a handrail around the chimney; altered canopy stays; a leading left hand sandbox and smaller buffers. *Sidlesham* fell to the breaker's torch (along with *Hesperus*) in 1932, some three years before the line (known as the West Sussex Railway after 1924) closed. (*John Scott Morgan Collection*)

W/N 50 of 1862 began life as an ordinary '12 in' variant of the 'Old I' class delivered on 20 June 1862 to J. T. Leather, Waterloo Main Colliery, Leeds. Its subsequent history is well detailed in the text, but to complete the picture, this works photograph, showing the locomotive after its 1916 rebuild, is included here. (*Col. Stephens Museum, Tenterden*)

As early as the 1860s, the need for a more powerful standard locomotive than the Old Class 'I' and 'K' was being felt and the solution to this deficiency arrived on the scene in June 1863 with the delivery of the first 'M', W/N 75 *Morlais*, to Dowlais Iron Co. at Merthyr Tydfil. This locomotive was fitted with 14in by 18in cylinders and 3ft wheels, but it retained many of the features of its precursor designs, including the classic domeless boiler; angular cornered saddle tank; lift-up smokebox door; warming valve for the tank; double-boss cast-iron wheel centres and compensating beam suspension for the leading and intermediate axles. The class proved to be an instant success with (principally) colliery/ironworks enterprises and contractors alike, although the prevailing standard cylinder stroke was revised downwards to 13in whilst between W/Ns 230 and 290 a semi-circular, rather than flat-sided tank was the prevailing order of the day. Some 157 'official' members of the 'M' class were turned out; the last of which was W/N 1860 in 1914. Of these, eighteen were built to 5ft. 6in. gauge; two to 5ft gauge and two were built with side tanks (W/N 1005-6) to the requirements of T.A. Walker and these were otherwise largely in conformity with the normal path of evolution of the class. Some thirteen additional locomotives, all built for the same customer in 1888 went further in additionally employing boilers fitted with domes on their barrels. Strictly speaking, these locomotives would be outside the spirit of the scope of this work, save for the fact that improvements to their standard components were incorporated into the 'mainstream' line of evolution. This entailed all of the modifications referred to earlier in connection with the 'L' class, including the use of 'round' tank corners; cabs (both special and standard); refinements to mainframe and cylinder design; the use of circular, as opposed to lift-up smokebox doors; the use, where required, of steam braking; the superseding of the 'double boss' wheel centre in favour of a more conventional pattern and the fitting of Isaacson valve gear in certain cases. One feature that was applied new to

This view shows W/N 52 of 1862 *Merion* (delivered in August to Thomas Savin, contractor for the Aberystwyth & West Coast Railway) at Aberdovey Harbour. The locomotive became No. 17 in the Cambrian Railways' list, being sold to Brynkinalt Colliery near Chirk in 1875, being last reported at nearby Black Park Colliery in 1900. This photograph illustrates well the distinctive early features of the 'Old I' class such as the classic Wilson-pattern chimney; the saddle tank fashioned from sheet iron and angles, with the only curves being the upper surface and the recess for the boiler; the abundance of snap head rivets; the columnar fluted safety valve cover; the leading weatherboard 'sculpted' to fit the spectacles and pressure gauge (a feature found today on *Sir Berkeley* W/N 1210 of 1891); the lift-up smokebox door (in this case, as with *La Portena* equipped with sealing strap); rear bunker without upper flare, and rectangular Railway Foundry-pattern worksplates. Note also the buffer beams extending above footplate level supported by upward projecting mainframe extensions; 'cotter pin' coupling rods and 'double-boss' wheel centres (all as per the Dursley locomotive). Two further important points should be noted about this photograph, which appears to date from shortly after the locomotive's delivery. Firstly, the rear weatherboard (a non-standard feature) is of similar design to the leading one, albeit lower, with a middle projection offering little extra protection, and secondly water feed on the left hand side is by means of a pump, contrary to slightly later Manning Wardle practice with early 'standards' and others which had an injector on this side.

W/N 1860 was what may be termed the 'Austerity' cab (with simple rectangular cut-out). This first appeared on some Manning Wardle locomotives in 1914 (owing to the limitations imposed by wartime conditions) and can be seen today on the preserved 'long boiler' 0-6-0ST *The Welshman* (W/N 1207 of 1890), having been acquired during a 1922 rebuild. After 1914, nine de facto class members were built, the last pair of which, W/Ns 2045-6 appeared in 1926. Additionally, three '13in by 20in' long wheelbase 0-6-0STs (W/Ns 1224-5 of 1891 and 1274 of 1893) also come within the ambit of this volume. A non-standard 5ft 6in gauge '13 in' inside cylinder class with a wheelbase of only 9ft 6in was built in 1911-13 for use in India, but sadly no maker's photograph appears to have survived. This design would have incorporated a firebox mounted over, rather than ahead of, the trailing axle, a design change the implications of which will be considered in later paragraphs.

Manning Wardle 'Old I' class 0-6-0ST W/N 57 was a 'Guy Fawkes day' delivery in 1862 to the River Wear Commissioners. It was described as, 'same as No. 35 but with special frames, hornblocks, sliding firehole door and two sets of volute spring buffers on each buffer beam'. The locomotive is seen here as RWC No. 2 having undergone sundry modifications including a headlamp mounted, rather unusually, on the right hand side of the smokebox; a 'home-made' cab and an upward bunker extension (discernible by the change in rivet spacing above the original vertical limit). This locomotive has an injector mounted on the right hand side, probably a non-original feature, and many features, apart from the 'double' buffer sets are similar to W/N 52 as would be expected, including the classic wooden toolbox on the leading right hand running board. Two 'personalized' features for this particular owner are of interest, namely the 'sextant' emblem on the sandbox and lining on the coupling rods, although none was applied to the spokes. A new set of 11in diameter cylinders was supplied under Order 32615 on 15 March 1892.

Manning Wardle made two attempts to produce a standard 0-6-0ST class with 14in by 20in cylinders and 3ft 6in wheels. The first of these was designated the 'N' class and amounted to only to five members constructed between 1873 and 1879. Although designed in the maker's typical mould, with a domeless boiler barrel and raised firebox wrapper for steam collection, some difficulties were apparently expressed with 'priming' (excessive carry-over of liquid water into the cylinders from the boiler) and these five locomotives all eventually appeared with domes on their boiler barrels, W/N 387 presumably having been modified in this way at an early date that goes unrecorded. This design alteration took the locomotives outside the main thrust of the maker's 'standard 0-6-0ST' philosophy and in consequence their standard class status was withdrawn. What was originally the re-launched 'N' class (equipped with a domeless boiler barrel and shorter wheelbase) commenced with W/N 547 in 1875. After completion of the first three class members, these locomotives were re-designated 'Q' (an unnecessary move, given that their de-classified precursors were fitted with domed boilers) and eventually some twenty-one of these locomotives were turned out, progressively incorporating the customary refinements, to which must be added two domed boiler side tank variants for T.A. Walker in 1888. The last-built specimen, W/N 1966, was built for Logan & Hemingway and although built as late as 1918, reflected this customer's distaste for cabs, instead incorporating only a weatherboard, albeit of the curved variety. Where necessary, vacuum braking was fitted and three class members came into main line ownership; perhaps the most handsome of the three was W/N 1555 of 1902 in its (sadly short-lived) final form prior to withdrawal by the Southern Railway in 1932. Two closely-related designs to the 'Q' class were also built. These were W/Ns 1508 of 1901 and 1866 of 1914 and both had longer cylinder stokes than the standard class (20in and 22in respectively).

If the standard Manning Wardle 0-6-0ST had a major Achilles heel, it was the fact that locating the firebox between the intermediate and trailing axles dictated the use of a wheelbase that was longer than many industrial users would have desired, given the sharp curves that prevailed on their systems. In order to mitigate this, some locomotives were provided with side play in their (usually leading and/or trailing) axle journals, or in some cases were fitted with translation slides giving side play in their leading and/or trailing axleboxes, as has already been noted. A solution to the 'long wheelbase' difficulty grew more necessary, however, with progressive enlargement of the standard designs and as far as the basic 'Q' class specification was concerned, the first move in this direction was made in 1898. The resultant locomotive, W/N 1407 was supplied in July of that year to a local customer, Farnley Iron Co. of Leeds, and incorporated a wheelbase shortened from the class standard by 1ft 6in at the rear to 10ft 6in allied to a firebox that sat over the rear axle, fitted with a sloping rather than a horizontal foundation ring. Two more examples followed in similar vein before a revised specification, with a wheelbase of 10ft, followed with W/N 1844 in 1914.

Manning Wardle 'Old I' class W/N 67 of 1863 was delivered as *Perseverance* to Messrs Brassey & Field who the contractors working on the widening of the Shrewsbury-Hereford section of the West Midland Railway. Following completion of this work, the engine passed into the hands of another contractor, T. Mackay for work on the Cantref Reservoir whence it was sold into 'mainstream' industrial service in the form of H. Leetham & Sons Ltd., the owners of Hungate Flour Mills in York. The locomotive's final owner was Hadfields (Hope & Caldon Low Quarries Ltd.) where, as *Neptune* it survived at Hope Quarry until circa 1939. This 1938 view illustrates well the combination of the early pattern 'angular' saddle tank (complete with snap head rivets) and later pattern smokebox with circular door (and leading bufferbeam modified to suit), fitted during a rebuild by the makers in 1910. The motion bracket, once again also doing duty as a boiler support, can also be seen to advantage. (*B. D. Stoyel*)

As with *Sidlesham*, Works Number 178 of 1866 was also built for a contractor, in this case T.B. Crampton for work at Fenny Crompton. The locomotive became East & West Junction Railway (later the Stratford-upon-Avon & Midland Junction Railway) No. 1 and was sold to another Colonel Stephens line, the Shropshire & Montgomeryshire Railway in 1910 where it became No.4 *Morous*. In this photograph, the locomotive is seen at Kinnerley circa 1921 with 0-4-2ST No. 2 *Severn* visible in the background on the right hand side. The non-standard 'wrap-over' roof (wider than the maker's usual pattern) and replacement injector (with waste pipe passing through the area bounded by the intermediate spring) as much in evidence in this left hand view, as is the bunker rather worse for wear! (*John Scott Morgan Collection*)

This specification eventually amounted to six further locomotives, including the final new locomotive to leave the Boyne Engine Works, W/N 2047 on 9 August 1926. This locomotive is now preserved on the Severn Valley Railway. As with the mainstream 'Q' class, there was a '14 inch' variant of the 'short wheelbase' specification with a 22inch cylinder stroke, in this instance represented by W/Ns 1794 and 1803 *Nonslip* and their Kitson-built descendant, W/N 5459 of 1932 *Austin* No. 1 which happily also survives today.

The 'O' class, normally fitted with 15in by 22in cylinders and 3ft 9in wheels, but subject to individual minor variations, amounted to forty-eight locomotives in the 'mainstream' vein, together with W/N 797 which had a domed boiler barrel. Once again, there were the usual design refinements as construction of the class progressed. The last representative of the class to be built. W/N 1725 *Julia Sheffield* was built with Isaacson valve gear but was fitted with Stephenson motion at a later stage in its career before scrapping in 1959. The short wheelbase variant of the class began at the request of Ackton Hall Colliery (a previous customer for the 'mainstream' variety) which received W/N 1577 *Vulcan* on 11 November 1902, constructed on similar principles to W/N 1407, in this case with a wheelbase shortened by 1ft at the rear from class standard to 11ft. Some seven 'short wheelbase' variants of the 'O' class were turned out, culminating with W/N 2017, probably in 1921 although its dispatch date goes unrecorded. The odd one out of the group as regards its wheelbase was W/N 1955 of 1917 *Charwelton*, which had a 10ft 6in wheelbase. Today this locomotive survives on the Kent & East Sussex Railway.

In November 1924, *Morous* was transferred to the West Sussex Railway, where it is seen in this front right hand three-quarter view. A new boiler with circular smokebox door was fitted in 1895 and safety valve bonnet in 1905 at which time the boiler pitch and canopy were raised by approximately 4 inches. The feed pump originally fitted to this side of the locomotive has been replaced altogether by a second injector (of similar design to that found on the other side of the engine), whilst the wide 'wrap-over' sheet, rear lower left had lamp-iron (mounted on a leading portion of the bufferbeam) and the S&MR. ownership plate are also evident in this view. (*John Scott Morgan Collection*)

The largest Manning Wardle 'industrial' design to be built in any significant volume was the '16in by 22in' 0-6-0ST specification that commenced with W/N 1367 produced for Midland Coal & Coke Co. Ltd. in June 1897. This retained the 12ft wheelbase and associated wheelbase structure of the mainstream 'O' class, but owing to the dimensions of the boiler and firebox, it was necessary to mount the firebox over the trailing axle from the specification's debut, thereby introducing this method of construction to Manning Wardle practice. A design of 0-6-0ST locomotive with 16in by 24in cylinders, represented by W/Ns 1137 of 1889 and 1226 of 1891 incorporating a firebox mounted between the intermediate and rear axles possessed a wheelbase of 14ft 8in, which would certainly have proved unwieldy for most industrial use. The '16in by 22in' specification with some variations ultimately amounted to some twenty-three locomotives built by Manning Wardle, the last being the still-extant W/Ns 2009-10 in November 1921. The basic specification achieved its greatest popularity with the Frodingham Ironstone Mines site near Scunthorpe (six examples) and Stewarts & Lloyds near Corby (three examples). Following Manning Wardle's demise, a further representative followed from Kitson (W/N 5424) modified in design by the fitting of a Belpaire boiler (a design used for replacement boilers supplied to Frodingham for three of the Manning Wardle precursors of Kitson W/N 5424), accompanied by no less than seven more locomotives using the original pattern of boiler for Stewarts & Lloyds. This was

This rear three-quarter view of *Morous*, taken at the same time as the previous one shows the upper rear lamp-irons, rear stay for the 'wrap-over' sheet, and vacuum brake control (a non-original component) to advantage. *Morous* survived until the closure of the W.S.R. in 1935, was Lot No. 323 in the sale of the railway's effects, but found no buyer apart from the scrap breaker during the autumn of 1936. In the background, to the right of the locomotive and immediately in front of the shed, can be seen 'K' class locomotive *Ringing Rock* (Works No. 890 of 1883). New cylinders were in 1896, 1901 and 1925. (*John Scott Morgan Collection*)

General Flores (W/N 235) was a variant of the Old 'I' class built in 1867 for Uruguay. It exhibits notable non-standard features including the 'stovepipe' chimney; 3 ft. 6 in. wrought iron wheels and 'special' pillar canopy. Note also the E.B. Wilson copper-capped cast iron safety valve cover and 'warming valve' leading from the firebox wrapper to the tank. (*Hunslet Archive*)

The last 'Old I' class 0-6-0ST in service, in its home country at least, was W/N 241 *Thorncliffe*, supplied on 4 January 1868 to Newton Chambers & Co. Ltd., Thorncliffe Ironworks & Collieries. The engine ended its working career with Ferens & Love Ltd., Cornsay Colliery where it earned its keep until withdrawn and sold to a Darlington scrap Merchant in January 1952. It was rebuilt by the makers in 1902 and by Hudswell Clarke & Co. in 1932, the latter rebuild resulting in a much modified boiler design and a saddle tank of much 'rounder' cross-section than the original which covered the smokebox. Injectors of relatively modern pattern also replaced the feed pump. Nonetheless, several original design features still remained in this photograph, which was taken at Thorncliffe Colliery following the later rebuild, including the flared bunker, equalizing beams between the first and second axles, 'double boss' wheel centres and even the early pattern worksplate. (*The late F. Jones*)

followed by five more representatives for the same customer from Robert Stephenson & Hawthorn in 1940-1, the last locomotives of pure Manning Wardle design to be completed during the pre-preservation era. As one final observation on this class, it should be noted that an attempt was made to bestow on this specification the 'T' classification (notably W/Ns 1646,1758 and 1761-2), but this did not apparently prove permanent.

Only three further designs need to be considered here under the 0-6-0ST heading. The largest design produced from new to the classic 'trailing axle behind firebox' school of design was a '17 in' by 24 in' 'Special' with 4ft wheels for the East & West Yorkshire Union Railway. The locomotives concerned were W/Ns 1307-8 of 1895 and 1489 of 1900, respectively E&WYUR Nos. 1-3. Apart from the short-lived regular passenger service on the E&WYUR (which commenced and ceased in 1904 and for which No. 1 temporarily carried a vacuum ejector), these locomotives spent their lives on coal workings. No 3 was withdrawn in 1923 by the L&NER without renumbering, but Nos. 1-2 were renumbered 3112-3 respectively. The latter locomotive, which had received new stronger frames lengthened by 6in in 1915 (which sadly proved prone to fracture in service) was withdrawn in 1928 and the former in 1930. E&WYUR No. 4 had originally been constructed in 1898 as a 0-6-2ST and was rebuilt by the makers in 1919 as a 0-6-0ST retaining its 3ft 9in coupled wheels. The rebuild involved the fitting of new mainframes giving the same total wheelbase as Nos. 1-3 (but with the intermediate

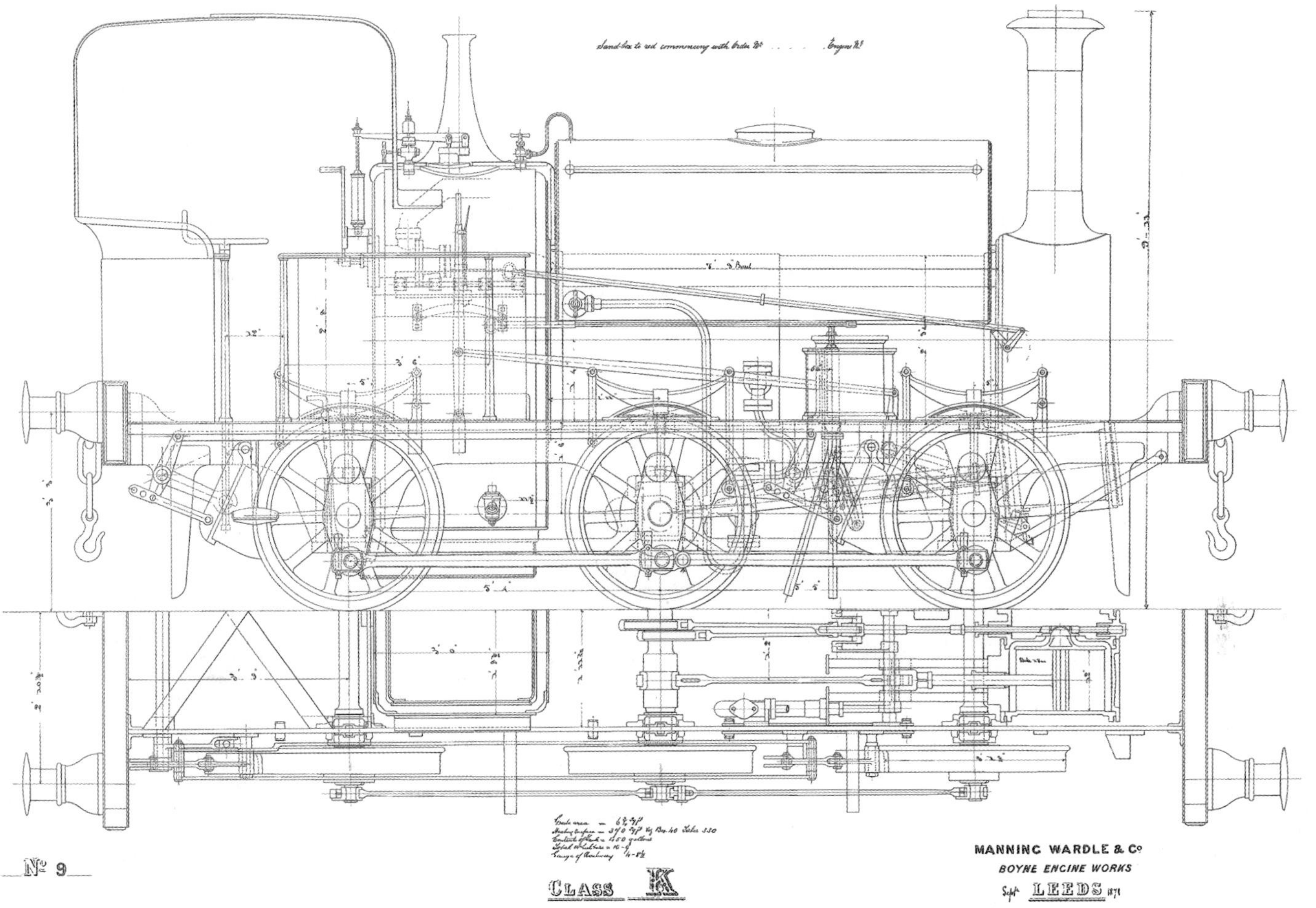

As shown in this September 1871 drawing, the 'K' class was basically a variant of the 'Old I' with the boiler barrel extended by six inches and the rear portion of the wheelbase correspondingly by the same amount. By this stage, the fluted safety valve cover was giving way to the simpler pattern shown (which was derived from those used on Wilson 'dummy crankshaft' locomotives), but the cross-bracing fitted between the side mainframes at the rear (a normal arrangement on the early standard six-coupled types) was still in evidence. Alternative pattern sandboxes are shown on this drawing. (*Hunslet Archive*)

axle 3in further forward to accommodate the original larger firebox wrapper) but unlike No. 2, these were not prone to fracture. The reason for the difference in behaviour is difficult to attribute but it may be that the steel used in No. 2's 1915 rebuild was of inferior quality owing to better quality steel being required for more direct war uses at the time. The rebuilt No. 4 was also supplied with a larger tank than Nos. 1-3 but this was replaced, along with other components at Doncaster in 1929 by items salvaged from the erstwhile No. 2 (3113) by which time the engine had become 3114. It was withdrawn in 1933.

The heaviest saddle tank design to be produced by Manning Wardle commenced with W/N 1759 in 1910, Littleton No. 4, and only two further examples were built: the short-lived A1 (W/N 1990) for Nine Mile Point Colliery in South Wales and W/N 2018 of 1922, Littleton No. 5. With 4ft wheels (4ft 2in in W/N 1990's case), 18in by 24in cylinders and a wheelbase of 13ft, this design was in many respects an enlargement of the abortive 'T' class referred to earlier (an unsurprising fact given that Littleton Collieries Ltd. was a customer for that class) and the family resemblance was very much in evidence. Unlike the earlier class, however, the wheelbase was equally divided, the brake hanger pivots were below rather than above the axle centrelines and a rounded cab roof was provided, necessitated by the proportions of the locomotive. Thankfully Littleton No. 5 survives to the present day at the Avon Valley Railway although the locomotive is not currently in working order.

The early pattern transitional 'Old I to K' class locomotive is represented by Works No. 140 of 1865, originally supplied as *Alyn* to a Mr. France, contractor on the Potteries, Shrewsbury and North Wales Railway. The locomotive was sold to the Mawddwy Railway in Mid-Wales two years later, becoming *Mawddwy*. Spares supplied included new block pistons in February 1890 and 12-plate springs in January 1891. When repaired under Order No. 33880 (February 1893), the engine lost its original lift-up smokebox door as a consequence of a new boiler, firebox and smokebox being fitted, along with new drawgear and a No. 40 Combination Ejector for vacuum brake operation. The last spares order (No. 66044) for a new pair of cylinders was dated 11 October 1910. Passing successively to the Cambrian Railway in 1911 and the Great Western in 1923, the locomotive remained in existence until 1940. This view shows the engine after acquiring its 1893 boiler, probably around 1900. At this stage, *Mawddwy* still retained its original E.B. Wilson pattern fluted safety valve cover. (*John Scott-Morgan Collection*)

Manning Wardle's first locomotive product, *Little Nell* (W/N of 1859) was described as a 3ft. gauge 0-4-0ST with 8in outside cylinders which was dispatched on 5 February 1859 to Dunstan & Barlow, Chesterfield. Although a narrow-gauge locomotive (which was ultimately destined to be converted to standard gauge by Markham of Chesterfield), its significance can be deduced from a Catalogue description of W/N 60, which was exhibited at the London Exhibition of 1862:

> 'LOCOMOTIVE MINERAL TANK ENGINE – Outside cylinders 9in diameter by 14in stroke; wheels 2ft 9in all coupled, copper firebox and brass tubes, boiler, axles and wheel tires (sic) of best Yorkshire iron. The tank holds 250 gallons, weight in working trim 10.25 tons.
>
> 'This little tank engine was designed expressly for the mineral traffic at iron works, collieries, etc. and will go round any curve where an ordinary railway wagon will pass.
>
> It is also admirably suited for contractors' purposes; the wheels being small it will ascend steep gradients, and, from its lightness, may readily be worked over contractors' metals, where a larger engine could not safely be used.
>
> 'The engine can be constructed for lines of 3ft gauge and upwards, and the buffers placed to suit any special mineral or ballast wagons.'

Another 'transitional' locomotive, W/N 163 of 1865 was an Australian export and spent some of its career working on a breakwater railway on the Clarence River, New South Wales. (*Bruce Macdonald Collection*)

Significantly, therefore, W/N 1 was constructed on the same principles as the later standard gauge standard designs (apart from the need for a 'waisted in' firebox wrapper to fit between the mainframes), thereby establishing these principles as part of Manning Wardle practice even before the Boyne Engine Works manufacturer had acquired its collection of E.B. Wilson drawings on 2 September 1859. As mentioned in Chapter Eight, these principles appear to have been based on the idea of a 'scaled down' version of *La Portena* in coupled form (Manning Wardle went on to build a coupled version of this design for the Western Railway of Buenos Aires as W/Ns 202-3) or possibly *Solferino*. Be all of this as it may, the earliest Manning Wardle 0-4-0ST locomotive to receive an official standard classification was W/N 13 of 1860 (8in by 14in cylinders) which eventually received the designation 'D', followed by W/N 14 (9½ in by 14in) which became the prototype of the 'E' class. Before giving greater consideration to the standard 0-4-0ST designs and their immediate relatives, one important point needs to be made; the solitary standard gauge locomotive to receive a permanent 'A' classification, W/N 270 of 1869, belonged to the cylindrical firebox/equal overhang school of design and is therefore outside the scope of this volume.

The smallest of the standard gauge standard designs was the 'B' class (6in by 12in cylinders) and in all, thirteen true members of this class were completed between 1863 and 1872. The earliest pair were built without running boards ahead of the driving area, with 2ft 3in wheels and with a 4ft 6in wheelbase. The class standard dimensions became established with W/N 97 and the final five class locomotives of this group were all exported: four to Peru and one to Brazil. One of the Peruvian exports, W/N 349 possessed features that included an enlarged tank extending over the smokebox; a donkey pump and a special pillar canopy. The groundwork for the introduction of the 'C' class was laid with the building of W/N 322 which appeared in November 1870 for export to Peru. Although nominally another 'B' class, its cylinder bore was increased to 7½in. In the event, only two 'C' (7in by 12in) class locomotives were built for standard gauge use: W/Ns 759 and 770, both of which appeared in 1880. Unlike the earliest 'B' class locomotives, these had contemporary refinements such as rounded, as opposed to angular, tank corners and a Manning Wardle injector. A latter-day incarnation of the spirit of the 'C' class came was the oil-burning W/N 1910 of 1916 *Sir Edward*, which possessed the same cylinder dimensions, but a rather larger boiler, which necessitated a correspondingly reduced tank capacity. It was also equipped with an 'Austerity' pattern cab, and mainframes and cylinders of a design commensurate with its date of construction.

A work-weary 'K' class 0-6-0ST is pictured seeing out its last days at Stewarts & Lloyds Minerals Ltd., Harston, on 11 September 1959. W/N 556 outshopped on 14 June 1875 began life as Cannock No. 1 at Norton Cannock Colliery, being sold in 1910 on the cessation of mining at this location to Holwell Iron Co. where the engine became Holwell No. 7. After a somewhat nomadic career, this locomotive came into the ownership of Stewarts & Lloyds, working firstly at Eaton Quarries from February 1954 and migrating to Harston Quarries in October 1957. Out of use by the time the photograph was taken, Holwell No. 7 was scrapped a year afterwards. Certain relatively modern features, such as Ross 'pop' safety valves and mechanical lubricator, were fitted to the engine during its career. The most intriguing feature about this locomotive is that despite the fact that original pattern compensating beams were still fitted at this stage, the mainframe design is totally unlike the pattern normally associated with the 'K' class, being 'rectangular' in its lower profile and hence the frames would have been non-Manning Wardle replacements. (*The late James Peden*) 'K' class locomotive

The 'D' class proved to be a popular design with contractors and industrial installations alike during the latter part of the nineteenth century, and over a thirty-nine-year period some fifty-four specimens were produced, with the design undergoing some important modifications including steam and exhaust piping relocated totally above the cylinders; the raising of running board level to dispense with splashers; dispensing with the angular corners on the saddle tank; redesigned mainframes and other chassis alterations and the use of a circular, rather than lift-up smokebox door. The contractor Lucas & Aird was an important customer during the 1880s and dictated certain detail requirements for its locomotives; one of these locomotives, W/N 941, apparently reached Suakin during the S&BR campaign of 1885 prior to return to the UK. Only three much modified derivatives, all to 5ft 6in gauge, were built after 1899 and these were supplied in 1905-7 to Argentina. The 'E' class proved to be nearly twice as numerous, amounting to some 103 members completed over a period of nearly forty-three years (excluding W/N 736 which was a rebuild of earlier classmate W/N 213), with a cylinder bore of 9in eventually proving to be the prevailing standard dimension despite some thirty-six class members being constructed with a corresponding dimension of 9½in Four of these locomotives were built to gauges of greater than standard: two of 5ft gauge; one of 5ft 3in and one of 5ft 6in. Most of the

Works No. 608 of 1876 was built for the contractor Logan & Hemingway and originally sent to Melbourne in Derbyshire. It was subsequently sold to the Manchester, Sheffield & Lincolnshire Railway where it is illustrated here as No. 537. Apart from the latter company's number plate, the engine appears to be in virtually original condition, retaining both its lift-up smokebox door and its E.B. Wilson-pattern weatherboard (a fitting apparently favoured by Logan & Hemingway). It was scrapped in October 1903. (*John Scott-Morgan Collection*)

'K' class 0-6-0ST W/N 620 left the Boyne Engine Works on 22 August 1876 to begin its career with the contractor J. Barnes at Chatburn Lancs., bearing the name *Lulu*. It is seen here some years later with another contractor, Mackay & Davies, near Saunderton having been renamed *Helen*. This locomotive appears to have been a fairly typical example of its type, incorporating both conventional and 'block' buffers, the latter to facilitate the handling of what the makers termed 'earth wagons' by contractors' locomotives. The only other details warranting special consideration are the fact that the smokebox rivets are all countersunk, the sandpipes actually face rearwards towards the intermediate wheelset (rather than straight down as on earlier locomotives) and the toolbox is on the left-hand side. (*Industrial Railway Society*)

The oldest surviving member of the 'K' class today is Works No. 641 of 1877, which started life as *Soloman* with G. Decon at Kettering. The following completion of work at this site, the engine was sold to another contractor, J.T. Fairbank of Darlington, who renamed it *Sharpthorn* and used it on construction of the Lewes-East Grinstead section of the L.B. & S.C.R. (part of which forms part of the present day Bluebell Railway). After passing through the hands of another contractor, William Rigby, W/N 641 fell into the hands of the dealer C.D. Phillips of Newport by 1889 whence it was sold to Samuel Williams Ltd. of Dagenham Dock, becoming this concern's No. 4. Here, the engine put in some 69 years of service, even acquiring a radio telephone in 1954, before being withdrawn and preserved by the owners in 1958. After a period on load to Bressingham Steam Museum at Diss, Norfolk (which came to an end in 1981), W/N 641 was loaned out again, this time to the Bluebell Railway where it arrived in time for the centenary of the opening in 1982, subsequently being purchased (sadly without any service records) by the latter entity from Williams' liquidator for £1500. This photograph shows the locomotive at work at Dagenham during the 1950s and well illustrates the modifications received during the locomotive's working life. Replaced components include the heavy 'girder pattern' cab steps; the boiler (with manhole in the firebox wrapper and circular smokebox door); the chimney, and the injector on the right hand side in lieu of feed pump. The engine is certainly a well-used machine and any scheme to restore it to working order on the line it once helped to build will necessarily be a costly one, especially is anything approximating to its original appearance is to be achieved. (*John Scott-Morgan Collection*)

remarks pertaining to customer base and design refinements that apply to the 'D' class apply to the 'E', save for three important points: firstly, the circular smokebox door never became a standard fitting on the 'E' class as built, in spite of its longer period of construction than the 'D'; secondly unlike the 'D' class, two 'E' class locomotives (W/Ns 1574 & 1582) were supplied with cabs when new; and thirdly, the 'single-boss' wheel centre was designated a standard component for the class as built for domestic customers, albeit only being fitted to the last-built of such locomotives, W/N 1610 *Nipper*. An important point relating to W/Ns 1574 & 1582 concerns the fact that the problem of priming once again raised its ugly head. This was initially cured by the fitting of a bulbous projection on the left-hand side of the firebox wrapper from which steam was taken to the cylinders.

Works Number 641 was not the only locomotive of its class to have been employed on construction of the Lewes-East Grinstead line and in 1879 J.T. Fairbank took delivery of Works Number 725 *Grinstead*. This locomotive eventually found its way into the hands of William Rigby of Driffield in 1899 who, as *Middleton*, used it on the Chichester-Grove Park track widening contract and then on railway extension work at Folkestone Harbour. Sold to the South Eastern & Chatham Railway for £520 in 1904, it was repaired, between April 1904 and March 1905, fitted with a new commodious cab, painted in S.E. & C.R. Wainwright-era livery and, after trials at Ashford, allocated to Folkestone Harbour. A new boiler was fitted in 1911 and new cylinders (supplied by the makers) in May 1913. Numbered 752 by the SE&CR, the former *Grinstead* is seen at Folkestone Harbour after reboilering circa 1912. the aesthetic effect had being spoilt by the new smokebox, which, as with the illustration of W/N 620, did not have 'snap head' rivets (apart from on the door) to match the tank. (*John Scott-Morgan Collection*)

Two photographs survive of W/N 1582 having suffered serious impact damage, mainly at the rear end, and the fact that the wrapper-mounted projection appears in one of these suggests that this damage took place at the Boyne Engine Works, given that no mention of it, nor the consequent repairs, can be found in the Loco Details. These repairs were almost certainly carried out when a proper dome was fitted to the wrapper in 1907. Two 'Special' 5ft 6in gauge 0-4-0ST locomotives with 9in by 14in cylinders were built in 1912 for C.H. Walker Ltd. in connection with the Buenos Aires Harbour Works and their other dimensions were little different from the 'E' class standards. These did incorporate rail-washing gear (as did all the BAHW locomotives), cabs, single-boss wheel centres and other details commensurate with their date of construction. They were also fitted with Isaacson valve gear, a feature of all Manning Wardle locomotives supplied for use on this particular C. H. Walker contract.

The 'F' class, with its standard cylinder dimensions of 10in by 16in (six class members being built new with a bore of 10½in) amounted to some 145 members in various forms. Having been introduced in 1869, none of

The erstwhile *Grinstead* is seen here in final SE&CR condition, by this stage stripped of its ornate livery and chimney cap circa 1919, having lost the latter in June the previous year. Apart from short spells at Tonbridge and on the Hawkhust Branch No. 752 remained a Folkestone-based locomotive throughout its 'Main Line' career. The locomotive survived to be absorbed into Southern Railway stock in 1923 as A752, being sold to Northfleet Deep Water Wharf in August 1925. Here, as *Dolphin*, it put in nearly two decades or so or work before the cylinders were condemned in the spring of 1943, being scrapped in March 1945. (*John Scott-Morgan Collection*)

This locomotive, *Burham* (W/N 730 of 1879) was originally built for Burham Brick & Cement Co. of Aylesford, Kent and finished its working life under APCM ownership. It was distinctive in being built with the early pattern of brackets ('skirting' the spectacles) on its Diamond canopy. (*John Scott-Morgan Collection*)

Another well-known 'K' class, Works Number 890 of 1883 originally built as *Vida* for the contractor J.C. Billups of Cardiff and re-sold to Pauling & Co. Following a spell in Government ownership during World War One, this locomotive was purchased by Lt. Col Stephens and used on the West Sussex Railway where it acquired the *Ringing Rock* nameplate from the much-rebuilt 'Q' class locomotive (W/N 630 of 1876) based on another Colonel Stephens line, the Kent & East Sussex Railway (and which had been involved in a flooding-related derailment in 1921). This view emphasizes the generally decrepit condition of the locomotive during the later 1920s and early 1930s as exemplified by close examination of the smokebox and bunker areas. *Ringing Rock* remained in use until the line's closure in 1935, being put 'beyond use' thereafter by having a wedge driven into the boiler barrel and it was scrapped before the 1936 auction of effects. (*John Scott-Morgan Collection*)

these locomotives possessed steam and exhaust pipes beneath the cylinders or angular-cornered saddle tanks when new and despite the fact that the earliest representative, W/N 275 was built with 3ft wheels, 2ft 9in. became the prevailing standard, although W/N 288 was built with 4ft wheels and other dimensions were used. The 'F' class was built over a fifty-six-year period stretching almost to the end of locomotive production at Boyne Engine Works and there were myriad detail differences, including two locomotives (W/Ns 712 & 722) built with condensing gear and side tanks for use by J. Dickson Jnr., the contractor for the conversion of the Swansea & Mumbles Railway for the use of steam motive power. Six members of a variant group with a lengthened wheelbase of 6ft (as opposed to 4ft 9in) were supplied to the Norwegian Trunk Railway between 1875 and 1892 and the second of these, W/N 576 of 1875, was noteworthy in being with first of the group to be built new with a circular smokebox door, some three decades before the practice became standard for the class as a whole. W/N 576 is still extant, but sadly not restored it its original condition, a daunting task experienced with sister locomotive W/N 1248 of 1892 which has been returned to working condition. Eight of the class members were built to 5ft 6in gauge: the last four of these were supplied in 1911-13 to C.H. Walker Ltd. for use in Buenos Aires. Owing to the long period of construction, there was much updating of the basic 'F' specification and by the time the last class member, W/N 2044 appeared, cabs; deeper mainframes; the use

This locomotive, W/N 968, was delivered on 21 April 1885 to the War Department was part of a specific order for nine 'K' class locomotives for the abortive Suakin-Berber Railway Expedition in Sudan. Since the order for the abandonment of the campaign was given a week later, it is unlikely that the locomotive ever reached Suakin. These locomotives were intended to be used with separate four-wheel water tenders and armoured 'bodies' above footplate level (with canvass sheeting below), and examples of the former were later used on the Royal Arsenal Railways at Woolwich as mobile oil tanks. After a two to three-year period of storage at the Royal Arsenal's 'Berber' site on Plumstead Marshes, W/N 968 saw out its career with the War Department with the Royal Artillery at Lydd, being disposed of circa 1907, after which further trace of the locomotive appears to have been lost. In this view, the engine is seen at Lydd running, sans leading coupling rods, as a 2-4-0ST. (*Industrial Railway Society*)

of two injectors and no pump; double-apron cylinders; 'single boss' wheel centres and other contemporary 'up-to-date' features were the order of the day.

Two locomotives that may be termed 'semi-F' class' with 10in by 18in cylinders were built in 1882 (W/Ns 838-9) to 5ft gauge for a Russian customer, who never took delivery. These were later re-gauged to standard for the domestic market, which for these outside cylinder locomotives must have involved axle replacement and a fair amount of 'surgery' to the pump stretcher and bufferbeams. From the point of view of inside cylinder designs, although design adaptation for 5ft gauge was not easy, 5ft 6in could often be accomplished (mainly) by using longer axles and hornblock/axlebox assemblies mounted outboard of the mainframes, with buffers centred at 6ft 5in. Two surviving ex-Walker/Buenos Aires 'M' class 0-6-0STs in Spain are classic examples of this last-mentioned method of adaptation.

Although a drawing exists for the 'G' class, no standard gauge locomotive was ever constructed to this basic plan and only one 5ft 6in gauge de facto example comes within the scope of this volume, Argentine export W/N 1176 of 1890; 4ft. 4in gauge locomotives for use in Brazil were built to a similar specification. By way of contrast, the 'H' class (12in by 18in cylinders) proved more popular with customers with 182 examples, of which five were of 5ft 6in gauge and one was a crane locomotive, being constructed between 1867 and 1925, to which must be added W/N 284 of 1869, originally built in modified

This view, taken at the Shoeburyness Military Railway in 1901, is believed to show another locomotive originally intended for the Suakin-Berber Railway, W/N 969, which was delivered to the War Department on 1 May 1885. Transferred to Shoeburyness after its period of storage on Plumstead Marshes, this locomotive received a new boiler (with a side hinged circular smokebox door) from the makers in 1911 and was advertised for sale in 1921, being scrapped shortly afterwards. (*Author's Collection*)

By the late 1890's, the Manning Wardle standard classes had largely taken on their mature form and Works No. 1416 *Emily*, supplied on 28 February 1899 to contractor J.D. Nowell & Son at Holme near Peterborough was a fine representative example. By 1917, *Emily* had passed to the Austin Motor Co. at Longbridge works, Birmingham where it spent the rest of its working life, being withdrawn and scrapped circa 1956. *Emily* is seen here at Longbridge on 19 July 1950 in a fine external state of turnout, the only drawback being the repair to the lower part of the smokebox door. The engine exhibits features typical of its date of construction, including the enclosed cab with integral trailing bunker and rectangular cutouts with radiused upper corners. The saddle tank is straight sided but is no longer 'angular' and its rivets are now countersunk. The Wilson-pattern chimney found on the early standard locomotives has now given way to the elegant Manning Wardle 'house' variety, whilst the smokebox would have incorporated a circular dished door from new. The sandboxes are now placed at each end of the running boards, whilst below footplate level, the characteristic early pattern 'double-boss' wheel centres are no more, although they continued to be incorporated into some locomotives into the twentieth century, apparently to use up existing stocks. (*The Late Ken Cooper*)

A slightly more modern locomotive than *Emily* was W/N 1590 of 1903, although there was little substantive difference between the two locomotives. This locomotive ended its days with Samuel Williams & Sons Ltd. at Dagenham where it is shown here. (*John Scott-Morgan Collection*)

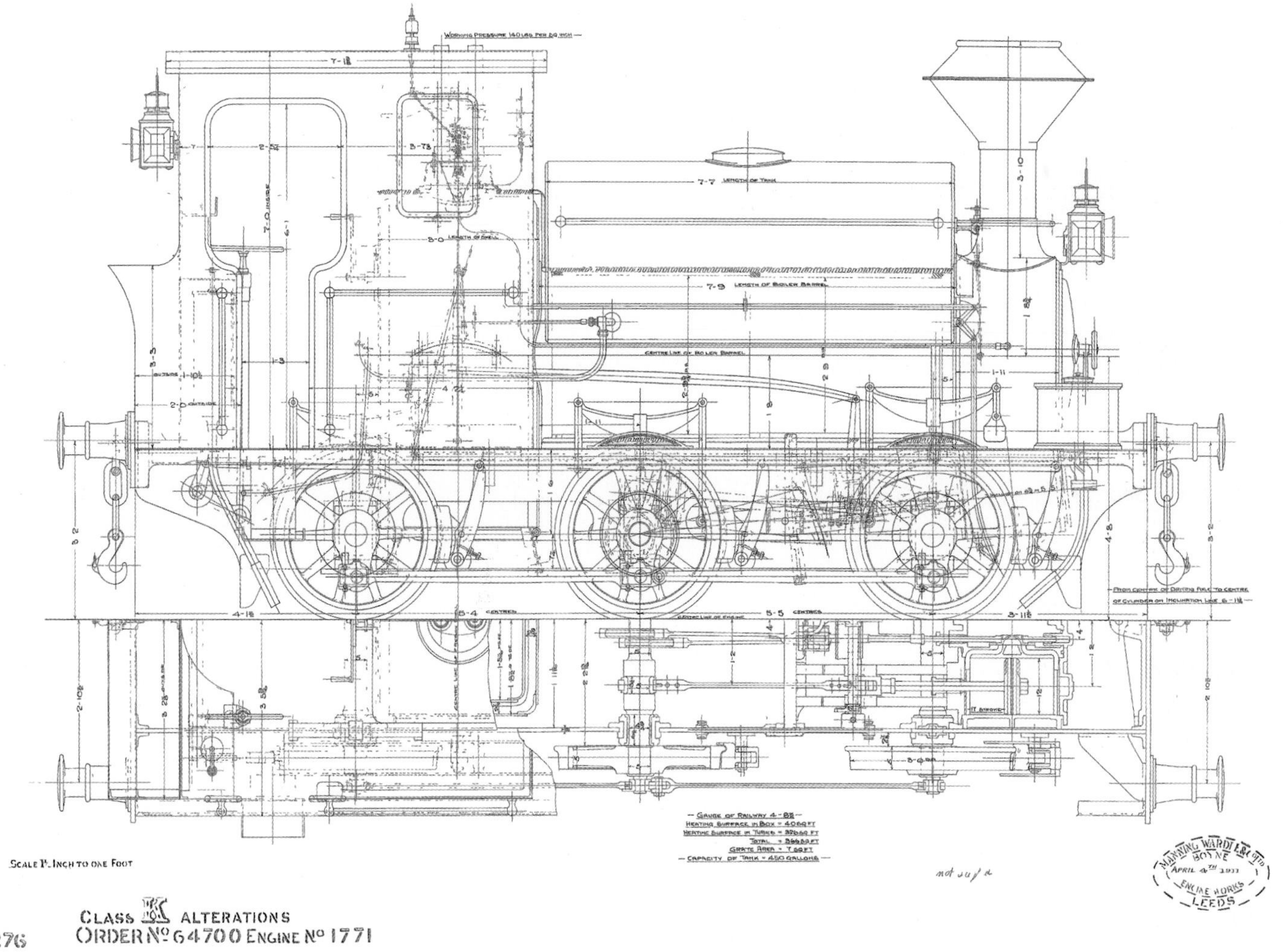

The significant later features found on most of the later members of the 'K' class can be seen in this drawing of W/N 1771 of 1911 *Helgeby* built for a Norwegian customer, for whom a special non-standard type of cab, more akin to some of the maker's locomotives for Russia, was fitted. (*Hunslet Archive*)

Old 'L' class Manning Wardle W/N 731 *Resolute* was supplied on 4 May 1881 to the contractor J.M. Smith at Bury, passing through the hands of another contractor, Gabbott & Owen at Huddersfield before being sold to Amalgamated Anthracite Co.'s Yniscedwyn Colliery. The Burry, Port & Gwendraeth Railway acquired the locomotive in late 1894, renaming it Cwm Mawr, eventually selling it to Avonside Engine Co. of Bristol in August 1904. Avonside rebuilt the locomotive with a new cab and extended the tank over the smokebox. In this form, it became No. 3 *Weston* of the Weston, Clevedon and Portishead Railway and is seen here in a spot of bother with a freight working at Portishead, probably during the 1920s. Note the leading sandboxes of non-Manning Wardle pattern and the ungainly stovepipe chimney, also the vacuum braking to handle the line's passenger traffic. Weston survived until the line's closure in 1940. (*E.N.C. Shorto*)

form to 4ft 1in gauge for the Middleton Railway and re-gauged in 1881, together with a 5ft 6in de facto duplicate of W/N 2043 of 1925 built by Kitson in 1928. The 'H' class *may* have been in spirit the oldest of the Manning Wardle four-coupled standard classes, assuming that the theory about *Solferino*'s design put forward in Chapter Seven is correct. In design development over the years, the path of evolution generally followed that of the 'F' class, but there were some important differences. A refinement introduced with W/N 514 of 1875 and fitted to a small number of class members was the single composite iron/timber block buffer, fitted at each end in conjunction with a pivoted drawbar to facilitate the negotiation of sharp curves. This type of drawgear is perhaps most associated with the Royal Arsenal at Woolwich and all Manning Wardle locomotives specifically built for use there, including a single 'F' class (W/N 961 of 1885), were fitted with this feature. The final 'H' built for use at the Royal Arsenal, W/N 953 of 1886 went a stage further in being additionally built with a shortened wheelbase of 4ft 9in, as was the next class member, W/N 984 of 1886 for Portsmouth Dockyard. This modification had already found a niche in relation to the '14 inch' classes as will be seen later. Over a three-decade period commencing in 1871 with W/N 333, an interesting and in some cases fairly long-lived group of six locomotives with 3ft 6in wheels were produced for

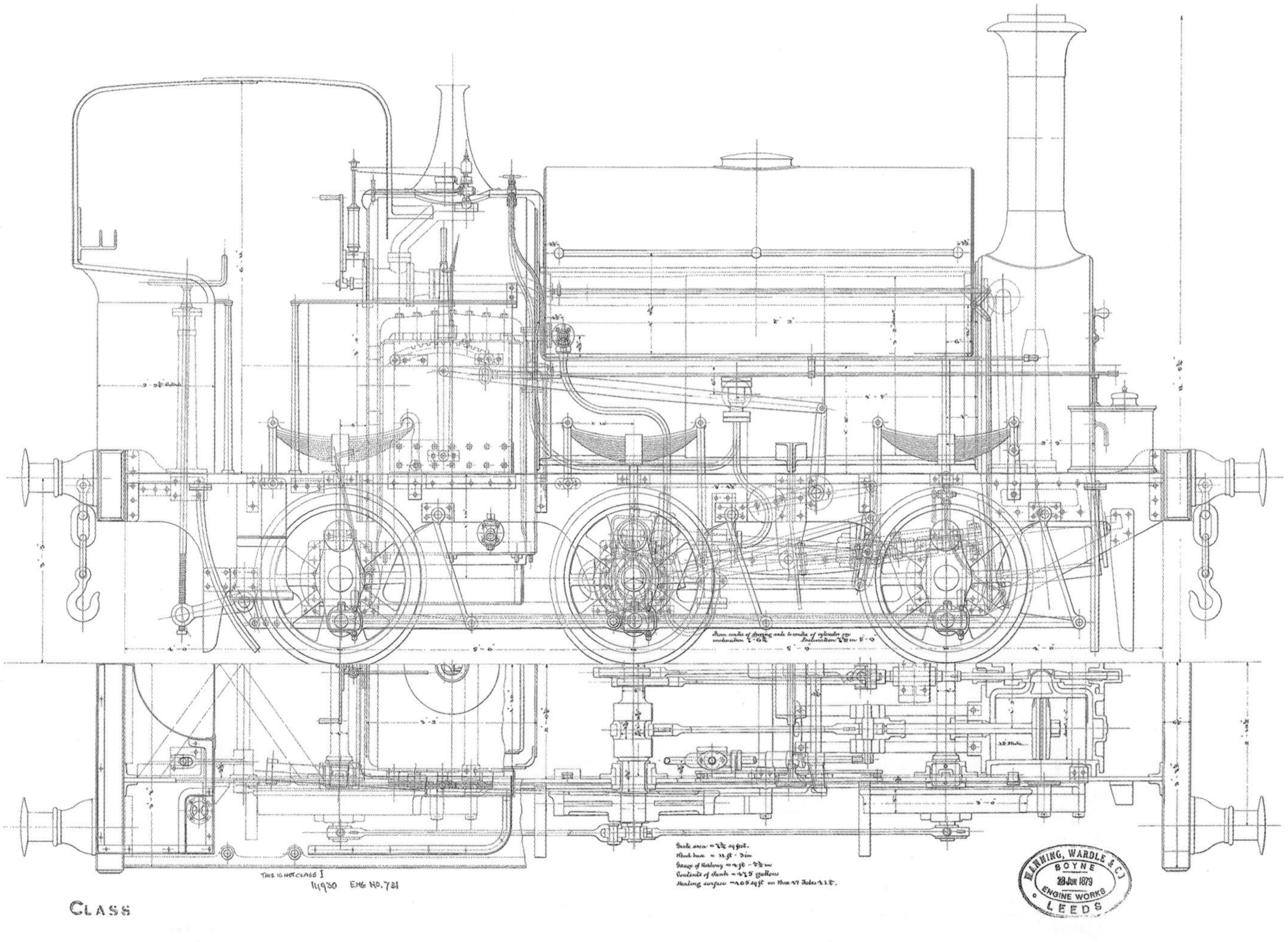

This 0-6-0ST drawing dated 28 June 1879 contains annotations showing that it was used for W/N 731of 1881 *Resolute* as built. The valve gear arrangement was different from that used on the 'Old I' and 'K' classes in that the reversing drop link bellcranks pointed forwards from the weighshaft, with the balance weights trailing. The eccentrics would therefore have been set at 180 degrees displacement from their counterparts on those classes as the reversing lever and reach rod arrangement was not altered. At this stage, the lift-up smokebox door, 'wrap over' roof and 'one feedpump, one injector' arrangements were still the order of the day. (*Hunslet Archive*)

Gjers, Mills & Co. and these worked at the Ayresome Ironworks near Middlesbrough. Photographs of some of these locomotives taken during the latter stages of their careers show, *inter alia* the large cast-iron one-piece block buffers with which they were fitted. In an attempt to improve the performance of the 'H' class generally, the boiler tube arrangement was revised from the 73-tube configuration hitherto used to an 81-tube configuration from W/N 1847 onwards, whilst Isaacson valve gear was fitted to W/N 1846. Most significantly, W/N 345 of 1871 earned the distinction of being the last traditional early-pattern four-coupled standard gauge Manning Wardle locomotive extant in the United Kingdom when it was scrapped in 1964.

There are a few 'oddities' that can be dealt with at this stage. Firstly, W/N 1727 of 1908, which was built with 2ft 9in wheels, Isaacson valve gear and a 4ft 9in wheelbase to the requirements of Portsmouth Dockyard. This locomotive possessed equal leading and trailing frame overhangs, a feature which, as has been seen, is normally associated with locomotives equipped with cylindrical fireboxes. W/N 1931 of 1918 was even more distinctive in being a 'crane locomotive' whose boiler and chassis dimensions were clearly inspired by the post-1914 'H' class. Finally, two '12 inch' 0-4-0STs were built in 1904 and 1911 to 5ft 6in gauge for Rose-Innes, Cox & Co. in Chile. Their general dimensions were similar but not identical to the 'H' class and both were

This locomotive is probably the best-known of the New 'L' class 0-6-0STs, being Works No. 1210 in 1891. It was originally built for Logan & Hemingway of No. 30 and delivered to Dunstan & Barlow's siding near Chesterfield for construction work on the Manchester, Sheffield & Lincolnshire Railway's lines in Derbyshire, afterwards being transferred to Nottingham for work on the London Extension that transformed the MS&LR into the Great Central Railway. Later renumbered 10, the locomotive remained in Logan & Hemingway ownership until the company's liquidation in 1935, seeing service on further contracts in connection with the GCR at Wath Concentration Sidings in 1905-7 and Doncaster Avoiding Lines in 1908-9, after which the engine returned to Leeds for a rebuild which included a new boiler. Further contract work in 'Great Central' territory followed, at Frodingham in 1910-12; Keadby Deviation in 1912-15 and a line serving Thoresby Colliery in 1925-6. The feed pump had been replaced by an injector supplied by the Makers in 1918. Next, the locomotive was transferred to LM&SR territory, seeing use at Barnt Green in 1926-7 and the Doe Lea Branch near Staveley before returning to Thoresby Colliery in August 1927. Three months later, the engine returned to former GCR territory in the form of assisting in the 'quadrupling' of the Manchester-Sheffield Main Line between Mottram & Broadbottom and Godley Junction Stations. No. 10's contracting 'swan song' was work on the Great Western Railway's Westbury and Frome avoiding lines between 1930 and 1935. The photograph shows it on a GWR "Crocodile" low-centre wagon at Westbury awaiting return to Logan & Hemingway's depot in Doncaster after completion of this work, after which it was sold to Cranfield Ironstone Co. Ltd. near Kettering in Northamptonshire. Here the locomotive acquired the *Sir Berkeley* nameplates from the Midland Ironstone Co.'s 'O' class (W/N 1631 of 1904) that had been scrapped after a short working life. The newly-renamed Sir Berkeley remained in use on the Northamptonshire system, latterly as spare engine, into the early 1960s, receiving an open-backed cab (in lieu of weatherboard) in 1957 along with various other minor modifications. It was subsequently acquired for preservation and moved to the Keighley & Worth Valley Railway in January 1965, being restored to working order over the next three years and steamed in public preservation for the first time on 11 February 1968. (*John Scott-Morgan Collection*)

Sir Berkeley is currently owned by the Vintage Carriages trust and for several years has been based on the Middleton Railway where this September 2006 view was taken. (*Author*)

Two classic New ''L' class locomotives, both fitted with the Diamond canopy, are shown in this view taken at Brookes Ltd.'s Tuck Royd Quarries circa 1897. In the foreground is W/N 1330 of 1897 *Silex*, whilst on the right in the distance can be found the second-hand W/N 1310 of 1896 *Nonslip*, formerly *Vulcan*. (*S.A. Leleux*)

The North Sunderland linked Chathill, some ten miles north of Alnmouth on the main Newcastle-Edinburgh Line, with Seahouses. On 23 June 1898, this little railway took delivery of *Bamburgh*, (Works Number 1394), a variant of the New 'L' class of the period fitted with a Westinghouse brake on the right hand side (necessitating the relocation of the handbrake column to the other side), 3ft 6in diameter wheels, redesigned frame ends and other sundry modifications. There were three members of the basic '3ft 6in' variant class, the other two being W/N 1360 of 1897 for the Cawood, Wistow & Selby Light Railway, and 1456 of 1899 for the Isle of Axholme Light Railway. *Bamburgh* led a relatively uneventful life, having its feed pump replaced by a second No. 6 Injector in 1920 and losing its wooden toolbox prior to a repaint apparently carried out early in 1934. This view was taken at Seahouses Station apparently in the late 1920s after the rear (non-matching) pair of cutout screens had been fitted. The concave face of the air brake reservoir can be seen beneath the rear end of the left hand mainframe, whilst the 'equalizing' beam is visible between the leading and intermediate axles. (*John Scott-Morgan Collection*)

reported extant in Santiago in recent years. The first attempt at a standard '13in by 18in' 0-4-0ST came with four locomotives built in 1874-5 that were eventually classified New 'I' in the Order Book and 'P' in the Loco Details. Essentially, they possessed the larger boiler and 550-gallon tank capacity of the 'P' class, but the 13 inch cylinders of the New 'I' and can be designated 'I'/'P' class. The New 'I' class proper began with W/N 659 in 1877 and in all, some eight examples appeared during the years up to 1905. The usual design revisions, such as circular smokebox door; cab; independent fastening of smokebox and cylinders; redesigned frames, and, on the last-built example (W/N 1659), cylinders increased by ½ inch in diameter took place during the period of construction of the class. One 'special' 0-4-0ST with 13in by 20in cylinders (W/N 2034) was constructed as late as 1924 incorporating such contemporaneous features as a steam brake; rail-washing gear; two injectors (no pump) and a full set of cylinder cocks. It survived until 1955.

Bamburgh is seen here in 1934 following the aforementioned repaint and the fitting of its leading pair of cutout screens. This view reveals several important details, such as the smokebox lamp iron; the Roscoe lubricator (on the left side of the tank front); the Westinghouse pump (on the right hand side partly obscured by the smokebox); the leading frame ends (of different configuration to W/N 1210), and the wheel splashers (of 'K' class pattern and hence not vertically 'centre' with the axles). It remained with the railway until October 1949 when it was sold to Motherwell Machinery & Scrap Co. Ltd. for breaking up. (*John Scott Morgan Collection*)

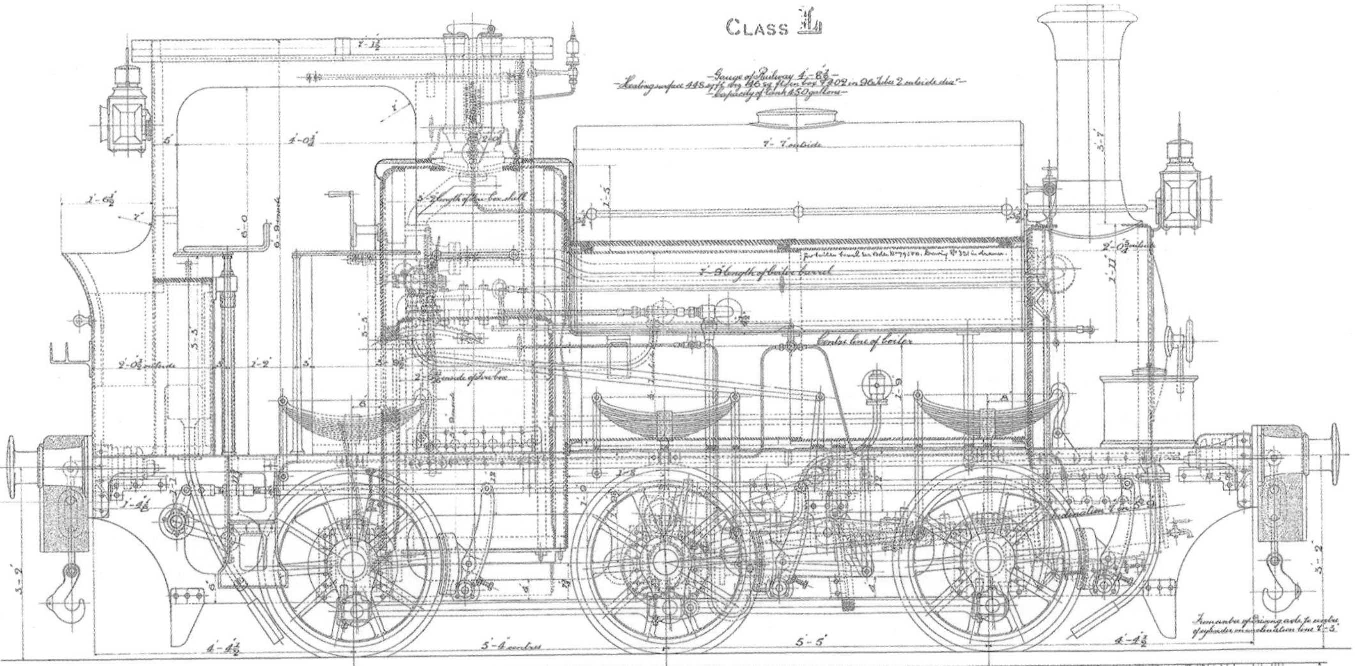

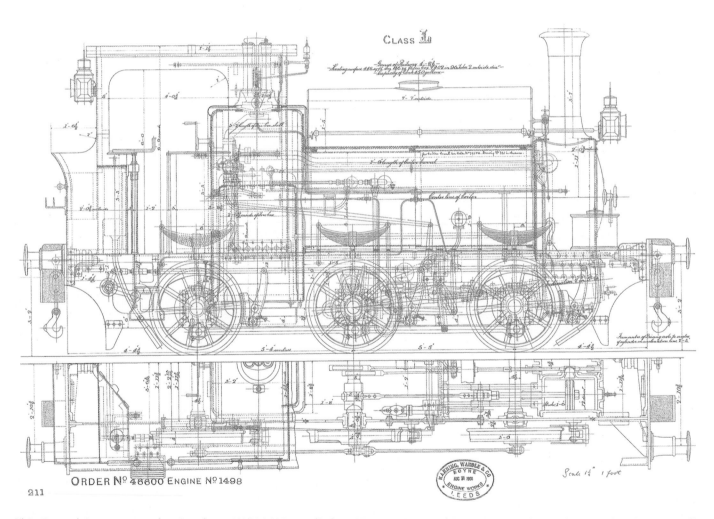

This General Arrangement drawing shows W/N 1498 supplied on 27 June 1900 to the contractor John Aird & Co. This drawing well represents the New 'L' class in its mature form with its fin de siècle cab incorporating upper radiused cutouts and conventional pattern wheel centres in place of the 'double boss' variety. Rail-washing gear was fitted to this locomotive but the internal handrail, attached to the rear spectacle plate, found on many other Manning Wardle locomotives of the period, was not apparently fitted to this example. Note also the combination of ordinary and 'block' buffers, a common feature of the company's locomotives built for contractors. (*Hunslet Archive*)

A classic New 'L' class in its mature form is Works No. 1601, outshopped on 8 May 1903 for the contractor John Aird & Co. Ltd. at Avonmouth as No. 138. After a period in the ownership of another contractor, Perry & Co. (Bow) Ltd. working on the GWR Oxley-Kingswinford contract the locomotive, by then named *Arthur*, passed to the Austin Motor Works at Longbridge until sold to another contractor, P. & W. Anderson Ltd. in 1919 for construction work in relation to the Kent Portland Cement Co.'s (later part of APCM) Kent Works at Stone near Greenhithe. Following completion of the work in 1921, Anderson sold *Arthur* to the Cement Company and the engine worked there until withdrawal and eventual acquisition by the Kent & East Sussex Railway Preservation Society in the early 1960s. (*The late Frank Jones Collection, Industrial Railway Society*)

Arthur was eventually sold by the K&ESRPS and today is to be found on the Middleton Railway, having been renamed *Matthew Murray*. The locomotive is seen here outside the railway's running shed with steam escaping from the overflow of a Pemberthy injector that has replaced the original 'in house' Manning Wardle pattern. (*Author*)

An atmospheric view of W/N 1657 of 1905 *Apex* (with *Arthur* in the background) in steam in front of the shed at APCM Ltd.'s works, Stone, Kent. (*John Scott-Morgan Collection*)

The classic late New 'L' class is represented here by *Azo* (W/N 1895), one of a pair of locomotives supplied in 1916 to Brookes Ltd. of Lightcliffe. A copy of this photograph was presented to Mr. W.A.N. Brooke at the engine's naming ceremony on 25 March of that year. Note that unlike *Arthur*, the cab now extends to meet the saddle tank. (*S.A Leleux*)

Three Brookes New 'L' class locomotives are seen in this view taken outside the company's 1917-built locomotive shed shortly after it was constructed. In the foreground is *Azo's* sister *Nitro* (W/N 1894 of 1916), whilst on the extreme left is *Azo* and in the middle of the photograph is *Silex*. (*S.A Leleux*)

In order to replace the rebuilt W/N 50 *Hecate* and as soon as the cessation of hostilities would permit, Lt. Col. Holman F. Stephens ordered a replacement locomotive for the W.C. & P.R. and this came in the form of modified de facto New 'L' class W/N 1970. The new locomotive, which became No. 5, is seen here at Clevedon Sheds and certain details, notably the raised boiler pitch and disc wheels, were clearly inspired by *Hecate*. Note also the pipe for the vacuum ejector (entering the smokebox on the right-hand side) and the spectacles hinged at an oblique angle to clear the 670-gallon saddle tank. (*Colonel Stephens Museum*)

WC&PR No.5 is seen in this view from the left-hand side, showing traces of its original lined-out livery, although the right-hand spectacle glass is broken. Given the design of the water tank, the location would appear to be Weston at an earlier date than the previous view. (*Colonel Stephens Museum*)

Despite the fact that the 'L' classification had fallen out of use by the time of its construction, there is no doubting the pedigree of de facto New 'L' class W/N 2025 of 1923 *Winston Churchill* currently on display at the Black Country Museum in Dudley, where it is seen on 22 November 2016. (*Author*)

Two de facto New 'L' class locomotives were constructed by Kitson and the second of these, W/N 5458 of 1932 is seen in this view. (*Industrial Railway Society*)

Works No. 341 was a long-lived locomotive, originally delivered on 24 1871 to the contractor Eckersley & Bayliss as *Scotby* for use in the construction of the Settle & Carlisle Railway. Following completion of this work, *Scotby* was sold into colliery service, passing into the hands of Newton, Chambers & Co. Ltd. (Thorncliffe Ironworks & Collieries), Yorkshire, where it was renamed *Silkstone*, thence to Malton Colliery & Coke Ovens near Lanchester in June 1946, becoming National Coal Board (No.5 Area) property in 1947. *Silkstone* was subsequently transferred to Bearpark Colliery in May 1956 and to East Hedley Hope Colliery near Tow Law during August the same year. Although rebuilt three times; 1903, 1925 (by Newton, Chambers & Co.) and 1935, the engine's Manning Wardle origins stood out to the end. In this view, the original rectangular maker's plate can be seen on the waist sheet. Latterly fitted with a cab, *Silkstone* was scrapped on site by D.S. Bowran Ltd. of Gateshead in April 1959. (*John Scott-Morgan Collection*)

Manning Wardle W/N 75 *Morlais* was delivered on 26 June 1863 to Dowlais Iron Co. Apart from having 14in by 18in cylinders in lieu of the class standard, it was in all respects the prototype 'M' class locomotive and it possessed many features typical of its date of construction, including the configuration of wheel centres; boiler and firebox design; leading compensating levers; 'angular' tank with snap head rivets and preheater, and early Manning Wardle chimney. (*Makers' Photograph via Industrial Railway Society*)

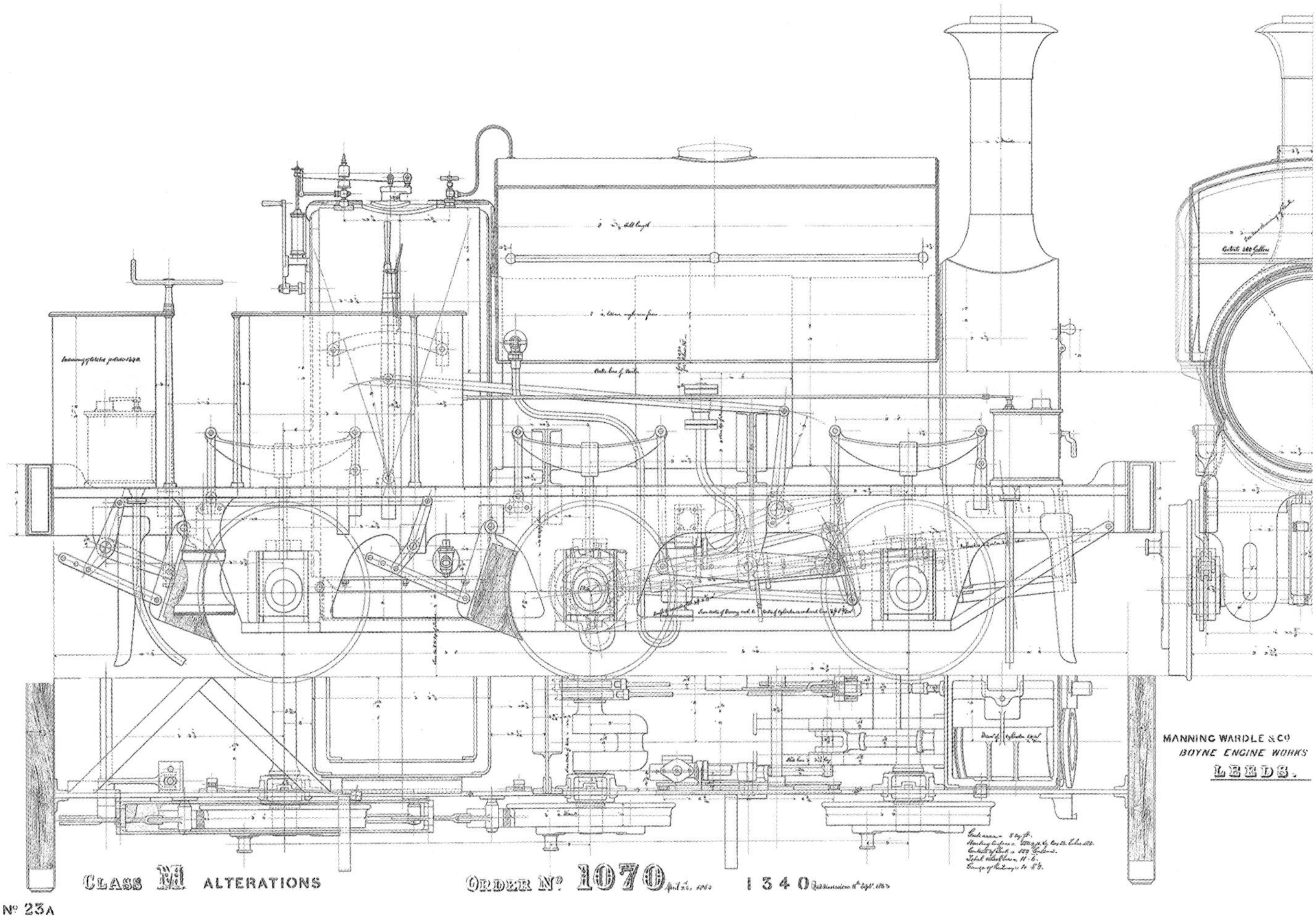

This is the General Arrangement drawing for W/N 75. (*Hunslet Archive*)

Works No. 654 was delivered on 27 April 1877 to Chesterfield & Boythorpe Colliery Co. Ltd as *Alvechurch*. The locomotive worked at Ramshaw and Boythorpe Collieries before being purchased by the makers and re-sold to Oxted Greystone Lime Co. Ltd., Surrey in 1921. It is seen here at Kinnerley on the Shropshire & Montgomeryshire Railway in War Department ownership over two decades later. (*John Scott-Morgan Collection*)

This rather sad photograph shows Manning Wardle W/N 654 on its final journey at Clarkefield (L.M.S.) on 12 May 1946. No longer required by the War Department following the cessation of hostilities during the previous year, it was making a one-way trip to Steel Breaking & Dismantling Co. Ltd. at Chesterfield. Note the rather untidy arrangement of the 'wrap over' accommodation for the locomotive's crew. (*B. Roberts*)

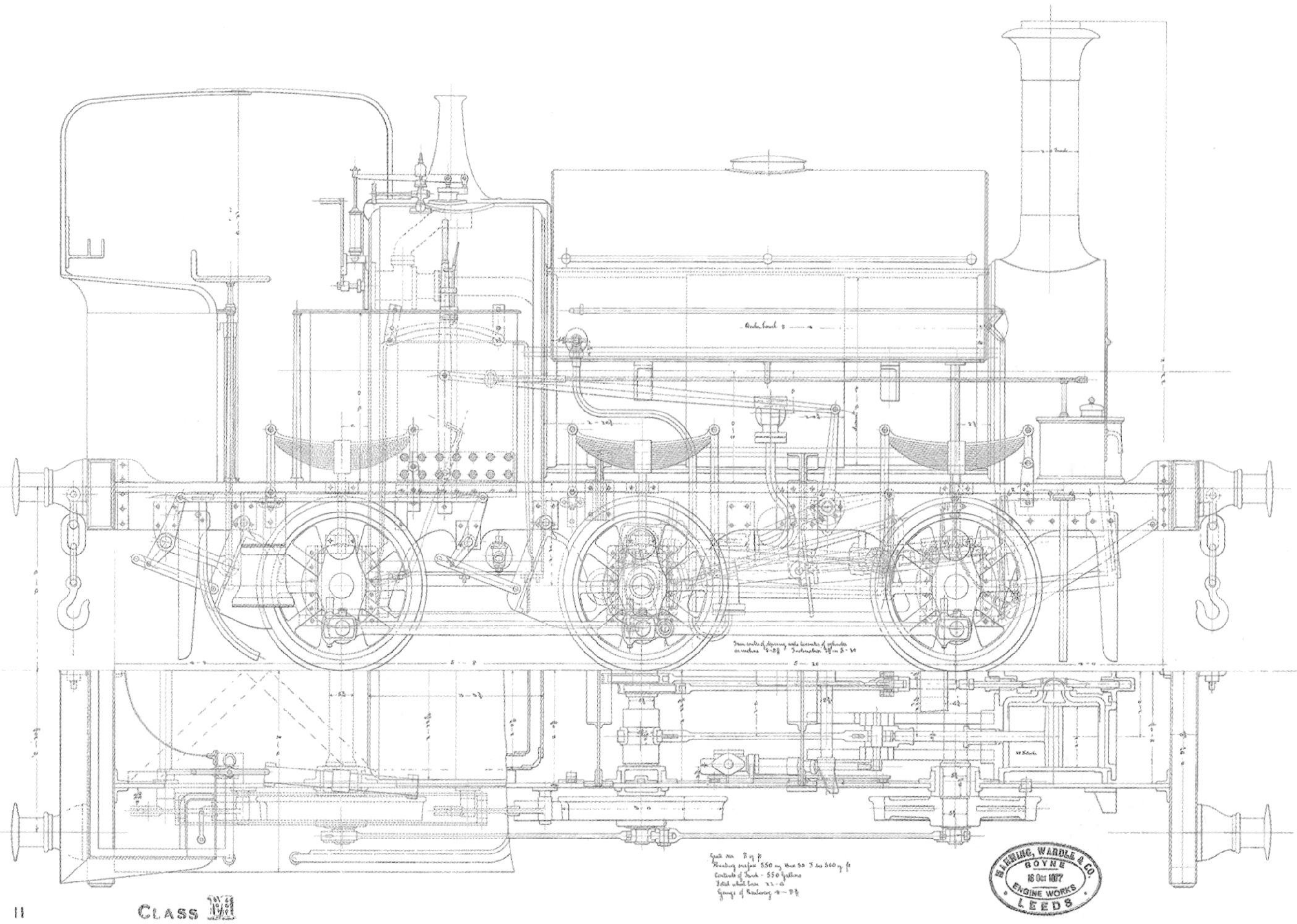

This General Arrangement shows the stage of evolution of the 'M' class shortly after the construction of W/N 641. (*Hunslet Archive*)

Works No. 860 was built in 1883 for Clugston Cawood Colliery in Lincolnshire and was rebuilt by Kitson & Co. Ltd. in 1928. It is seen here in this rear left hand view in 1955 during the final period of its career. It was scrapped, under N.C.B. ownership, shortly afterwards. (*Author's Collection formerly Robert Price*)

This view of the other side of the locomotive shows much detail in close-up, including the simple straight chamfered frame ends, the rail-washing gear, the pipework and controls (inside the cab) associated with the injector and blower, and the rail washing gear. (*Author's Collection formerly Robert Price*)

If one considers the 'I'/'P' class locomotives as a separate group, then there were twenty-nine '14 inch' officially classified 'P' class locomotives (excluding W/N 760), of which five were built with a wheelbase of less than the class standard, to which must be added two de facto members built after the classification was dropped. Of the short-wheelbase locomotives, four were built with a 4ft 9in wheelbase for one customer, namely Moira Colliery in Leicestershire, and these were equipped with single composite block buffers and associated drawgear. Given the survival of three of these locomotives into the 1950s, it is pleasing to record that although none of the five locomotives built for the Royal Arsenal with this buffer/drawgear arrangement is believed to have survived the 1920s, their spirit lingered on in Leicestershire for more than a generation afterwards. In addition to the mainstream design developments over the years, it should be remembered that three customers in particular had specialist requirements, namely Millwall Dock Co. in London; Carron & Co. Ltd. in Glasgow, and Gjers, Mills & Co., whose four specimens incorporated 3ft 6in wheels and design modifications similar to contemporaneous 'H' class locomotives produced for this customer.

Although the 'P' class specification was built in its various forms until 1917, in 1911-12 a new '14 inch' class, with an increased cylinder stroke of 20in and other comparable dimensions, appeared. Given its relatively late appearance, at a time when the classification system was beginning to fragment, it was not surprising that no official classification was allocated, although W/N 1842 was tentatively called 'No. 2 class' in the Order Book. The class amounted to some fourteen locomotives, together with a single extra specimen modified in design to incorporate a 4ft 9in wheelbase. Steam braking was standard and, apart from the use of two injectors and no pump on some class members, and the increased

'M' class Manning Wardle 0-6-0ST W/N 1379 began life as a contractor's locomotive with Price & Wills at Battle, Sussex on 1 July 1898. Originally named *Sidley*, this engine passed through the hands of Topham, Jones & Railton in 1907 thence to Rosyth Dockyard circa 1916 where it was renamed *Allenby* before putting in a spell of work on the Nidd Valley Railway (1921-34). Subsequently sold to another contractor, Sir Lindsay Parkinson, *Allenby* was numbered 206 and used, with several other locomotives, in the construction of ROF Chorley. Apart from a spell on loan to NCB Opencast Executive at Dalton Screens near Wakefield in the late 1940s, *Allenby* remained in the ownership of Sir Lindsay Parkinson until scrapped. The locomotive is seen here at Temple Newsam 8 June 1947 and exhibits all of the characteristics of a mature form 'M' class locomotive, save for the retention of the 'double boss' wheel centres (an interesting comparison with 'K' class locomotive *Emily*). A point to note is how the cross-sectional profile of the saddle tank 'clips' the circular profile of the leading spectacles: the tendency of the forward view to be obscured in this way was a constant problem with Manning Wardle locomotives with '13 inch' cylinders or larger. In this photograph, *Allenby* is shown sandwiched between two Hudswell Clarke *Countess of Warwick* class 0-6-0STs (a direct competitor in the marketplace to the 'M' class): the leading one being *No. 42 Risley* and bringing up the rear No. 54 *Julia*. This latter locomotive (Hudswell W/N 1682 of 1937) would, for the want of £400, have become Easingwold Railway No. 3 in 1947 and survives today under restoration at Ruddington on the outskirts of Nottingham. (*C. A. Appleton*)

cylinder diameter on W/N 1828, there were comparatively few other significant variations among a class that was constructed over little more than a decade. Three, including the last-built (W/N 2028) were built for Moira Colliery, of which two incorporated the distinctive 'Royal Arsenal' pattern buffers and drawgear, although none were built with a 4ft 9in wheelbase. Today, W/N 1795 of 1912 survives at Barrow Hill Roundhouse, although it has yet to return to working order.

One '14 inch' 0-4-0ST of non-standard type, W/N 1509 of 1900 was built to 5ft 6in for export to India. This locomotive had a relatively long cylinder stroke of 22in. The '15 inch' 0-4-0ST's were very much a mixed bag, ranging from two classic nineteenth century types, W/N 581 *Gunner* for the Royal Arsenal and modified 'P' class W/N 780, through two early twentieth century 'oddments', including W/N 1521 of 1901, which was equipped with drawgear that catered for the mixed standard/3ft 10in gauge system of the Low Moor Iron Co. Ltd. at Bradford, to four representatives a what could have become a standard class had Manning Wardle survived longer. Sadly, before they were withdrawn, the last

By 1921, the 'M' classification had ceased to be used for new locomotives at the Boyne Engine Works, although six locomotives (W/Ns 2001-6) supplied to Bombay Port Trust as Nos. 12-17 respectively between 14 May and 18 June 1921 were 'run of the mill' 'M' class locomotives in all but name save for the fact that they were built with Isaacson's valve gear. W/Ns 2004-6 were purchased by T. W. Ward for £500 each in Bombay and shipped them to its depot at Grays in Esssex. Two of these locomotives subsequently saw home service on the Wissington Light Railway and W/N 2004 worked there on hire in 1935 and 1936, being purchased by this concern in May 1938 for £1350 where it received the spurious identity N.F.F.2. Sold by the Wissington system shortly before the end of the Second World War, the locomotive worked at Frodingham Slag Tip in Scunthorpe in 1945 and was on loan to Crosby Ironstone Co. in 1947-8 prior to being re-purchased by Wards (this time at Templeborough, Sheffield) for £455 during the April of the latter year. Further hirings-out followed: to Constables Matlock Quarries (September 1949); A. Monk & Co., Warrington (Autumn 1951), and finally N.C.B. Harworth Coke Ovens in the autumn of 1954 where a cylinder end cover was pushed out. In the summer of 1955, W/N 2004 returned to the Sheffield depot and is illustrated there in April 1959. It had been scrapped by March 1963. Although fitted from new with a best mild steel (rather than Yorkshire Iron) boiler and a No. 2 Pattern Wakefield sight feed lubricator, this locomotive's direct descent from *Morlais* is self-evident. Further 'modern' features include the design of wheel centres and the shape of the frame ends and bufferbeams (associated with 'dual' spring and block buffers when built: only the former survived to the end), but classic early design features were retained, such as the provision of a feed pump (later replaced by a second injector) and compensating beams. The leading spectacles, unlike those on W/N 1379, fully 'cleared' the saddle tank and the rail washing gear with which the engine was built was removed during its working career. Sister engine W/N 2006 was also purchased by British Sugar Corporation for the Wissington Railway in 1938 (following hirings in 1932, 1935, 1936 and 1937) and remained there until scrapped on site in August 1965. (*The late Frank Jones*)

three locomotives of this group, which worked on the Lambton, Hetton & Joicey Collieries system in County Durham, all lost their characteristic Manning Wardle domeless boilers in favour of the Robert Stephenson & Hawthorn pattern domed variety. No locomotives from this group survive today.

The 'Magnum Opus' of Manning Wardle outside-cylindered 0-4-0ST's first appeared in 1912 with W/N 1802 *Cyclops* for Vickers Ltd., Barrow-in-Furness. The locomotive in question was equipped with 16in by 24in cylinders and 3ft 8in wheels and had the distinction of being the first Manning Wardle locomotive to be built

Works No. 2015 of 7 December 1921 began life as *Abernant* with Cardiff Corporation Waterworks at Cefn and as built was similar to the locomotive in the previous illustration, save for being built with Stephenson valve gear. This resulted in *Abernant* being a totally standard 'M' class although the classification was never officially bestowed. The compensating beam suspension linking the leading and intermediate wheelsets was retained at this stage. By December 1927 through the efforts of T.W. Ward Ltd., *Abernant* was in the hands of the Austin Motor Works, Birmingham, where at some stage between 19 July 1950 (when it was photographed) and 20 November 1963 (when it was sold to John Cashmore of Great Bridge for scrap) it was given a new boiler and its graceful 'waisted in' smokebox was exchanged for a more utilitarian straight sided variety, similar to the later 'K' class pattern as found on *Emily*. Fortunately, *Abernant* was not scrapped but endured a period in Ashted Walk Playground at Duddeston, where it became disfigured by graffiti until transferred to the Standard Gauge Steam Trust at Tysley on 13 July 1989. A decade later the engine was in store at North Woolwich and it now awaits restoration at Ruddington where this photograph was taken on 16 August 2014. Sadly, the years of open storage have taken their toll and much renewal of platework will be necessary in addition to mechanical refurbishment. (*Author*)

using Whitworth screw thread standards. It was in all respects a modern design for the period with two injectors and no pump, and steam braking and three more class members appeared over the succeeding period of a little over six years. One of these, W/N 1888 again suffered the indignity of receiving a domed boiler, whilst it and its two sisters that remained on British soil are now no more. Following the 1918 Armistice, however, W/N 1802 found a new home on the other side of the globe at Lithgow, New South Wales where it was renamed *Possum*. Following withdrawal from service with C. & G. Hoskins Iron Works in 1969, it was presented to the local Eskbank House Museum and remains there on static display to this day.

The precursor to the 'Q' class was the five-strong 'N' class which, as referred to in the text, had difficulties with 'priming' and were therefore fitted with domes on their boiler barrels. The pioneer of this class, W/N 387 of 1873 is shown here whilst running as MS&LR No. 407. (*Author's Collection*)

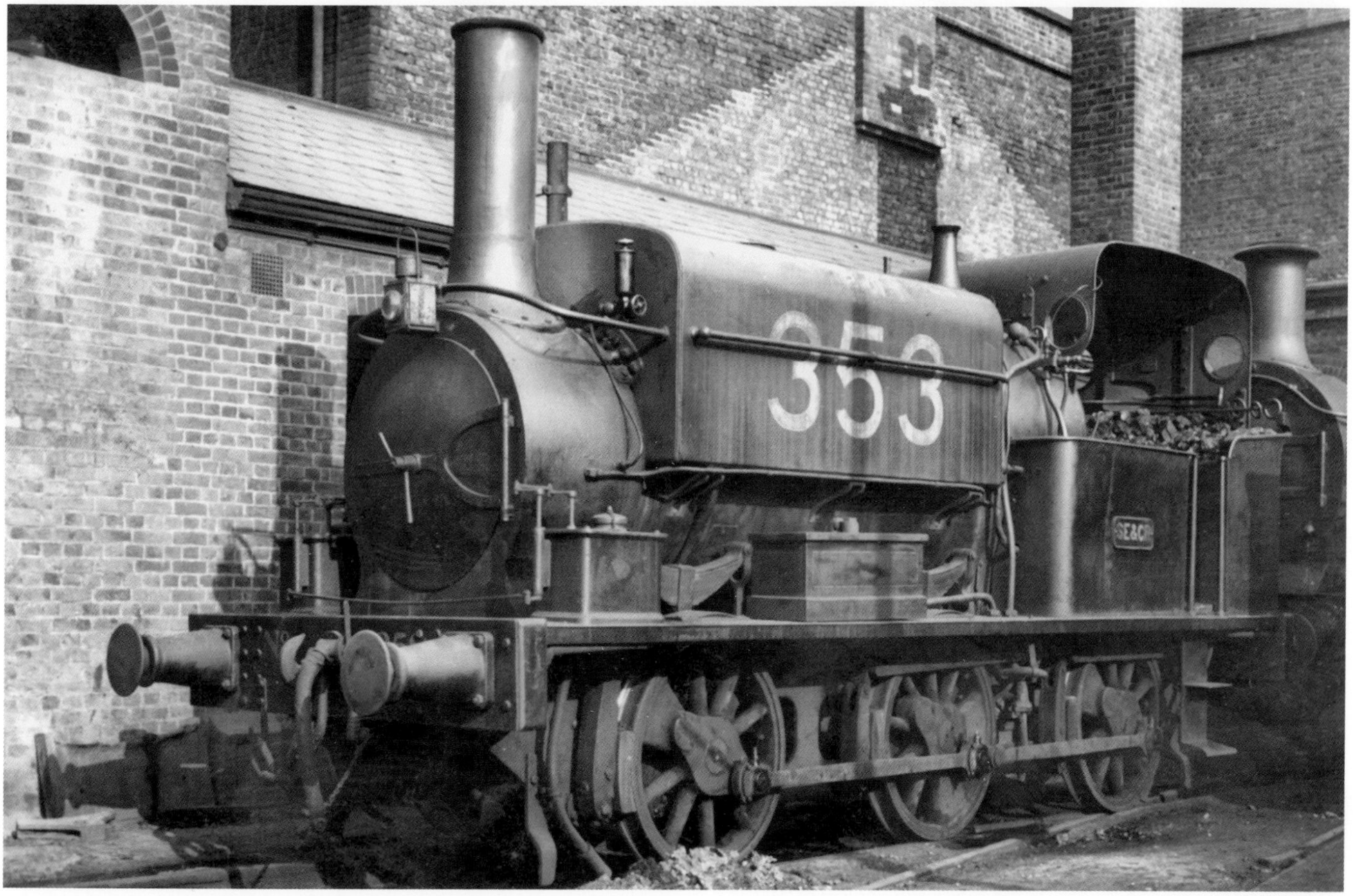

Works No. 1154 of 1890 was supplied on 4 September 1890 to the South Eastern Railway at Ashford for pilot duties at the Carriage & wagon Works there. Numbered 353 by its owners, it was a typical 'Q' class of the period, save for the fact that it was fitted with vacuum brake equipment from new, along with a Jenny Lind pattern smokebox door hinge, a feature revived on some new Manning Wardle locomotives during the 1880s and 1890s. It was little altered during its operational career, receiving SE&CR livery in October 1899; new cylinders in May 1901, and the austere grey livery with stovepipe chimney in March 1917. The injectors also appear to have been repositioned below footplate level at some stage. Note also the leading sandbox linkage. (*John Scott-Morgan Collection*)

353
SE&CR

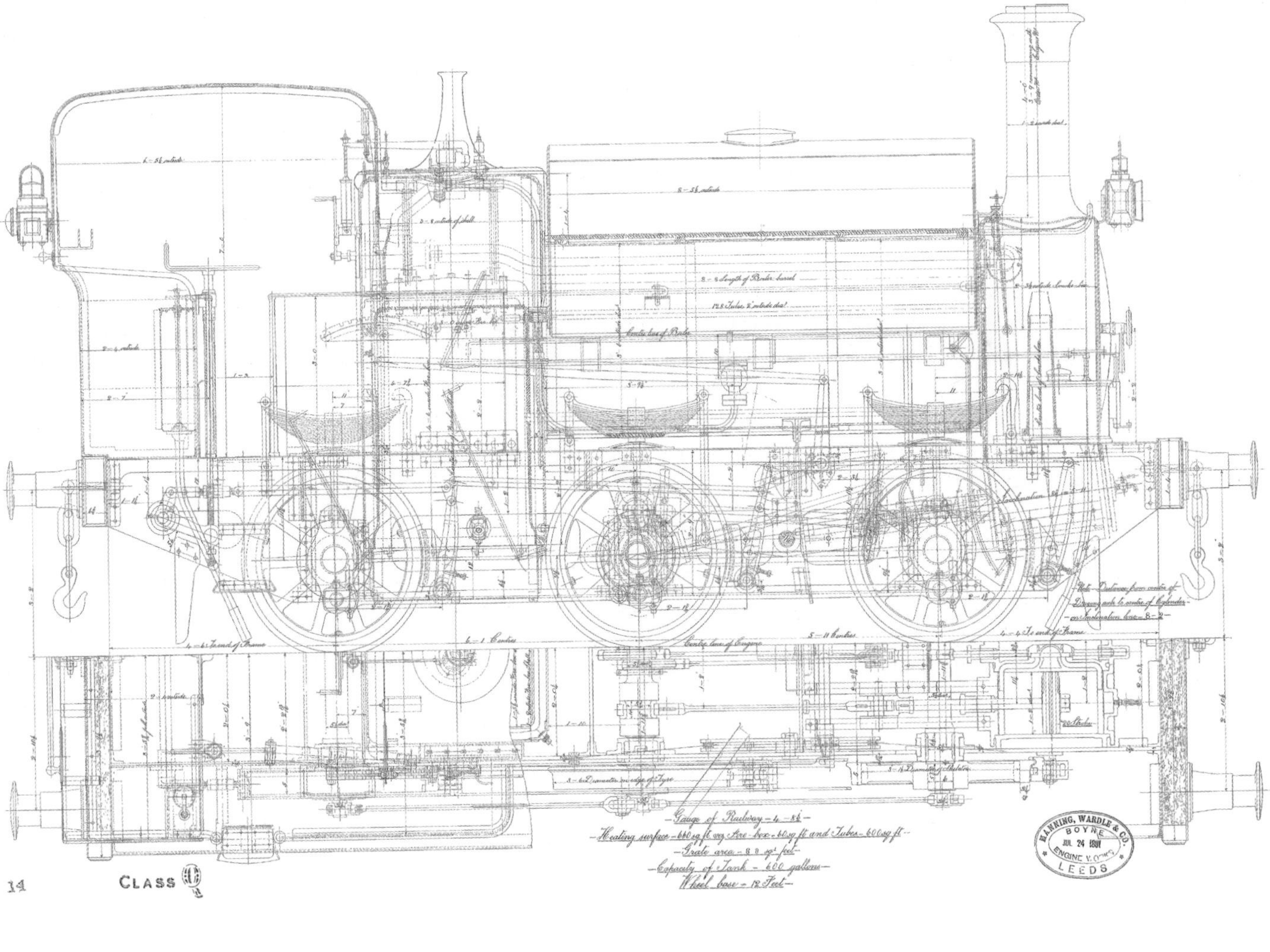
–Gauge of Railway – 4 – 8½ –
–Heating surface – 660 sq ft viz Fire box – 60 sq ft and Tubes – 600 sq ft –
–Grate area – 8 0 sq feet –
–Capacity of Tank – 600 gallons –
Wheel base – 12 Feet –
MANNING, WARDLE & CO.
BOYNE
LEEDS
14
CLASS O

Above: One of the major 'celebrities' amongst the 'Q' class was W/N 1555 (28 February 1902) originally ordered as *Northolt* No. 56 by the contractor Pauling & Co. Ltd. for construction work on the Great Central & Great Western Joint Railway. Remaining in Pauling's hands after the opening of this railway, the engine was eventually sold on June 4th 1913 for £725 to the Freshwater, Yarmouth & Newport Railway on the Isle of Wight. The locomotive is pictured in this view in pre-Grouping days at Freshwater in company with the line's other locomotive, a second hand ex-LB&SCR 'Terrier', formerly *Newington* No. 46. W/N 1555 was a classic 'mature period' standard Manning Wardle, with its circular leading cab spectacles and rectangular cut-outs 'radiused' only at their upper corners. The Roscoe lubricator was mounted lower down on the right hand side of the smokebox (rather than on the tank), whilst Ramsbottom safety valves had superseded the earlier Salter pattern. The leading sandbox linkages were mounted beneath footplate level (where they were less susceptible to damage), whilst 'double boss' wheel centres were still utilized at this relatively late stage. Apart from painting in emerald green livery with black bands and white lining (the FY&NR livery), the only other major pre-grouping modification was to dual-fit the engine for both Westinghouse and vacuum braking (the former was standard on most of the Island, whilst the latter was used by the FY&NR). (*John Scott-Morgan Collection*)

Opposite above: A side view of No. 353, also taken after 1917 at Ashford, where the engine remained at work until withdrawn under Southern Railway ownership in December 1929, being scrapped in 1932. The boiler was sold to a Canterbury greenhouse owner for heating purposes, but it too had been scrapped by August 1947. (*John Scott-Morgan Collection*)

Opposite below: This Manning Wardle works drawing shows the 'Q' class at the stage of development reached by 1891 and is a close match for W/N 1154 of 1890 as built (a copy was held by the S.E.R. and its successors). As can be seen from the accompanying illustrations, the development of the class mirrored that of the other standard six-coupled classes produced at Boyne Engine Works over the years during which production took place. (*Hunslet Archive*)

Following the Grouping, the locomotive was repainted in Southern Railway 'Maunsell green' livery in May 1924, becoming W1 in which form it is seen here. As can be seen in the illustration, the second set of piping associated with the vacuum brake had also been removed at this stage. It was re-assigned to become the Medina Wharf shunter, becoming *Medina* in 1928. At this stage, the upper cab profile was remodelled to produce a fully 'radiused' 'square' cut-out profile, making the engine one of the most handsome Manning Wardles to see service. (*John Scott-Morgan Collection*)

Sadly, *Medina was* to be short-lived in its final form, falling victim to the Southern Railway's locomotive standardization policy on the Island in favour of ex-L&SWR 'O2s' and ex-L.B. & S.C.R. 'Terriers' and 'E1s'. It was withdrawn in June 1932 and broken up on the Mainland at Eastleigh in July 1933. (*Industrial Railway Society*)

W/N 1966 was delivered on 22 May 1918 to the contractors Logan & Hemingway at Doncaster as No. 3 and later found employment with Midland Ironstone Co. Ltd. at Crosby Ironstone Mines as Beauchamp. As built the engine had a 'retro' feel in that it was only fitted with a leading weatherboard, although it was equipped with Ramsbottom safety valves and conventional wheel centres. By the end of its career, as shown in this photograph, it had acquired an enclosed cab although it had lost the upper part of its chimney cap. It was scrapped in March 1966 (*Author's Collection*)

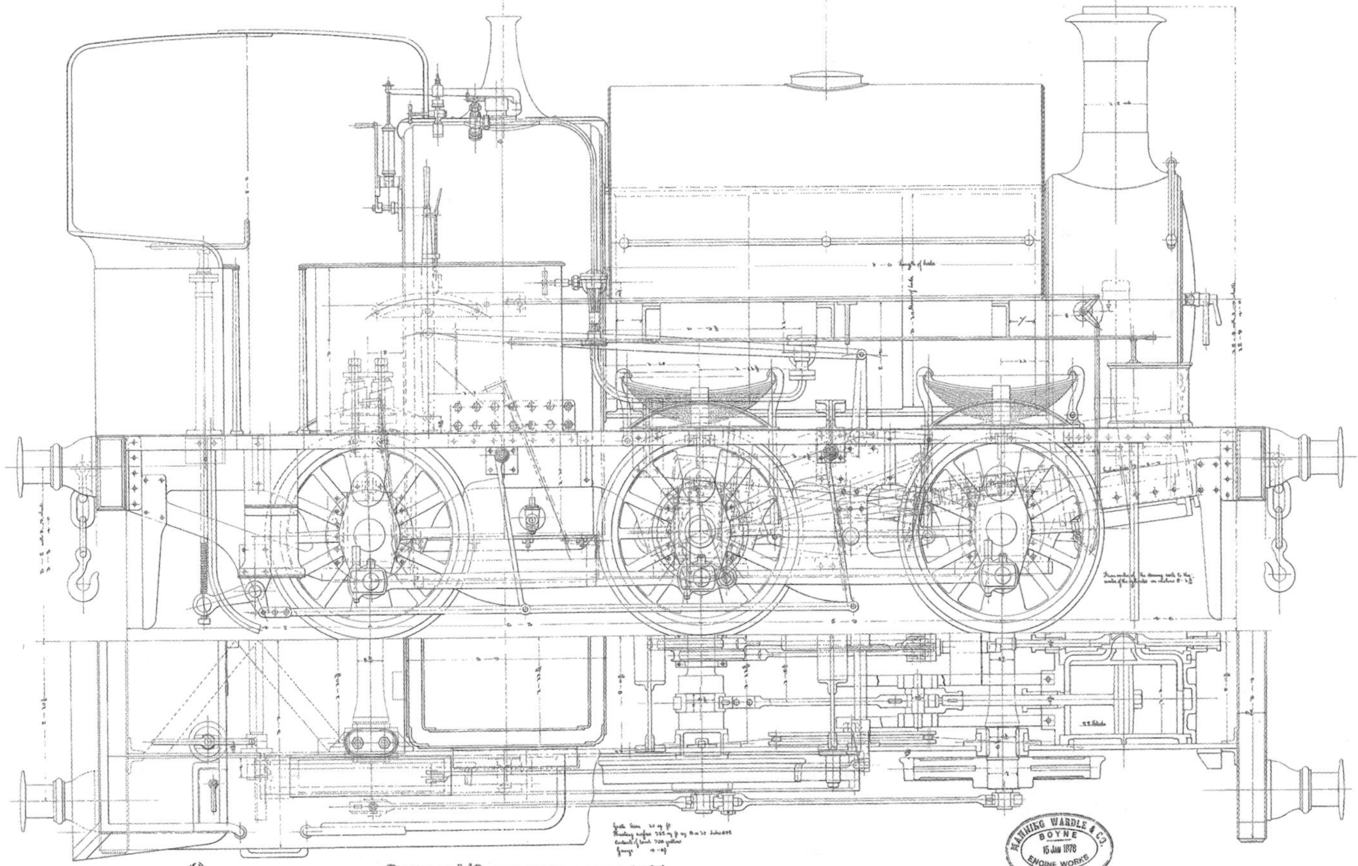

This is the maker's drawing, dated 15 June 1878, for the 'O' class locomotive W/N 681 *Sydney* delivered on 18 February the previous year to John Williams & Co. of Sydney, New South Wales. Although an enlargement of the general design principles found in the 'Old I' class, the use of the conventional pattern side hinged smokebox door was established on this design from an early stage, as was the use of two injectors. The use of coil springs for the trailing axle was another feature of note, as was the lack of brake blocks on the leading axle, although this was remedied on later members of the class. (*Hunslet Archive*)

This early 'O' class locomotive, W/N 462 *Henry Briggs* was supplied on 27 October 1873 to H. Briggs Son & Co. Ltd. at Waterhaigh Colliery and passed into NCB ownership (No. 8 Area Division 3) on 1 January 1947, being scrapped after over eight decades of work in 1955. The locomotive was rebuilt by Hudswell Clarke in 1932 (including the provision of a new boiler with Ross 'pop' safety valve and saddle tank), whilst the mainframes have been modified, if not renewed outright whilst the 'double bosses' on the intermediate wheel centres have been strengthened (a feature also found on another long-lived Briggs 'O' class, W/N 611 of 1876 *Mexboro* which was rebuilt by Hudswell Clarke in 1912). The original pattern of brake rigging, acting on the rear and intermediate wheelsets only, has endured however. The photograph was taken on 7 May 1950. (*The Late Frank Jones*)

This 'O' class locomotive, W/N 480 *Hamsteels* began its career on 20 January 1874 at Hamsteels Colliery in County Durham. In this view, taken circa 1900, the locomotive is in virtually original condition save for the fact that the safety valve bonnet is missing. Unlike W/Ns 462 and 611 *Hamsteels* was not particularly long lived, being scrapped between 1910 and 1924. (*Industrial Railway Society*)

Conduit No. 3 was W/N 1180 of 26 November 1890 for Conduit Colliery Ltd., Staffordshire. The locomotive is little different in appearance from W/N 681 as depicted in the General Arrangement drawing, the most easily apparent difference being the provision of braking for the leading wheelset. In this right-hand profile view, one of the two Littleton Colliery '18 inch' Manning Wardle 0-6-0STs can be seen in the centre left background. (*Chasewater Railway Preservation Society*)

Conduit No. 3 proved to be a long-lived locomotive and after a 1920 rebuild by the makers passed to Littleton Colliery in 1931 and to N.C.B. West Midlands Division No. 2 Area on 1 January 1947. The Engine was rebuilt at Cannock Central Workshops in 1956-7 acquiring several components (including the enclosed cab and maker's plate) of sister engine Conduit No. 4 (W/N 1326 of 1896). Following further colliery transfers within Staffordshire, Conduit No. 3 in its 'hybrid' condition ended its operational career with Cannock & Rugeley Collieries based at Rawnsley Shed in July 1963 and was eventually scrapped in December 1964. It and several other historic locomotives based there at the time deserved a better fate! (*Chasewater Railway Preservation Society*)

Above: Progressive enlargement of the basic Manning Wardle specification eventually stumbled on a problem: placing the firebox neatly between the intermediate and trailing axles meant that wheelbases expanded in a fashion commensurate with enlargement resulting in difficulties where prospective customers possessed railway systems with sharp curves. The solution to this problem was to adopt an inclined foundation ring surmounting the rear axle so that the rear portion of the wheelbase could be shortened. In consequence, a design with '16 inch' cylinders, later designated the 'T' class appeared in 1897. W/Ns 1503-4 were delivered on 15 October 1900 as *Earlstown* and November 14th the same year as *Newtown* to R. Evans, Haydock Colliery Co. Ltd. Both locomotives had careers of respectable length, coming under N.C.B. ownership on 1 January 1947: W/N 1503 never left its original workplace and was scrapped there in June 1965 by J. K. Holt & Gordon Ltd., whilst W/N 1504 was latterly transferred to Lea Green Colliery and broken up by the same scrap merchant as its sister at Chequerbent in March 1966. This locomotive is seen here on 17 June 1965 at Lea Green Colliery with its leading bufferbeam removed. It had acquired the distinction of being fitted with a Giesel ejector during its NCB career. (*Author's Collection*)

Opposite above: Manning Wardle's first locomotive Littleton No. 1 for the Staffordshire-based Littleton Collieries (W/N 1515 of 10 November 1901), was constructed to a similar design and the engine is seen here on 8 February 1958 by which time it was under the jurisdiction of N.C.B. Cannock Area. It was scrapped on site in September 1961. Works No. 1596 of 4 March 1903 Littleton No. 2 (whose identity No. 1 temporarily assumed in 1946) was scrapped in late 1960. (*Ken Cooper*)

Opposite below: 'T' class locomotive *Dolobran* (W/N 1762 of 20 October 1910) was the first member of its class to be supplied to Lloyds Ironstone Co. Ltd., of Corby, Northants. The type proved popular with this customer, and its successor, Stewarts & Lloyds Ltd., who purchased similar locomotives from Kitson and Robert Stephenson & Hawthorns after the demise of Manning Wardle.

LITTLETON
No1

DOLOBRAN
1762

Following withdrawal from ordinary service in the late 1960s, *Dolobran* was stored at Rolvenden (Kent & East Sussex Railway), North Woolwich and on the Cholsey & Wallingford Railway before being transferred to the premises of the Great Central Railway (North) at Ruddington near Nottingham. Restoration to working order is currently well advanced at this latter venue as this photograph, taken in August 2014, shows. (*Author*)

Two 'T' class 0-6-0STs (respectively W/Ns 1929-30 of 18th and 25th July 1917) were supplied to the Inland Waterways & Docks Department at Sandwich in Kent. These were built with 'austerity' cabs and no leading waist sheets. Subsequently finding their way to the Air Ministry at Cranwell, they were eventually sold, via a dealer in Grantham to Foxfield Colliery, Staffordshire as its Nos. 1 and 2 respectively (receiving the names Blythe and Foxfield) and both passed to N.C.B. North Staffordshire Area in 1947. W/N 1930 was scrapped in 1952, but Blythe was a little more fortunate, working latterly at Parkhouse Colliery, Chesterton where it is seen here on 14 September 1965. It was scrapped shortly afterwards. (*D.N. Wignall*)

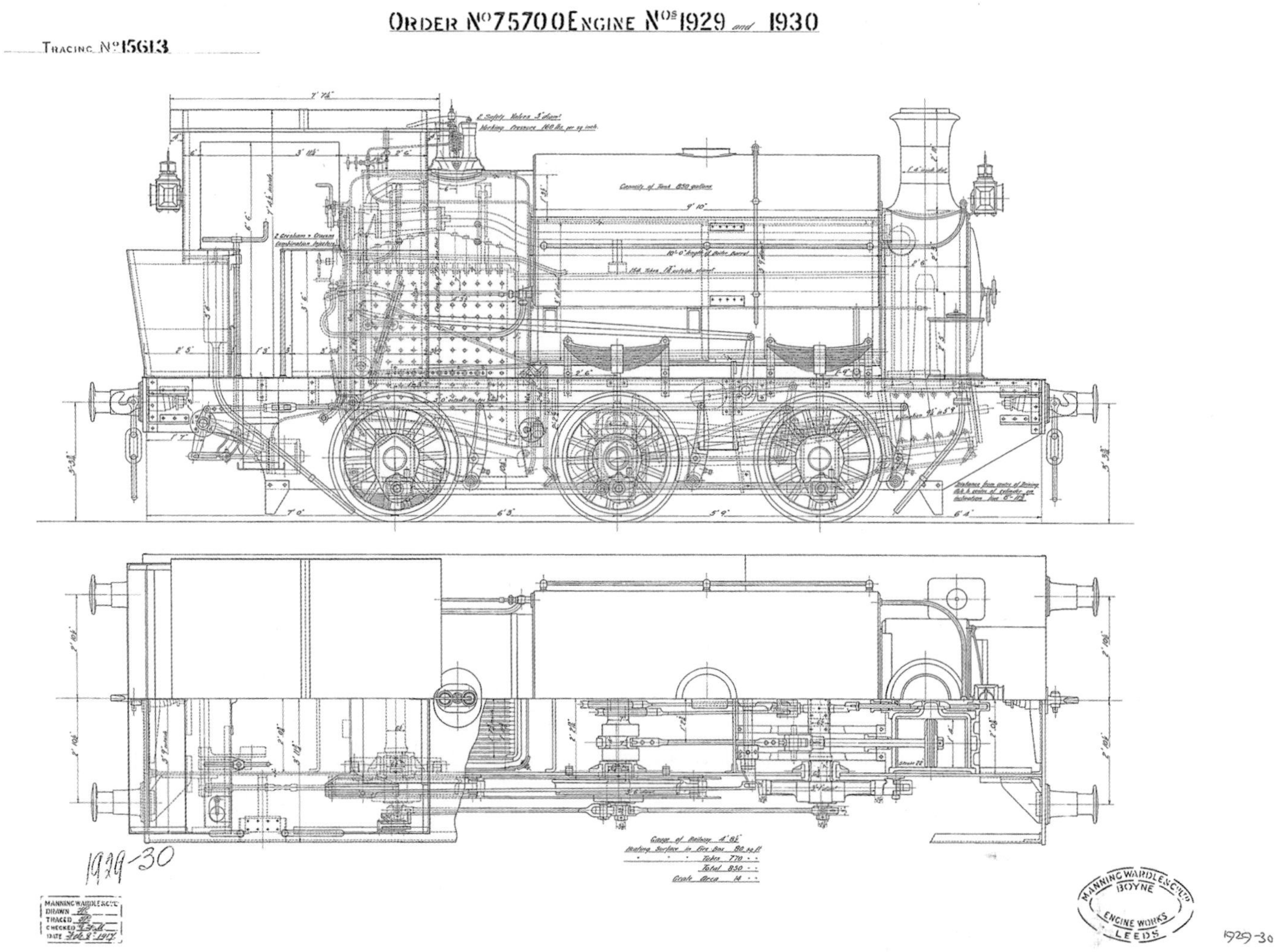

Fortunately, the General Arrangement drawing for W/Ns 1929-30 survives and it illustrates well the proportions of the 'T' class with its general 'chunky' appearance only being softened by the saddle tank profile with had lost much of the 'angular' appearance exhibited by many early Manning Wardle saddle tanks. The foundation ring (inclined to clear the rear axle), 'austerity' pattern cab and simple 'straight cut' leading frame ends (in contrast to *Dolobran* and Littleton No. 4 but later found on Littleton No. 5) are in evidence, as are the 'bottom pivoted' brake hangers. (*Hunslet Archive*)

Nonslip was delivered new to Brookes Ltd. of Lightcliffe, near Halifax in 1912 as W/N 1803, but remained with its original owner for little over four years before re-sale in January 1917, eventually finishing its career at Airedale Collieries near Castleford. Although the locomotive survived a boiler explosion in 1919, it was scrapped prior to the outbreak of World War Two. The design is represented in preservation, however, by Kitson W/N 5459 which is currently undergoing a major overhaul. (*Sidney Leleux Collection*)

Above: The largest locomotive design produced using the significant design principles embodied in the 'Old I' class was represented by three 0-6-0ST locomotives with 17 inch cylinders for the East & West Yorkshire Railway. The locomotive in the photograph, *E. & W.Y.U.R. No. 1* was briefly fitted with a vacuum ejector for working the railway's short-lived passenger service. At the Grouping, it was renumbered 3112 by the L&NER, whilst sister engine, E&WYUR No. 2 became 3113. The remaining member of the three-strong class, W/N 1489 was withdrawn in 1923 without renumbering and 3113 in 1928, leaving 3112 as the last survivor of the trio until 1930.

Opposite above: This General Arrangement drawing of W/Ns 1307-8 emphasizes the proportions of the design, along with the 8ft. spacing between the intermediate and trailing axles necessitated by the placing of the firebox ahead of, rather than over, the rear axle. Nonetheless, the design was a handsome one incorporating the classic 'pre-standard' Manning Wardle cab. (*Hunslet Archive*)

Opposite below: The ultimate development of the 'T' class was this design with 18in by 24in cylinders, 4ft wheels and 13ft wheelbase. Weighing 51 tons in full working order, the first of three class members was delivered on 26 August 1910 (W/N 1759) to Littleton Collieries, Staffordshire as Littleton No. 4. Most of the technical and aesthetic features associated with contemporaneous 'T' class locomotives (necessarily adjusted for the difference in overall size) were found on this locomotive, but loading gauge restrictions necessitated a 'rounded' cab cross-section and the brake hangers were attached to the mainframes above rather than below the axle centrelines. Following over half a century of service, *Littleton No. 4* was broken up in September 1961. The second locomotive of this design, W/N 1990, was delivered to Nine Mile Point Colliery on 20 November 1990, whilst the last, W/N 2018 of 13 November 1922, and still extant after disposal in October 1972, is Littleton No. 5. (*Hunslet Archive*)

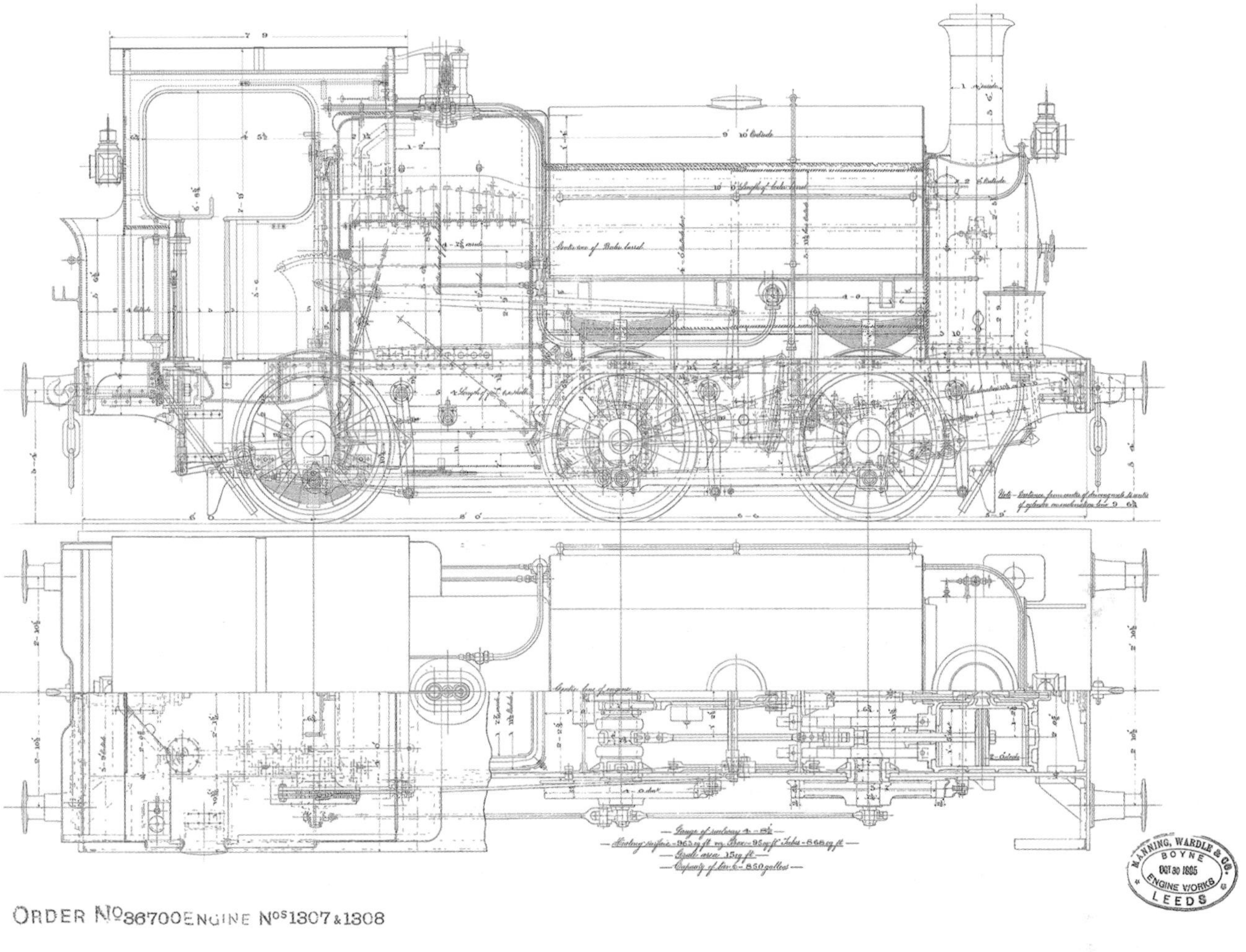
MANNING, WARDLE & CO.
BOYNE
ENGINE WORKS
LEEDS
ORDER No 36700 ENGINE Nos 1307 & 1308

1750

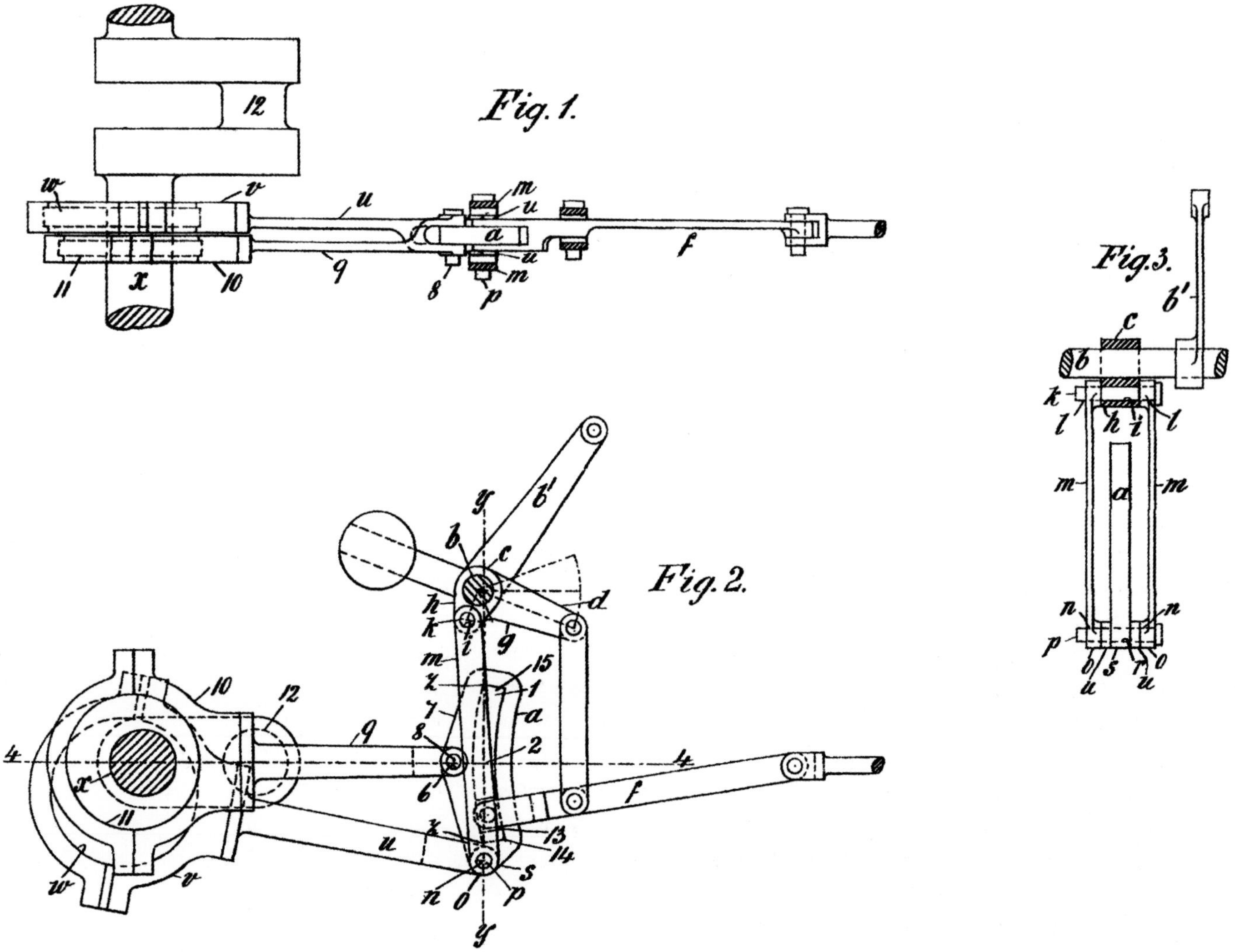

Following defeat in the 1906 lawsuit over the use of Marshall's valve gear, Manning Wardle was forced to turn to another avenue in its pursuit of innovation in this field. Accordingly, what has come to be known as Isaacson's valve gear was patented in 1908. Essentially, the main valve motion was provided by the action of the larger eccentric (marked 'w' in the diagram's Figure 2 and set at the required angle), which was connected to the lower end of the expansion link. This latter component was suspended from the drop-links ('m'), whose orientation could be altered between forward and reverse limits by means of a lug projecting outwards from the weighshaft. The lap/lead component of the motion was provided by the smaller eccentric ('11'), whilst the main reversing action was achieved by the raising or lowering of the valve rod ('f') by means of the bellcrank ('d') on the weighshaft and its associated drop links (the action of moving drop links 'm' being essentially corrective during the reversing process). The Patent claimed that this valve gear achieved virtually equal event characteristics at each end of the cylinder but whilst it found favour with a small, number of customers, such as C.H. Walker Ltd. and Bombay Port Trust, it did not achieve universal adoption. (Patent No. 1907/27899)

CHAPTER 10

THE CORPORATE HISTORY OF MANNING WARDLE & CO. LTD.

According to an obituary for Charles Weatherall Wardle, published in the *Leeds Mercury* for 4 July 1888, he passed away at the age of 67, having seen the departure of Alexander Campbell during the early 1870s and following the death of John Manning in 1874, the Boyne Engine Works passed solely to him and his son Edwin three years later. Information contained in obituary and other sources recorded that Charles Wardle, born at Rothwell, near Leeds on 25 April 1815, was the son of the Vicar of Beeston, who had latterly served as a Justice of the Peace for the Borough of Leeds and had learned his trade under Matthew Murray. Additionally, he married Anne Elizabeth Leather, a member of a very influential Leeds family and was admitted to membership of the Institution of Mechanical Engineers in 1856, by which time he was employed at the Railway Foundry following a period of employment with the Milton Ironworks, near Barnsley. During the years between 1877 and 1888, the unincorporated firm of Manning Wardle & Co. had become very much a family business, with 390 employees recorded in the 1881 Census, and it steadily established a reputation for the supply of reliable products, particularly locomotives for the use of railway contractors as has been noted. This strategy was continued by the only son amongst his six children, Edwin (born 1850) and the net profit of £20,567 attained in 1899 may have been the most successful trading result ever achieved by the Boyne Engine Works. Edwin was keen, however, during the early years of the twentieth century, to exploit the advantages offered by the limited liability, a trend followed by other Leeds-based engineering concerns at the time. By means of an Incorporation Certificate dated 17 February 1905, therefore, Manning Wardle & Company Ltd. came into being and this took over the assets of the formerly unincorporated enterprise by means of a contract dated 31 March 1905. During the previous year, the surveyors, Messrs. Martin & Fenwick had valued the Freehold Boyne Engine Works site at £16,500 whilst the goodwill (individually valued at £20,000), buildings, stock-in-trade, machinery and other items were valued by Messrs. Bramwell & Harris at £118,920 1s. 7 d., giving a total of £135,000 1s. 7d. A report of the firm's profits during the period leading up to incorporation was supplied by its auditors, Messrs. H.W. & J. Blackburn (Chartered Accountants) of Leeds and Bradford. The detail is contained in Appendix Two. The average profit during the period 1897-1904 was £11,335 15s. 10d., of which £3,000 per annum would have been required to service the interest on the £60,000 stock envisaged for the new company. The security for this sum amounted to a revised figure of £140,420 from the earlier valuation, plus £10,750 of additional working capital and the average of the preceding five years' book debts, namely £15,273 19s. 7d., giving a total of £161,443 19s. 7d. Some £100,000 of share capital was authorised, of which £88,500 in 8,850 shares of £10 nominal value was actually paid-up, initially to Edwin Wardle along with £47,000 in cash as consideration by the company for the undertaking. Article 97 of the Articles of Association provided that:

> '... the said Edwin Wardle shall be Managing Director of the Company so long as he is a director thereof or until he resigns such office of Managing Director and such resignation shall not unless it be otherwise expressed in his notice to the Company of such resignation be deemed a resignation of his office as a Director.'

It was additionally provided that the qualifying shareholding for a director was a nominal £1,000 (shares which were allocated from Edwin Wardle's holding, the first block of which was to a Mr. Horace Sanderson, Edwin Wardle's nephew, as Commercial Director and Secretary of the Company) whilst the remuneration of individual directors was initially fixed at £100 per annum plus any further sums as may be determined by the Company in General Meeting, the first of which was held at Boyne

Engine Works on 16 May 1905. Although formed as a private company, it was stated by 23 June 1905 that a quotation on the Leeds Stock Exchange would be sought. One immediate effect of this decision under the Companies Acts as they were in force at the time was that a minimum number of seven shareholders was required. This required the issue of a further seven shares for £10 in cash each (including, rather strangely, a further share each to Edwin Wardle and Horace Sanderson). By 23 November 1910, the two original directors (respectively holding 8,451 and 101 shares) had been joined by Joseph Henry Evers (Engineer; 201 shares), a Leeds resident, and Alfred Harrison Smith (101 shares), a brewer resident in Workshop. The three non-director shareholders were Richard Evers, Henry Gaskell Blackburn and Henry St. John Sanderson, brother of Horace, (1 share each, making up the total of 8,857 shares). The £60,000 issue of 1st Mortgage Debenture Stock took place between 26 and 28 June 1905. By September 1912, Horace Sanderson and Joseph Henry Evers had resigned their directorships, to be replaced by John Thomas Middleton (most importantly, considering the company's customer base, a railway contractor) and Smethwick JP George Bean, who filled the post as Chairman. In addition, a fifth director, Harold Whitaker Deighton Fielding had been appointed and Frederick Smith filled the role of secretary. By 30 June 1912, the first year for which published accounts appear to survive, the share capital was divided into 2,500 6 per cent preference shares; 2,000 6 per cent second preference shares and 4,357 ordinary shares, all of £10 par value. Of these, some 500, 300 and 2,283 respectively of each type were in the hands of nominees (total value £30,830) and

Today, all that remains of the infrastructure that once made up the Boyne Engine Works are a pair of gate-posts, dated '1858', and the Office Building, one of whose walls can be seen behind the left-hand post in this view. The author is standing immediately in front of the right-hand post in the centre of the picture. (*Author*)

not available for corporate finance, thereby giving a total effective share value of £57,740. Only £50,000 of loan finance was raised by the Debenture Issue against the par value liability of £60,000. The surviving documentation suggest that the loan issue was split into a liability of £30,000 (plus interest) at par value and £28,000 (again plus interest) as security against the £20,000 balance of the loan advance, and £8,000 elsewhere. This latter £28,000 was eventually redeemed on 12 October 1924 as will be seen.

From the profit figures given in Appendix Two, it can be seen that during the years ended 30 June 1912 and 1913 both turned in net losses. This was despite the fact that there was a trading (gross) profit in both years, namely £2,661 15s. 0d. and £1,056 14s. 0d. respectively. In 1911-12, the problem was simply that debenture, bank and loan interest amounted to £2,970 1s. 3d., whilst in 1912-13, the picture was more complicated, with interest in its various forms amounting to £2,409 18s. 6d.; income tax £42 1s 11d.; directors' fees and expenses £816 15 s 0d. and payments for Trustees for the debenture stock holders £42 0s. 0d. The only mitigating factor, amounting to a mere £1 17 s. 6d. came in the form of transfer fees, nature unspecified. The company had been forced to raise more mortgage finance on 30 January 1912 from the National Provincial Bank against debts owed by the Earl of Ellesmere's Office, Manchester (£592 for a new boiler); the India Office in London (£2,360 in respect of locomotive W/Ns 1790-1), and all monies due or to become due to the company from Edwin Wardle, whose address was given as No. 11, Draycott Place, London S.W.

The onset of hostilities in 1914 brought with it an improvement in the company's trading position at a time when only thirty employees were present, although, as can be seen from Appendix Two, there was a distinct 'lagging effect' between the receipt of orders and any dramatic effect upon net profits as the high point of this period was only reached in 1920, nearly two years after the Armistice, and the only years under consideration when the preference dividend was paid were between June 1919 and June 1923, (respectively £,3000, £4,500, £300 and £1,500). The 1915-16 profit figure has however, been adjusted in Appendix Two to take account of the cost of £1,272 9s. 4d. for tool scrappage. The 1917 Director's Report stated that during the preceding year, the Works had been well charged with orders, but there had been difficulty obtaining the supply of the necessary materials and labour, which had hampered the company when attempting to take full advantage of the situation. From the practical point of view, this manifested itself in the use of steel for tubes and fireboxes where non-ferrous materials would previously have been used (these being required for shell-cases, for instance), and steel on occasions not being of the desired quality. The Register of Directors, apart from stating that John Thomas Middleton (of Walter Scott & Middleton Ltd.) had been elevated to the status of Vice-Chairman, revealed only one major development, namely the death of Edwin Wardle on 3 December 1919. Although not the final fatal blow for the company, the loss of the last director with the all-important family connection must have caused a major loss of morale on the part of the remaining directors. John Thomas Middleton died at his home in Woking, Surrey in June 1922 and his heir, Edgar Kershaw Middleton assumed a place on the board. As at 10 November 1922, the remaining directors were James Harry Price (partner in Price & Reeves, contractors, and director of Dundalk Ironworks Ltd.); Charles Lupton (Solicitor); Harold Whitaker Deighton Fielding; Sir George Bean (Chairman) and Alfred Harrison-Smith (Vice-Chairman). Apart from the two last-named, who died in January 1924 and on 25 February 1925 respectively, the remainder served in office until the company's demise. During the year ended 30 June 1922, the company was faced with a classic double-whammy. Firstly, the gross trading profit, which had reached £17,088 3s. 11d. during the previous year, had fallen to £7,178 7 s. 9d. during the year. The initial period of euphoria that had gripped the nation following the Armistice rapidly turned to disillusionment with a marked deterioration in the economic outlook in consequence, especially in heavy engineering. Secondly, the relatively inflated profits of the period from June 1919 to June 1921 attracted the attention of the tax authorities and during the year ended 30 June 1922, some £309 10s. 5d. in income tax was paid, in addition to £917 17s. 0d. of corporation tax for 1920 and 1921 along with £4,088 0s. 0d. excess profits tax for 1921.

The period from 1914 onwards manifested itself in another fashion, namely the fragmentation of the company's organizational structure. The progressive disintegration of the classification system for the standard locomotive designs was one indication of this trend, as was the irregular accounting period in 1913-15 and the late filing of the Annual Return for 1918 which was not filed until June 1919. The organization situation could not have been helped by the deaths during the company's latter years of three directors and the fact that at least as far as the standard locomotive designs were concerned, some manufacturing methods and materials (at least in peacetime conditions) may have improved over time, the company's main product was still in concept an 1850s item. The 1922 Director's Report refers to the importance of Messrs. Edgar Middleton and J. Harry Price on the board, given their connections to two of the company's most important customers, and also of the solicitor Charles Lupton (who formerly acted for Edwin Wardle) as representative of members of the Wardle family, at that stage the main ordinary shareholders. There was, however, a reluctance to accept reality as the report goes on to say:

> 'The results of the trading for the several preceding years indicate that with anything like favourable trading conditions the earning capacity of the company will be fully maintained.'

As has been seen, the directors then went on to recommend the payment of a full year's arrears of preference dividend despite a net loss for the year of £1,200 13s. 3d. calculated by means of the deduction of tax liabilities relating to 1920-1. By the time of the Directors' Report for the year ended 30 June 1923, the harsh reality of trading conditions of the period was beginning to sink in:

> 'There has been a loss on the year's working of £6,540 1s. 0d. This result may be attributed to the conditions of the Locomotive Industry, arising out of slackness of demand, and whilst the Company has secured a reasonable proportion of the business available, your Directors share, in common with others in the Locomotive trade, a general disappointment that the hopes of a revival with which we commenced the year just closed, are just deferred.'

No dividend was recommended, also the accounts show an amount for this of £1,500, presumably part of the previous arrears. The Report significantly went on to say, however:

> '...with a return to normal trading conditions, your Directors have every confidence in the future of the Company.'

The Directors' Report for the year ended 30 June 1924 was far more pessimistic. The net loss for the year was £12,264 14s.8d., and this not only reduced the accumulated balance on the Profit & Loss Account to £17,399 10s. 2d. but seriously depleted the liquid cash resources of the Company. It was therefore reluctantly decided to make a further £30,000 Debenture Issue to the company's bankers and redeem £28,000 of the original Debenture issue in order to give the bankers the necessary wider security (against the entire undertaking) for the business to continue. These transactions took place on 18 November and 12 October 1924 respectively. Despite the grim trading background, a new boiler shop came into operation during the period under review. Examination of the remaining net profit figures for the company's existence show that all attempts to stem the tide of the company's decline failed. Profitability was never restored, no further preference dividends were ever paid, let alone any dividends on the ordinary shares. During 1924, only eight locomotives (W/Ns 2032-9) were completed and during 1925 and 1926, the corresponding totals fell to four locomotives in each year (respectively W/Ns 2040-3 and 2044-7). No Directors' Fees were paid after 30 June 1924 and with effect from 31 August 1926, all work was transferred to Leeds neighbours, Kitson & Co. Ltd. with the last completed locomotive, W/N 2047 leaving the Boyne Engine Works some twenty-two days earlier. The final accounts were made up to 31 March 1927 and show that the loss incurred during the period from 31 August 1926 to that date amounted to £4,331 18s. 2d. The amount in principal and interest owing to debenture holders at that stage was £56,556 17s. 7d. in total. The situation was by this stage totally hopeless and on 29 September 1927, the debenture holders appointed Sir Leonard Knight Coates of 2, East Parade, Leeds as Receiver for the company, with its registered office being moved to this address on 25 February the following year. The period of receivership lasted until 11 December 1929 and the earliest transaction of major importance was the sale of the company's goodwill for £3,000 to Kitson & Co. Ltd. The plant and machinery were sold for £5,000 and, according to *The Locomotive* magazine, this was to T.W. Ward Ltd. of Sheffield. Although the buildings and office furniture fetched £13,150, nothing was mentioned in relation to the freehold value of the Boyne Engine works site, which presumably was included under this head. If so, the financial consequences for creditors and shareholders were nothing short of a disaster, given that the book value of freehold land, buildings and plant as per the last set of accounts was £105,638 3s. 9d. The resultant loss, £84,488 3s. 9d., is an indication of the catastrophic economic climate that faced the locomotive building trade during the 1920s. In all, some £730,897 7s. 4d. in cash was claimed by the receiver, of which £2,933 12s. 10d. was paid to Kitson in 1927-8 for work undertaken after August 1926. When all other disbursements were accounted for, the cash left on the receiver's hand amounted to £23,479 18s. 5d. which was paid to Midland Bank, the debenture holder. Manning Wardle & Co. Ltd. ceased to exist as a legal entity on 8 December 1931 when a notice to this effect was published in the *London Gazette*.

Kitson & Co. Ltd. continued to build locomotives to Manning Wardle designs, but this company fell into receivership in 1934, the receiver being none other than Sir Leonard Coates who had performed the same function for Manning Wardle's debenture holders a few years earlier. Although the *Railway Gazette* for 25 June 1937 recorded that the receivership had been ended by the injection of more capital by London-based merchant bank, Messrs Kinloch & Co. Ltd., in 1938 Kitson was persuaded to officially withdraw from locomotive manufacture altogether under an agreement with the Locomotive Manufacturers Association (in order to eliminate surplus capacity in the industry). Under this agreement, the goodwill, patterns and drawings for Kitson and Manning Wardle locomotives were then transferred to Robert Stephenson & Hawthorns Ltd., a concern based in Newcastle and Darlington formed by amalgamation of its two component manufacturers during the preceding year, subject to a 10 per cent levy on consequent sales payable by R.S. & H. Ltd. to the LMA. R.S. & H. Ltd. supplied five locomotives, of Manning Wardle 'T' specification with minor improvements, to Stewarts & Lloyds Ltd. of Corby, Northants. in 1940-1 and incorporated certain Manning Wardle features into a succeeding design for the same customer (albeit with a domed boiler barrel). Other spares came from this supplier for Manning Wardle products as late as the 1950s, including the aforementioned three domed boilers and accompanying round profile saddle tanks for '16 inch' 0-4-0STs on the Lambton, Hetton & Joicey Collieries system, totally altering the appearance of these locomotives. By the end of the 1950s, however, R.S. & H. had withdrawn from steam locomotive manufacture and following this decision, the Manning Wardle and Kitson goodwill passed appropriately to Hunslet Engine Co. Ltd. in 1960.

In the years following the demise of Manning Wardle & Co. Ltd., much of the former Boyne Engine Works site passed directly to Hunslet Engine Co. Ltd., including the new Boiler Shop referred to in the 1924 Directors' Report, and the Erecting Shop, which during the Second World War was put to use producing howitzers and was consequently known as the 'Gun Shop'. Other parts of the former Boyne Engine Works were used by J. & H. McLaren Ltd., a concern best-known for the manufacture of Diesel engines (and for whom Rupert John Isaacson had once worked), including products for locomotive builders such as Kerr, Stuart, Hudswell Clarke and Hunslet. Today, all that recognizably survives from the Boyne engine works site are the Offices and the adjacent Gateposts, still bearing their '1858' date of construction. In addition, a small number of locomotives covered by this volume still exist at home and overseas, whilst the most surviving Manning Wardle drawings and records are now held at Statfold Barn Museum, near Tamworth. The original Shepherd & Todd 'Quadrangle', once covered by Fretwell's lease, was subsequently leased to Kitson, thence to Hunslet between 1941 and 1947 (by which time Kitson's business had been taken over by J. & H. McLaren), being purchased outright by Hunslet during the following year. Today an original archway from 'Fretwell's Quadrangle' survives adjoining Pearson St. as a rare relic of E.B. Wilson's all-important Railway Foundry. It is through this arch that the pioneering 'Jenny Lind' would have emerged in 1846, although not, as has previously been contended, the Todd, Kitson and Laird-built *Lion* of 1838.

MANNING WARDLE LOCOMOTIVE DIMENSIONS

Four-Coupled Classes (0-4-0ST)													
Class	Cyls.	Wheelbase	Wheel	Boiler Details (5)			Heating Surface				Tank	Weights	
			Dia.	Length	Diameter	Pitch	W.P.	Tubes	Firebox	G.A.	Cap.	Empty	W.O.
B (1)	6in. × 12in	4ft 6in	2ft3in	6ft 9in	1ft 11in	3ft 6in	120psi	82 sq.ft	18 sq.ft	2.9 sq.ft	200 galls.		
B (2)	6in. × 12 in	4ft 7in	2ft 6in	6ft 9in	1ft 11in	3ft 6in	120psi	82 sq.ft	18 sq.ft	2.9 sq.ft	200 galls.		
W/N 1910	7in × 12in	4ft 6in	2ft 6in	7ft 0in	2ft 3in						160 galls.	9.75 tons	11.35 tons
C	7in × 12in	4ft 7in	2ft 6in	6ft 9in	1ft 11in	3ft 6in	120psi	104 sq.ft	21 sq.ft	3.0 sq.ft	200 galls.		
D (3)	8in × 14in	4ft 9in	2ft 9in		2ft 4in	3ft 10in.	120psi				200 galls.		
D (4)	8in × 14in	4ft 6in	2ft 8in	7ft 0in	2ft 1in	3ft 11.5in	120psi	153.5 sq.ft	23.5 sq.ft	3.5 sq.ft	200 galls.	8.5 tons	10.0 tons
E	9in × 14in (6)	4ft 9in	2ft 9in	7ft 3in	2ft 3 in	3ft 9.5in	120psi	217.5 sq.ft	30.5 sq.ft	5 sq.ft	250 galls.	9.15 tons	10.85 tons
F W/N 1756	10in × 16in	4ft 9in	2ft 9in	7ft 11in	2ft 7in	4ft 6.9in	120psi	264.5 sq.ft	32.5 sq.ft	5.5 sq.ft	350 galls.	13.4 tons	16.15 tons
G (7)	11in × 17in	5ft 0in	3ft 0in	8ft 3in	2ft 8in		120psi	315 sq.ft	35 sq.ft	5.5.sq.ft	400 galls.		
W/N 1727	12in × 18in	4ft 9in.	2ft 9in				150psi	370 sq.ft	41 sq.ft	6.28 sq.ft			
H	12in × 18in	5ft 4in	3ft 0in	8ft 3in	2ft 9in	4ft 11in	120psi	335 sq.ft	39 sq.ft	6.5 sq.ft	450 galls.	16.35 tons	19.85 tons
H W/N 1847	12in × 18 in	5ft 4in	3ft 1in				120psi	359 sq.ft	41 sq.ft	6.28 sq.ft	500 galls.		
W/N 1639*	12in × 18 in	5ft 6in	3ft 0in	8ft 6in	3ft 0in		140psi				450 galls.	17.15 tons	20.95 tons
I	13in × 18in	5ft 6in	3ft 0in	9ft 4in	2ft 10in	5ft 0in		428.25 sq.ft	43.5 sq.ft	6.5 sq.ft	500 galls.	16.4 tons	20.5 tons
P W/N 546	14in × 18in	4ft 9in	3ft 0in	8ft 7in	3ft 1in	5ft 0in		480.5 sq.ft	47 sq.ft	7.0 sq.ft	515 galls.		
P	14in × 18in	5ft 6in	3ft 0in	9ft 4in	3ft 1in	5ft 0in		503 sq.ft	47 sq.ft	7.0 sq.ft	550 galls.		
W/N 1773	14in × 20in	5ft 6in	3ft 1.5in				160psi	540 sq.ft	60 sq.ft	8.25 sq.ft	600 galls.		
W/N 581	15in × 20in	6ft 0in	3ft 1in	10ft 0in	3ft 3in			608 sq.ft	51 sq.ft	7.75 sq.ft	600 galls.		
W/N 1802	16in × 24in	6ft 6in	3ft 8in	12ft 0in	3ft 9in	6ft 6in	180psi	804 sq.ft	81 sq.ft		900 galls.	31.75 tons	37.25 tons

*5ft 6in gauge.

Six-Coupled Classes (0-6-0ST)

Class	Cyls.	Wheelbase	Wheel	Boiler Details (5)			Heating Surface				Tank	Weights	
			Dia.	Length	Diameter	Pitch	W.P.	Tubes	Firebox	G.A.	Cap.	Empty	W.O.
O.C.I.	11 or 12in × 17in	5ft. 5in. + 4ft 10in	3ft 1 .375in	7ft 3in	2ft 9in	4ft 4.5 in	120psi	305 sq.ft	40 sq.ft	6.75 sq.ft	420 galls.		
K (8)	12in × 17in	5ft 5in + 5ft 4in	3ft 1 .375in	7ft 9in	2ft 9in	4ft 4.75in	120psi	370 sq.ft	40 sq.ft	6.75 sq.ft	450 galls.		
K (9)	12in × 17in	5ft 5in + 5ft 4in	3ft	7ft 9in	2ft 9in	4ft 4.75in	120psi	366 sq.ft	40 sq.ft	7.0 sq.ft	450 galls.		
L	12in × 18in	5ft 5in + 5ft 4in	3ft (Some 3ft 6in)	7ft 9in	3ft 1in	5ft 0.5in	140psi	402 sq.ft	46 sq.ft	7.0 sq.ft	450 galls.		19.905 tons
O.C.L. W/N 731	13in × 18in	5ft 9in + 5ft 6in	3ft	8ft 2in	3ft 2in	5ft 3in		418 sq.ft	47 sq.ft	7.25 sq.ft	475 galls.	17.3 tons	20.55 tons
M	13in × 18in	5ft 10in + 5ft 8in	3ft (Some 3ft 6in)	8ft 2in	3ft 4in	5ft 4in		500 sq.ft	50 sq.ft	8.0 sq.ft	550 galls.	18.55 tons	24.5 tons
W/N 1844 (10)	14in × 20in	10ft total	3ft 6in	7ft 4in	3ft 6in		160psi	537 sq.ft	56 sq.ft	8.8 sq.ft	600 galls.		
Q	14in × 20in	5ft 11in + 6ft 1in	3ft 6in	8ft 8in	3ft 6in	5ft 10.5in	160psi	600 sq.ft	60 sq.ft	8.8	600 galls.		
W/N 1803 (10)	14in × 22in	9ft 6in total	3ft 6in				160psi	600 sq.ft	60 sq.ft	10 sq.ft	650 galls.		
W/N 1955 (10)	15in × 22in	11ft total	3ft 9in	8ft 3in	3ft 10in		160psi	670 sq.ft	62 sq.ft	10 sq.ft	700 galls		
O	15in × 22in	5ft 9in + 6ft 3in	3ft 9in	8ft 6in	3ft 10in	6ft 0.5in	160psi	692 sq.ft	70 sq.ft	10 sq.ft	700 galls.	23.2 tons	29.15 tons
T W/N 1929 (10)	16in × 22in	5ft 9in + 6ft 3in	3ft 6in	10ft 0in	3ft 9in	6ft 4.5in	160psi	770 sq.ft	80 sq.ft	14 sq.ft	850 galls.		
W/N 1307	17in × 24in	6ft 6in + 8ft 0in	4ft 0 in	10ft 0in	3ft 11.125in	6ft 9.5in	150psi	868 sq.ft	95 sq.ft	15 sq.ft	850 galls.		39.6 tons
W/N 1759 (10)	18in × 24in	6ft 6in + 6ft 6in	4ft 0 in	12ft 0in	4ft 4.125in		160 p.s.i	1068 sq.ft	113 sq.ft	19 sq.ft	1000 galls	41.15 tons	50.95 tons

Notes: (1) Class prototype (W/N 84); (2) Class B 'mainstream' dimensions; (3) 1862 London Exhibition locomotive (W/N 60); (4) Class 'D' mainstream dimensions; (5) Diameter measurement taken from smallest ring; (6) Several class E locomotives built with 9.5in by 14in cylinders; (7) Abortive design for standard gauge use: no order or works numbers ever allocated for such purposes. (8) Class K per1871 Drawing 9A; (9) Later Class 'K' dimensions as W/N 1771. (10) Rear axle beneath firebox (remaining featured classes have rear axle behind firebox).

Appendix 2

MANNING WARDLE PROFITS FOR SELECTED YEARS

A. Pre-Incorporation	
Year	**Profit/(Loss)**
1897	£8,862 10s. 1d.
1898	£4,632 6s. 6d.
1899	£20,566. 19s. 5d.
1900	£19,893 18s. 11d.
1901	£13,865. 15s. 5d.
1902	£8,367 8s. 8d.
1903	£8,871 13s. 11d.
1904	£5,625 13s. 8d.

B. Post-Incorporation	
Year	**Profit/(Loss)**
To 30/6/1912	(£308 6s. 3d.)
To 30/6/1913	(£2,252 3s. 11d.)
1/7/1913 To 28/8/1915	£2,327 14s. 0d.
To 30/6/1916	£1,836 10s 9d.
To 30/6/1917	£4,234 9 s. 9d.
To 30/6/1918	£6,416 6s. 10d.
To 30/6/1919	£9,815 18s. 11d.
To 30/6/1920	£13,258 18s. 8d.
To 30/6/1921	£13,005 19s. 3d.
To 30/6/1922	£3,805 3s. 9d.*
To 30/6/1923	(£6,450 1s. 0d.)
To 30/6/1924	(£12,264 14s. 8d.)
To 30/6/1925	(£7,585 17s 10d.)
To 31/8/1926	(£9,057. 1s. 4d.)
31/8/1926 To 31/3/1927	(£4,331 18s. 2d.)

Deduction of the Corporation Tax for 1920-1 and Excess Profits Tax for 1921 resulted in a revised net loss figure in the 1922 Directors' Report of £1200 13s. 3d. See Chapter 10.

BIBLIOGRAPHY

KITSON CLARK, Edward, *Kitsons Of Leeds, 1837-1937,* 1938.

RC&TS *Locomotives of the Great Western Railway Part 2,* 1953.

RC&TS *Locomotives of the Great Western Railway Part 3,* 1956.

ROLT, L.T.C., *A Hunslet Hundred,* 1964.

RC&TS *Locomotives of the Great Western Railway Part 10,* 1966.

RC&TS *Locomotives of the L.B.& S.C.R. Part 1,* 1969.

REDMAN, R.N., *The Railway Foundry Leeds,* 1972.

MABBOTT, F.W., *Manning Wardle & Company Ltd. – Locomotive Works List,* 1981.

GROVES, N., *Great Northern Locomotive History Volume 1,* 1986.

HARMAN, F.W., *Locomotives Built By Manning Wardle & Co. Volumes 1-3,* 1997-9.

TOWNSLEY, D.H., *The Hunslet Engine Works,* Plateway Press, 1998.

SIMPSON, J.E., *Locomotives of Quality: A Pictorial History of Manning Wardle & Co.,* 2000.

INDEX